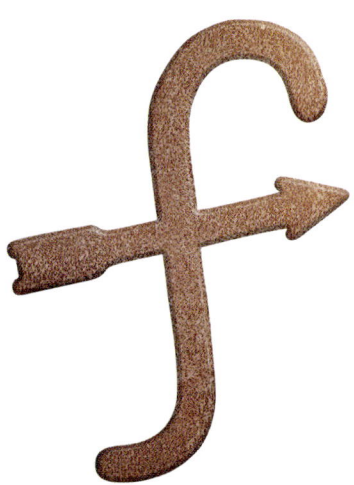

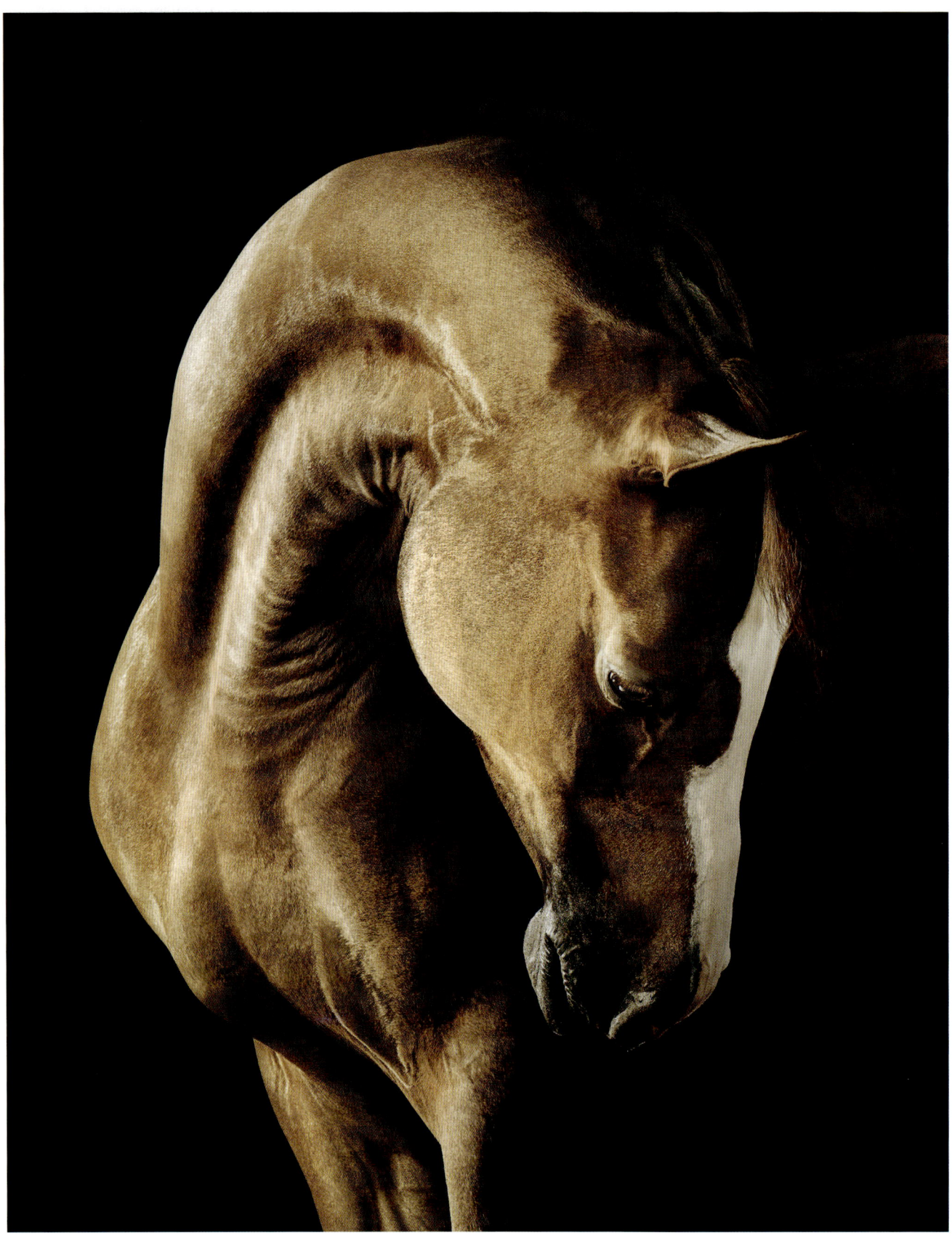

Peanut

SADDLEBRED ARABIAN MARE

FARM LIFE

A COLLECTION OF ANIMAL PORTRAITS

by Randal Ford

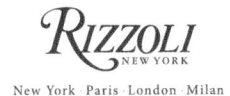

RIZZOLI
NEW YORK

New York · Paris · London · Milan

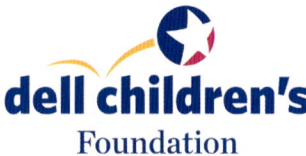

We are proud to donate a portion of book proceeds in support of Dell Children's Foundation, based in Austin, Texas.

Dell Children's Medical Center hospitals serve as the only comprehensive dedicated pediatric facilities in the Central Texas region. Since opening in 2007, Dell Children's has cared for a 46-county area, providing the only Level I Trauma Center and most specialized care for children and adolescents in the greater Austin metropolitan area. In 2023, Dell Children's opened a north location to expand the reach and impact of their world-class care. Dell Children's provides specialized pediatric health care to a population that is 70 percent under or uninsured and, as a nonprofit hospital, relies on philanthropy to support its mission to serve all children. Dell Children's is honored to have programs named in *U.S. News & World Report*'s Best Children's Hospital List, including Cardiology and Heart Surgery and Neonatal Intensive Care.

First published in the United States of America in 2024 by
Rizzoli International Publications, Inc.
49 West 27th Street
New York, NY 10001
www.rizzoliusa.com

Foreword by Brian Patrick Flynn

Publisher: Charles Miers
Associate Publisher: James Muschett
Managing Editor: Lynn Scrabis
Editor: Candice Fehrman
Design: DJ Stout and Stu Taylor, Pentagram Design

Printed in China

2026 2027 2028 2029 / 10 9 8 7 6 5 4 3

ISBN: 978-0-8478-3171-5

Library of Congress Control Number: 2024931473

The authorized representative in the EU for product safety and compliance is Mondadori Libri S.p.A., via Gian Battista Vico 42, 20123 Milan, Italy, www.mondadori.it

Visit us online:
Instagram.com/RizzoliBooks
Facebook.com/RizzoliNewYork
Youtube.com/user/RizzoliNY

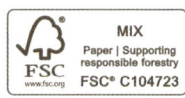

Dedicated to the farm animals—past, present, and future—
that enrich and sustain our daily lives.

FOREWORD

BY BRIAN PATRICK FLYNN

In photography, film, and television production, there's an old adage for staying sane and eliminating stress: "Never work with children or animals." Clearly, Randal Ford does not follow the latter half of this rule. In fact, his entire business is working with animals. As a production designer and art director, I have a massive appreciation for visual storytelling. And creating a narrative with animals who cannot read, write, or even speak with the human being tasked with directing them is some next-level storytelling.

From the time we're old enough to make noises and point at things, we seem to have a strong connection to animals. First, it's their shapes. Then it's how they move. And before you know it, our brains are connecting silhouettes and actions with sounds—cows moo, ducks quack, cats meow. But sound is not something that can be captured through a photograph. Ford must rely solely on shapes and movement for his method of storytelling, and he does so with such ease.

When I'm crafting a film set, I often include artwork with animals as the subjects. Come to think of it, probably every space I design has an animal in it, whether it's a brass bird sculpture, a framed oil portrait of a stately dog, or even pop art of an alpaca wearing pearls and a Marilyn Monroe–style wig. There's a social reason behind this decision as well. Animals are conversation starters, and when you stick a conversation starter in a room full of strangers, those strangers will leave the room as newly acquainted friends.

Animals have tons of personality, just like humans do. It's fair to say that the link between dogs and humans is the most popular and well-celebrated animal-and-person pairing on Earth. But when it comes to Ford, it's all about the cow. The photographer is quick to admit that this mainstay of the family farm is a true hallmark of his work. Ford says it's beyond just snapping a photo of a cow; it's about crafting a portrait that showcases the animal's quirks in a fresh, new light, revealing the bovine's true essence and thus allowing us to identify part of ourselves in it. I've had many travels in which I've similarly connected with an animal and found myself drawn to it. Hanging directly above my sofa is a photograph of a majestic Icelandic horse that was taken in winter and conveys a very quiet, cool, and confident vibe.

Every artist has their own aesthetics, and many artists can be verbose in trying to describe those aesthetics. Ford's explanation is easy: simplicity. While Ford directs and connects with each animal to show its complex personality and characteristics, his backgrounds have to remain very simple and not compete with other shapes or textures. And from a decorating point of view, this is what makes his artwork a perfect fit for interior design. The neutral backdrops allow each piece to fit effortlessly and harmoniously in almost any space in a home.

It may be true that dogs are known as "man's best friend," but I think it's safe to say the entire animal kingdom is Ford's best friend.

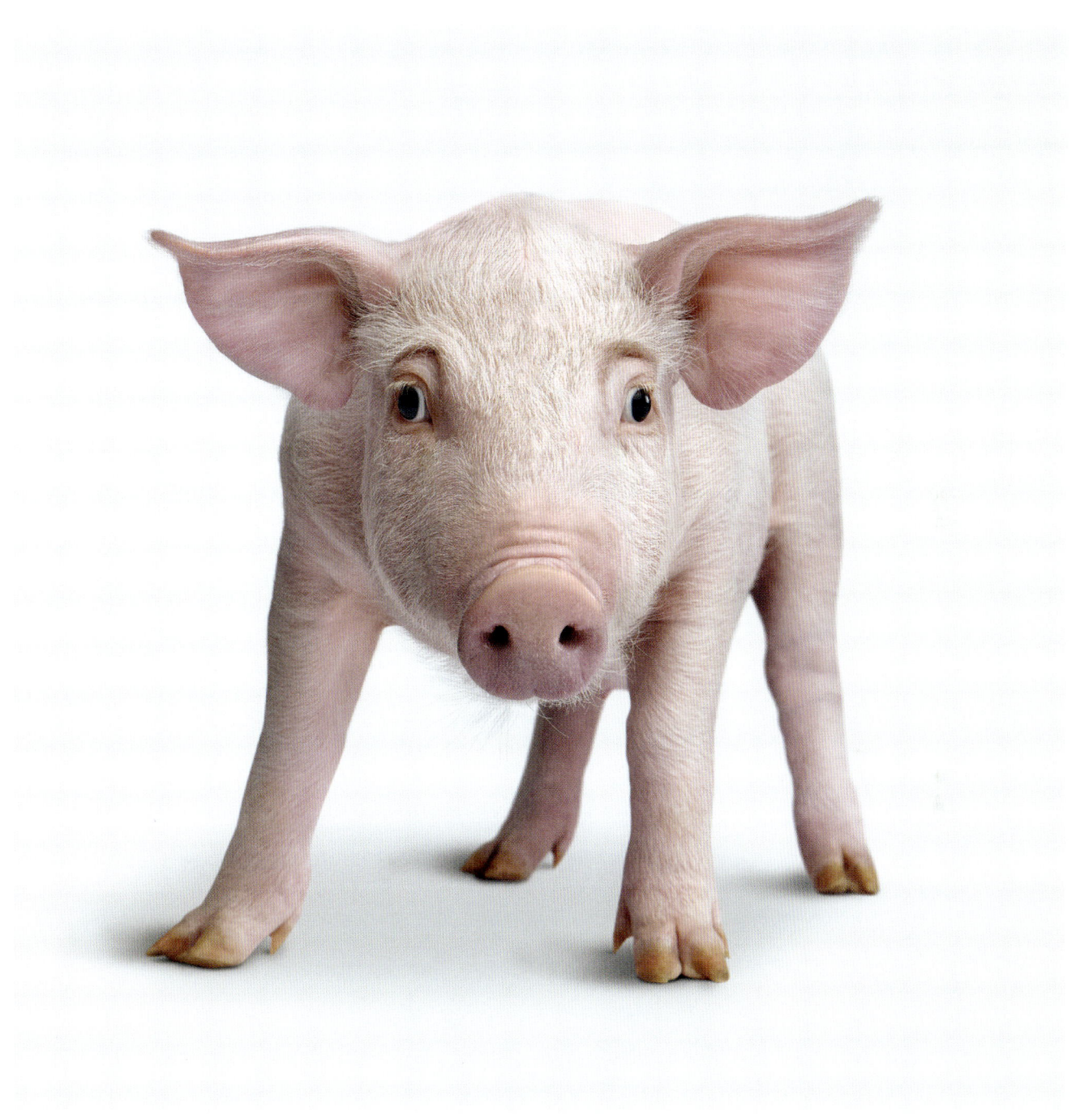

Ruby Rose

PINK PIGLET

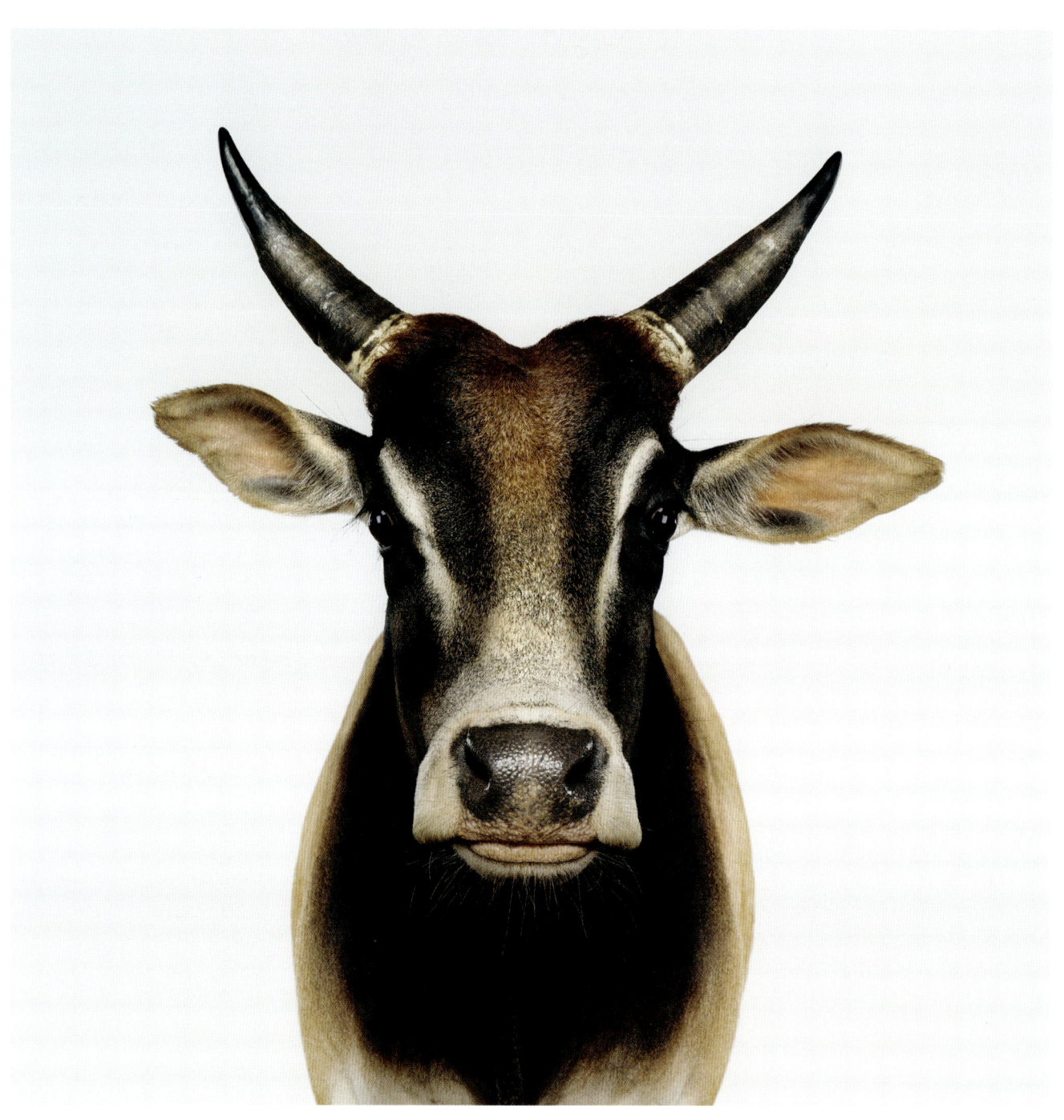

Swagger

ZEBU BULL

PASTORAL TRIBUTE

BY RANDAL FORD

It's the first morning of a three-day shoot on the farm. We arrive just before the sun does, which means we get to watch the blank fields slowly transform into an array of colors—first gray, then gold, then a rich amber as bright as fire. As I stand outside the rustic red barn, which we will spend the day transforming into our studio, I take a moment to soak in my surroundings.

I watch the low fog lay across the pasture like velvet as the symphony of farm life begins. The gentle lowing of cows can be heard in the distance; they are curiously making their way toward us. Beyond the fence line, cheerful chickens cluck beneath sprinkled seed, and a rooster announces the day. There are horse hooves tapping past me as they make their way out of the wooden stalls and into the green grass. As I step back inside the barn, it smells of leather saddles and sawdust and feels warm, like a home. And a home it is. The beauty of life on the farm comes in knowing that every hoof beat, every gentle nuzzle or mew, tells the story of trust, partnership, and the heartwarming rhythms of a relationship between human and animal.

My previous book, *Good Dog*, explored the world's first domesticated animal—man's best friend—and delved deep into the unbreakable bonds humans have shared with dogs throughout history. Each portrait captured the magic of our favorite companions and highlighted their loyalty, love, and unending devotion to their humans. In this latest book, I venture beyond our backyards and into the heartlands of America, embracing a diverse lineage of creatures that have been integral to our survival, our stories, and our shared history.

It is my hope that this collection of portraits serves as an everlasting tribute to the animals that have helped shape and sustain humanity. Through their eyes, we see not only their soul but also a reflection of the ancient wild within them. Whether clothes to keep us warm, strength and speed to keep us able, or life-giving food on our tables, farm animals deserve more than just a children's song. They deserve our recognition, respect, and gratitude. Let us celebrate their immense beauty, honor the indelible mark they've left on the landscape of human existence, and remain in awe of their enduring significance in the tapestry of farm life.

REFLECTION AND CONNECTION

BY RANDAL FORD

At the very heart of these pastoral portraits is a desire to celebrate the beauty of American farm life and pay a lasting tribute to the animals that allow us to grow, feed our families, and survive. *Farm Life* is a playful collection of personality, beauty, strength, and whimsy. With every unique image, the viewer is invited to look beyond the surface and into the very heart, soul, and spirit of these amazing animals.

Creating portraits of animals in the studio is both an art and a meticulous science. I believe simplicity is the ultimate sophistication, and it is this belief that drives me to use classic but neutral backgrounds, precise lighting, and intentional styling. Achieving the right balance between these elements allows the vibrant spirit and intrinsic beauty of each animal to take center stage without any distractions from its environment.

The eyes of these animals are always a significant focus in my work—they serve as a window into the unspoken parts of each creature and build connection. I believe that we not only see each animal in a new light but also discover a reflection of ourselves within them—our souls, our emotions, and our shared experiences. Animals continue to be an incredible presence in our lives, and I believe that is because of this mirror effect. As we witness their majesty and strength, we are able to notice the same things within ourselves. It is this overarching thesis that makes the images in this book meaningful to me, and hopefully to you as well. As we look upon each portrait, may we recognize not only the outer beauty of these creatures but also the inner courage, vitality, and force that have carried them across the land for millennia.

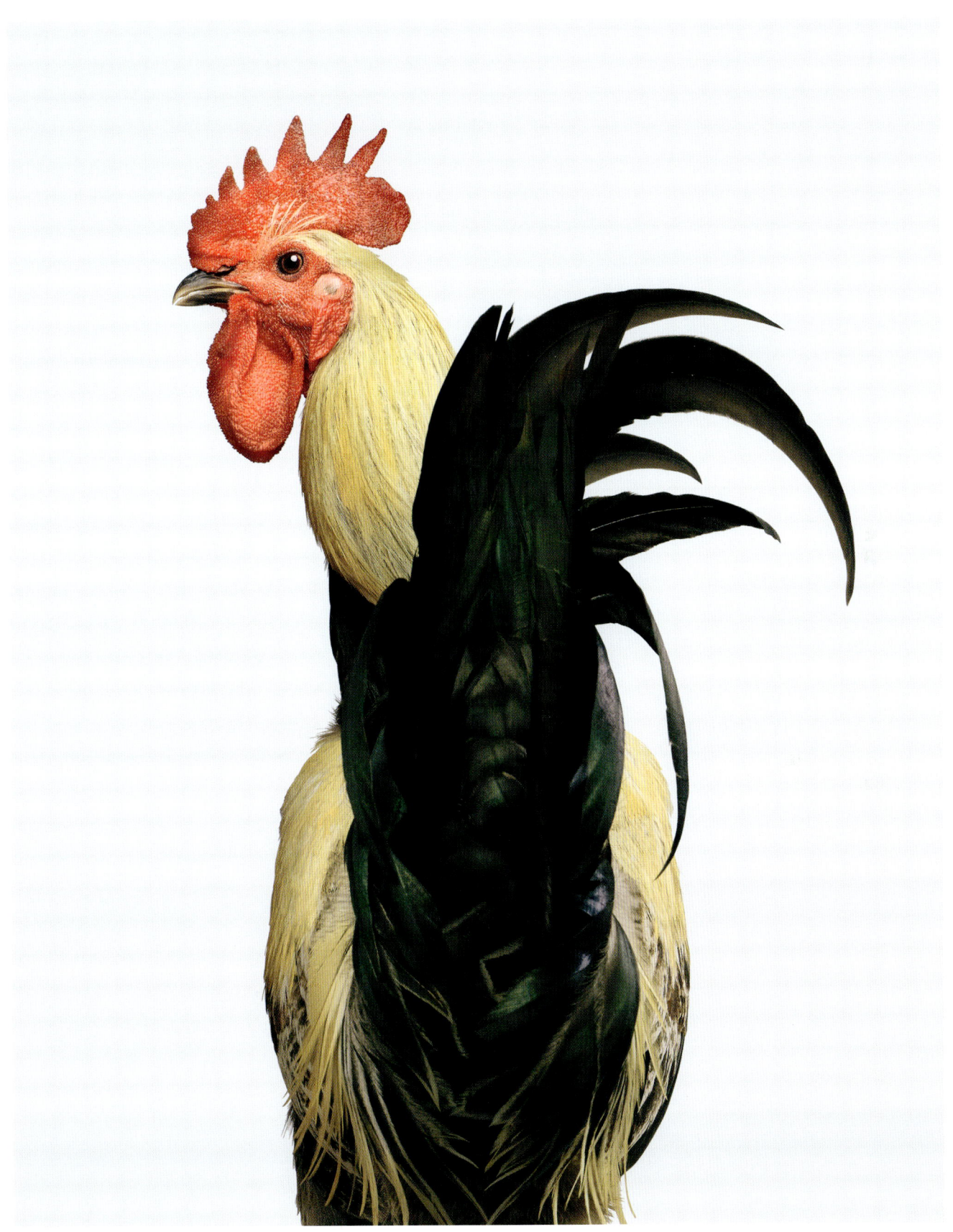

Duke

DENIZLI LONGCROWER ROOSTER

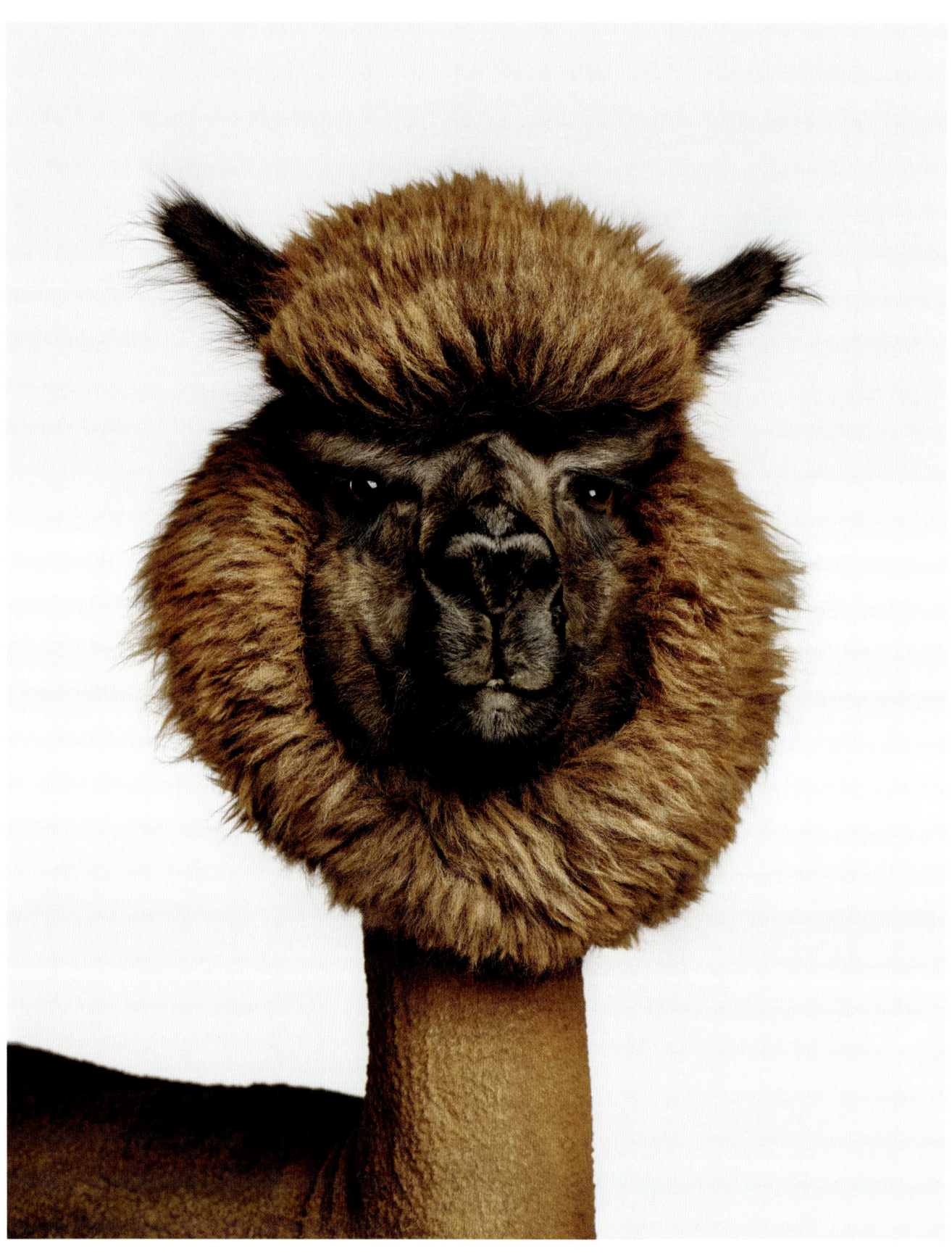

Christoph

HUACAYA ALPACA

PROCESS NOTES

The process of creating these portraits starts with the precision of light. Each animal—from the silken wool of a sheep to the dappled hide of a cow—has a unique texture that requires specific lighting adjustments to highlight it properly. Every subtle shift in light accentuates these textures in different ways, lending new depth and character to the portraits.

In the final stages of my process, and inspired by techniques dating back to old-world darkroom masters, each portrait is subtly finessed in Photoshop. Delicate adjustments in postproduction breathe life into each frame, making the portraits palpable and alluring without compromising their integrity or authenticity.

While technique and process are undeniably crucial, intuition and experience play an equally vital role. Animals, with their spontaneous expressions and moods, often offer a fleeting window into their essence. Capturing that elusive moment where their personality shines is the heart of my craft.

Ultimately, the narrative is led by the animals themselves. This collection is a showcase of my photography, but equally it is a tribute to the spirit of each animal.

Farm Life is an invitation to delve deeper, connect with these animals, and witness the stories they share with the lens. By applying my unique craft and meticulous studio portraiture practices, I was able to capture more than 150 compelling portraits that go beyond the barn and into the very heart of each animal. This playful yet powerful collection shines a lasting light on farm animals and boldly emphasizes their rightful place within it. It is an honor to share these portraits with you.

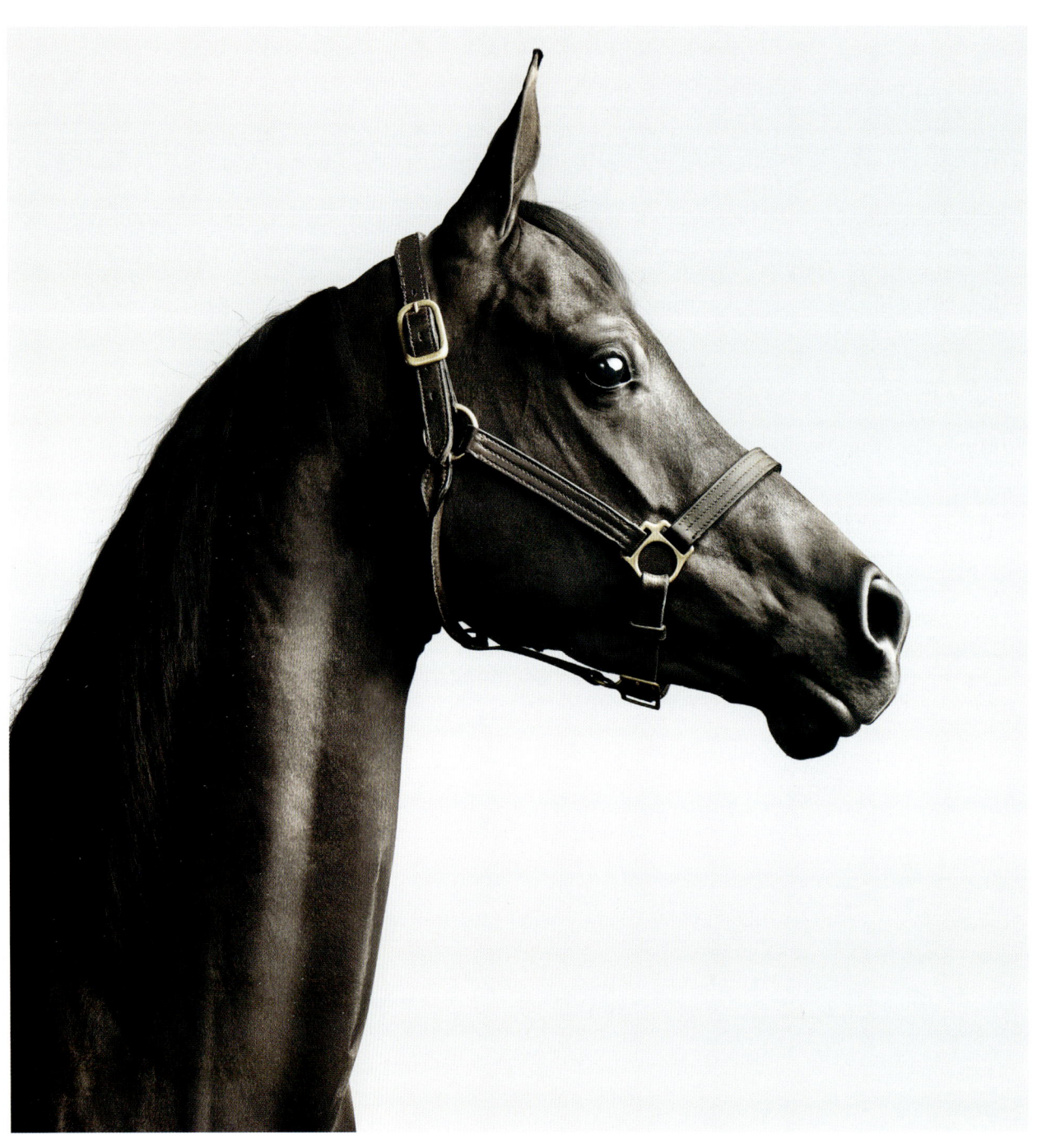

Suzie

BLACK ARABIAN MARE

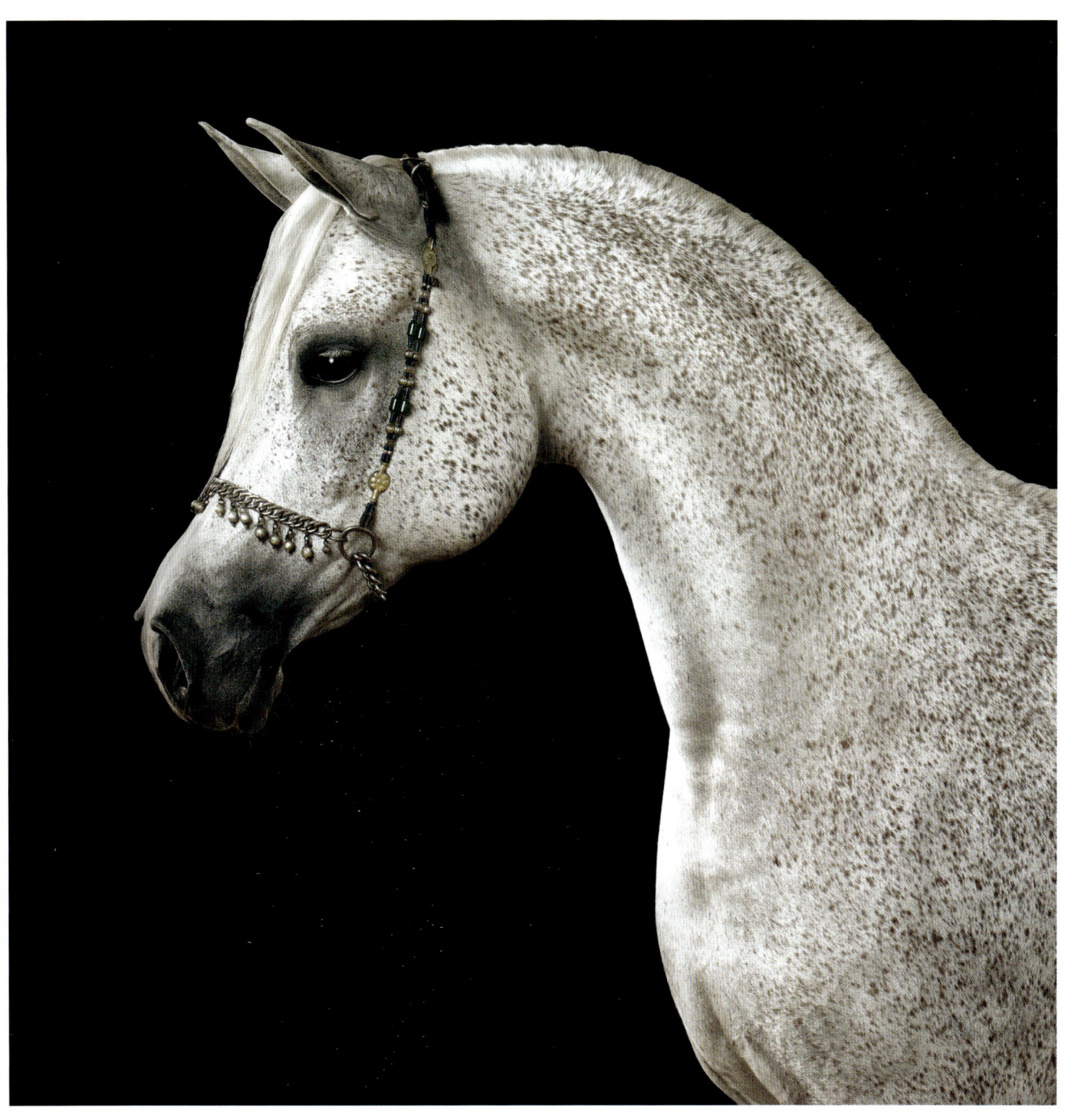

Marmaara

GREY ARABIAN MARE

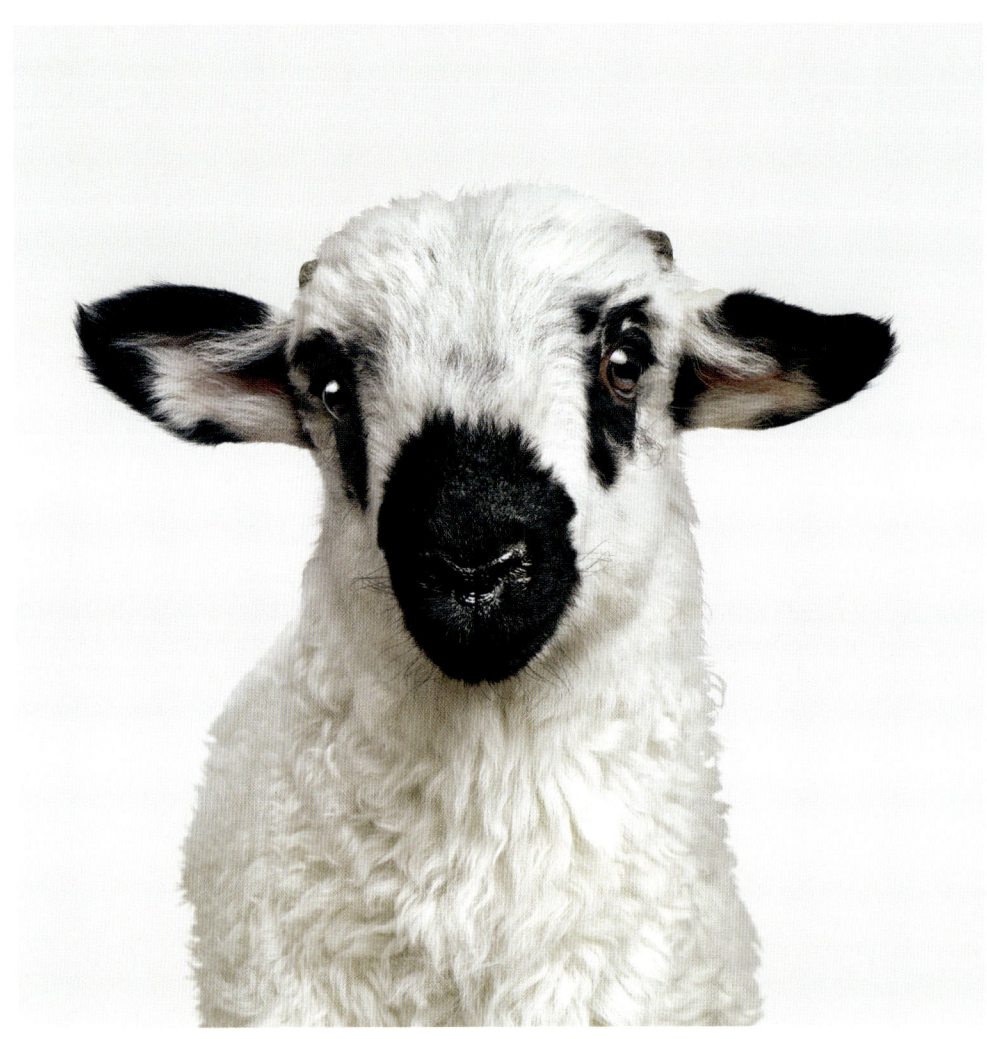

Kotton

F1 VALAIS BLACKNOSE LAMB

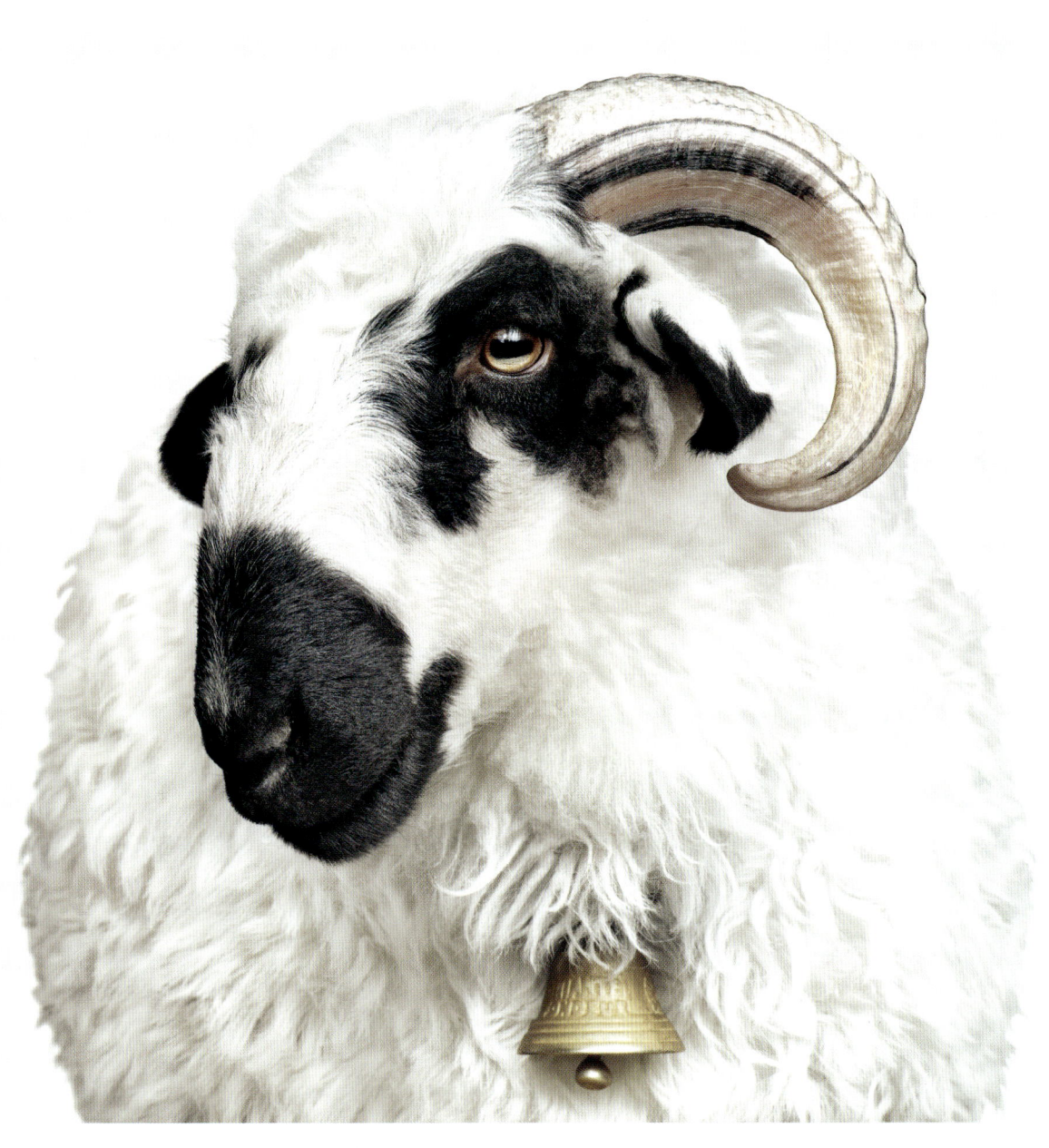

Juno

F1 VALAIS BLACKNOSE SHEEP

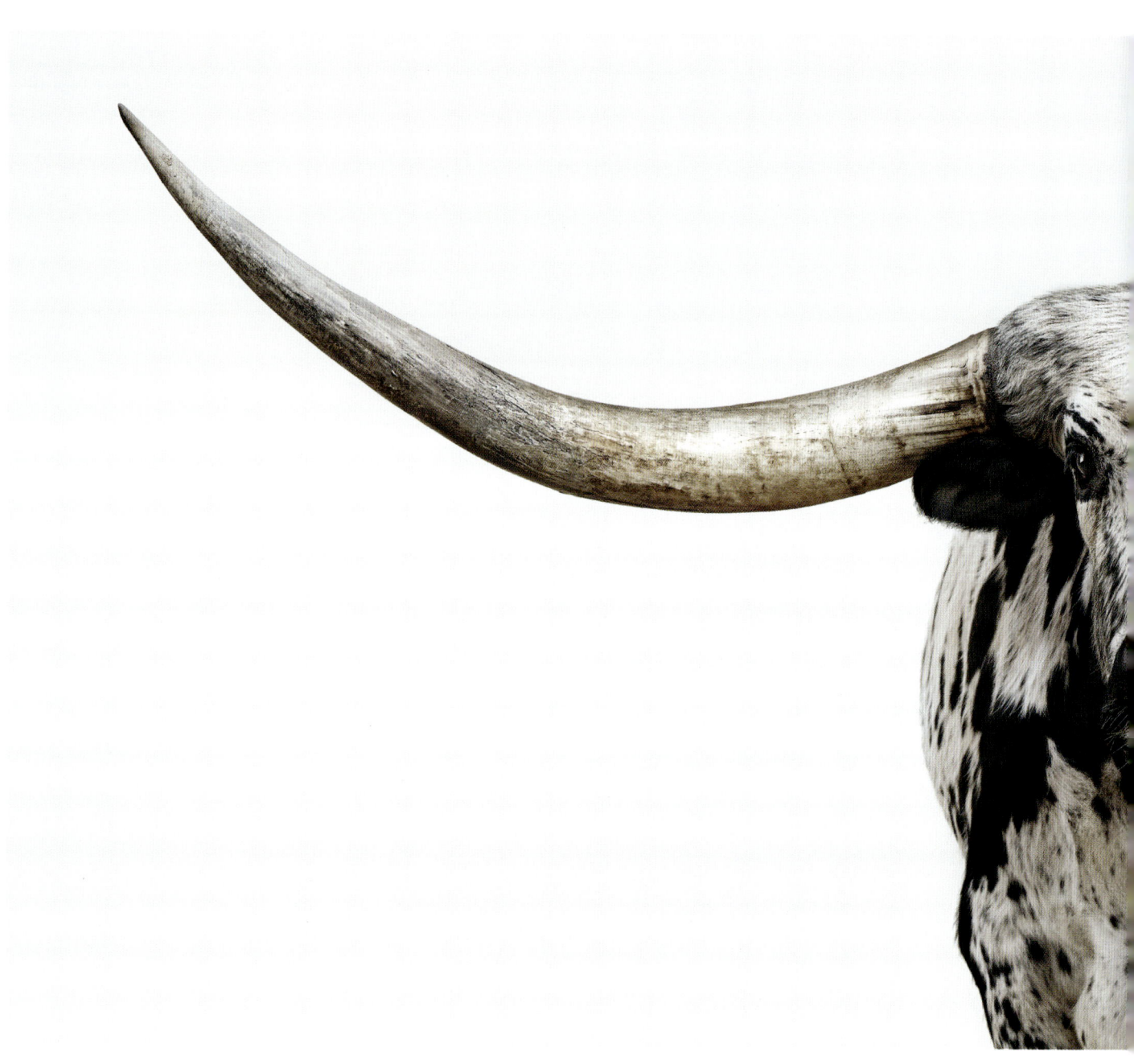

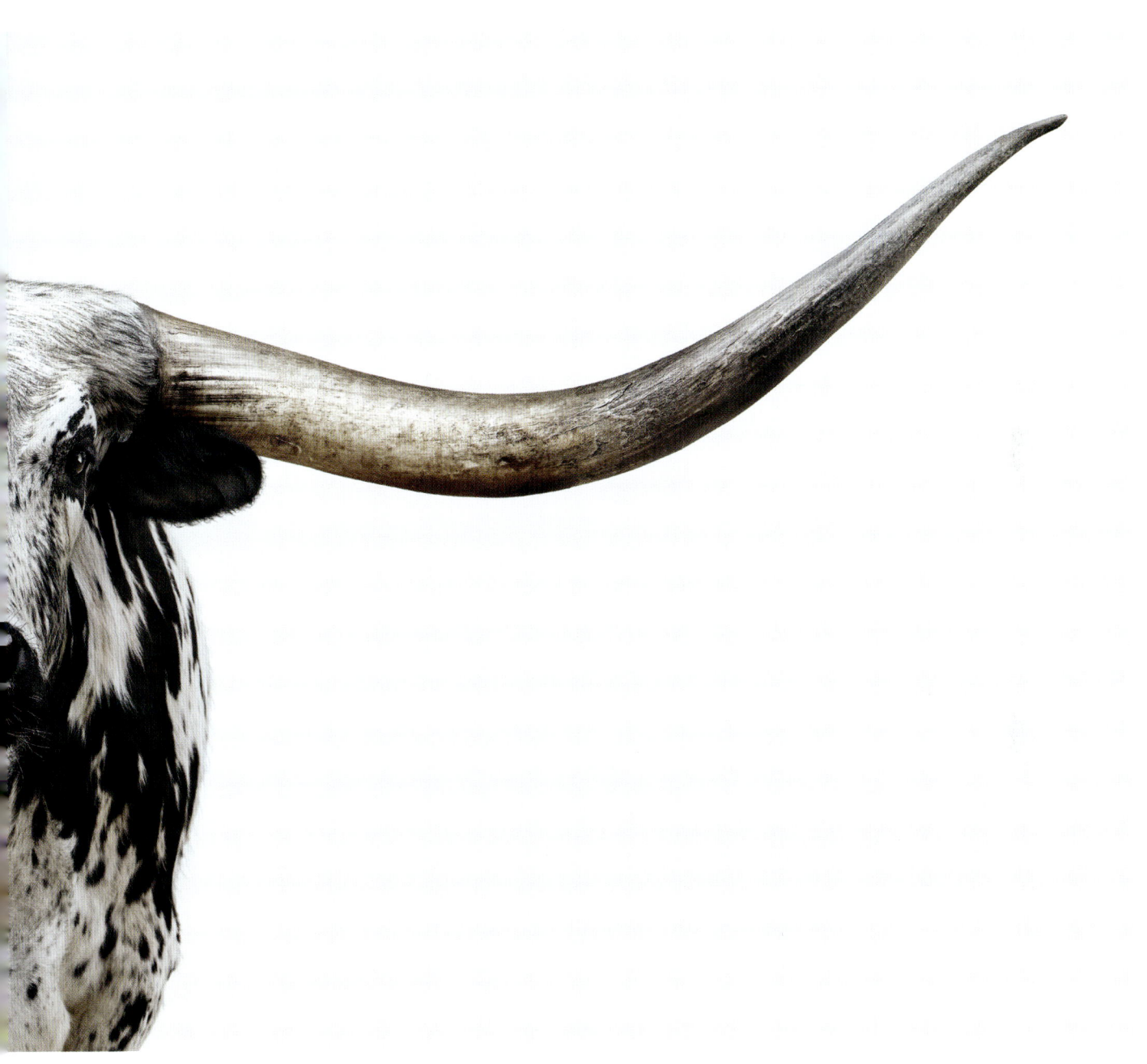

Dante

DAPPLED TEXAS LONGHORN

GOATS

A staple in agrarian cultures worldwide, goats owe much of their popularity to their easy nature and ability to adapt. Thriving in and among a variety of terrains—from mountains to deserts to lush hillsides—they are resilient animals that demand less care than other livestock. Their nourishing milk, tender meat, and durable leather grant many societies the ability to generate economic income to support their families and households.

Photographically, goats are incredibly captivating. Their floppy ears and intense, piercing eyes make for an interesting visual pairing—one that highlights their playful antics while also hinting at a more mischievous side. A goat's intrinsic essence speaks loudly in front of a lens and provides the viewer with a visceral—almost tangible—encounter.

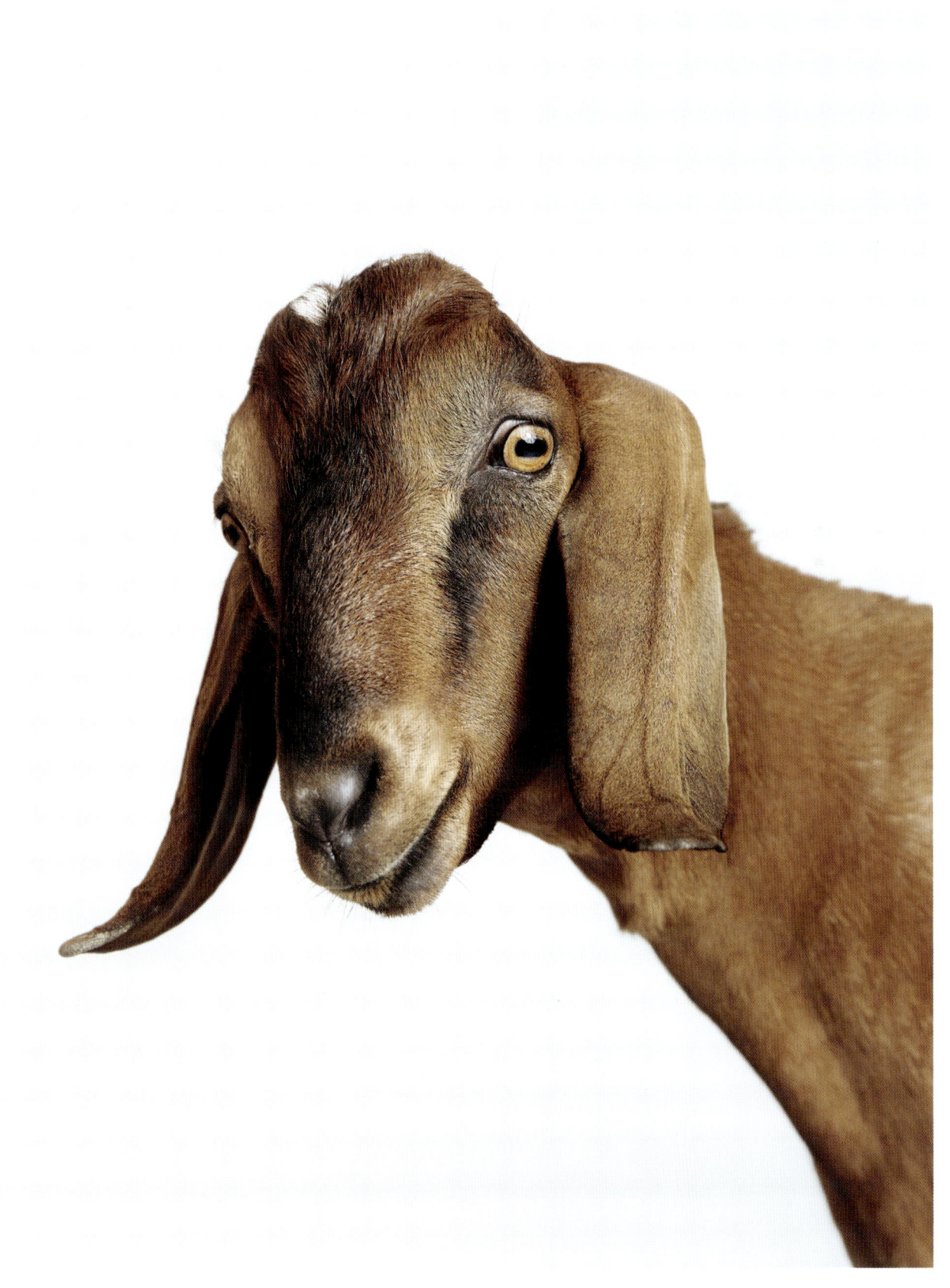

Sammy

BROWN GOAT

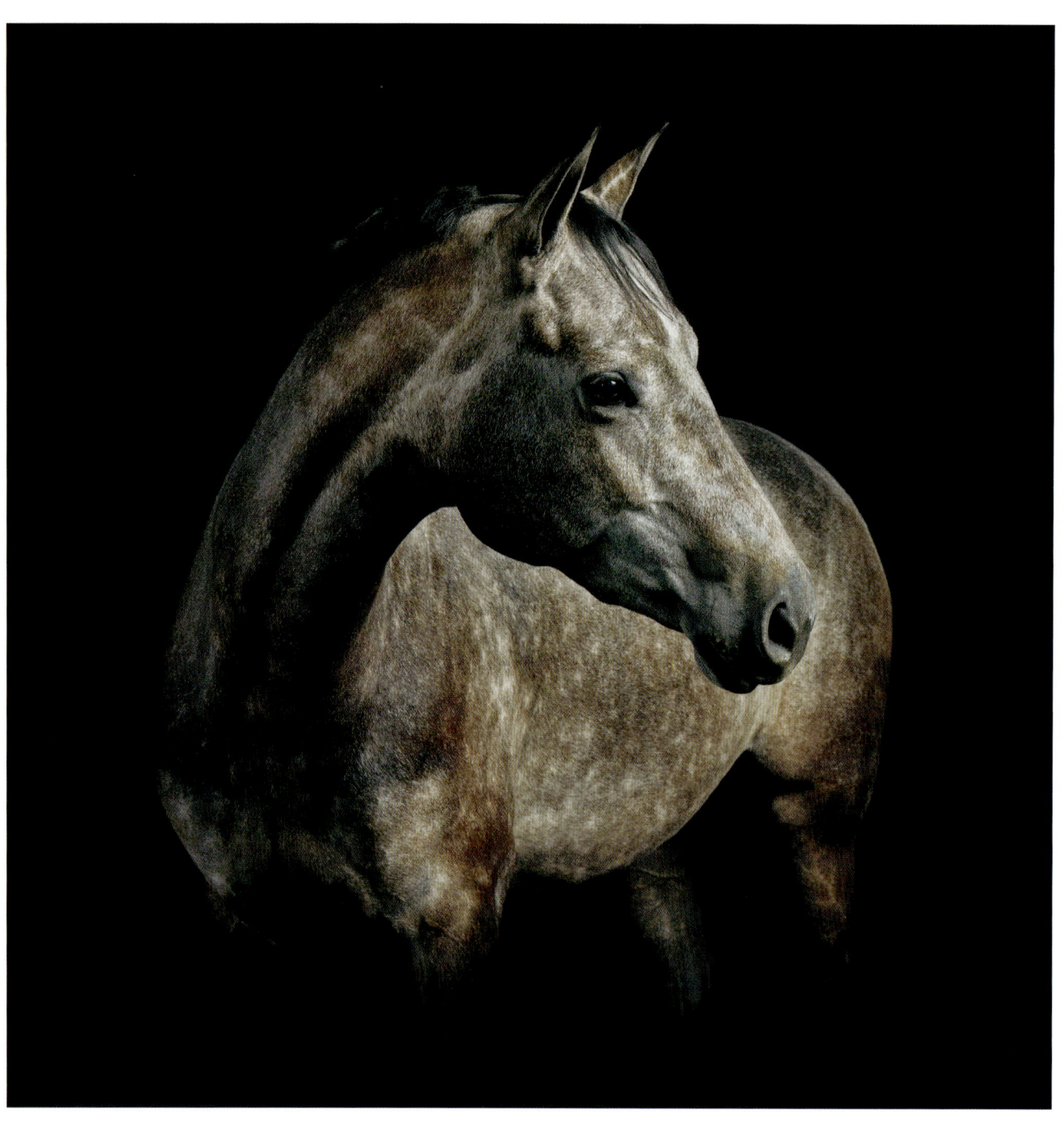

Beretta

GRAY QUARTER HORSE

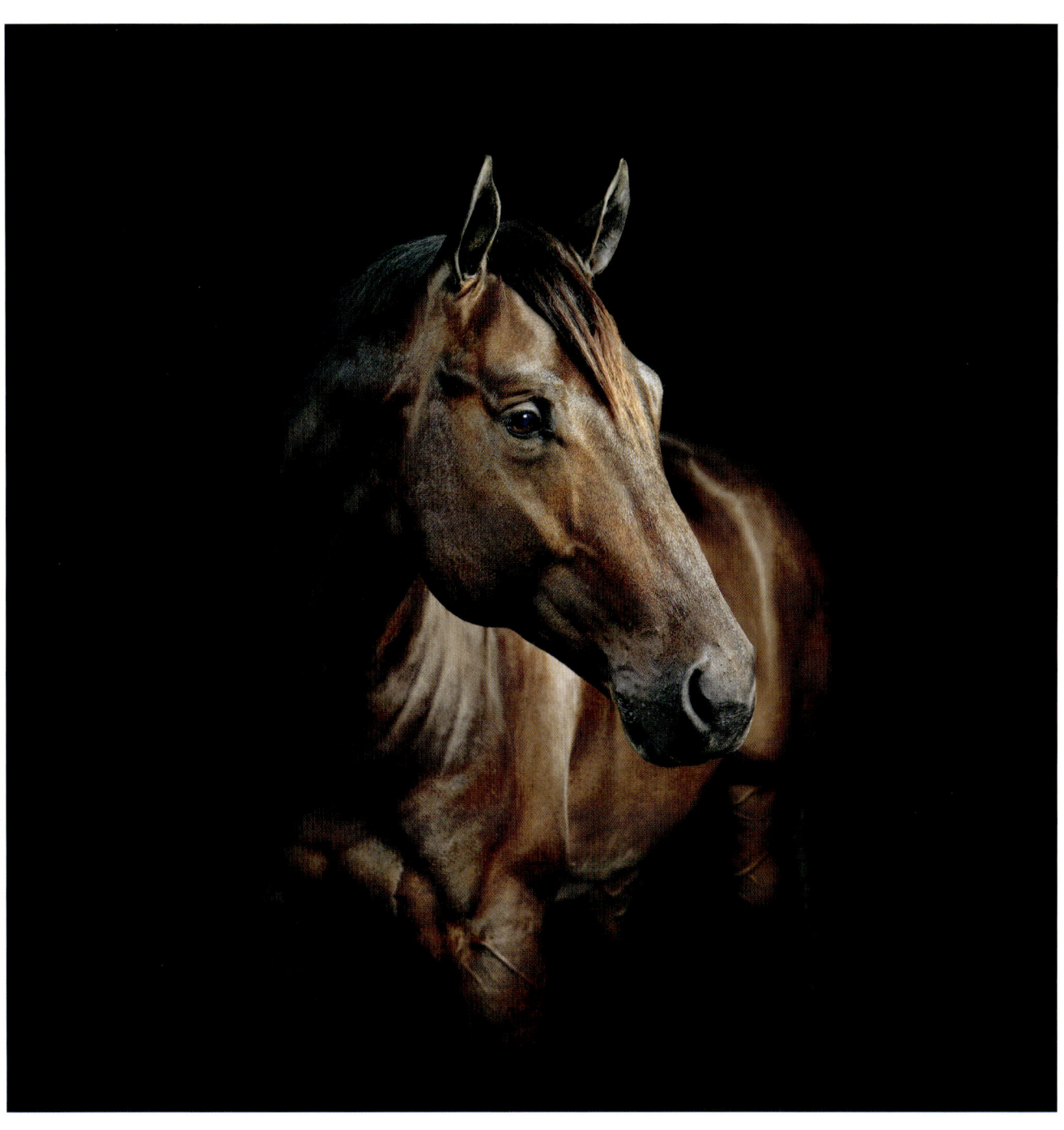

Elm

BROWN QUARTER HORSE

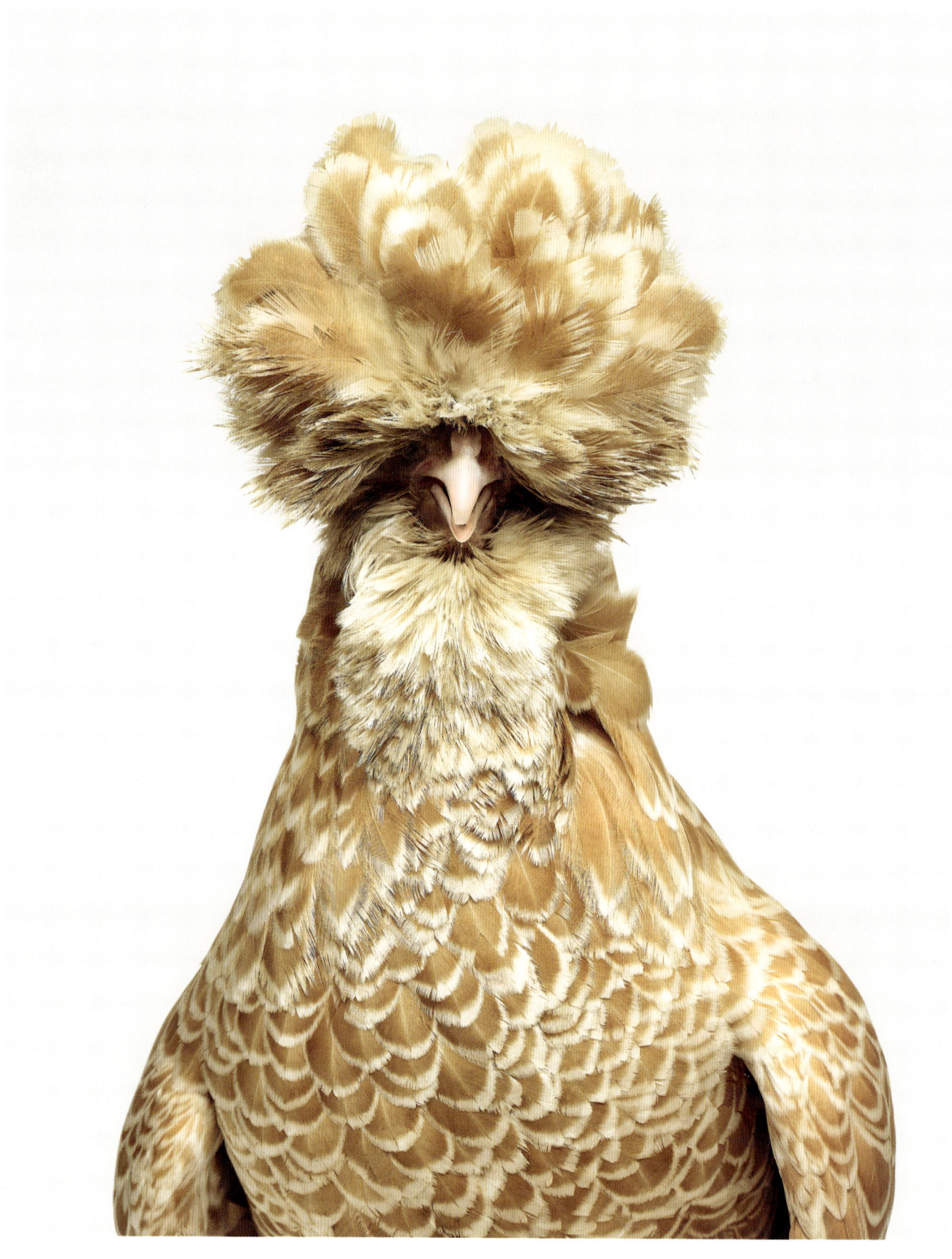

Latte

BANTAM BUFF LACED POLISH HEN

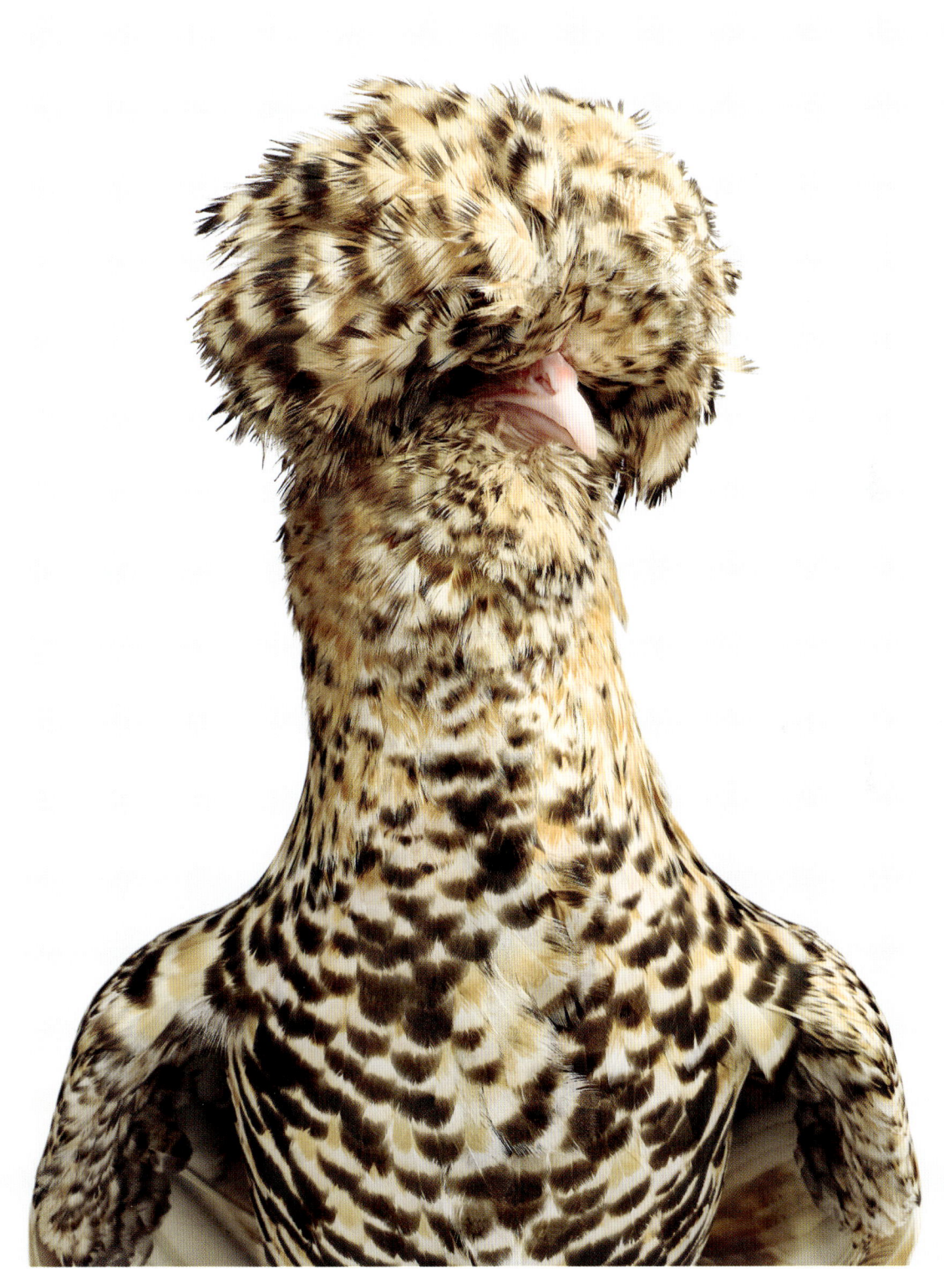

Doloris

CANDY CORN POLISH HEN

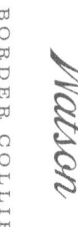

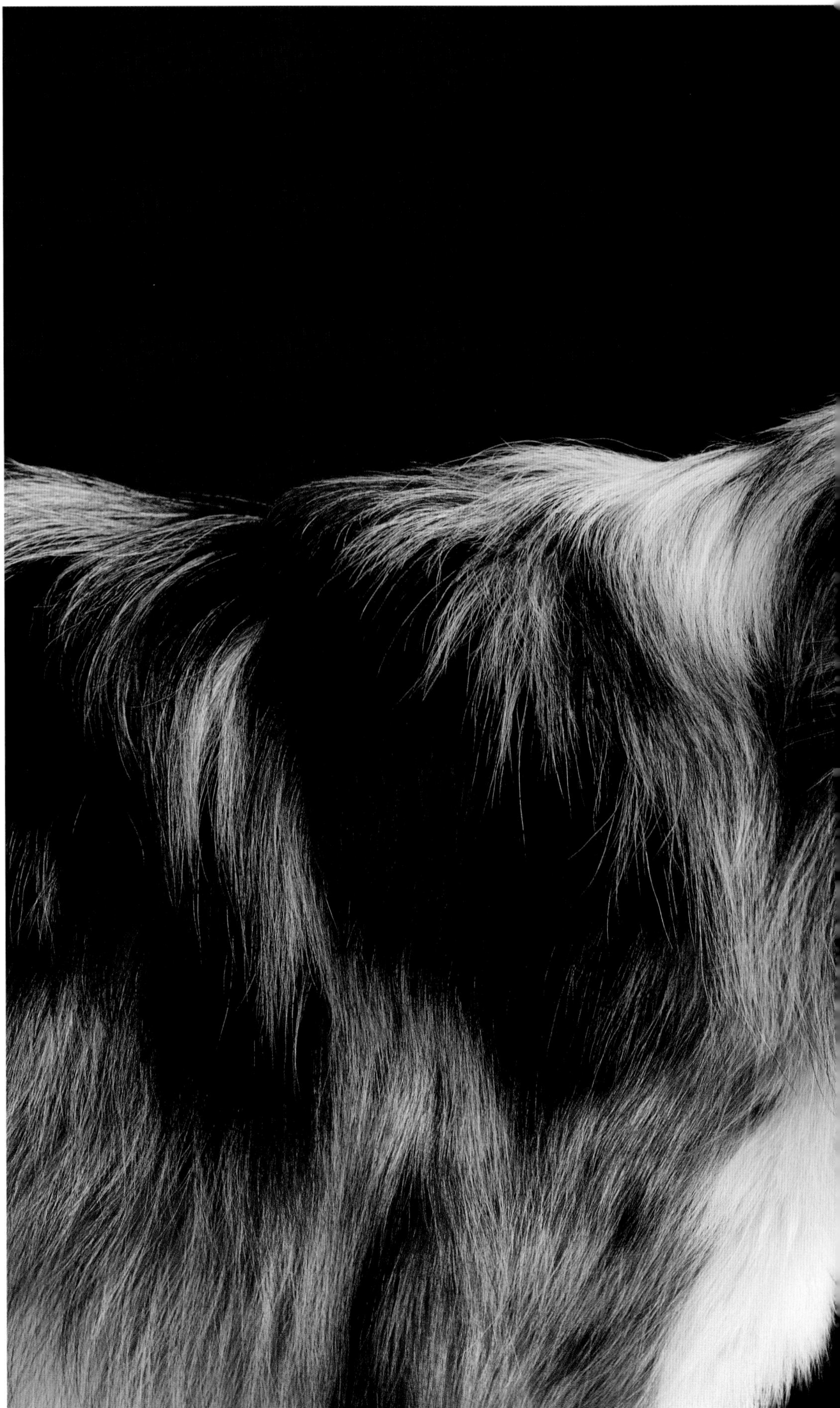

Watson

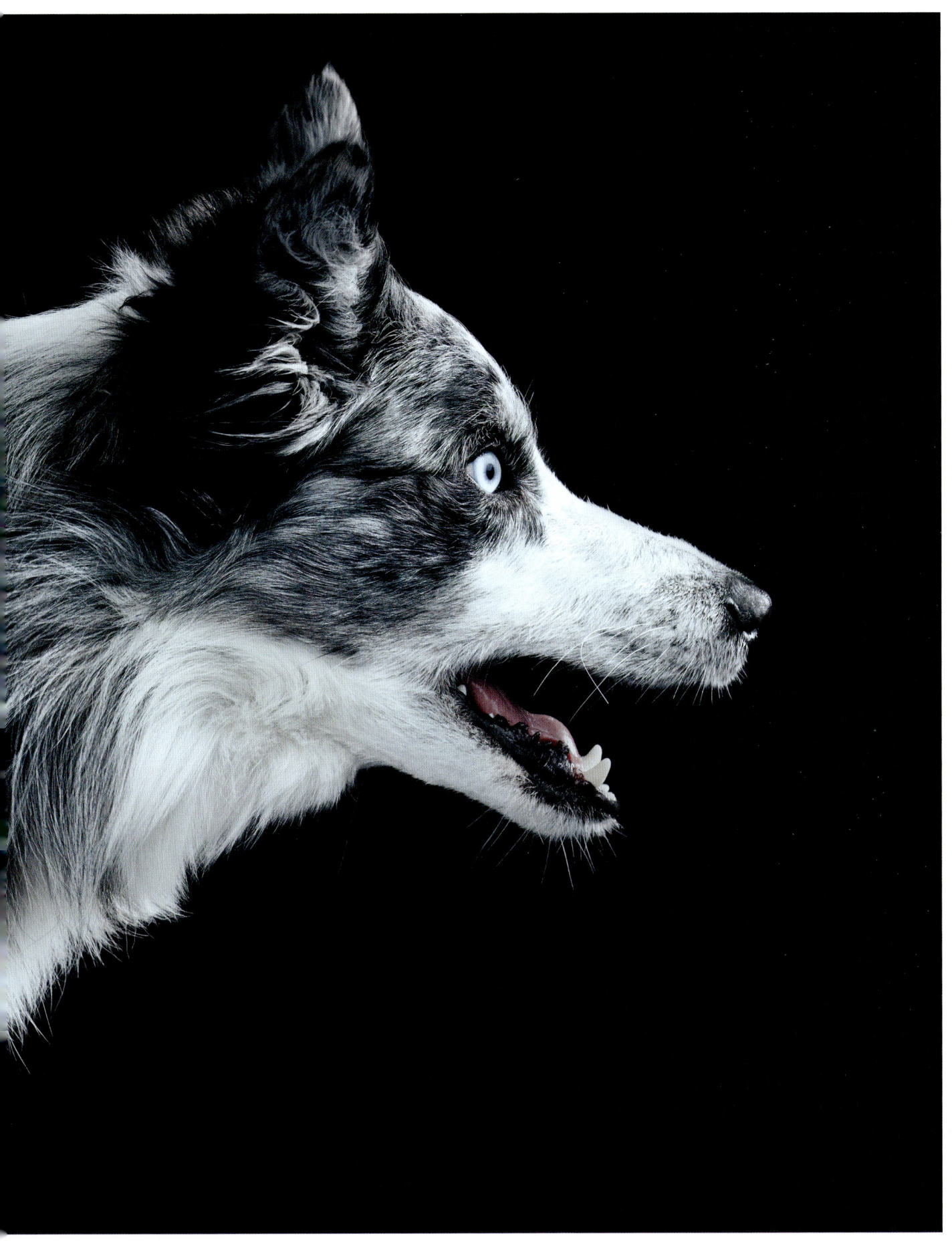

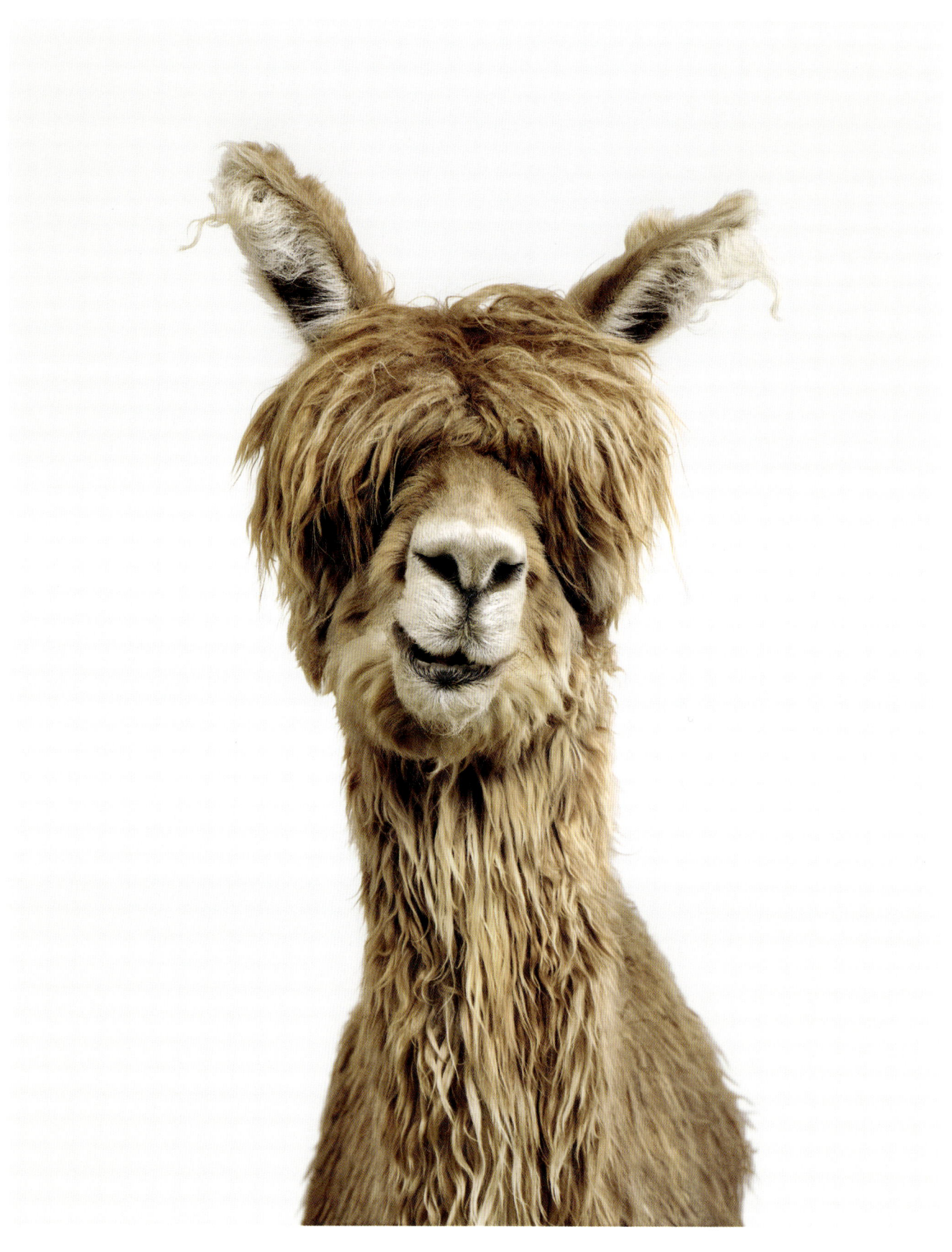

Goldfinch

SURI ALPACA

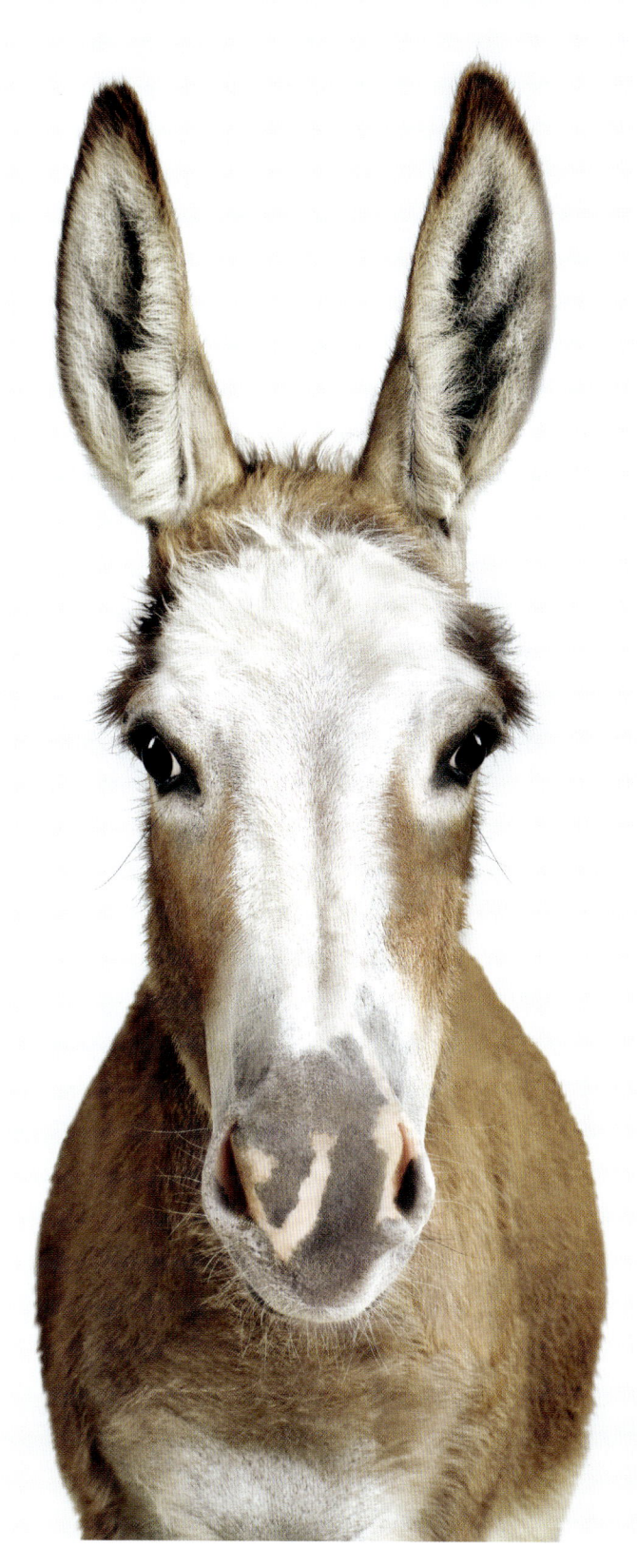

Daisy

DONKEY

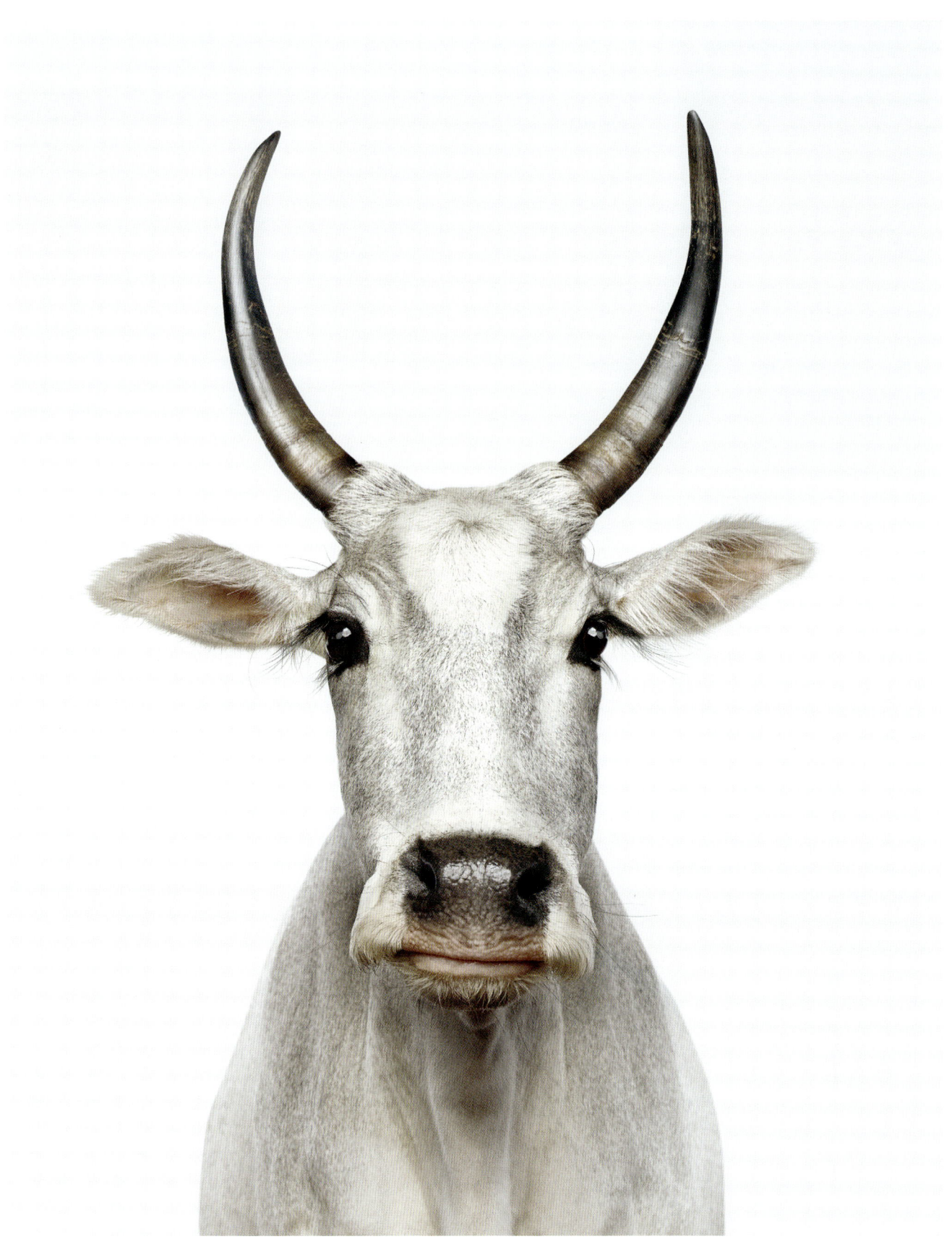

Notta Chance

ZEBU COW

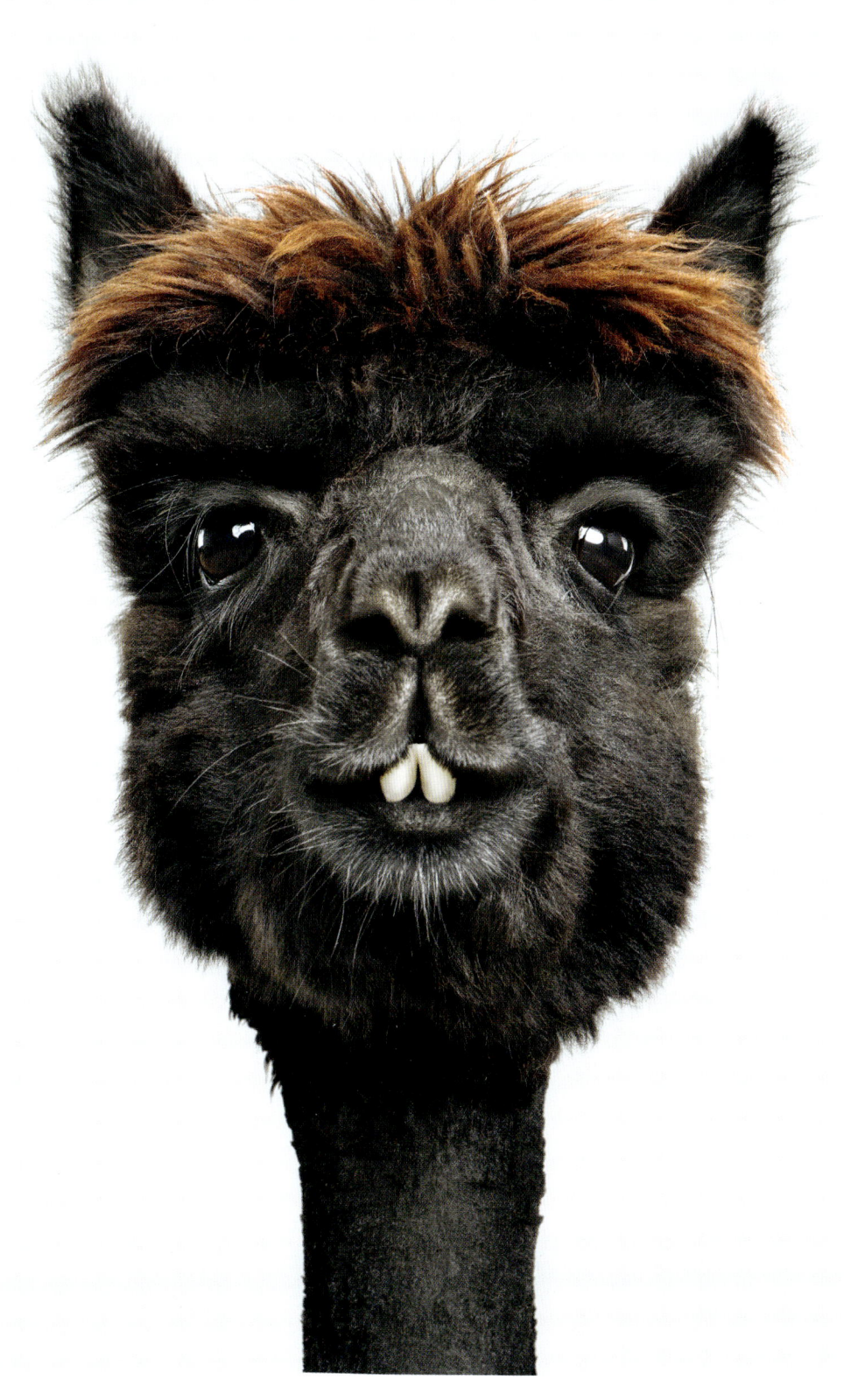

Venus

HUACAYA ALPACA

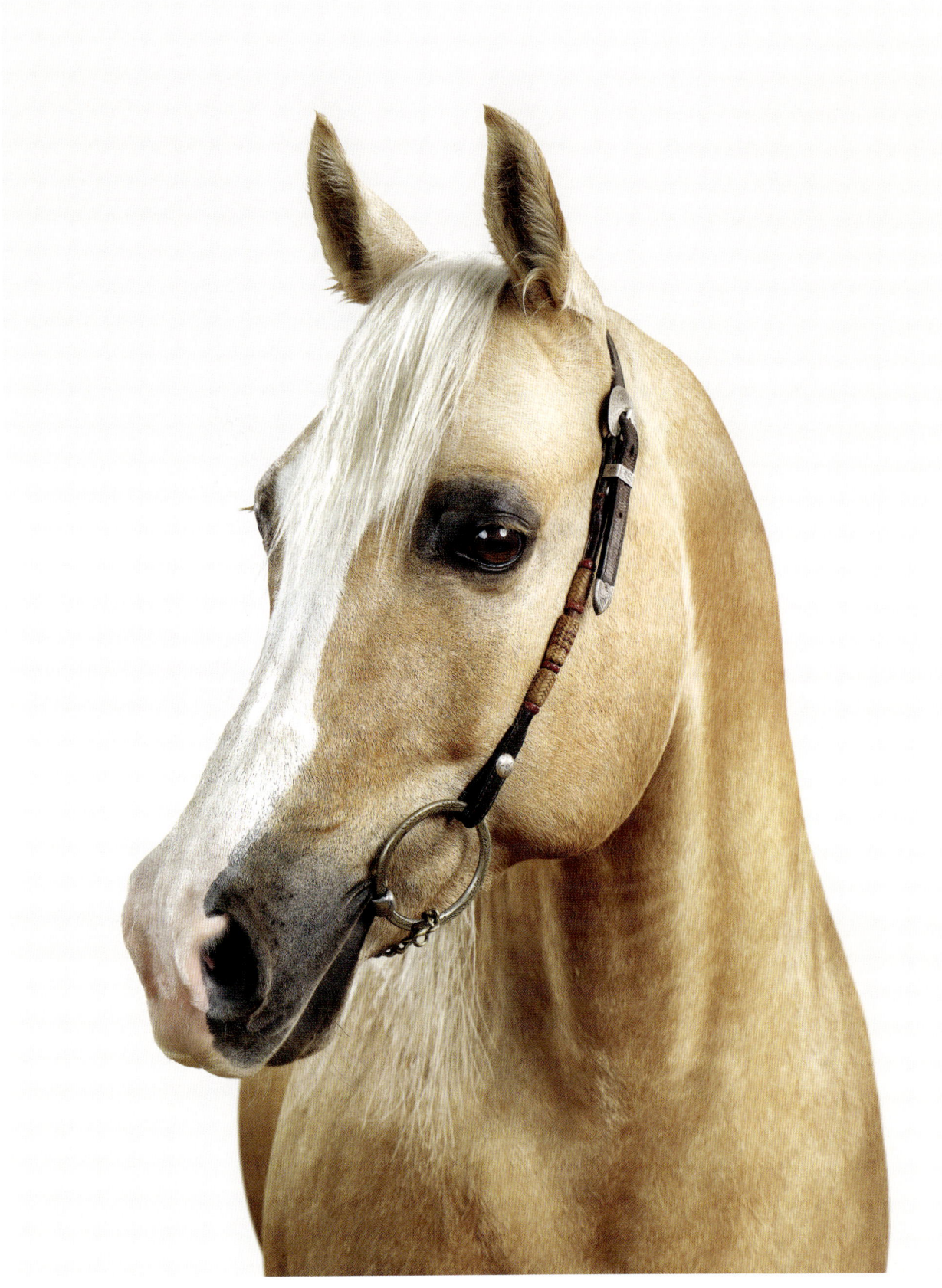

Rhapsody in Motion

PALOMINO ARABIAN HORSE

HORSES

With their rich and wild history woven into the fabric of human civilization, horses serve as monuments to partnership and progress. Long before engines roared, the booming gallop of dusty hooves led thousands of historic journeys, adventures, and discoveries. Yet, beyond transportation, horses have also been our trusted confidants, loyal companions, and honorable allies.

As an observer behind the lens, the profound intuition I witness in these animals is nothing short of mesmerizing. With an uncanny ability to sense the subtlest shift in mood or emotion, horses connect with us on a level that's both profound and palpable. This deep understanding between horse and human has fostered a bond that spans centuries.

In all of their beauty and grandeur, horses command awe and reverence. Their majestic, muscular stature is matched only by their gentle souls, a combination like no other in the animal kingdom. I aim to showcase horses as the epitome of strength and sensitivity—magnificent and powerful beasts with an unparalleled legacy of service, companionship, and intuitive connection.

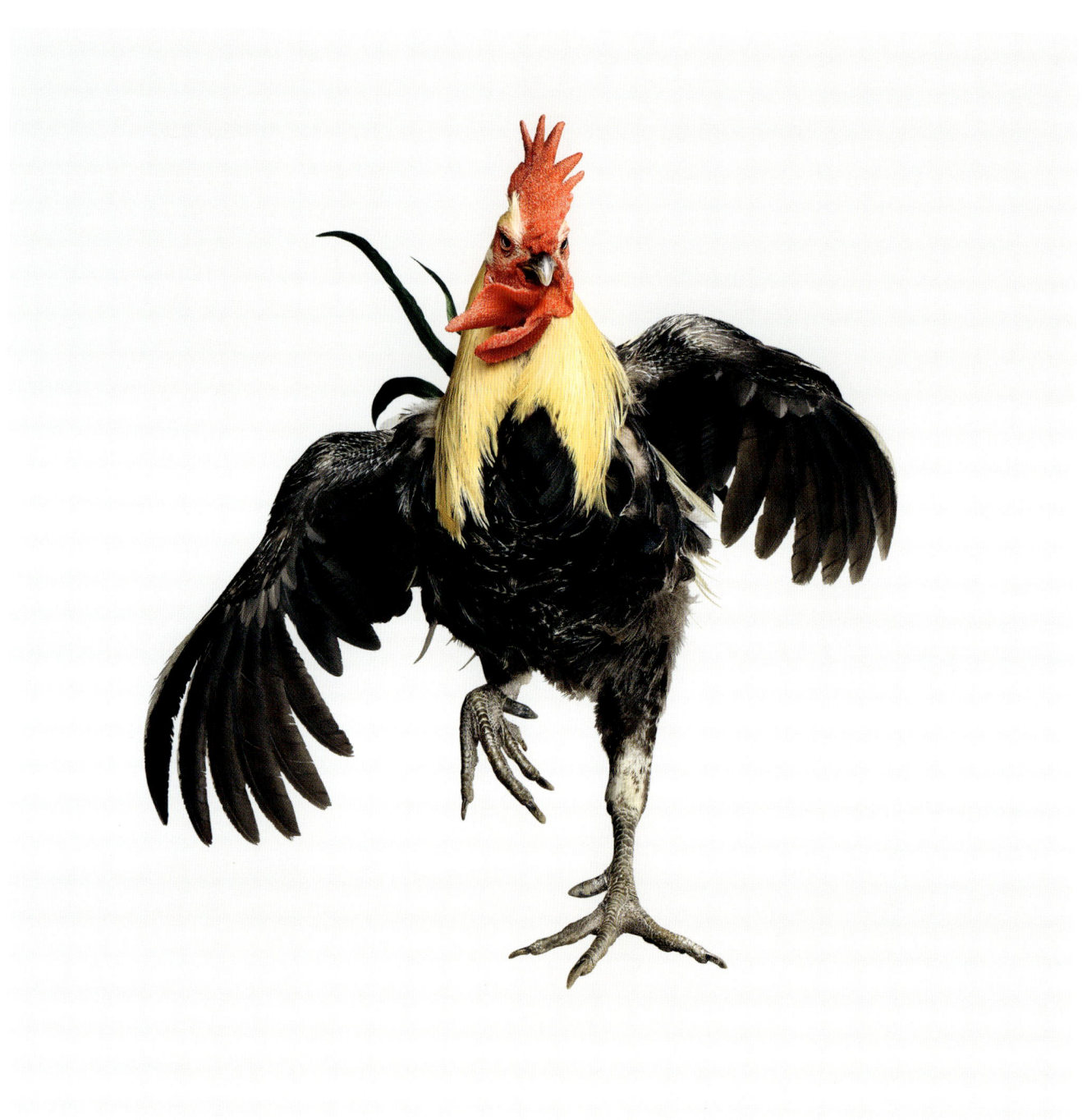

Duke

DENIZLI LONGCROWER ROOSTER

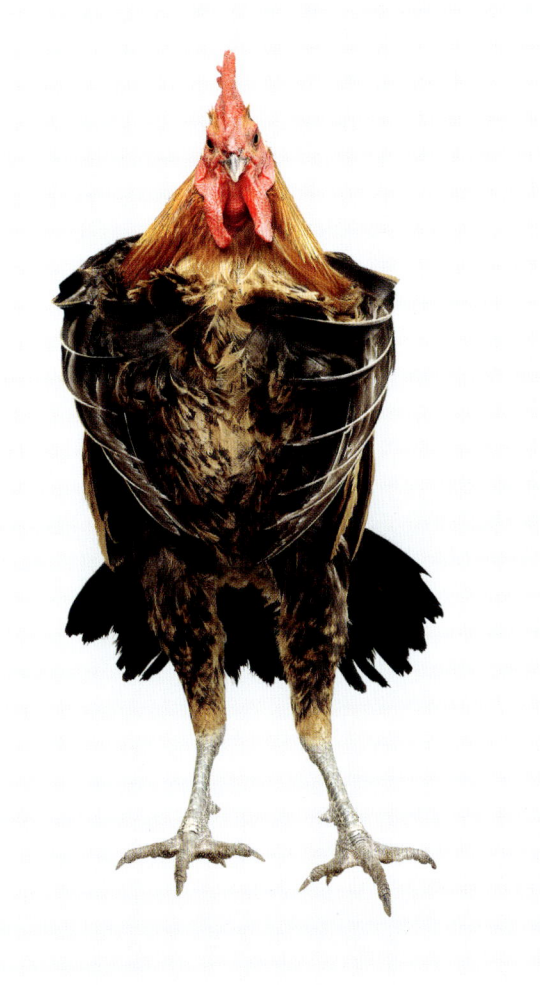

Orion

DENIZLI LONGCROWER ROOSTER

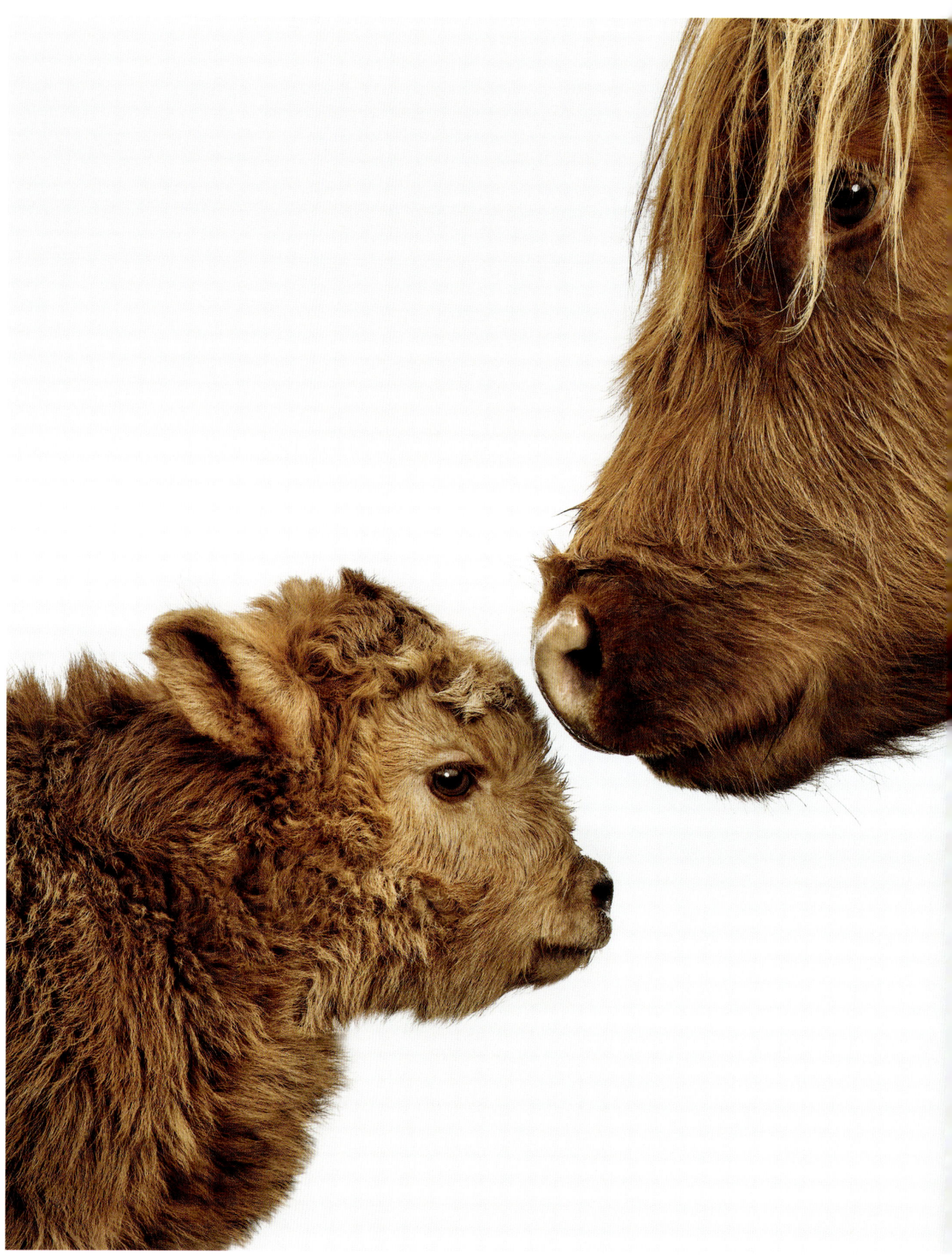

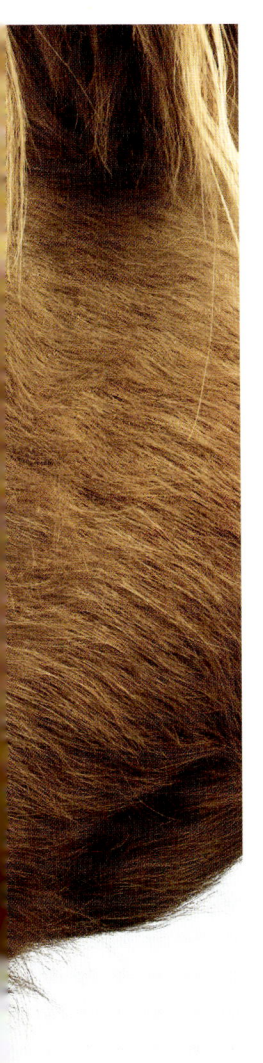

Sandy and Sunny

RED HIGHLAND COW AND CALF

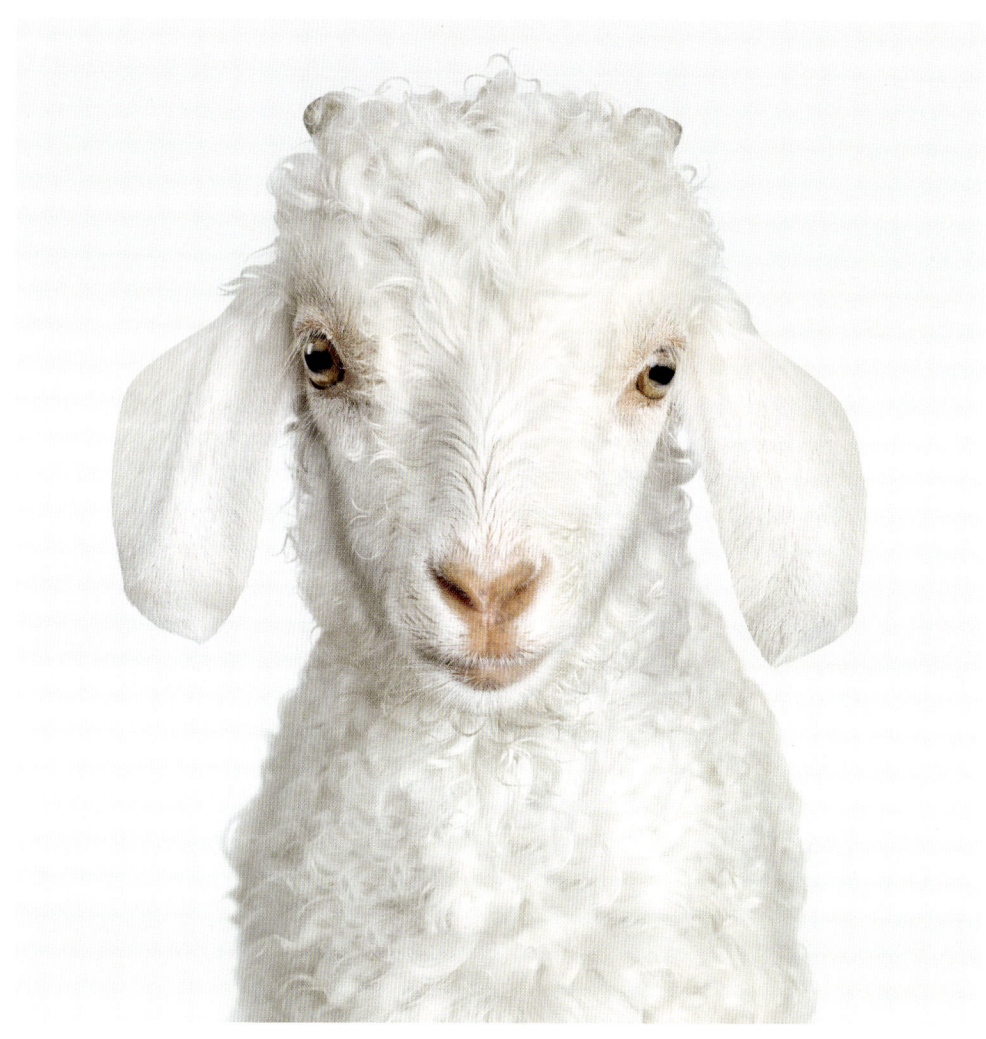

Clover

ANGORA DOELING GOAT

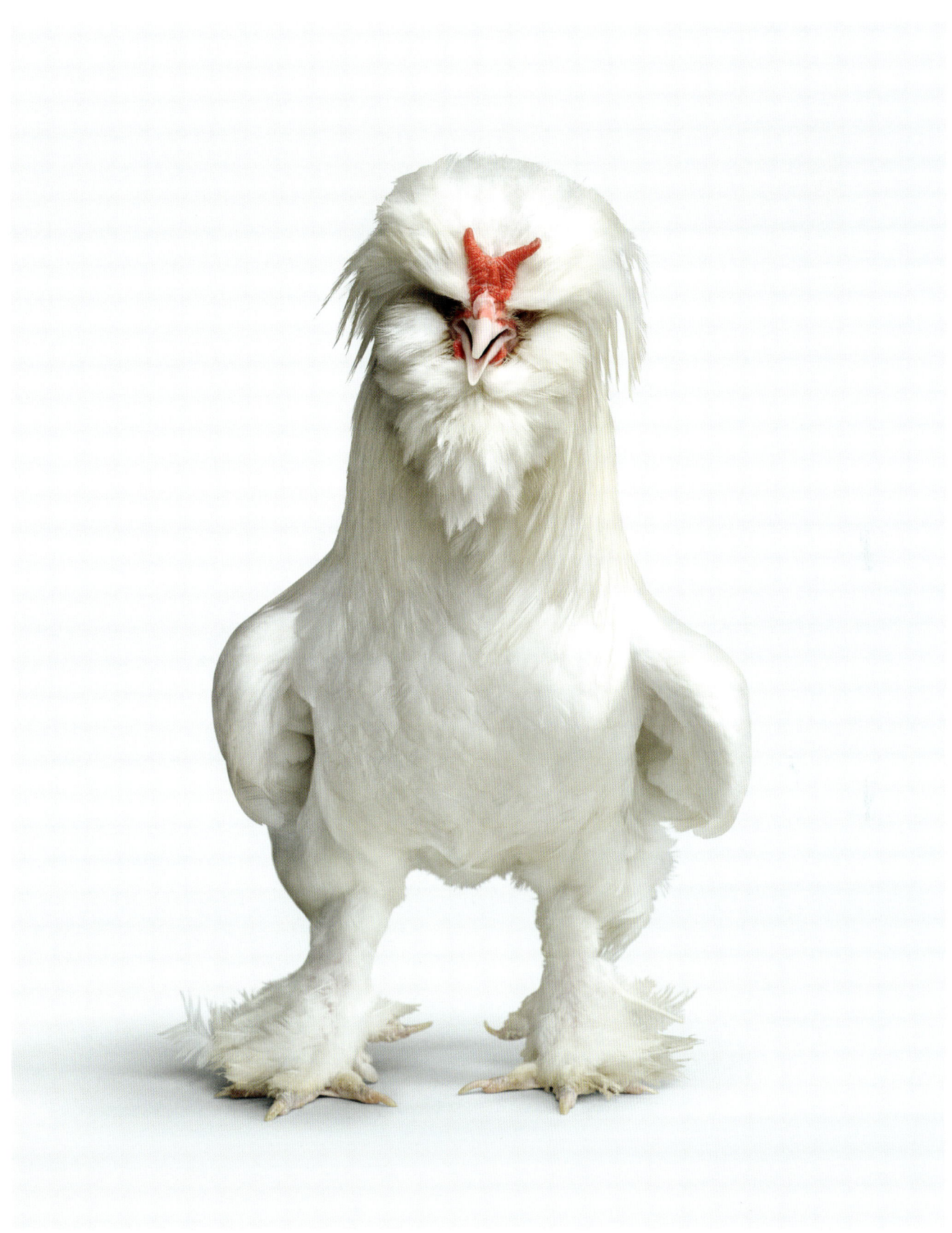

Aleister

WHITE SULTAN ROOSTER

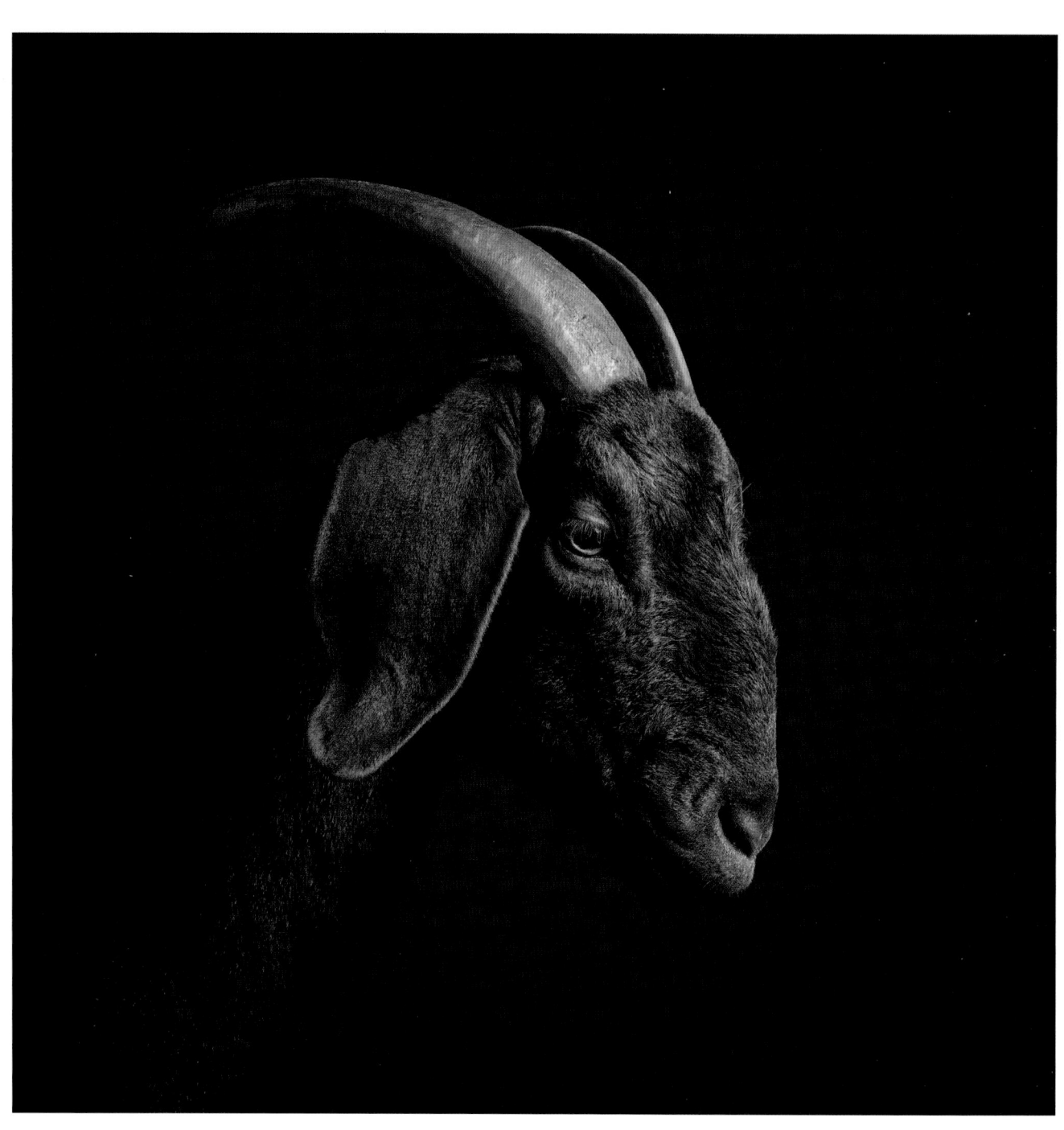

Oscuro

BLACK GOAT

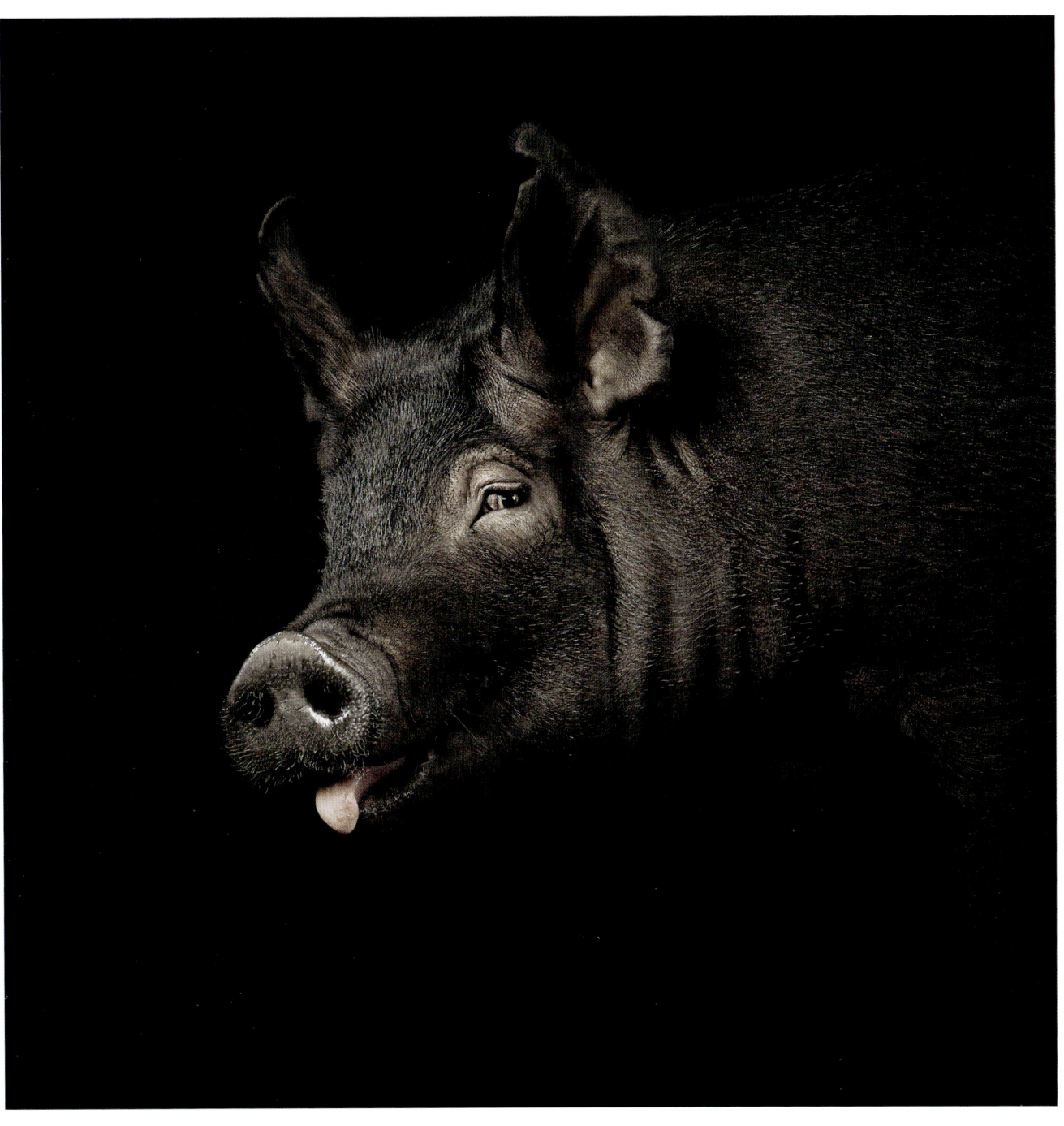

Jethro

BERKSHIRE PIG

CHICKENS

Despite their inability to fly, chickens bring an array of feathered whimsy to my portrait work. Their spirited expressions often evoke a lighthearted—even comedic—sentiment and bring a sense of playfulness to the set. Their colorful displays and lively demeanors offer a captivating array of personalities that's hard to overlook.

Amid the myriad of breeds, the stunning contrast between soft feathers and distinct textures of their combs and beaks draws me in.

These vibrant birds have not only colored my photography world with their beauty but also consistently put food on the table for generations of families. The daily gift of an egg, a symbol of sustenance and life, is a testament to their unending generosity.

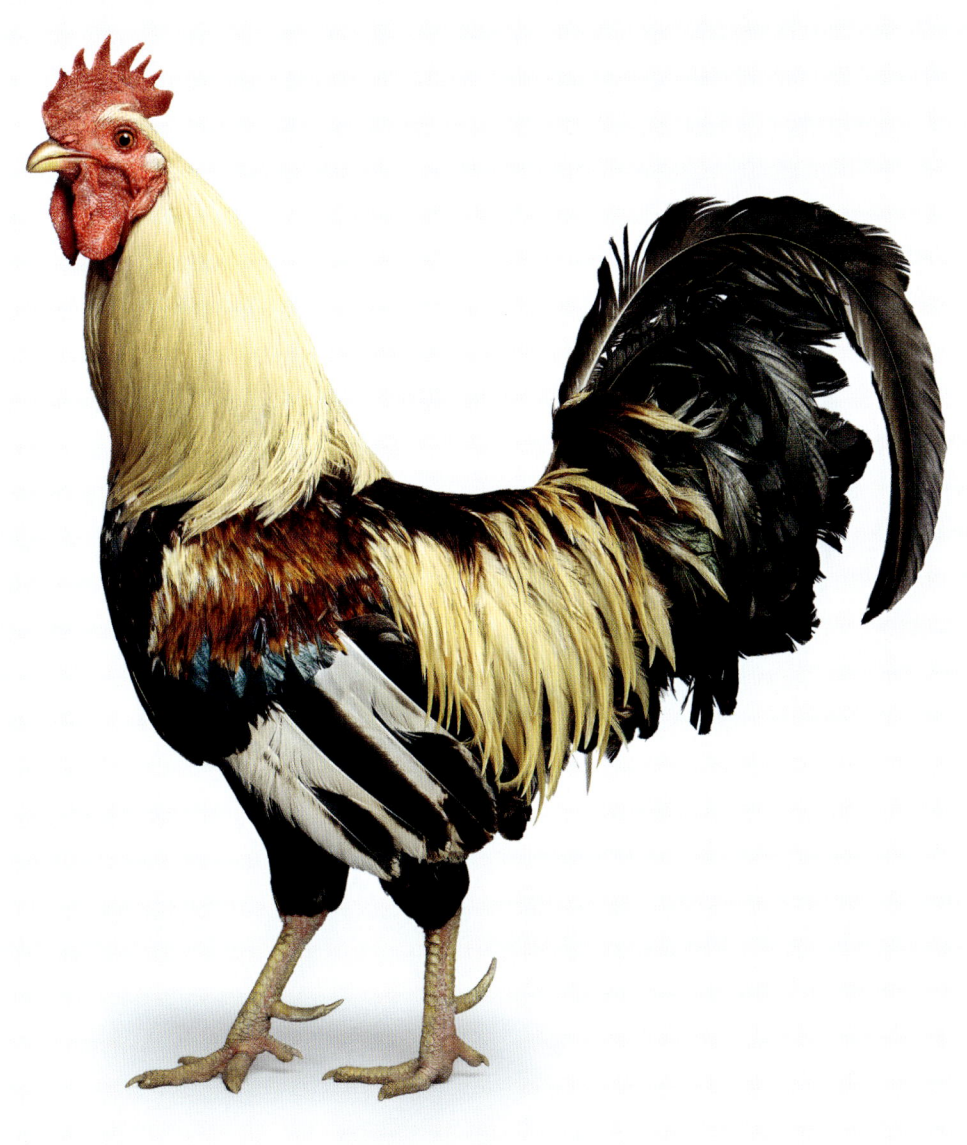

Garth

AMERICANA ROOSTER

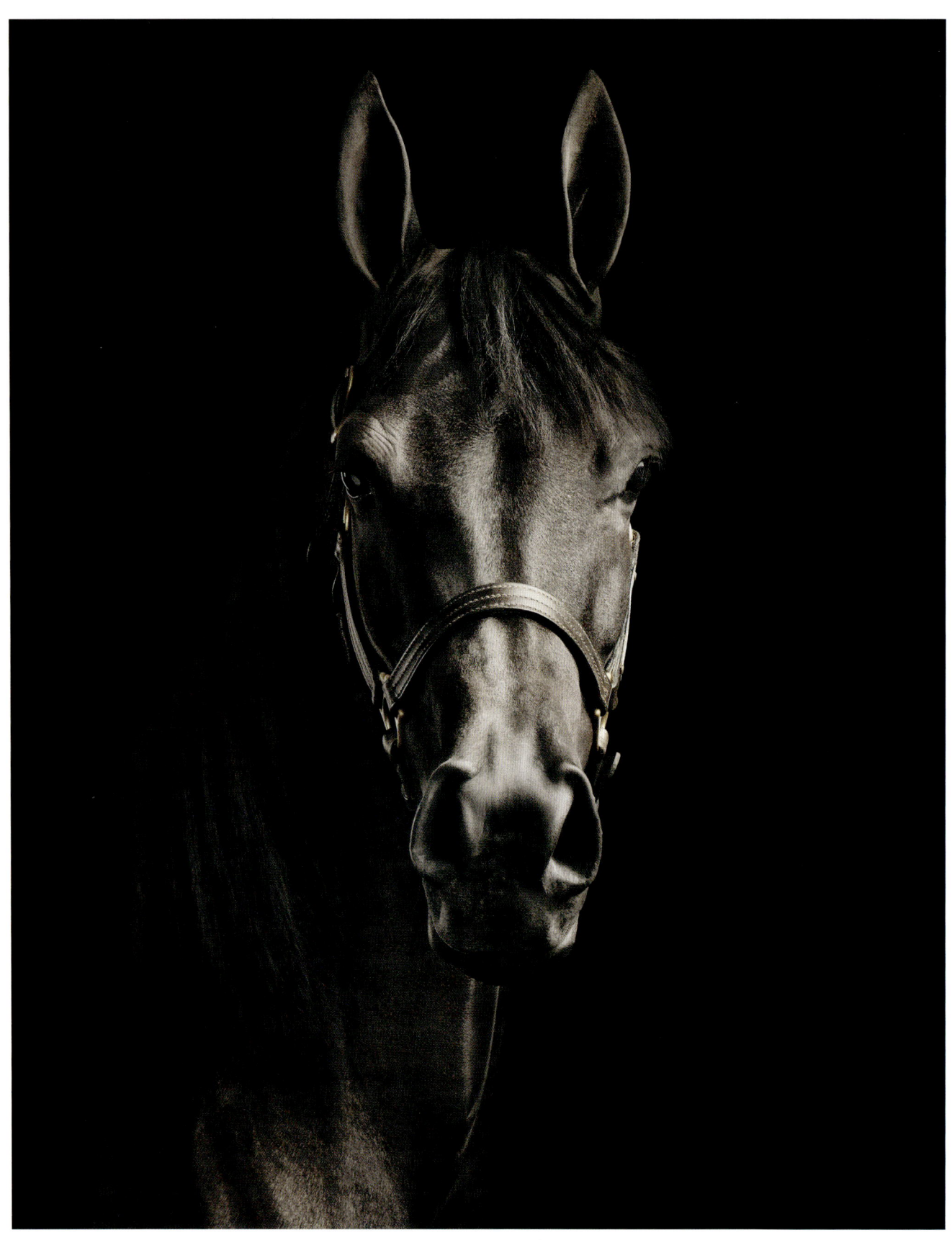

Suzie

BLACK ARABIAN MARE

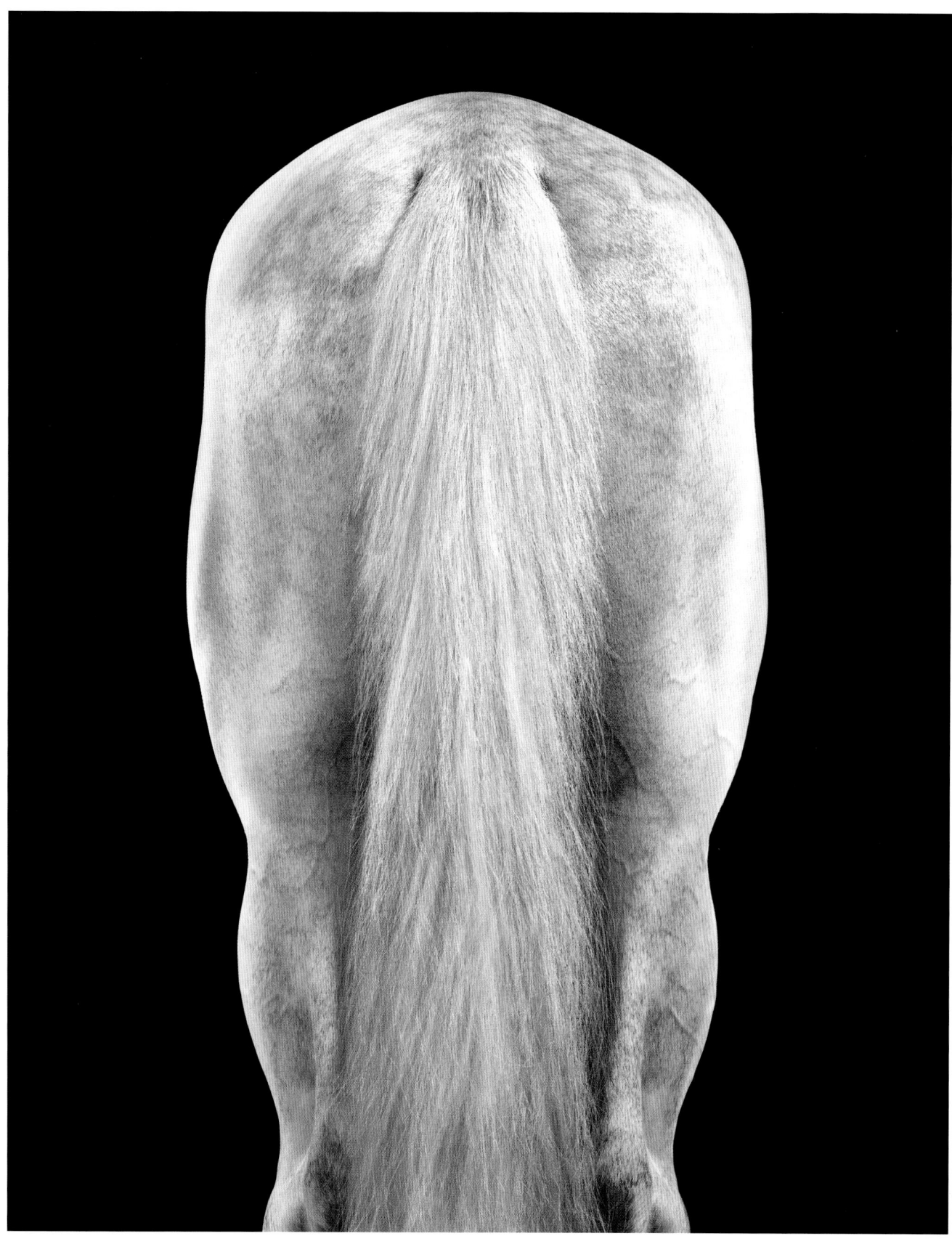

Parisii

WHITE ARABIAN STALLION

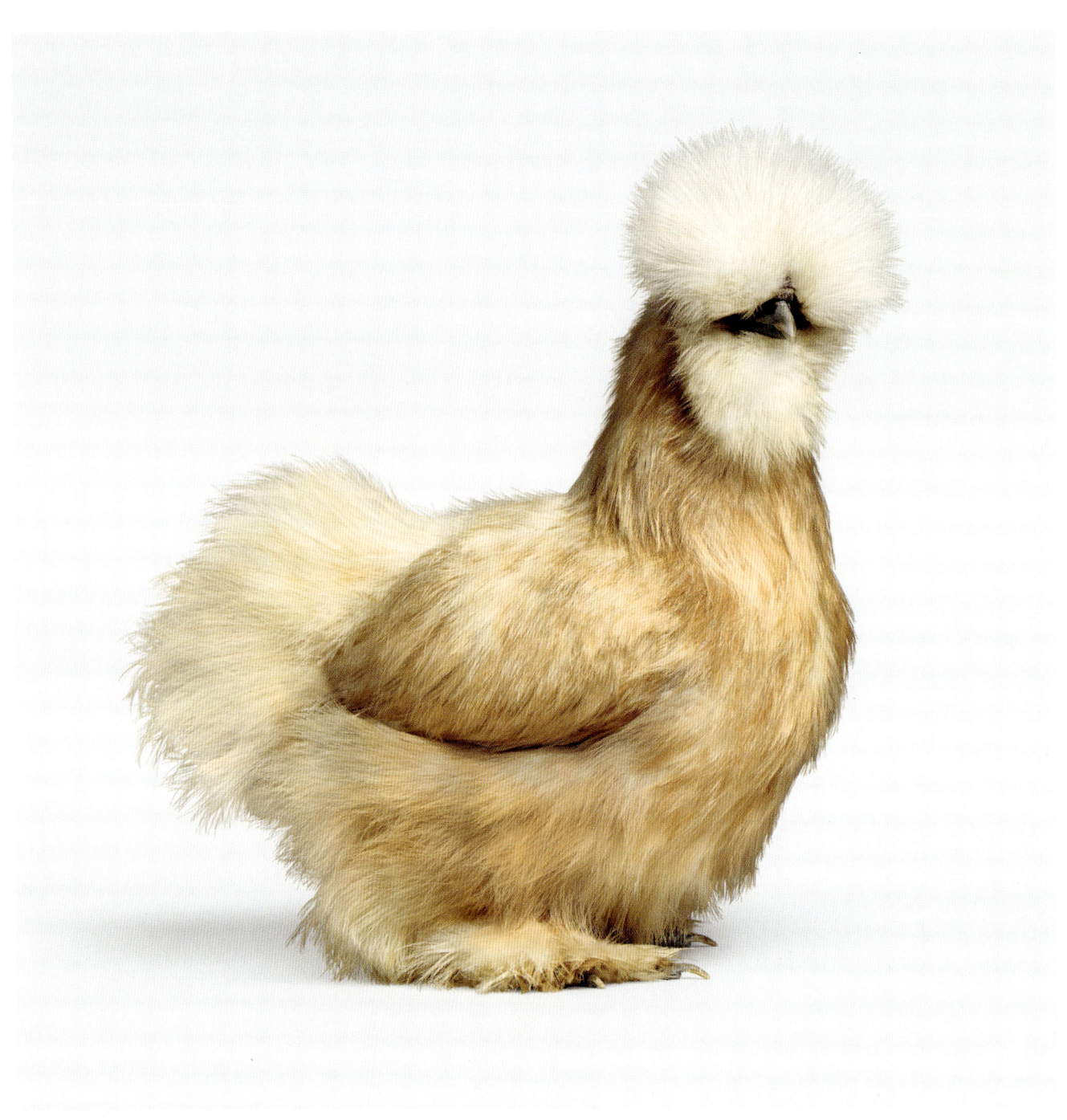

Carmela

BUFF SILKIE HEN

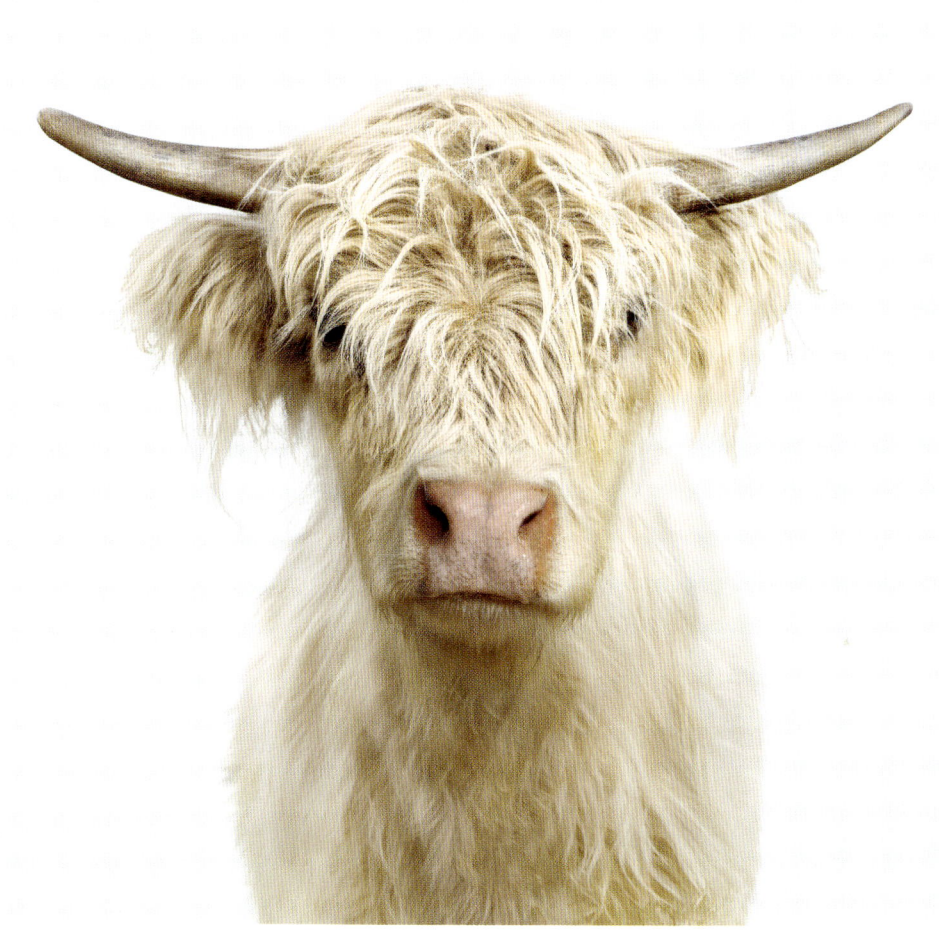

Rose

HIGHLAND COW YEARLING

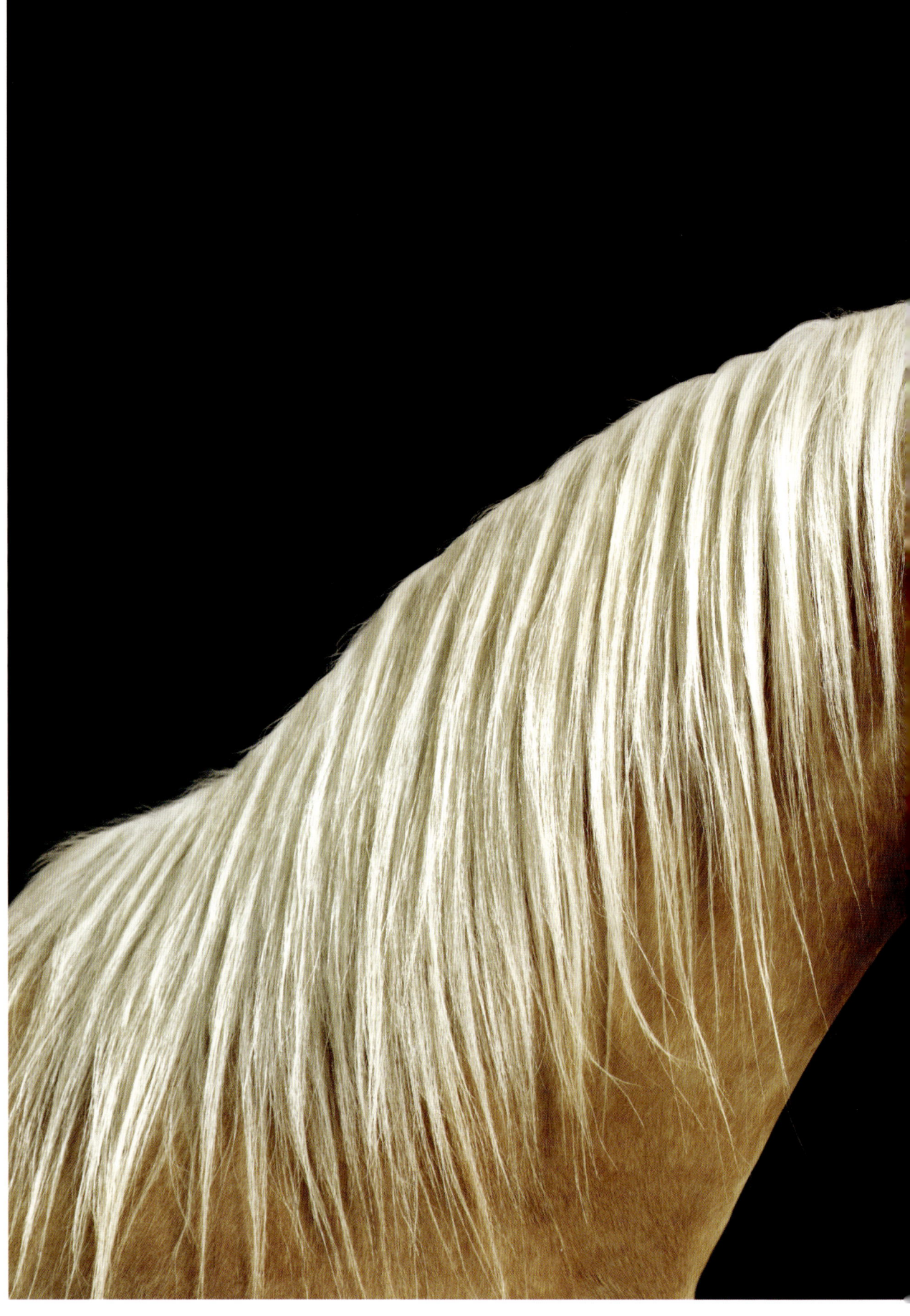

Rhapsody in Motion

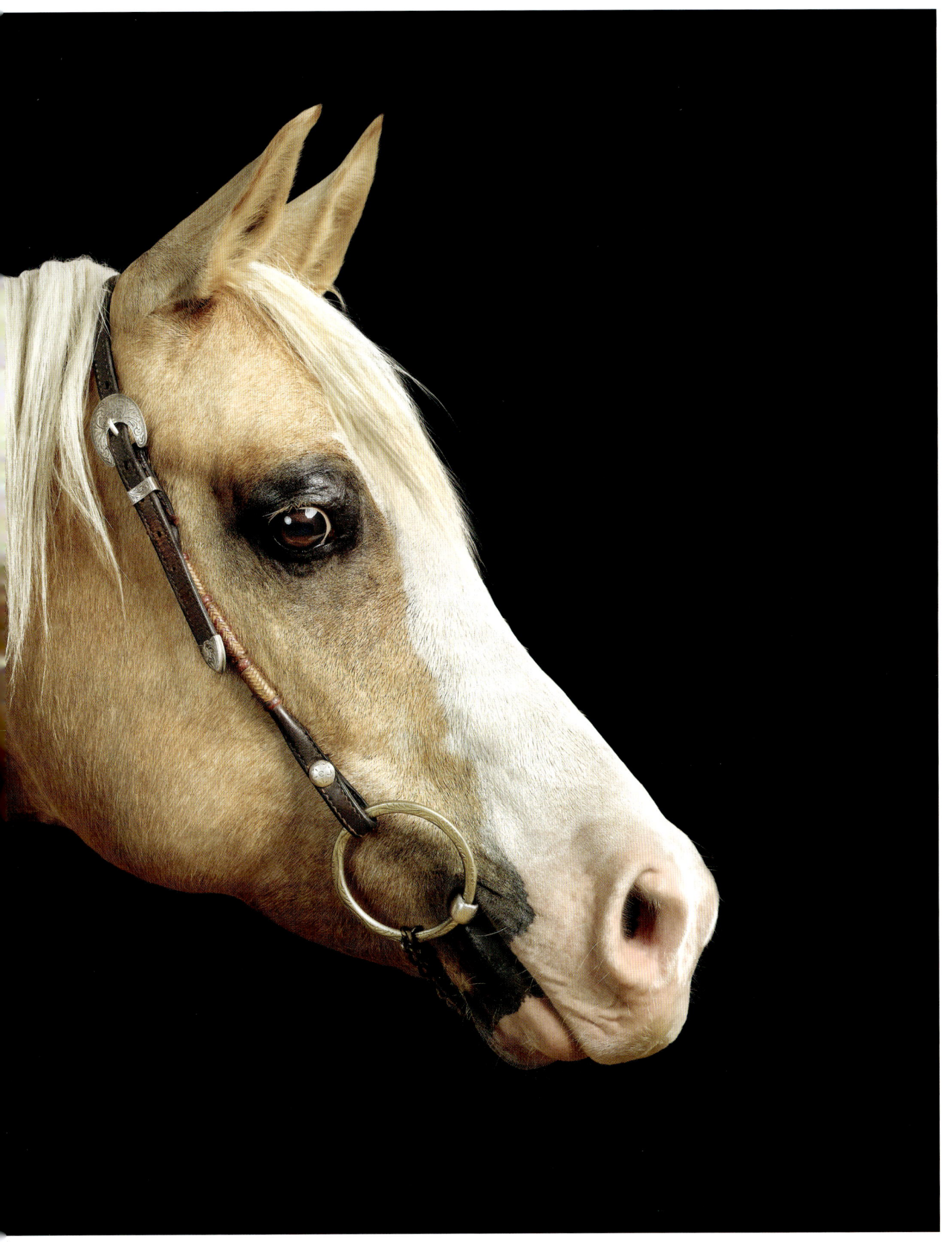

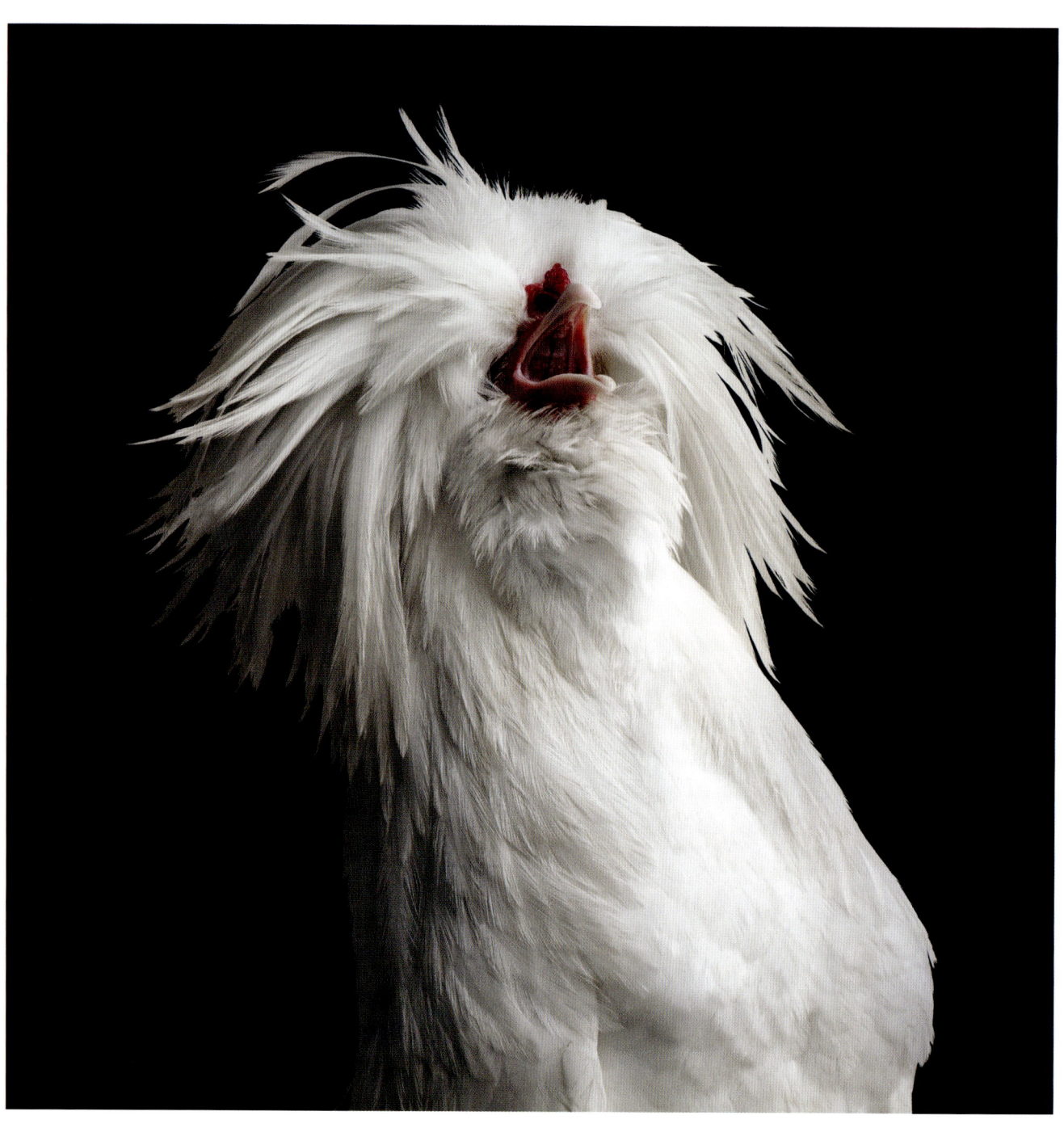

Denali

BANTAM WHITE POLISH HEN

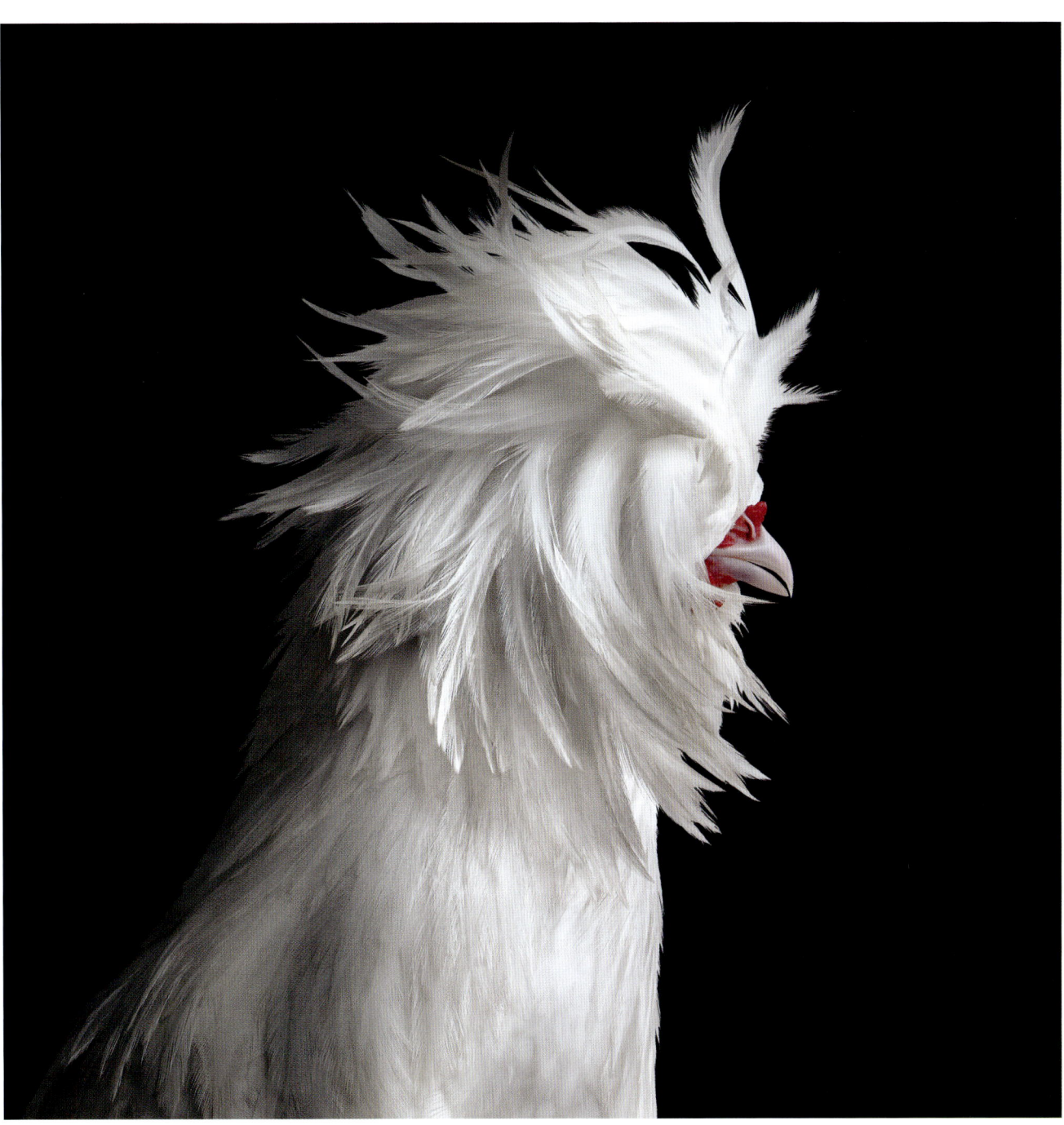

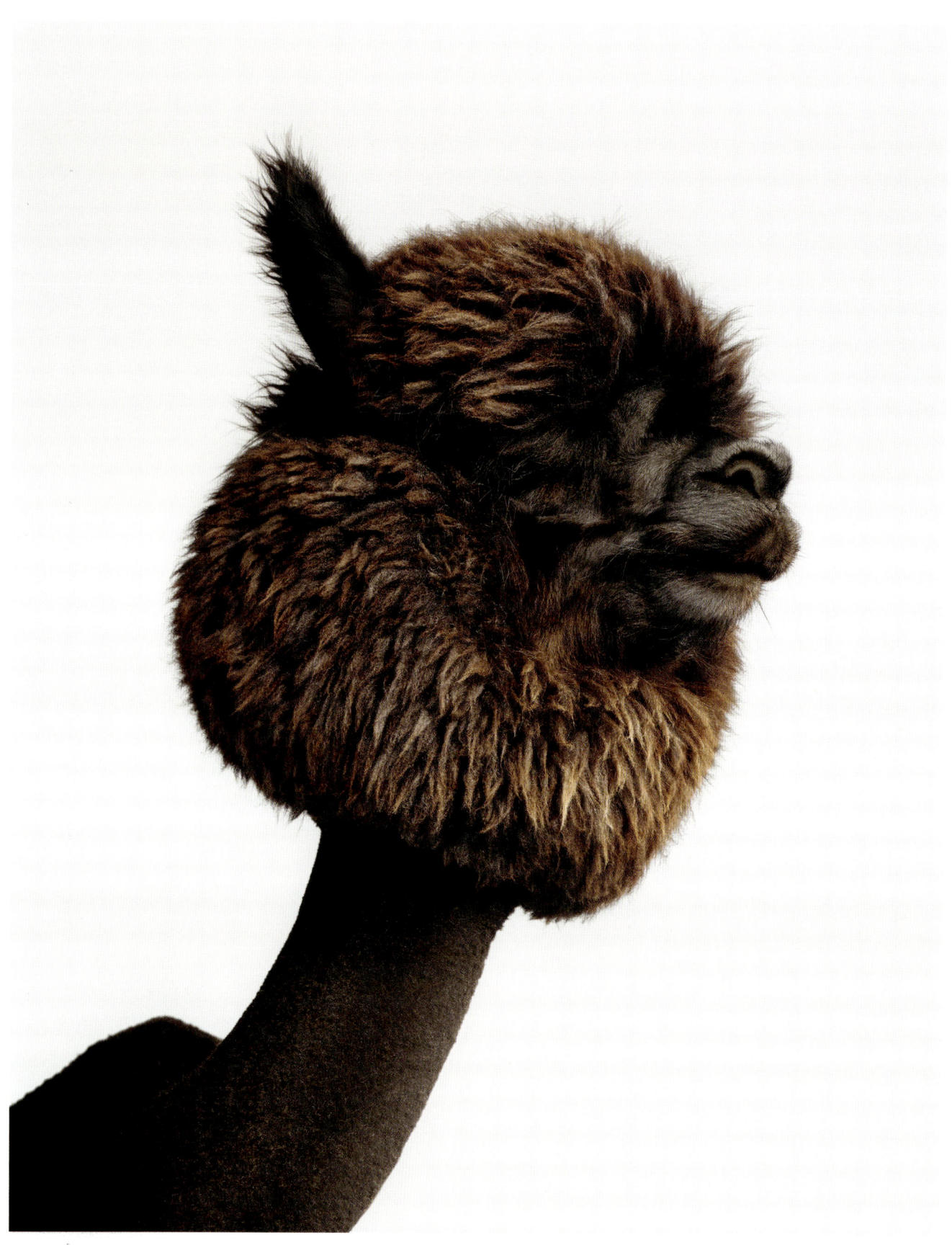

Pacheco

HUACAYA ALPACA

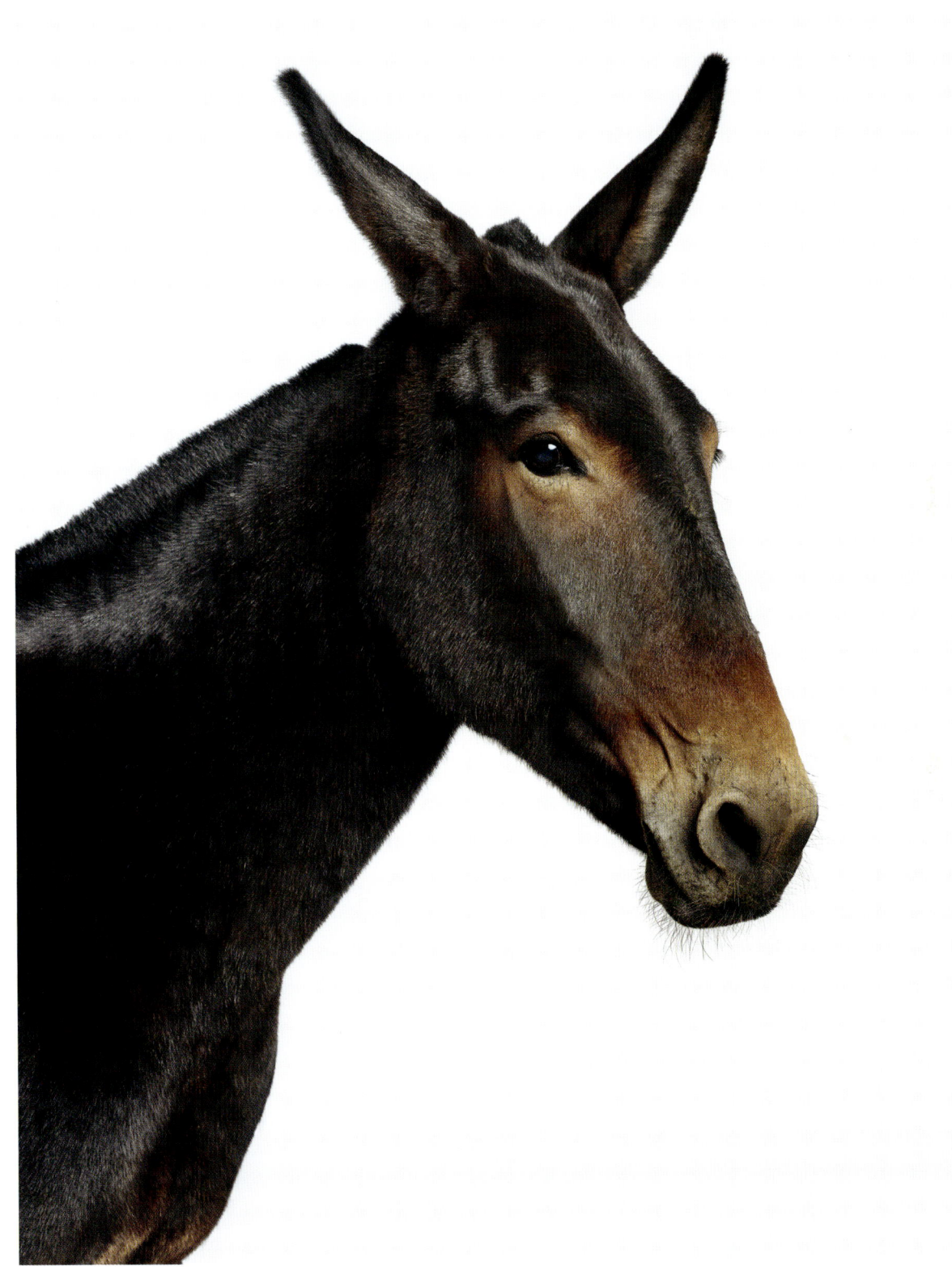

Milo

JOHN MULE

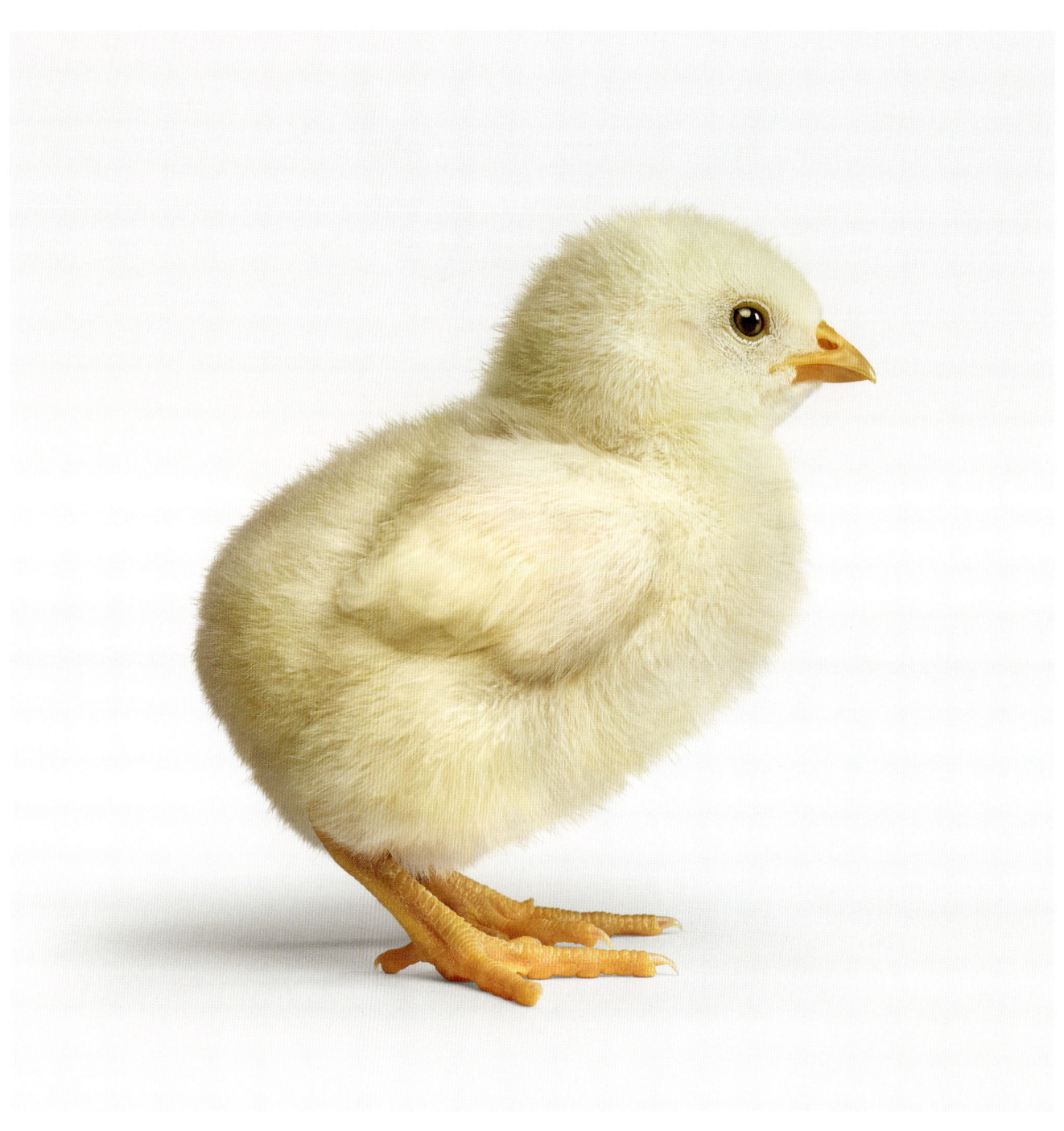

Curly

BUFF ORPINGTON CHICK

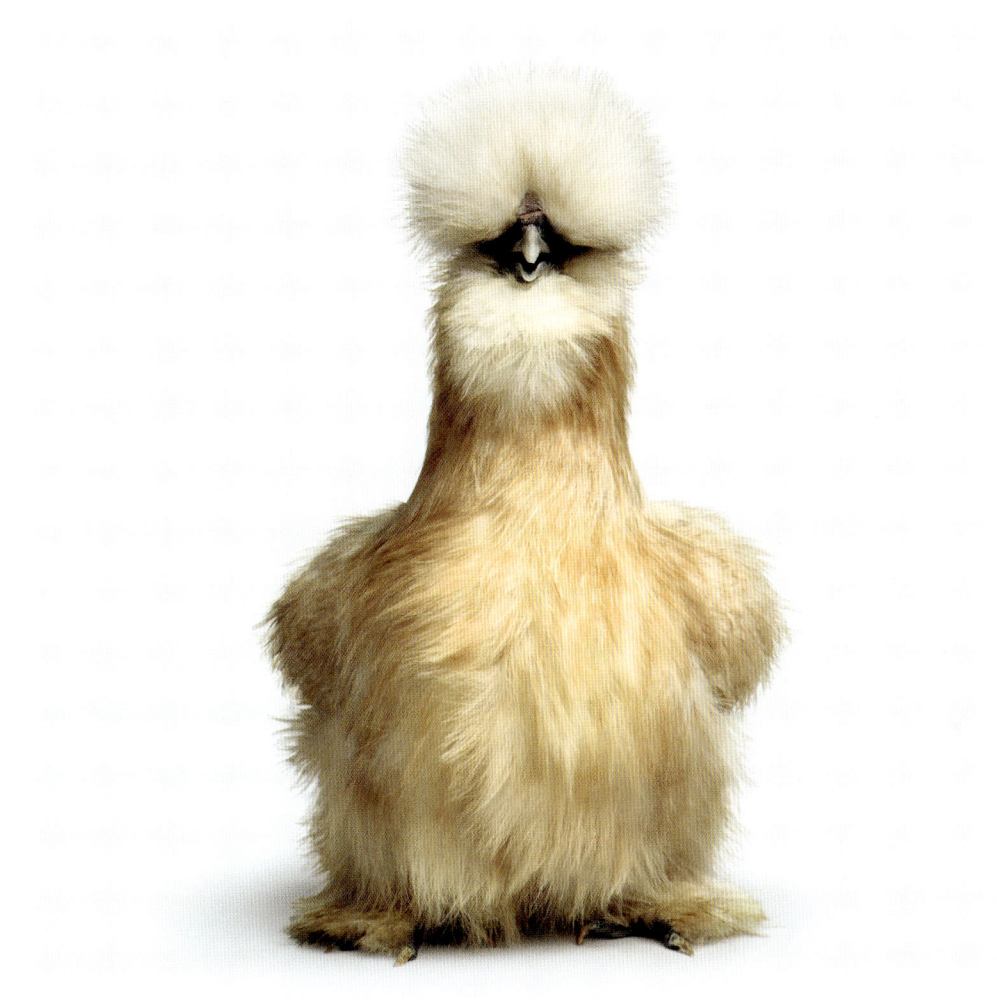

Carmela

BUFF SILKIE HEN

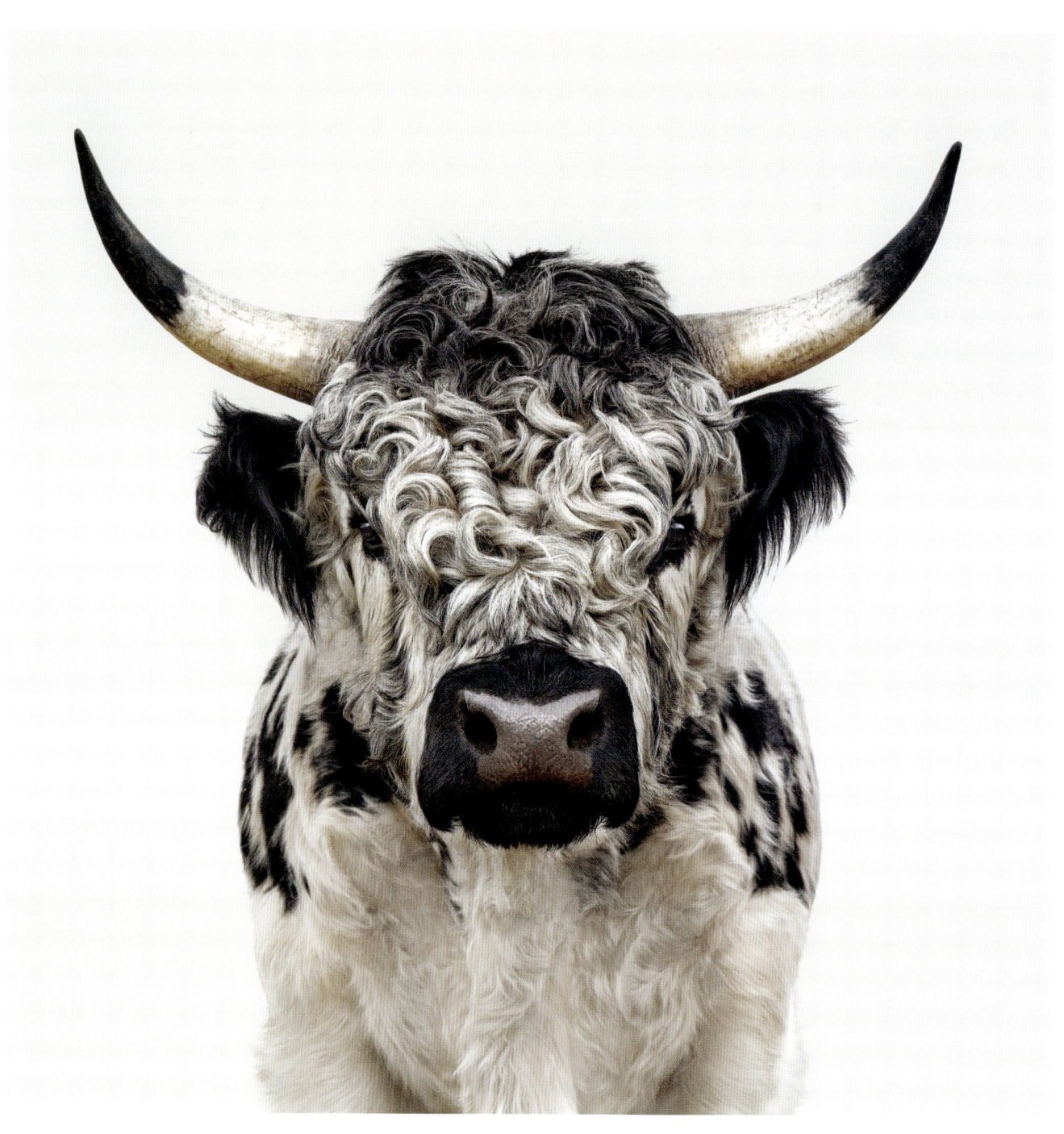

Murphy

HIGH PARK BULL

BULLS

If there is one thing I've learned, it's that a bull is not a cow and must be treated as such. Unlike cows or steers, bulls are domineering, testosterone-driven, and ruthlessly competitive. Their aggression is a survival switch that can flip swiftly, come without warning, and offer no apologies or second chances.

Photographing bulls is a dance with danger—one that requires both practical skill and an intuitive understanding of their primal instincts. Their deep snarls of intimidation and the sheer force behind every thunderous hoofbeat serve as reminders of their authority and dominance in the room.

The aura of a bull is not for the fainthearted. It's a thrilling encounter with a creature whose aggressive tendencies are as powerful as their unpredictable nature. Each portrait is a tribute to the primal essence of a bull and an homage to the untamed spirits roaming American pastures.

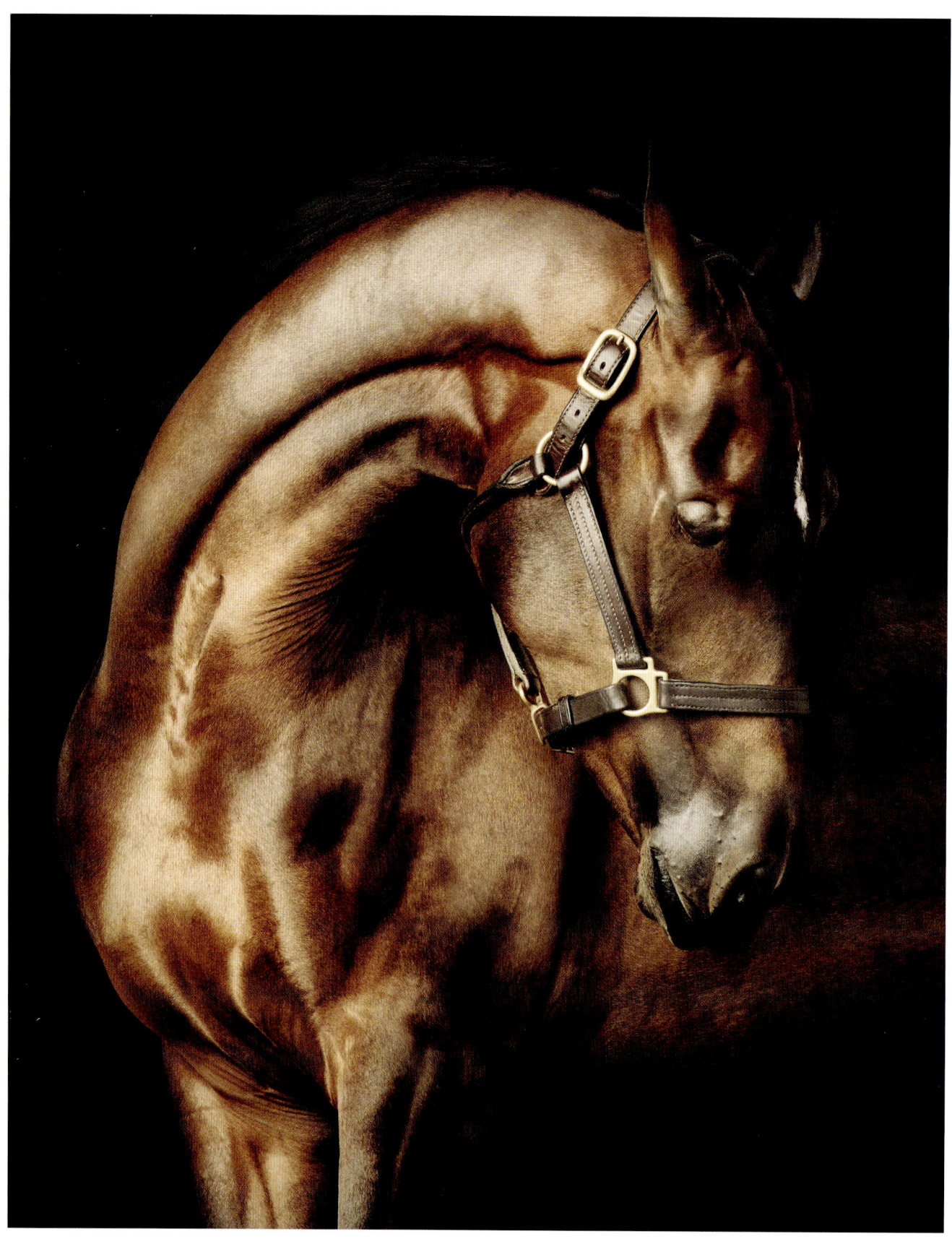

Ravioli

ARABIAN MARE

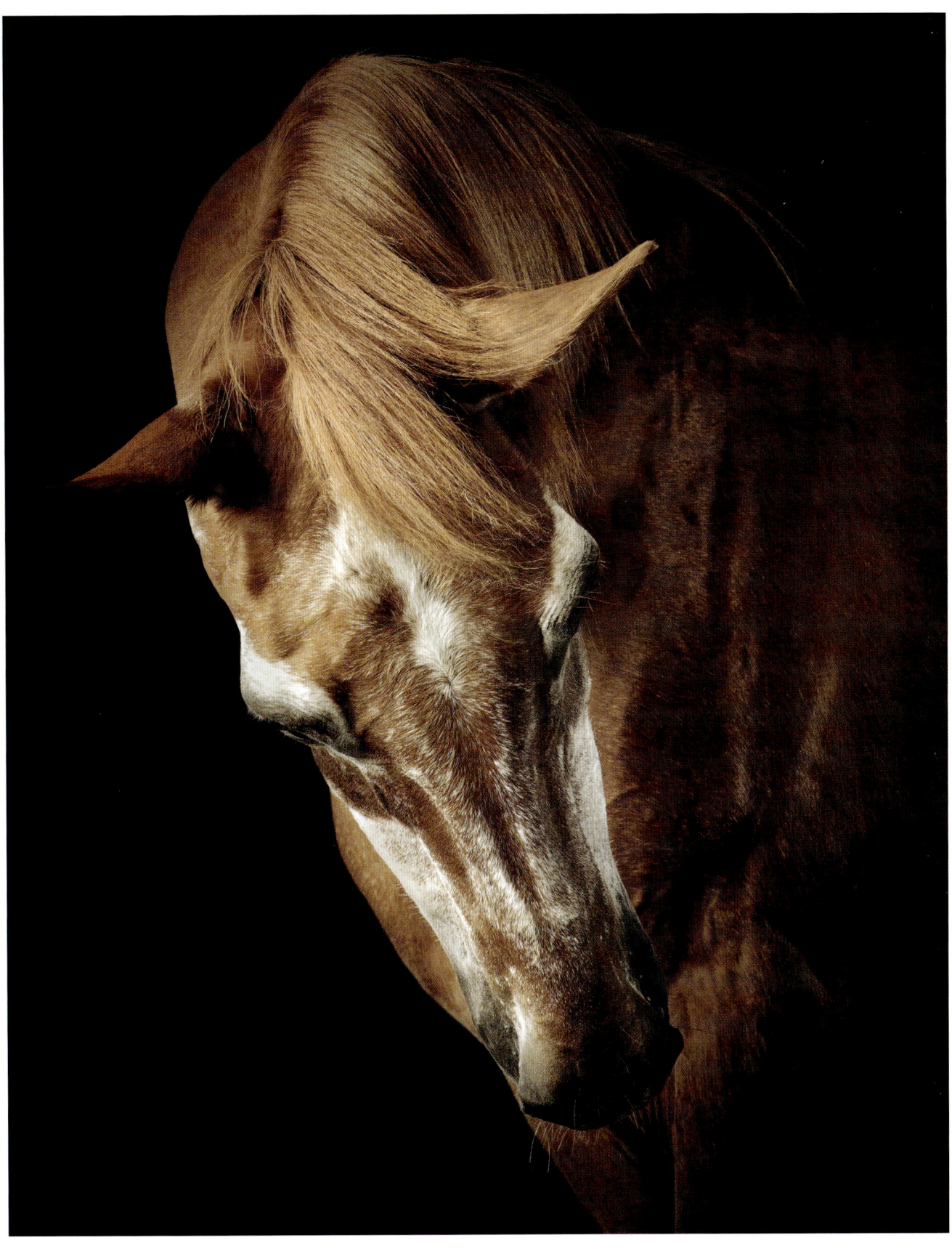

Aloha

SADDLEBRED ARABIAN MARE

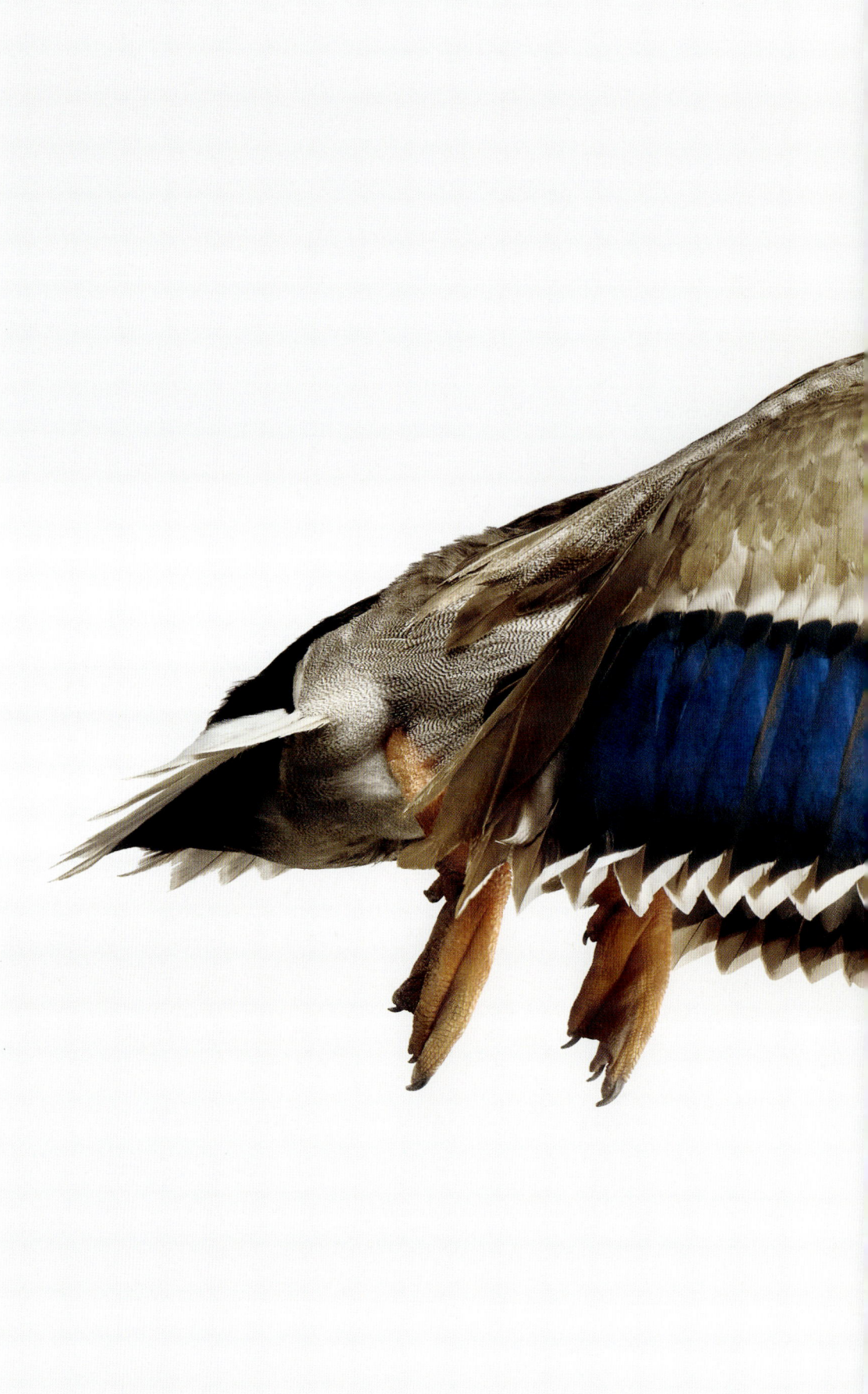

Jasper

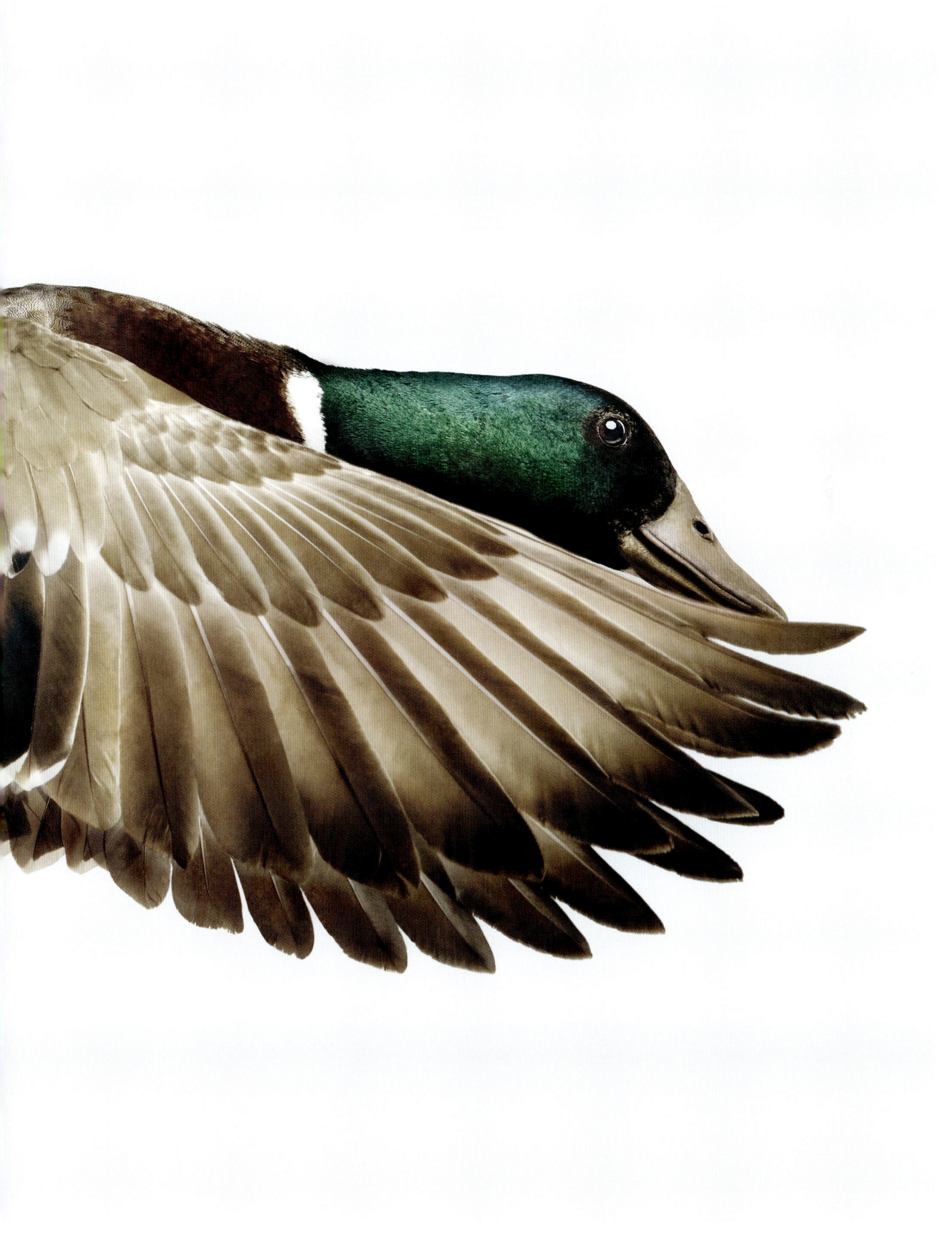

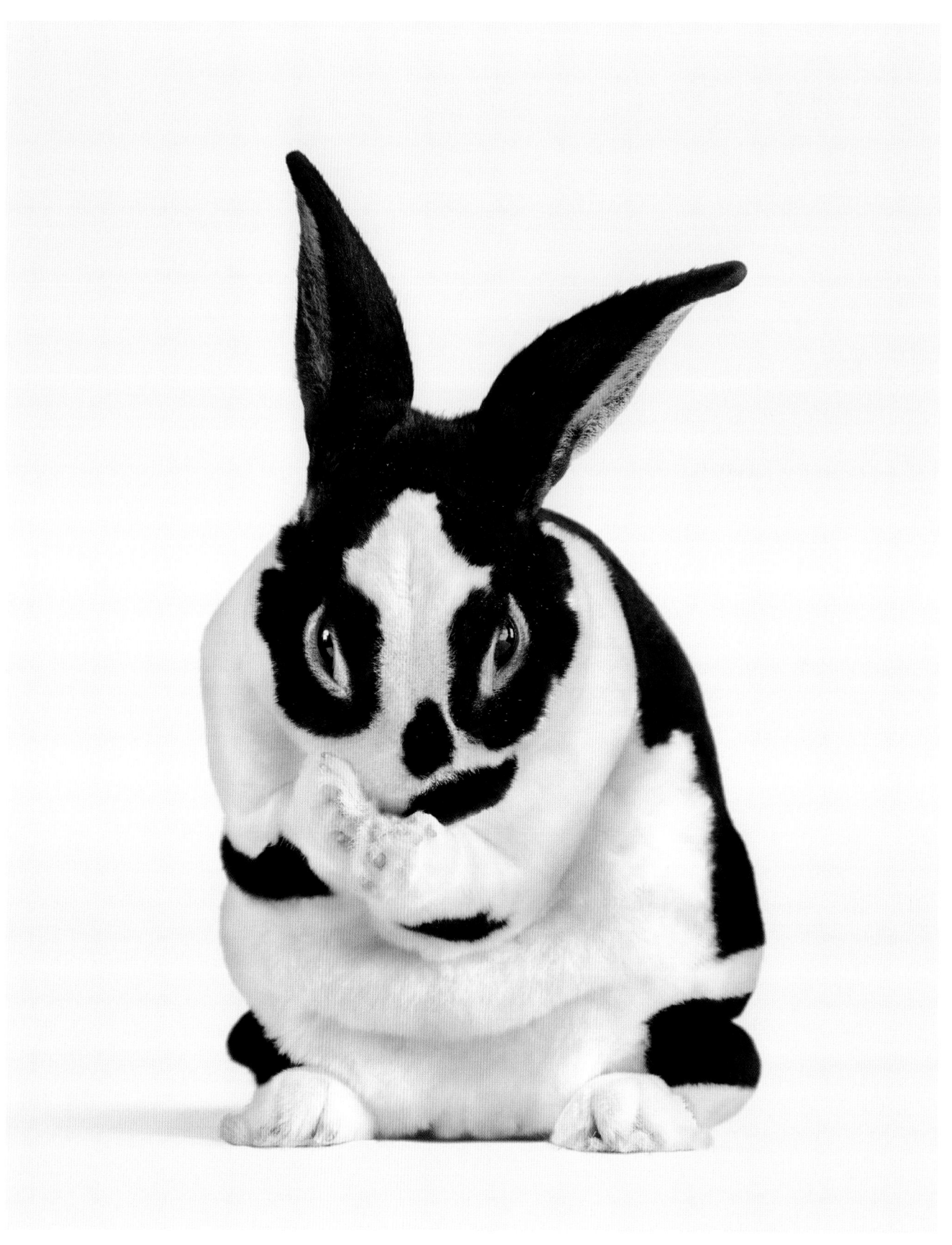

Dutton

MINI REX RABBIT

Dutton was always up to something.

Originally raised to be a show bunny, he

instead retired early due to his naughty

ways on the show table. Mischievous to

his core, Dutton is also known for being

quite the escape artist—always wondering

what's on the other side of the fence, always

wondering how he can stir things up. This

paw-to-face shot was a perfect portrayal

of his coy ways. You can't hide this time,

Dutton. His black splotches did a beautiful

job of highlighting his shape against the

white background.

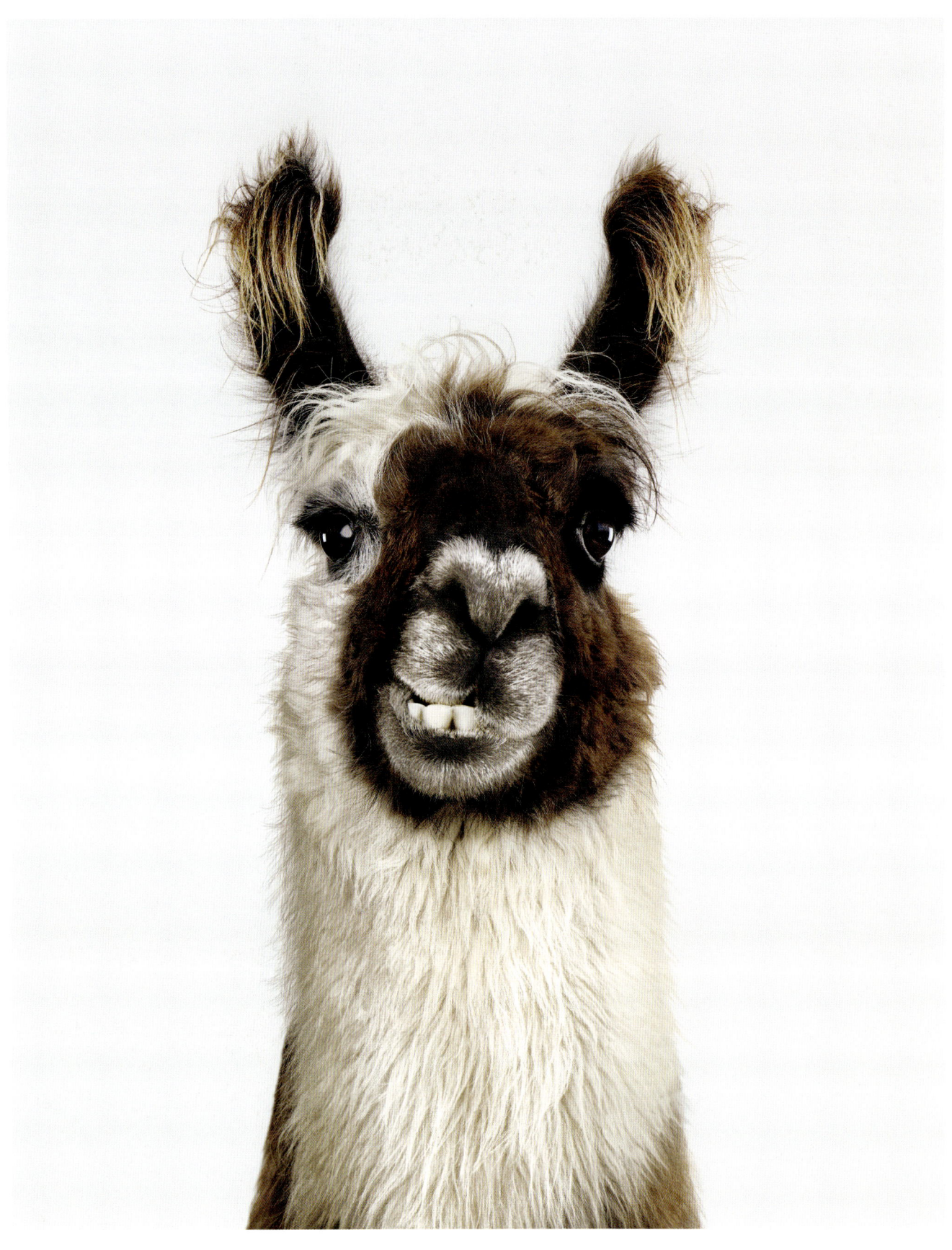

Hawk

LLAMA

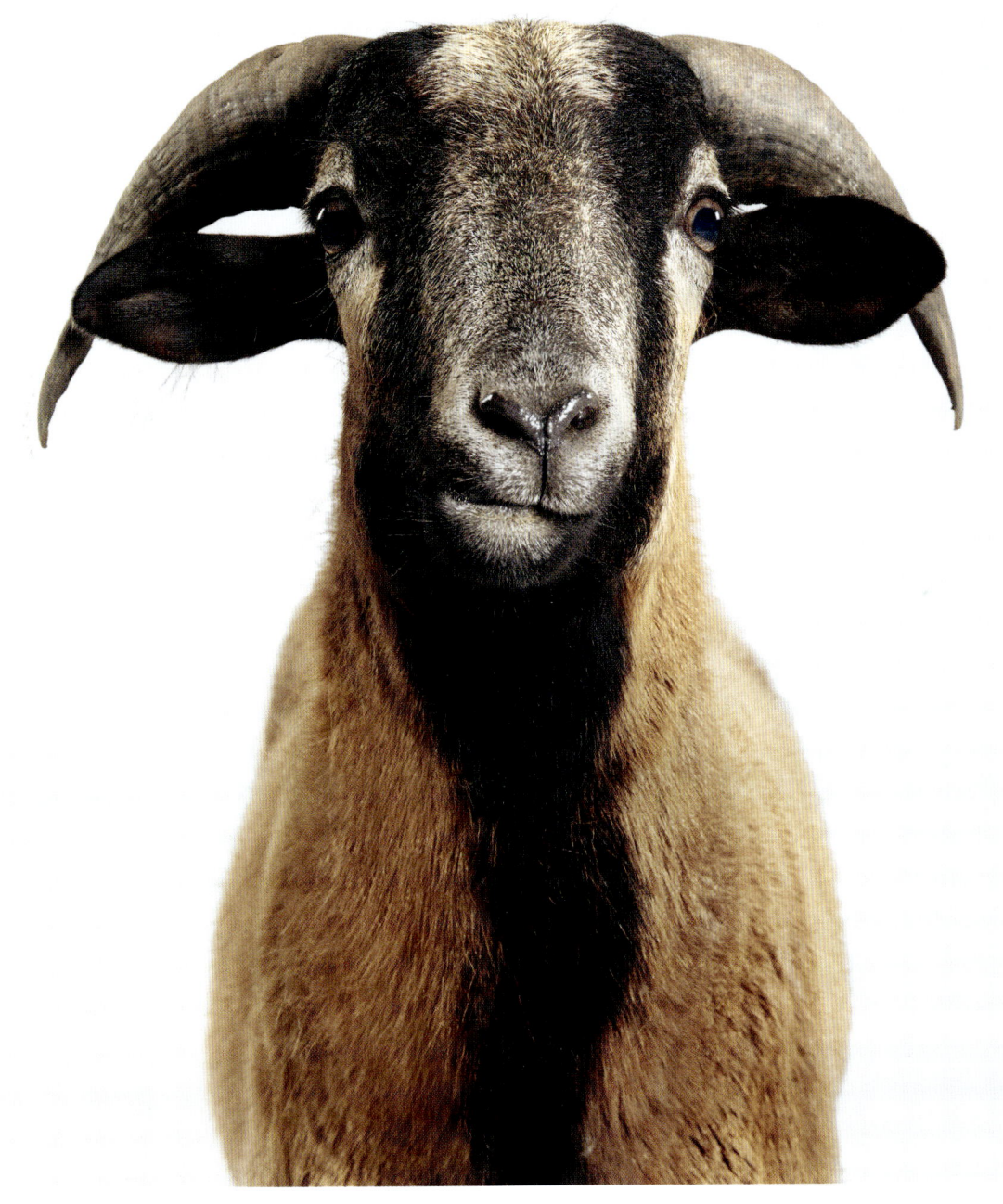

Octavius

BARBADOS BLACKBELLY SHEEP

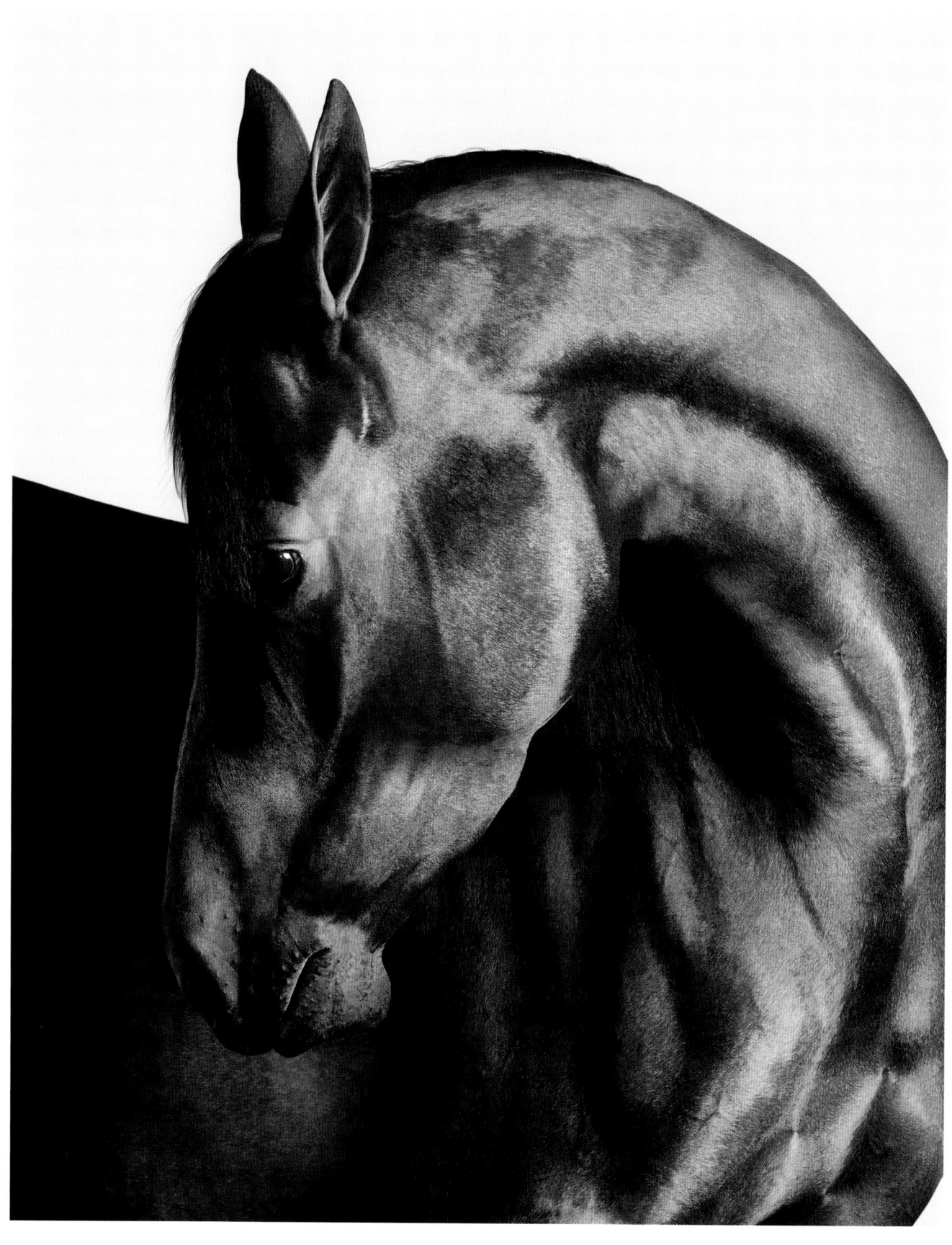

Suzie

BLACK ARABIAN MARE

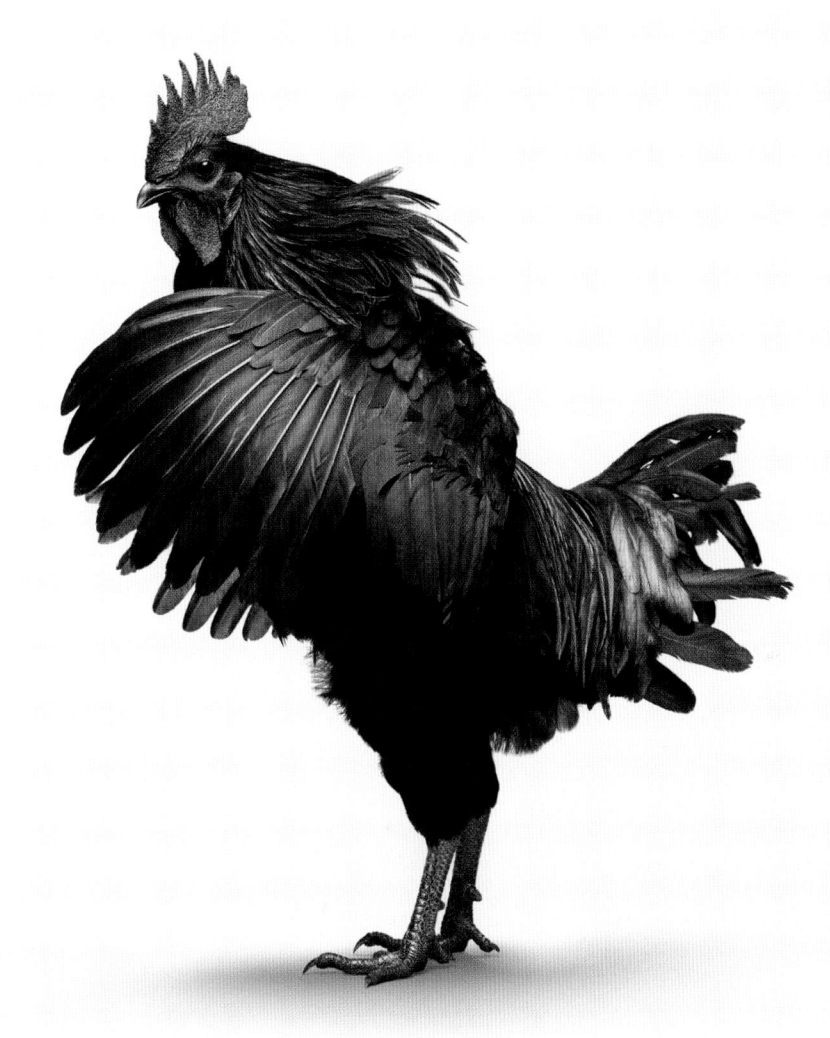

Krishna

AYAM CEMANI ROOSTER

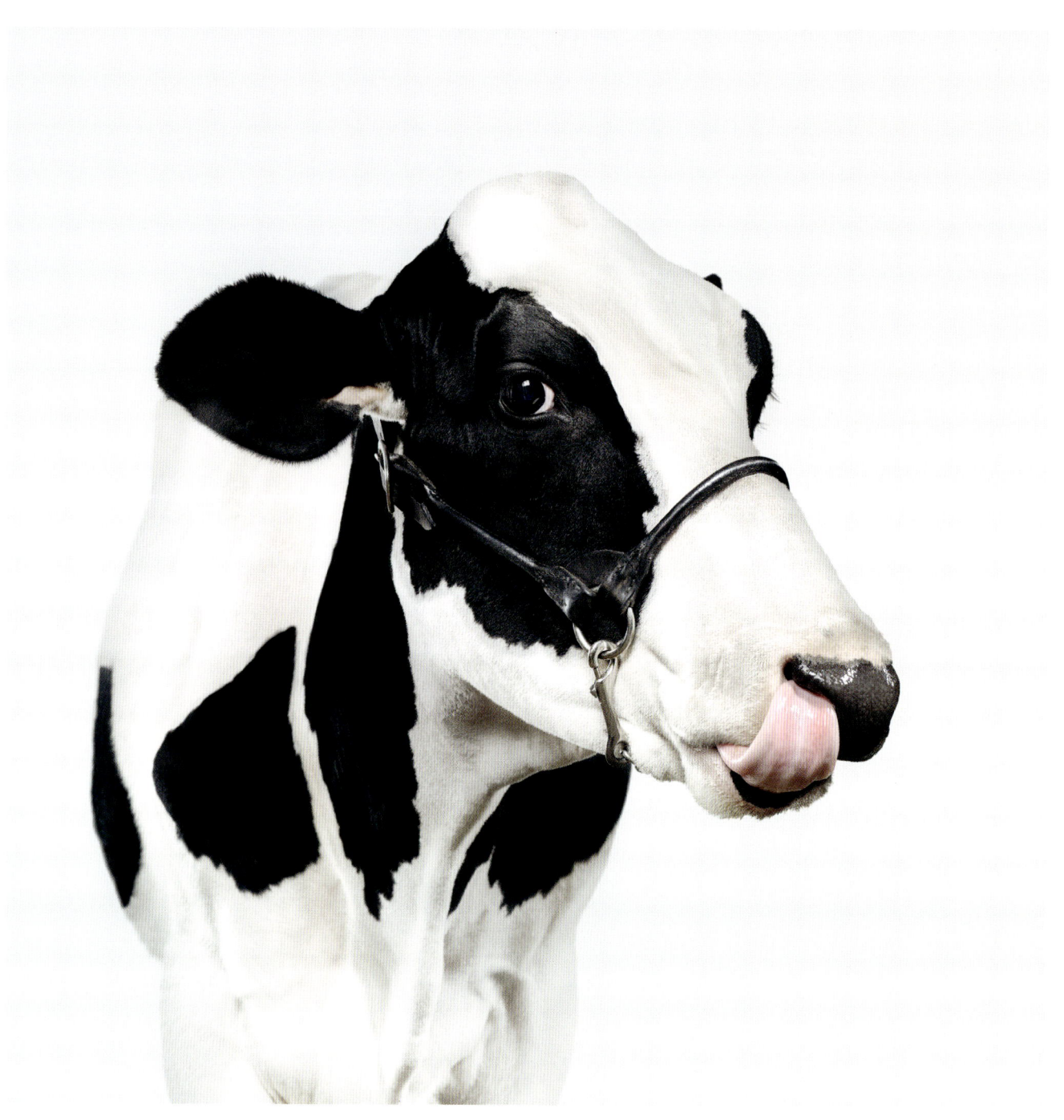

Shirley

HOLSTEIN COW

COWS

Cows hold a uniquely special place in my photographic journey, being the very first animals I photographed in a studio setting. Their inherent charm, affection, and friendly personalities transcend cultures, endearing them to audiences worldwide.

If there is a hallmark in my portraiture, it is undeniably my work with these quirky yet magnificent beings. I've often said that if I am renowned for anything, it is my portraits of cows.

Aside from being one of my favorite subjects, cows have also been pillars upon which civilizations have flourished. Their multifaceted contributions—be it the nourishing milk, the sustaining meat, or the durable hide—have been invaluable to humanity.

Beyond their physical offerings, cows have grown to become the quintessential farm animal, not only in this book but also in just about every civilization across the planet.

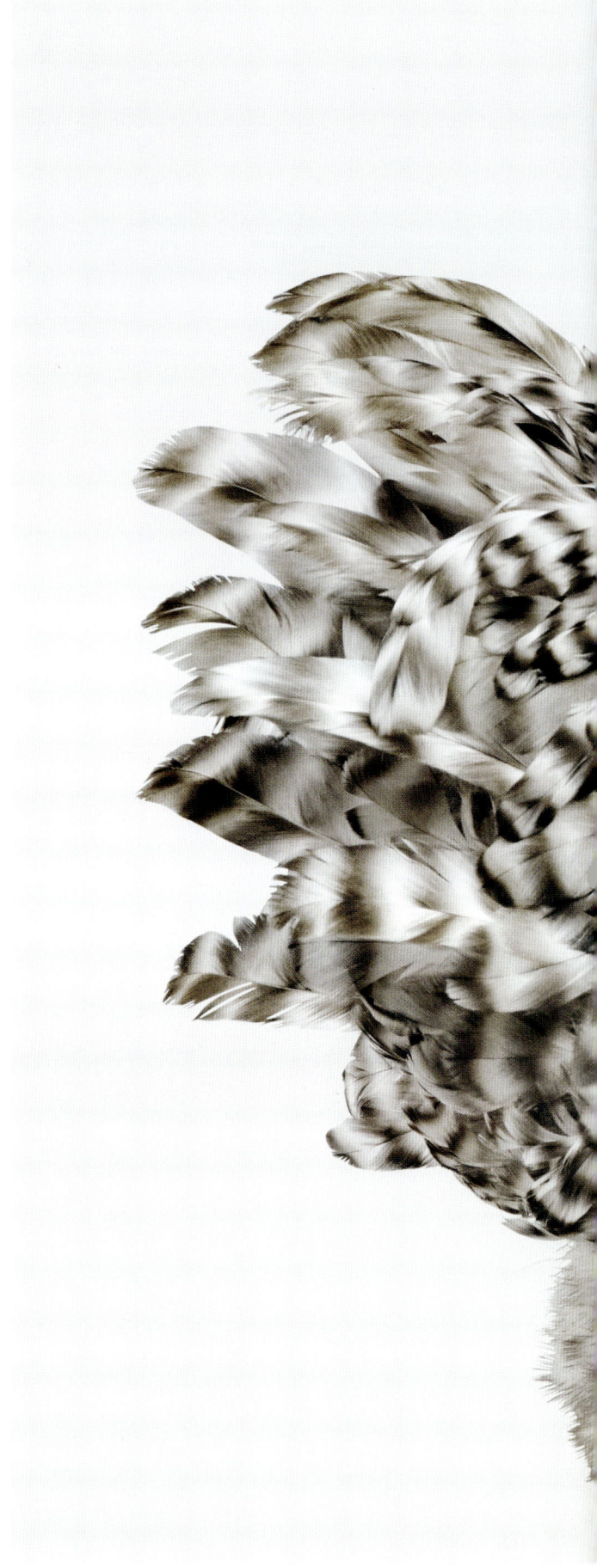

Opal

MECHELEN TURKEY HEAD HEN

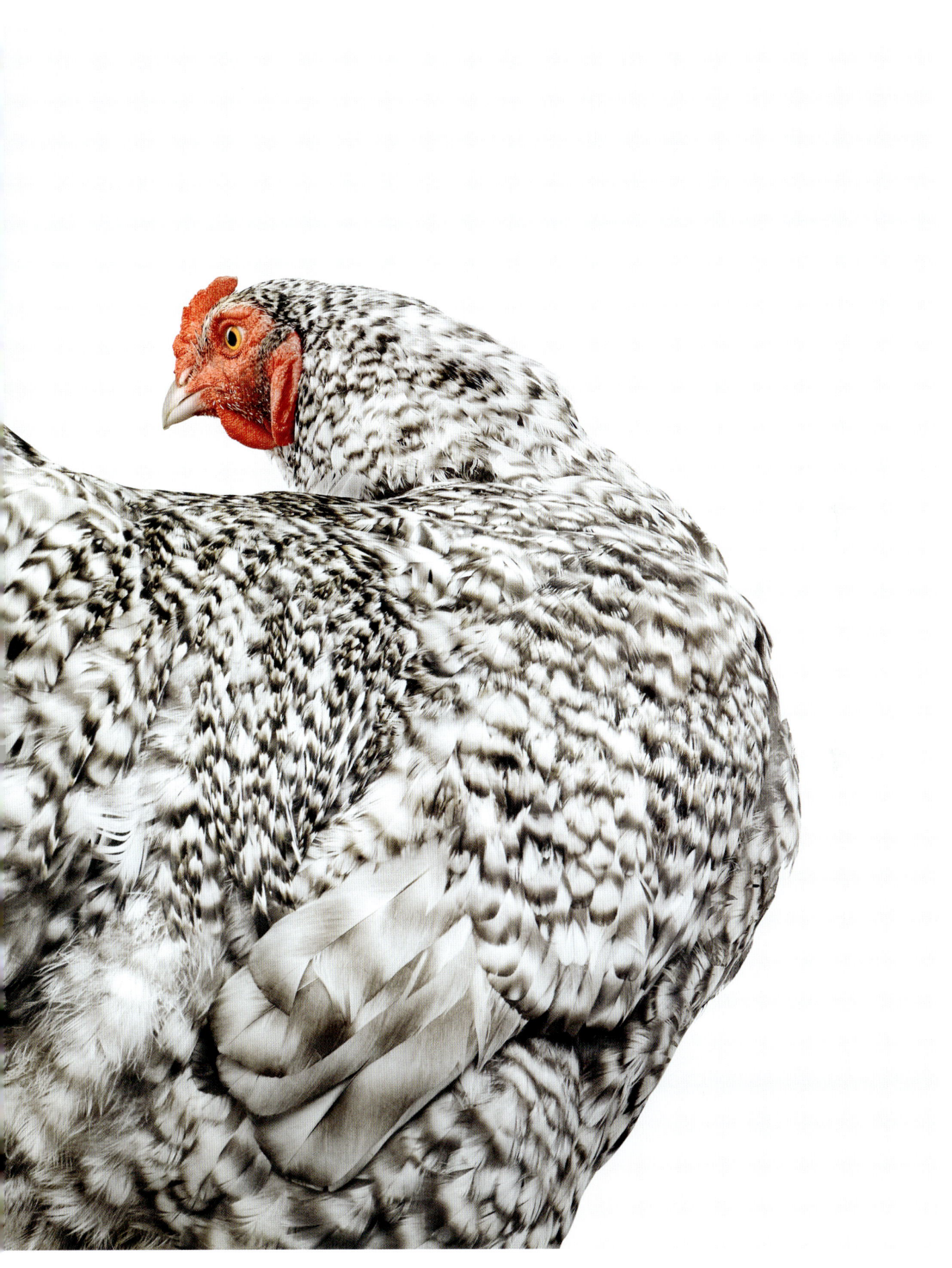

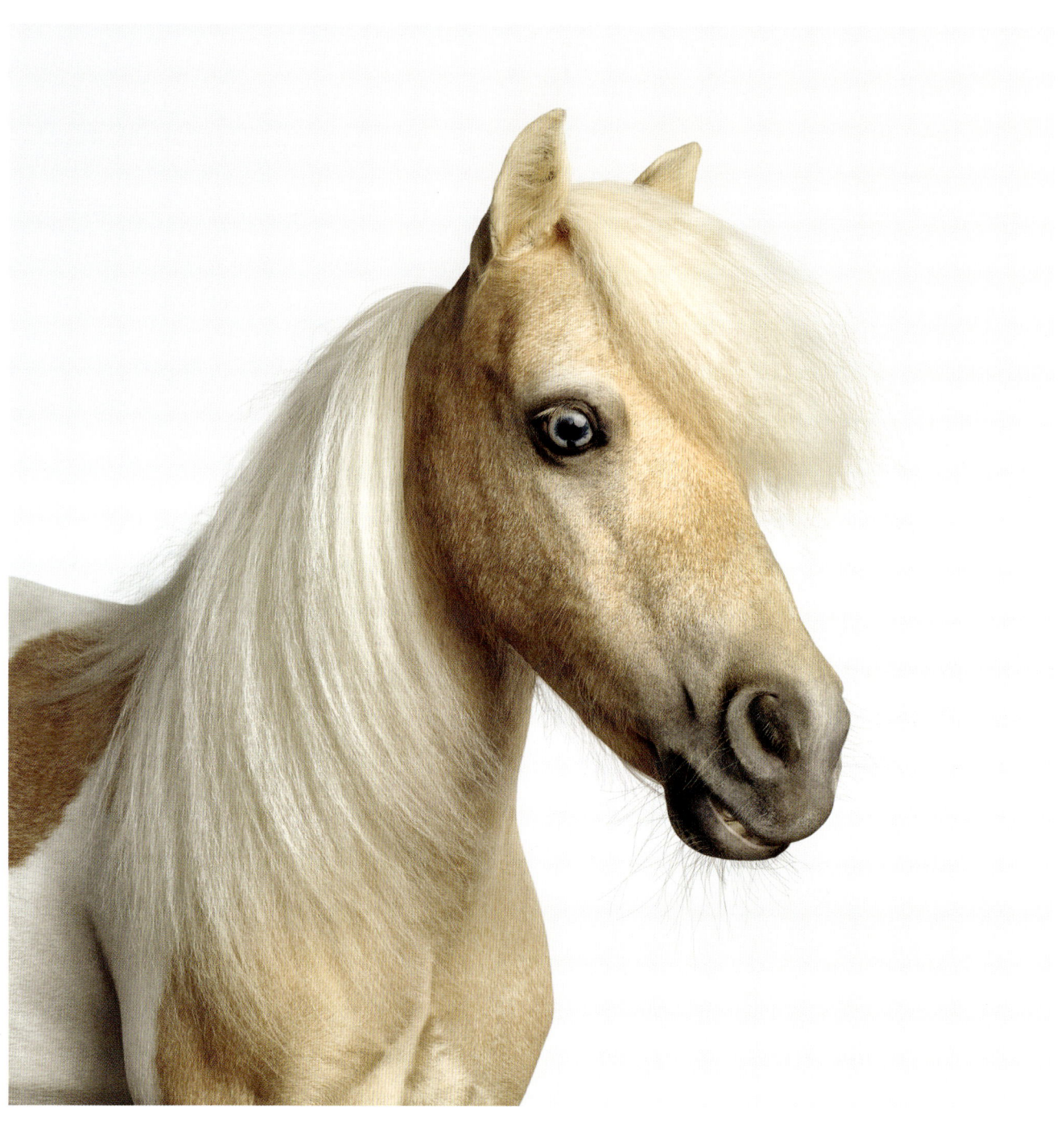

Lilly

MINIATURE HORSE

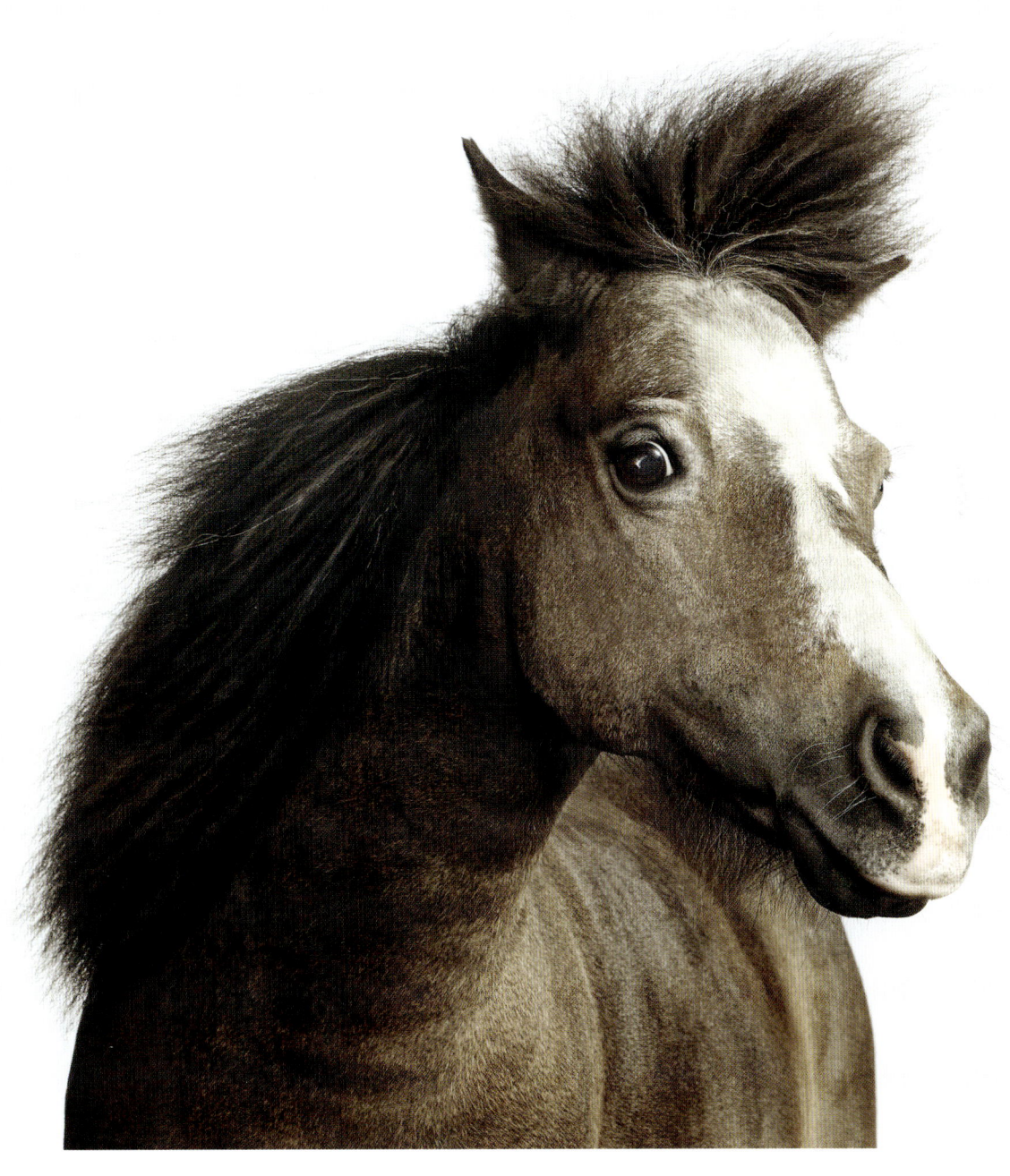

Polly

MINIATURE HORSE

ALPACAS AND LLAMAS

Alpacas and llamas, ambassadors of the Andean highlands, boast a blend of charm and peculiarity. No two look the same. Their saucerlike eyes, distinct buck teeth, and doglike snouts offer a plethora of visual treats, not to mention the endless—and endlessly entertaining—haircut possibilities when it comes time for spring shearing.

In front of my lens, alpaca antics often oscillate between a charming curiosity (often aimed at my camera) and a playful yet abrupt high-speed spitting habit. Thankfully, my lens was only spat on one time!

In addition to these oddities lies another perplexing eccentricity—that is, the designated dung piles each animal returns to for its bathroom breaks. This quirky behavior, aside from being a great conversational icebreaker, also hints at an innate sense of order and cleanliness, as well as a desire to keep their private business to themselves. I think we can all respect that.

Photographing alpacas and llamas is a unique dance between appreciating their gentle spirits and navigating their whimsical quirks. In the world of farm life, these adorable mammals weave affection with oddity, resulting in a special creature that has captured the hearts of many.

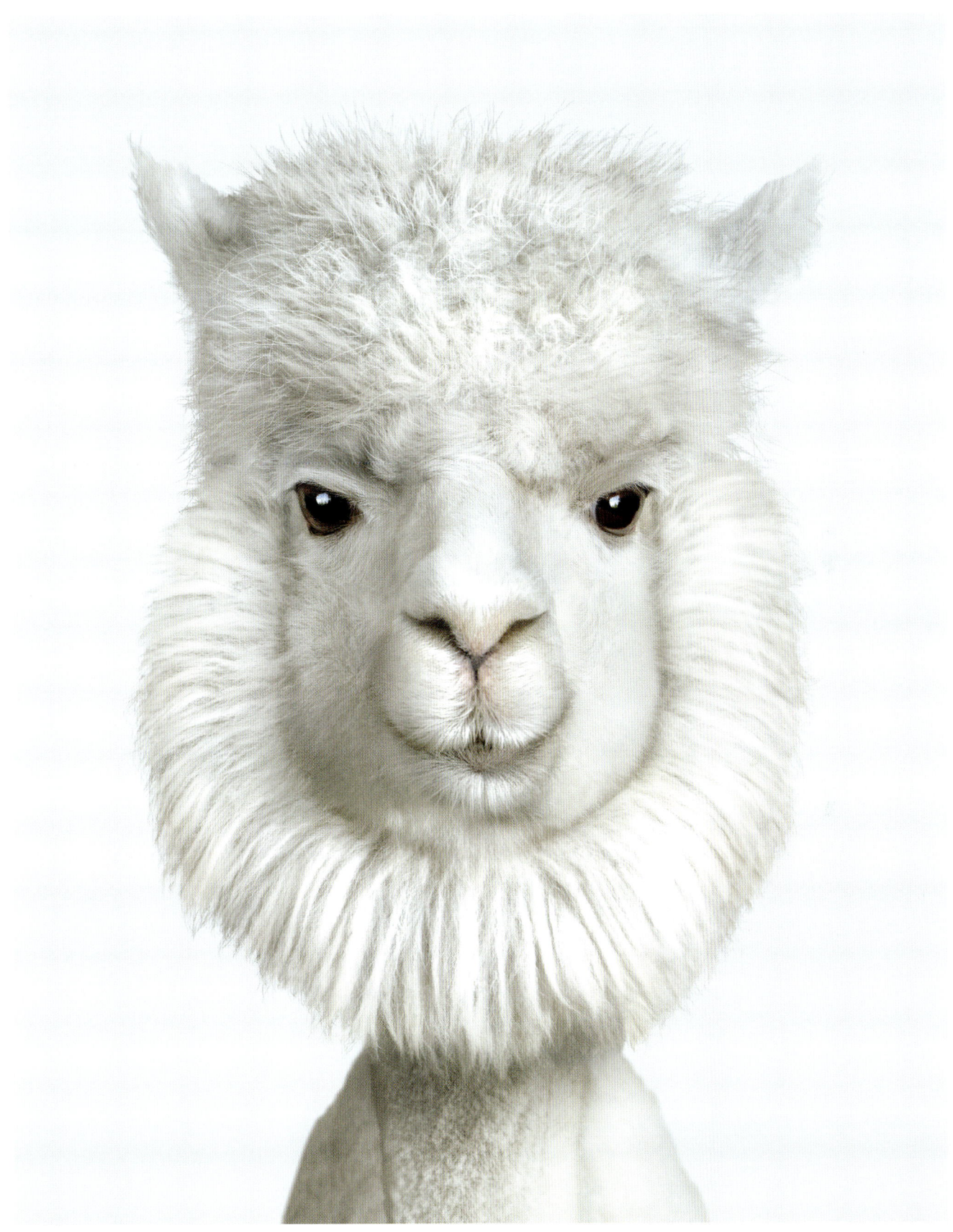

Lily

HUACAYA ALPACA

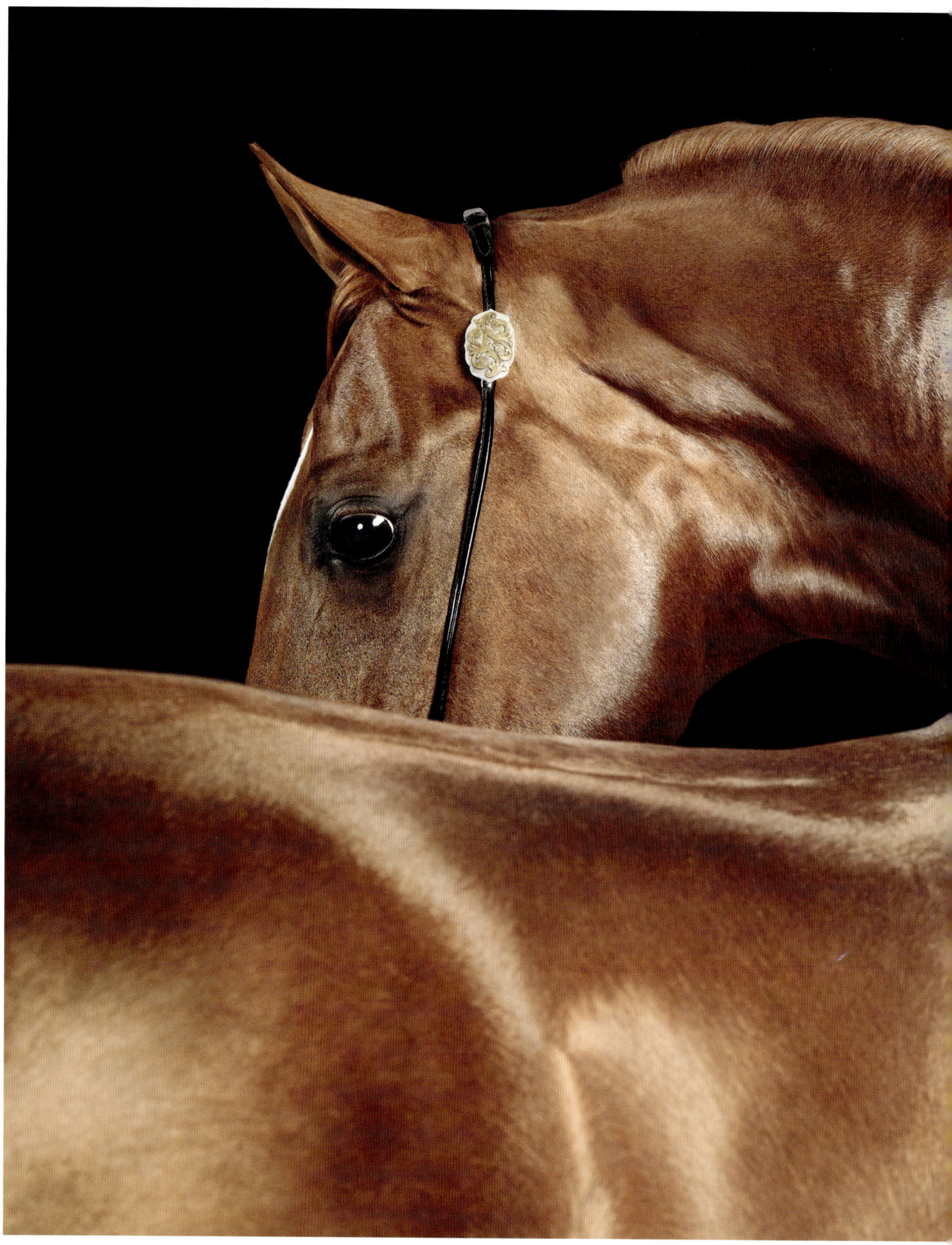

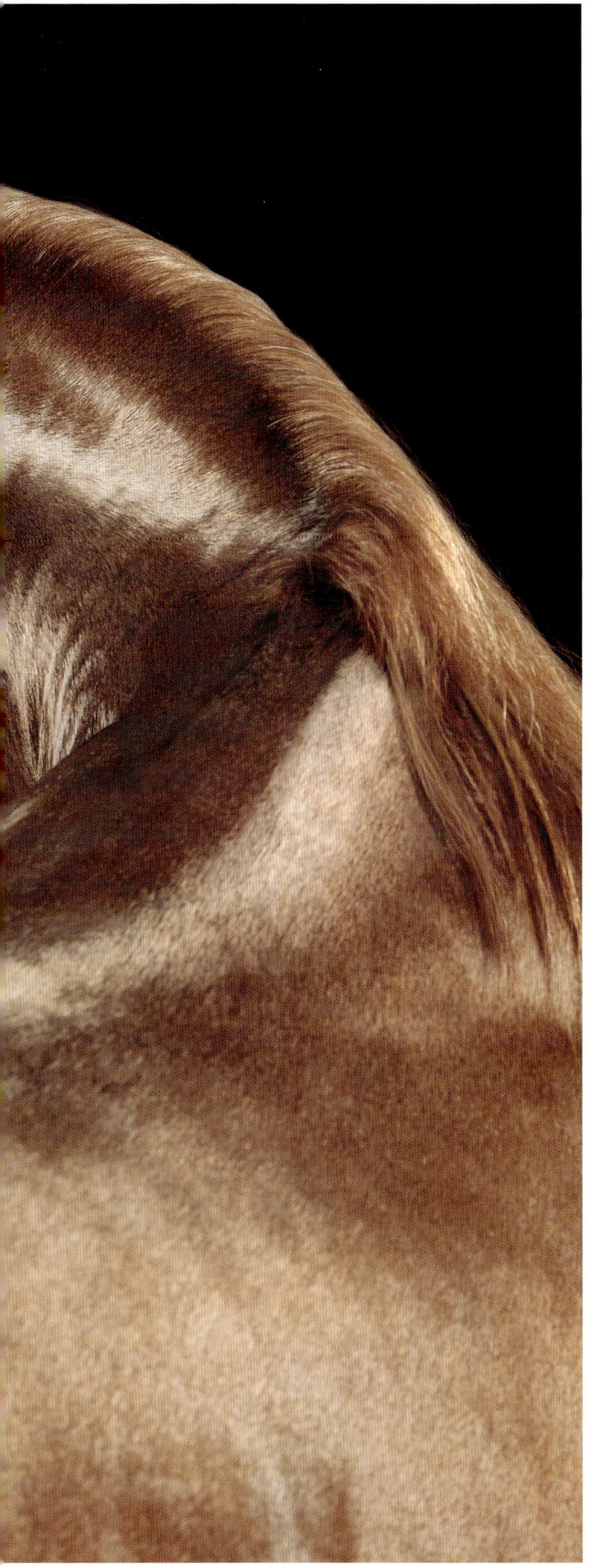

Lahab Albidayer

RED ARABIAN STALLION

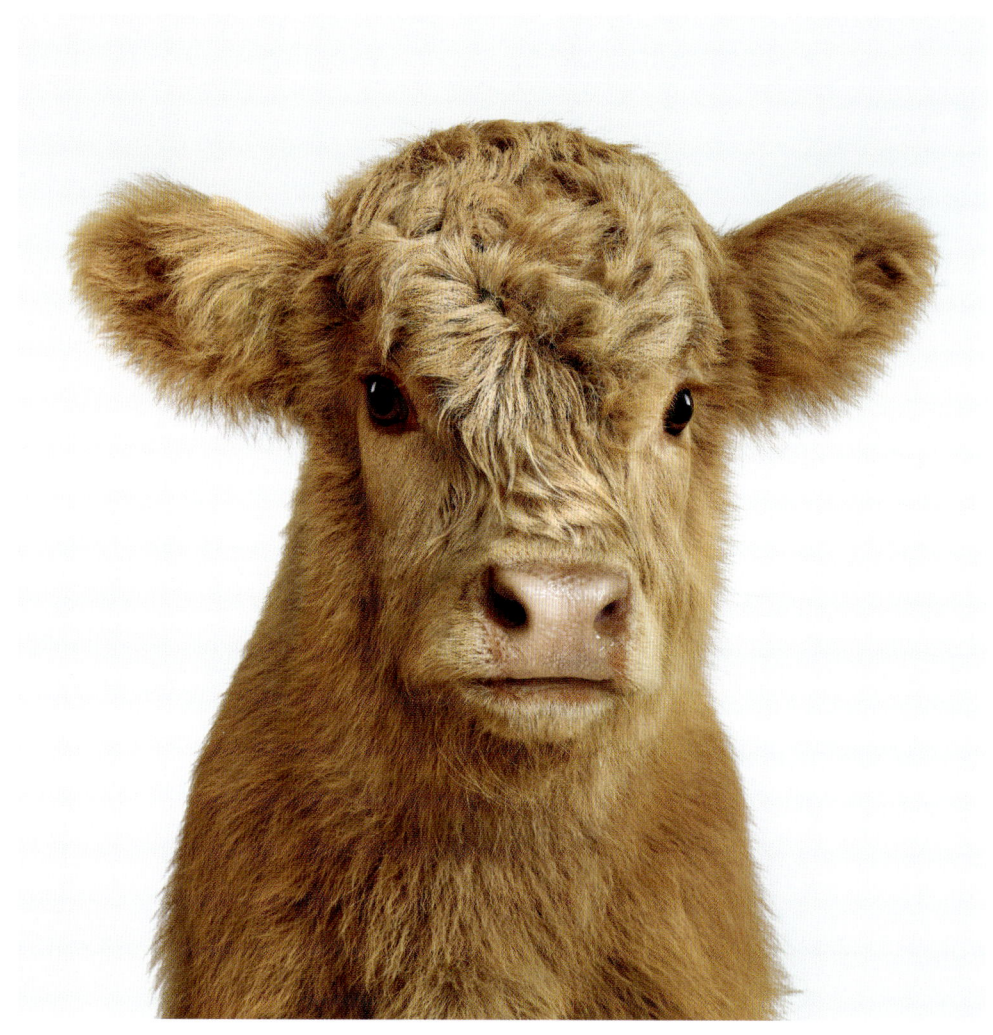

Marigold

HIGHLAND CALF

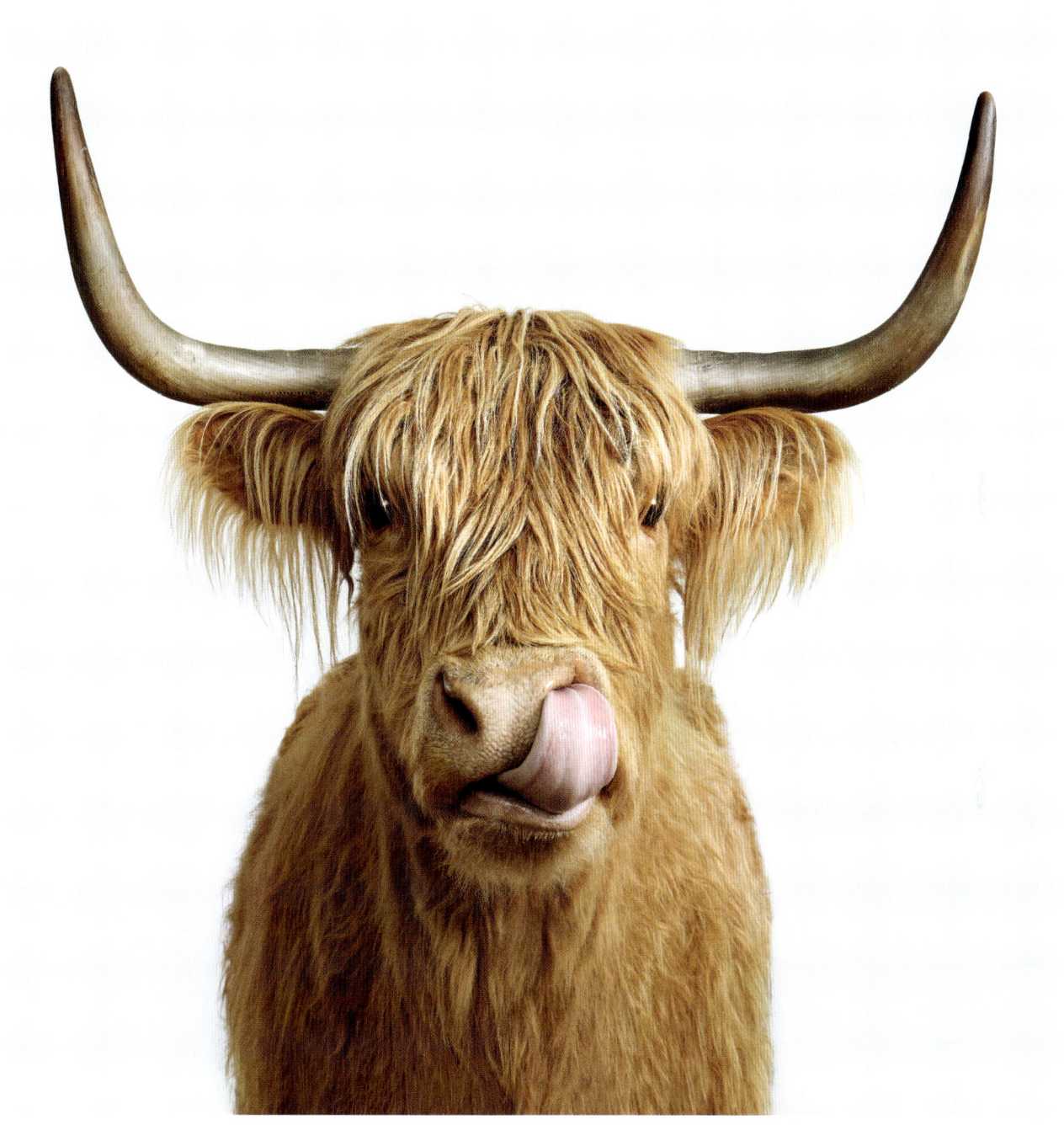

Ellie

HIGHLAND COW

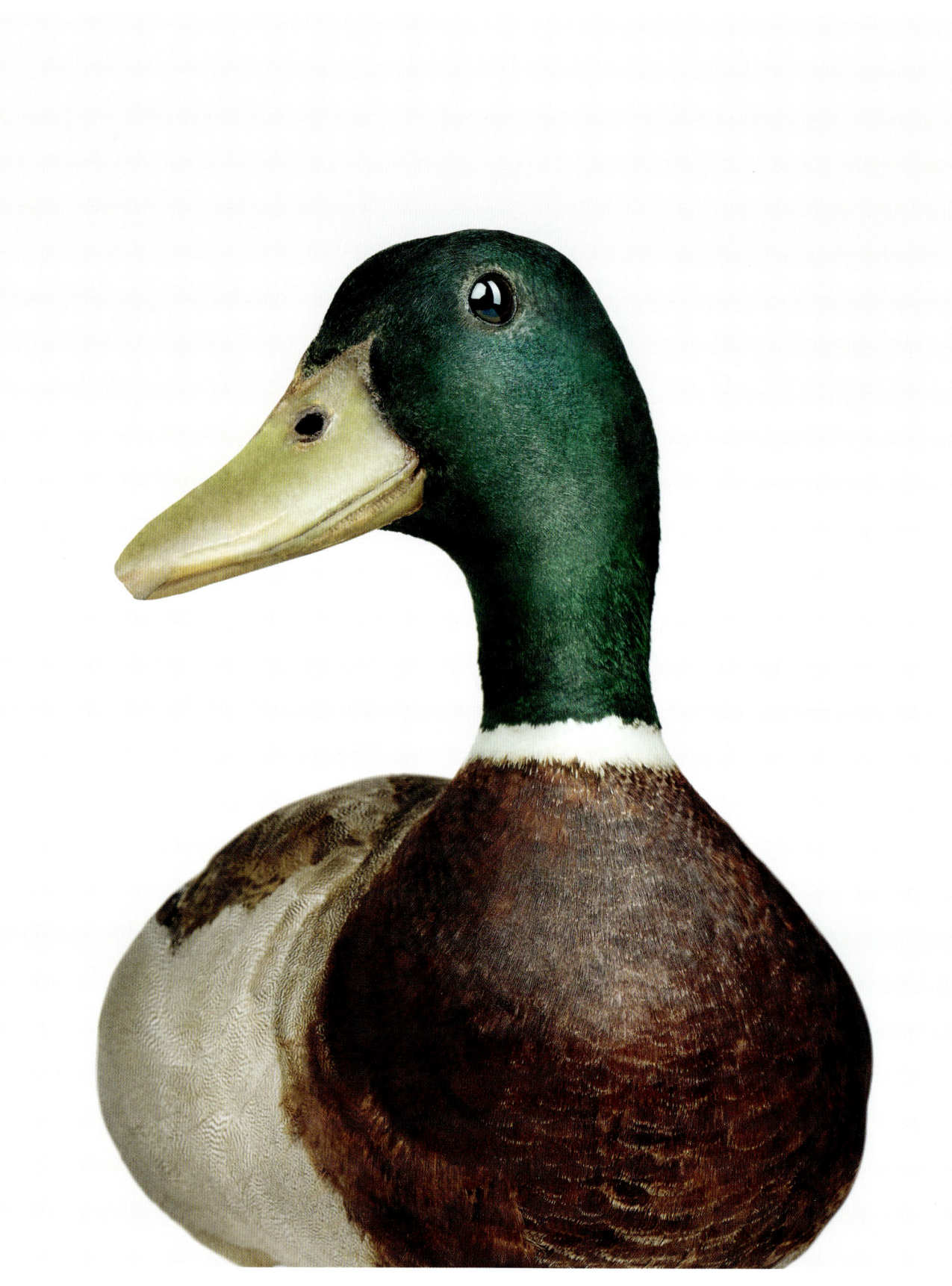

Jasper

GRAY MALLARD DUCK

DUCKS

For generations, ducks have held a soft spot in the hearts of humanity. Beyond their picturesque forms in flight, they remind us to seek solace in the gentle rhythms of nature. A symbol of calm, these winged creatures so often accompany our quiet moments of contemplation, whether sitting on a soft blanket in the park or taking a slow walk around the pond.

No matter where they may meet us, ducks always carry with them an ethos of profound simplicity and invite us to embrace life's currents with patience and adaptability. Their symbolic presence in folklore, art, and literature reflects their timeless significance, symbolizing everything from freedom and independence to unity and community.

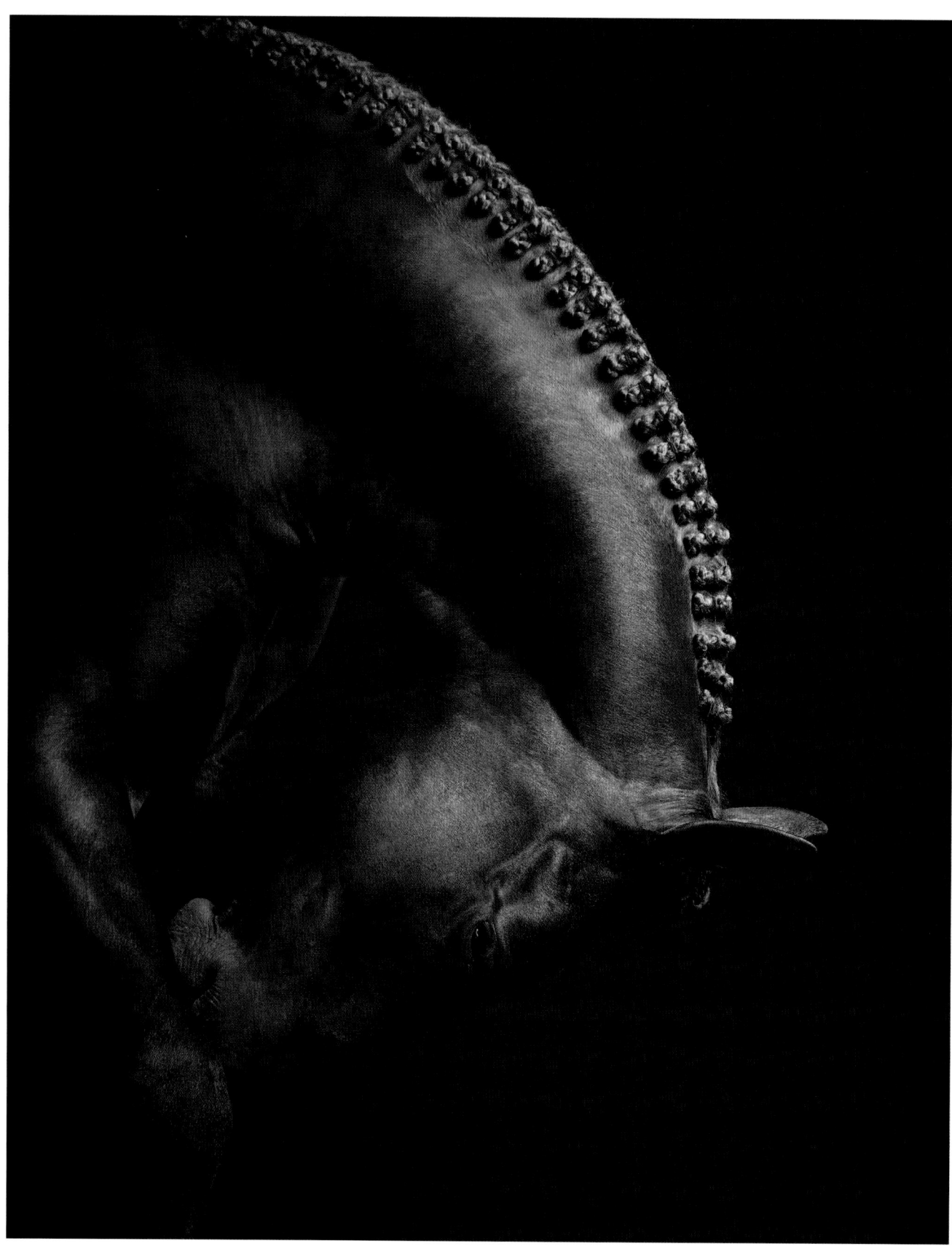

Black Betty

BLACK QUARTER HORSE MARE

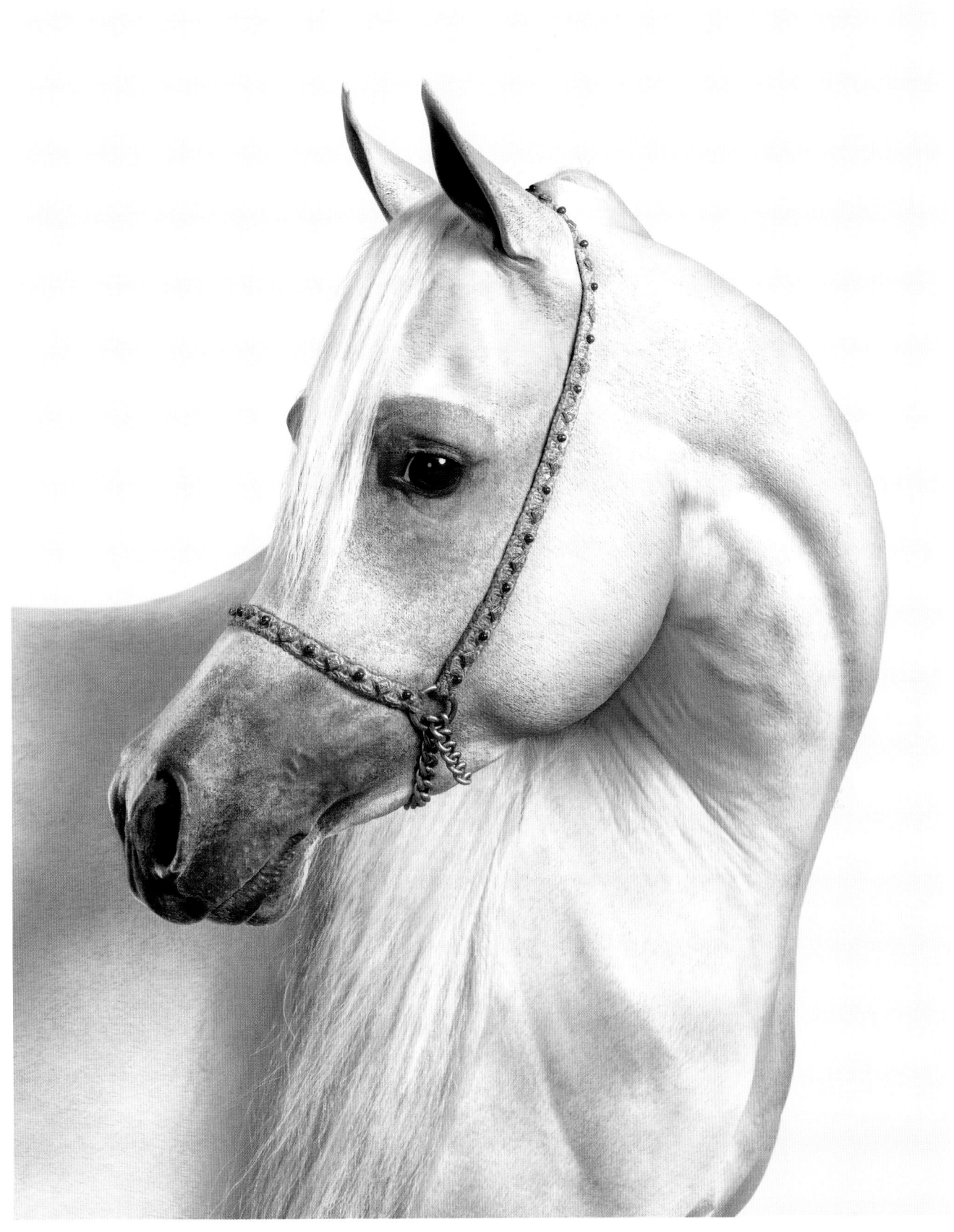

Parisii

WHITE ARABIAN STALLION

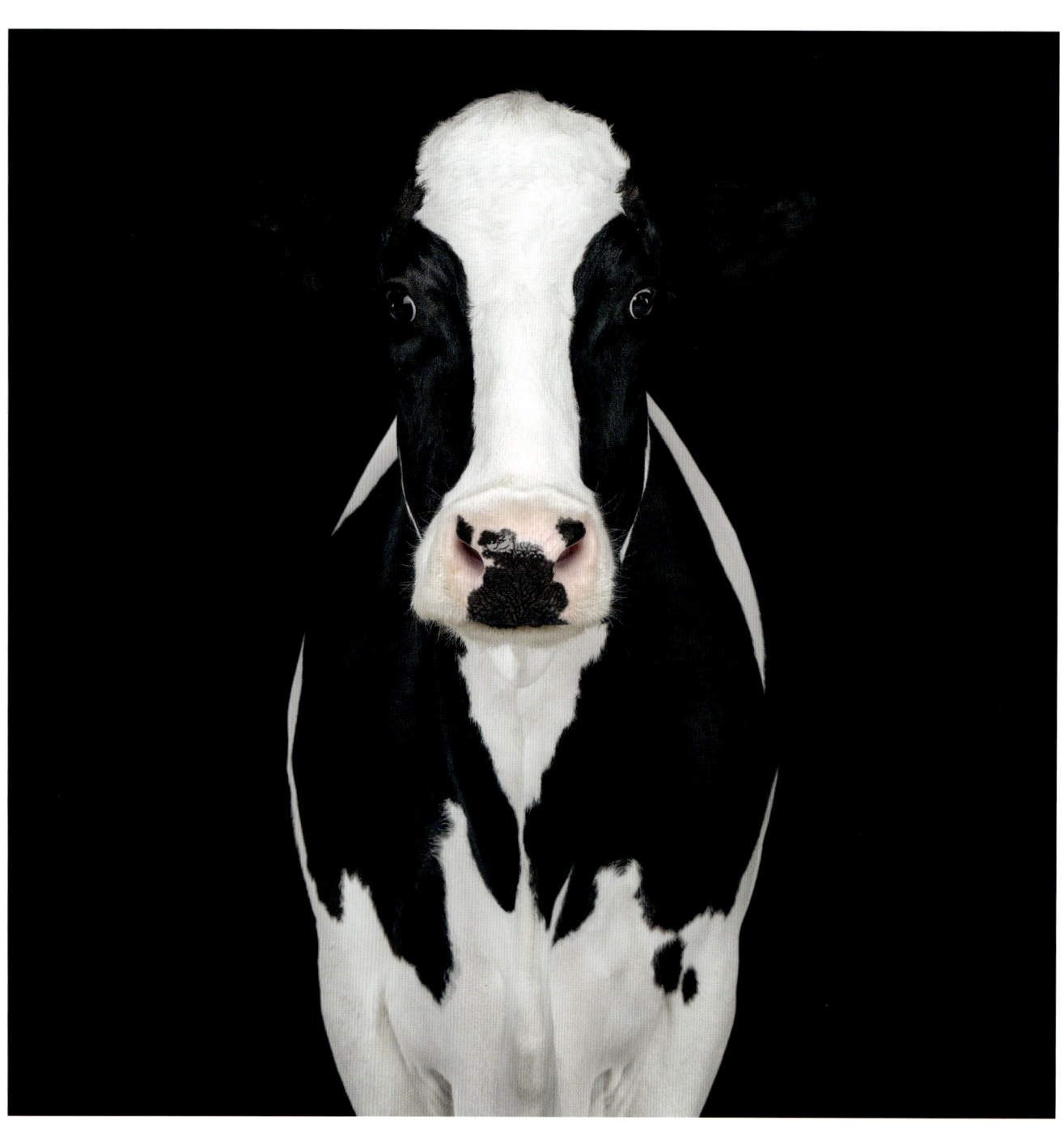

Freckles

HOLSTEIN COW

Dairy cows are the quintessential animals of the American farm. Because we are so familiar with this particular breed and see them frequently grazing along roadside pastures, painted on billboards, or talking in storybooks, it can be easy to forget how uniquely beautiful they truly are. Freckles was a pristine example of the traditional cow we all know and love. Her symmetrical splotches and iconic, charming expression endeared her to all of us and reignited my appreciation for these amazing animals.

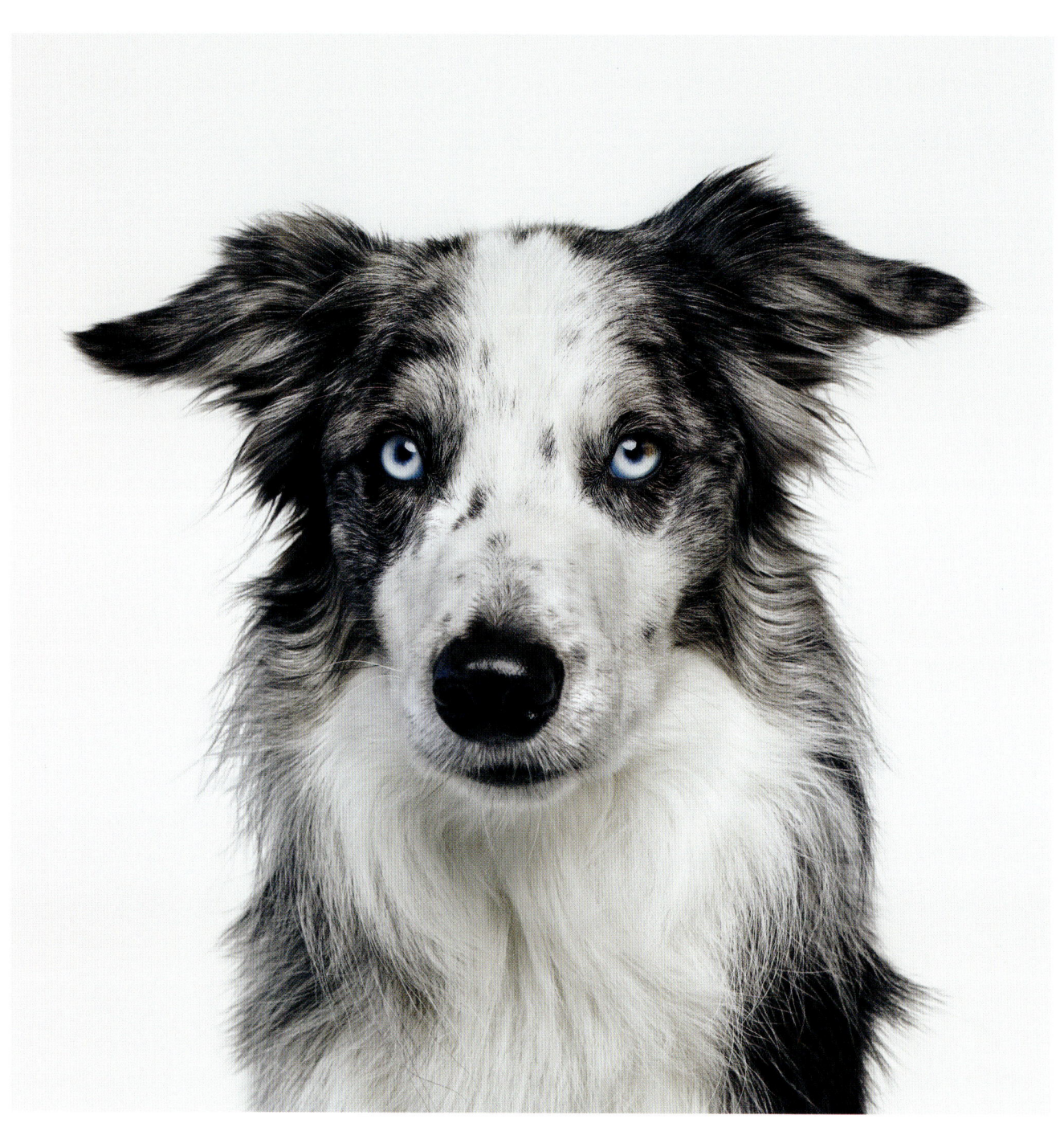

Watson

BORDER COLLIE

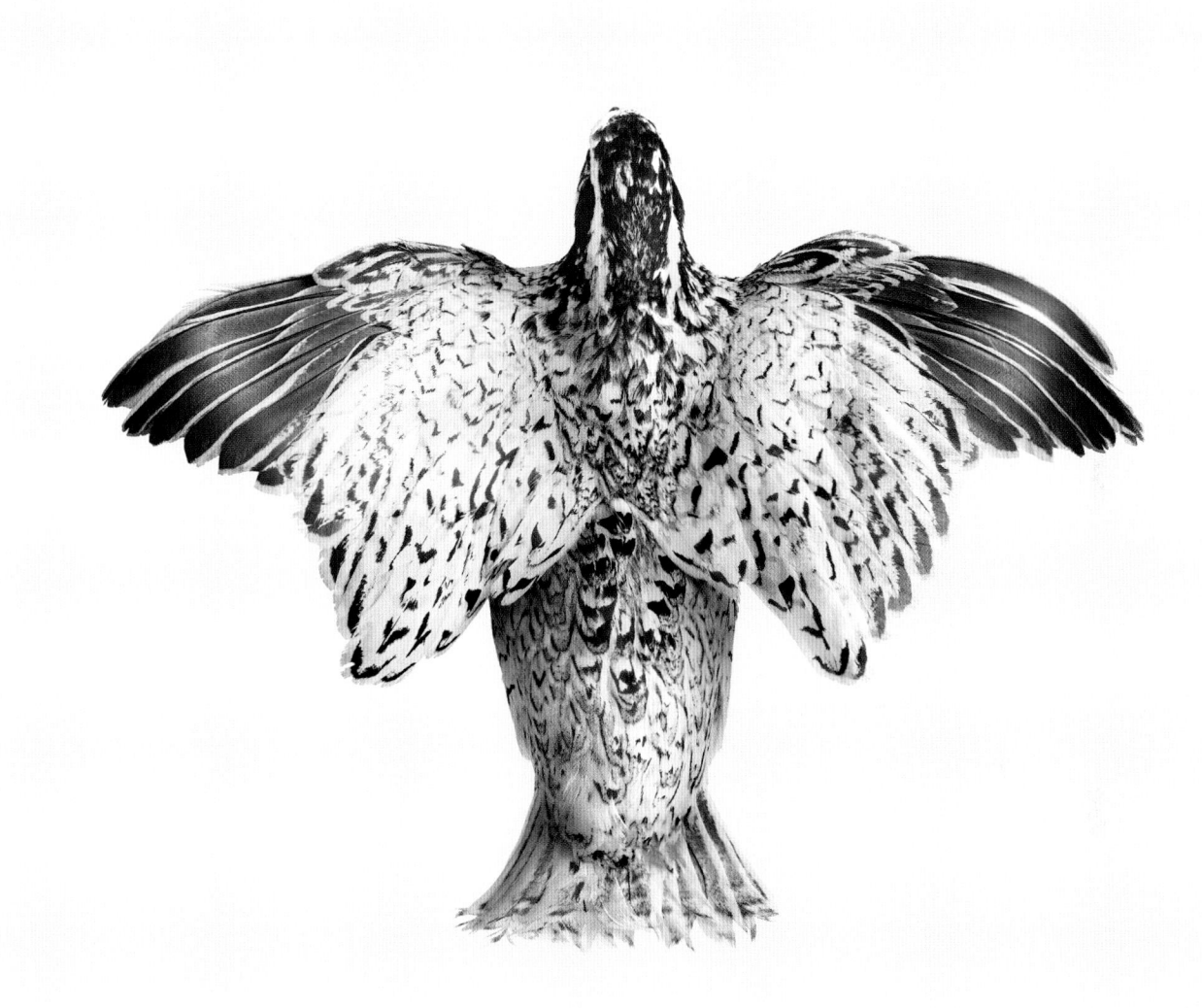

Tux

SNOWFLAKE BOBWHITE QUAIL

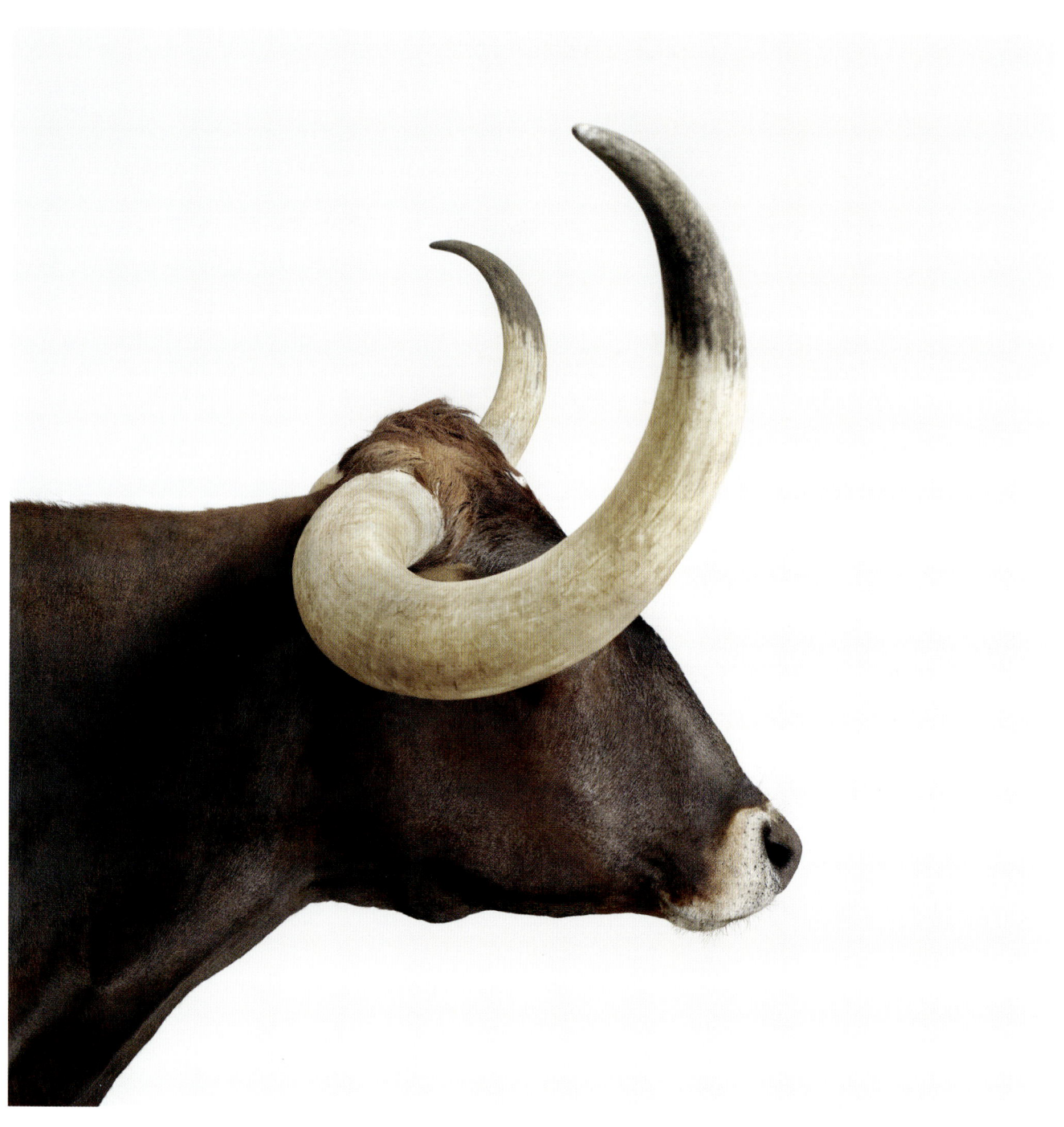

Maverick

TEXAS LONGHORN

TEXAS LONGHORNS

As an iconic symbol of the American West, the Texas longhorn holds a special place in my portrait work. These majestic creatures—their lineage tracing back to the earliest Spanish settlers—have been deeply integrated into the core of ranching heritage. Their stunning horns serve as a true work of art and grow ceaselessly throughout their lives, sometimes reaching upward of 10 feet across with magnificent and unique curvatures. Yet beneath the intimidating spread of ivory bone lies a surprising demeanor of gentleness.

The docile nature of a Texas longhorn is a testament to the ways they have grown closer to humans throughout history. Photographing them becomes a journey through time and captures the juxtaposition of power and grace. In the vast landscape of livestock, the Texas longhorn stands out for its iconic silhouette, enduring spirit, and gentle heart.

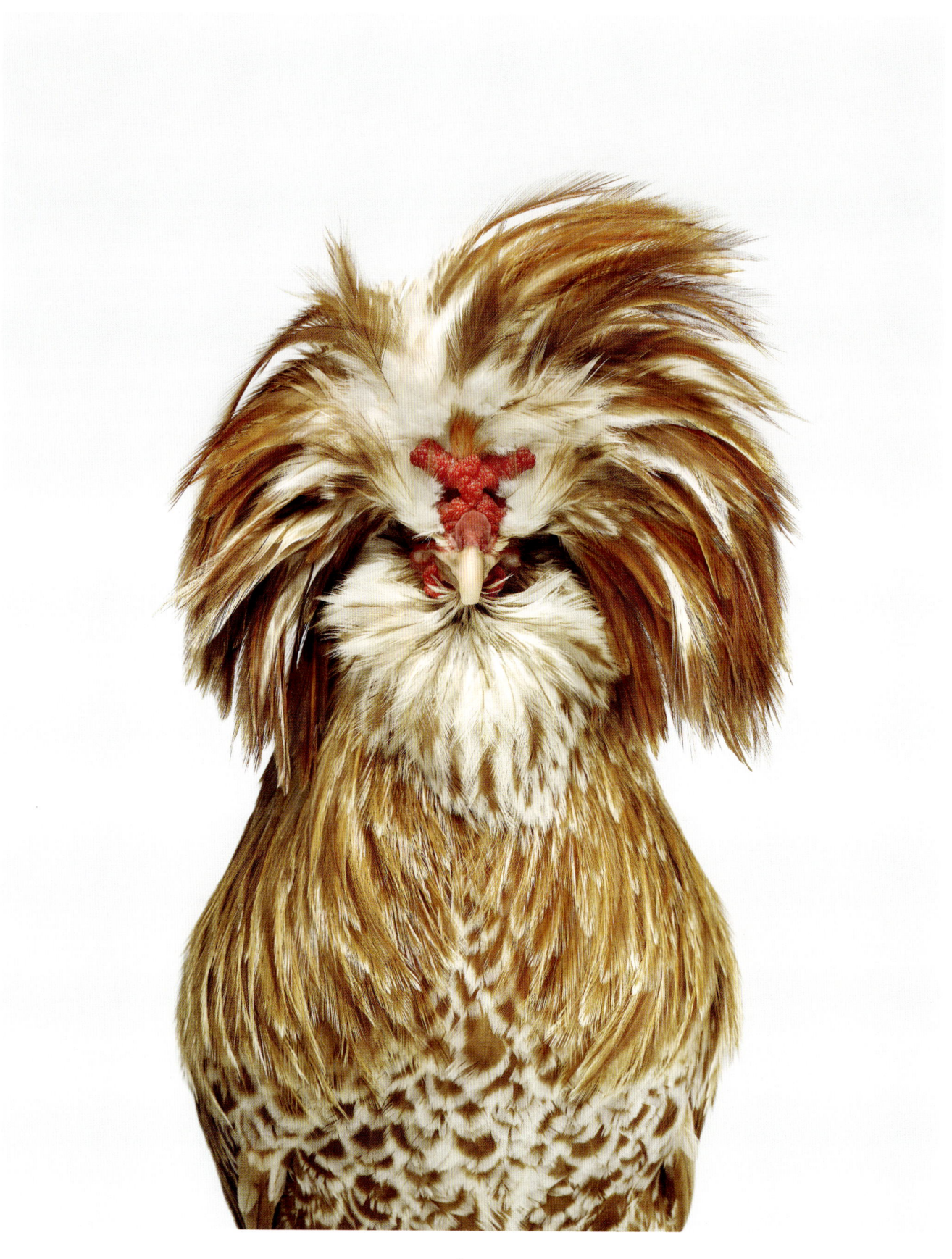

Blaze

BUFF LACED POLISH ROOSTER

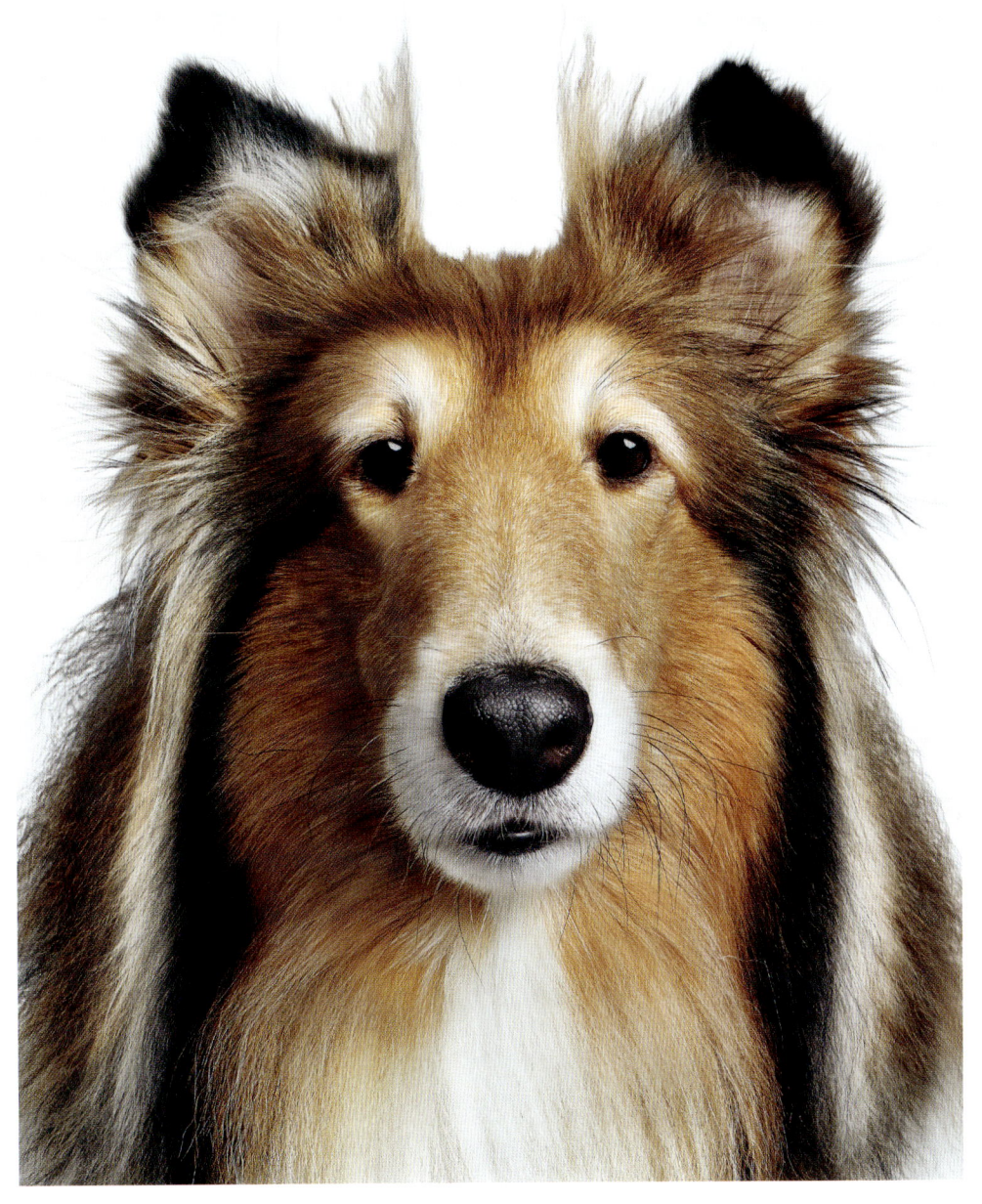

Reveille

ROUGH COLLIE

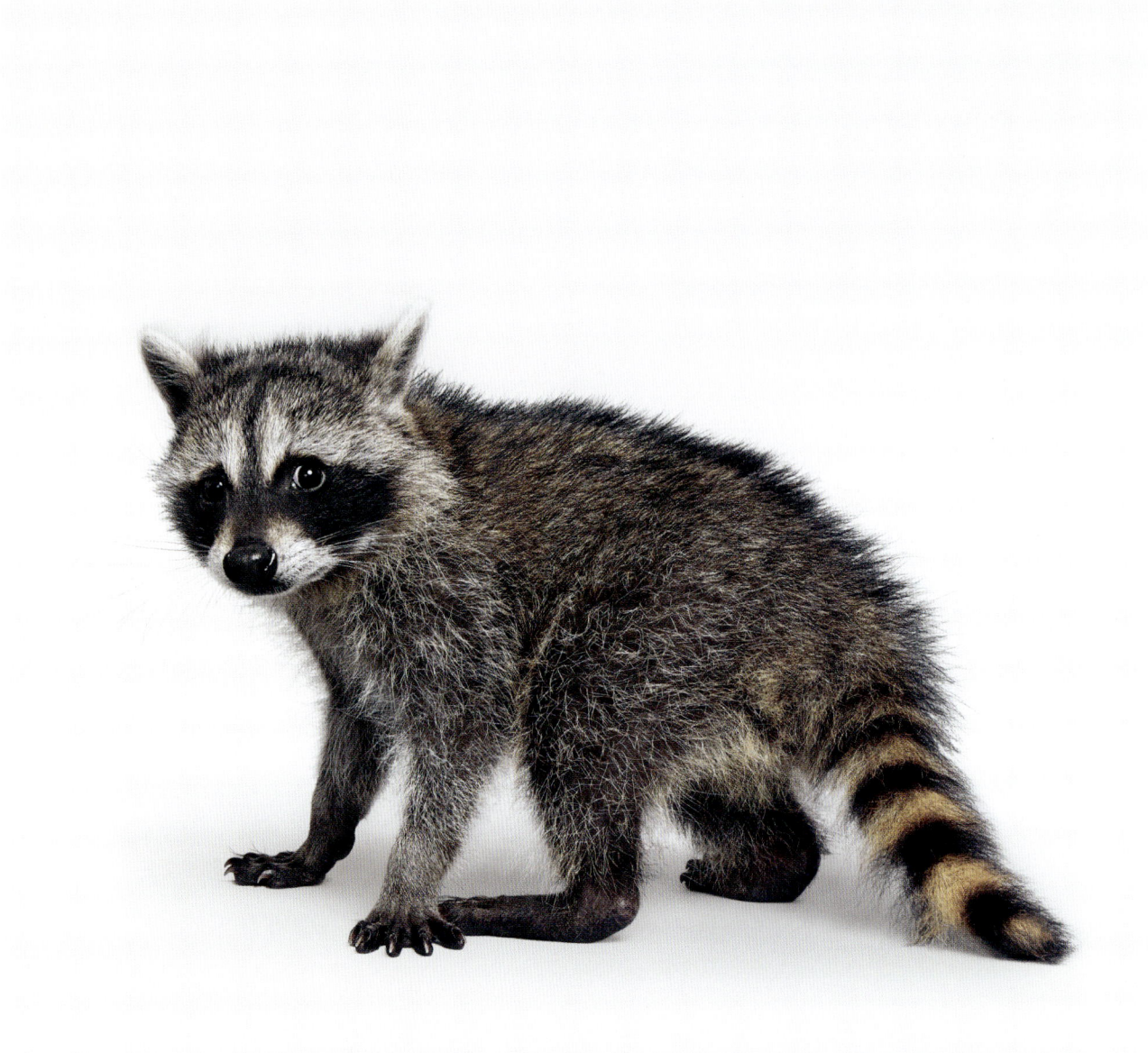

Lewis

BABY RACCOON

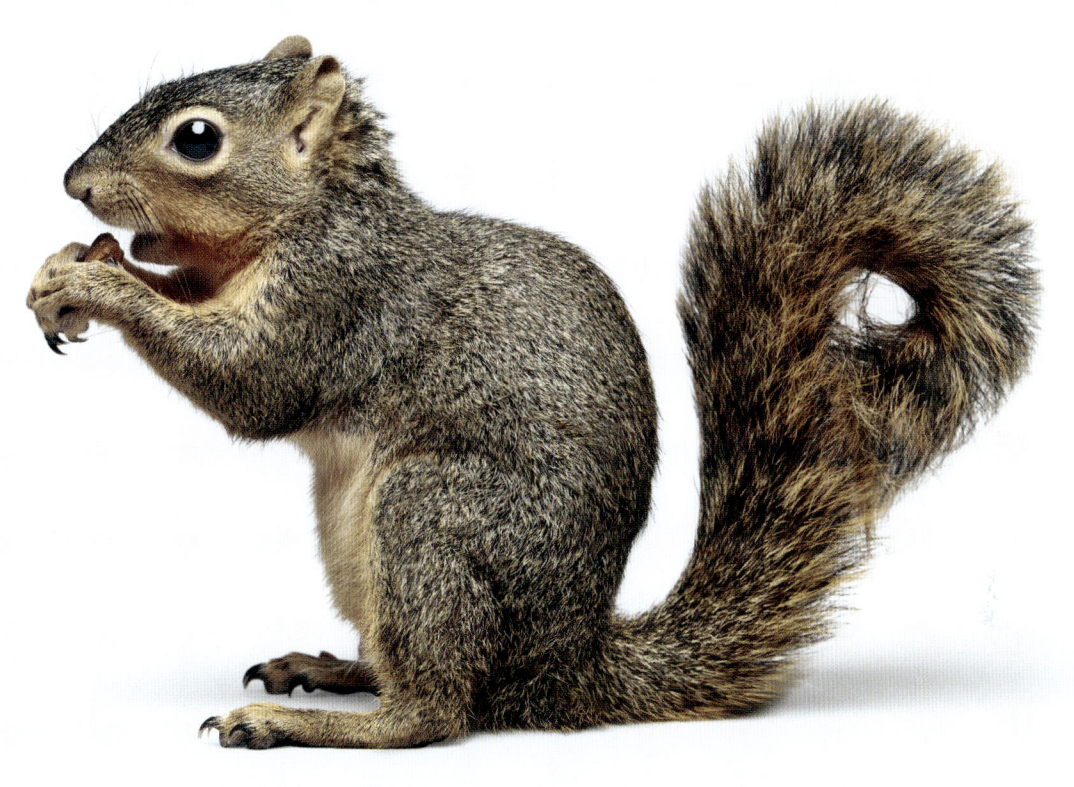

Merle

SQUIRREL

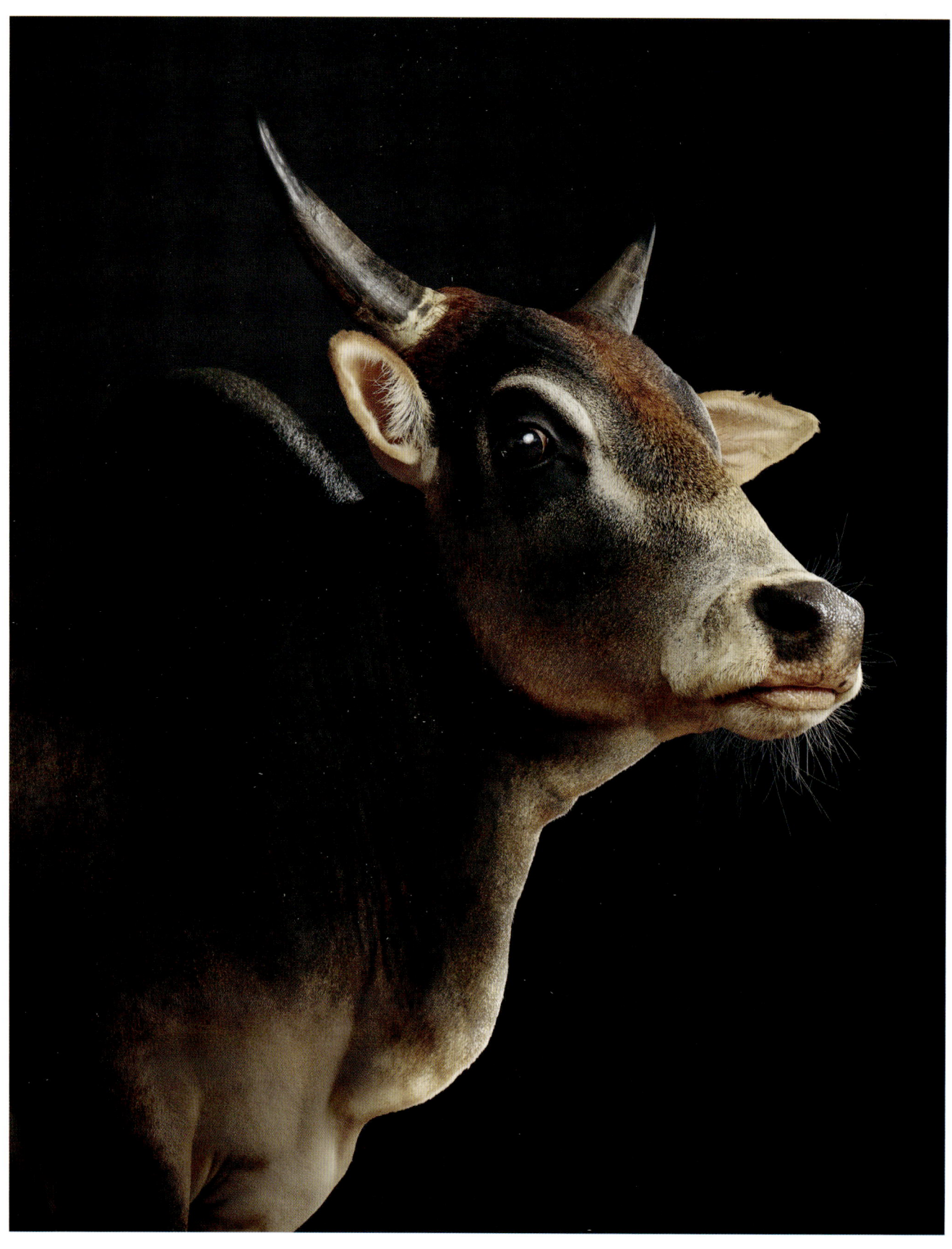

Swagger

ZEBU BULL

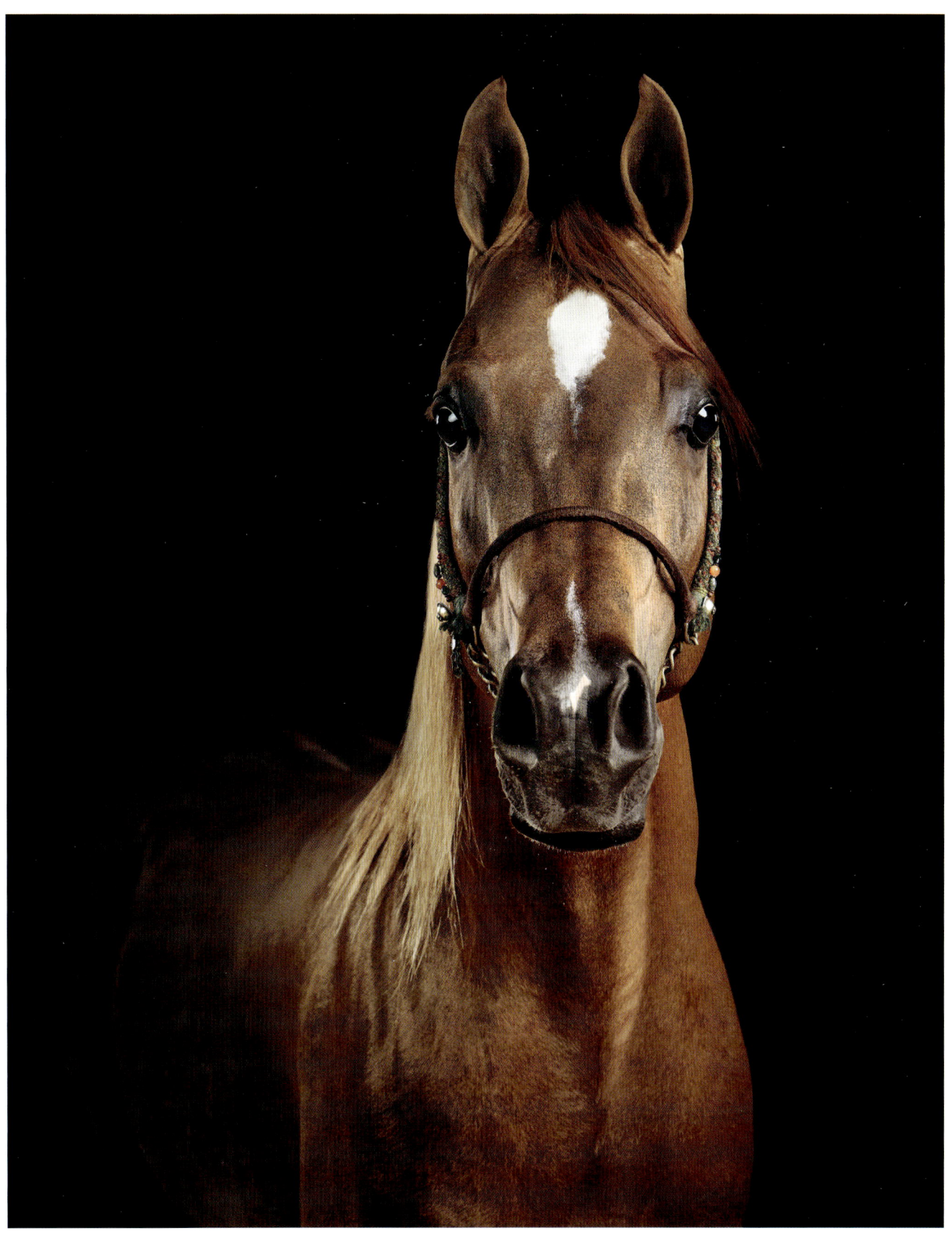

Lahab Albidayer

RED ARABIAN STALLION

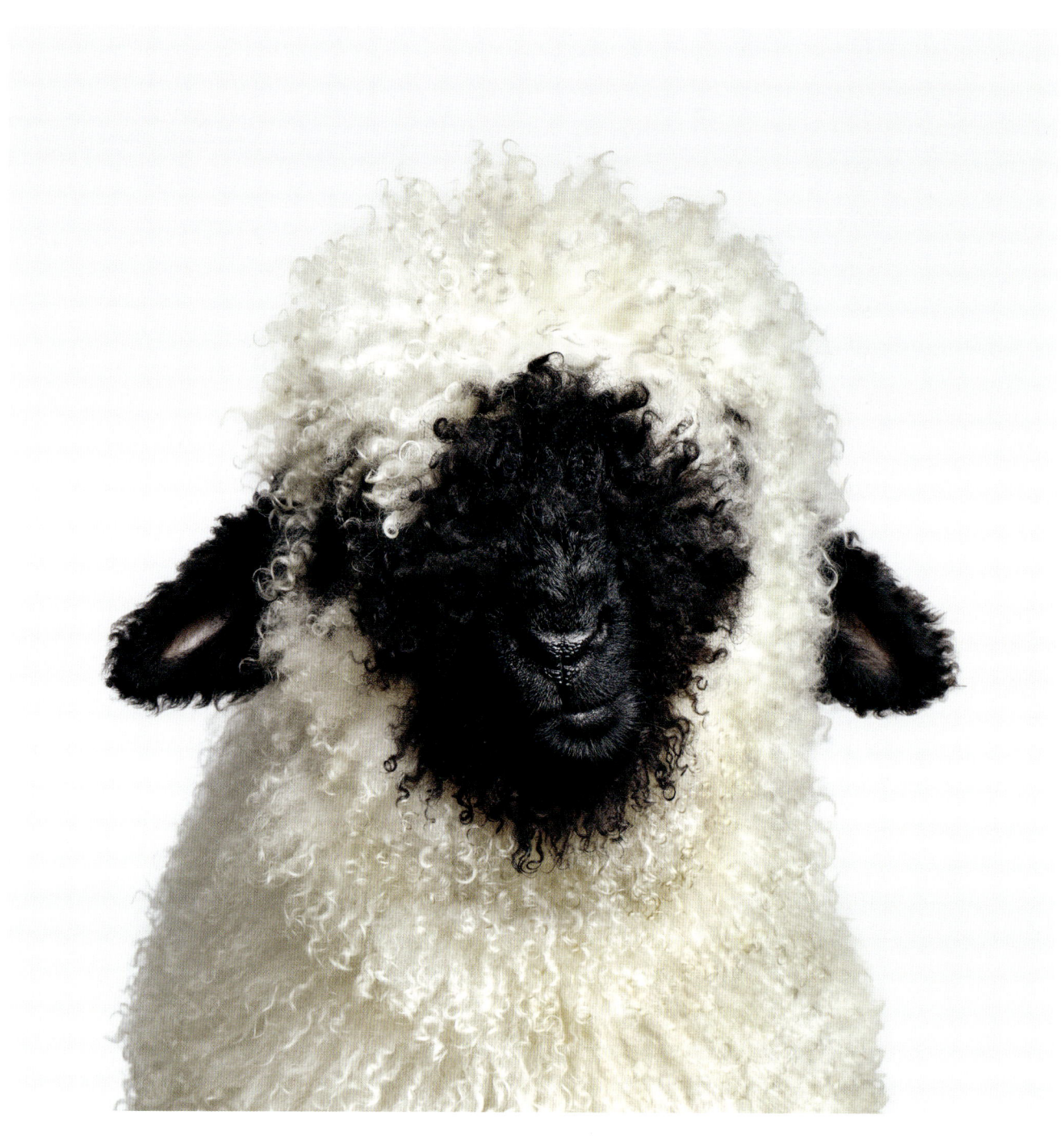

Kipply

SWISS VALAIS BLACKNOSE SHEEP

Kipply is as special as his breed. Originating

in Switzerland, Valais Blacknose sheep

remain extremely rare and important to

the Swiss people. Finding not one but two

(twins even!) was an exciting moment, one

that had me traveling across the country

to photograph them. Per Swiss tradition,

Kipply and his twin, Klover, were both

named according to the yearly naming

calendar, which determines a designated

letter for each year. These beauties were

born in 2023—the year of the K.

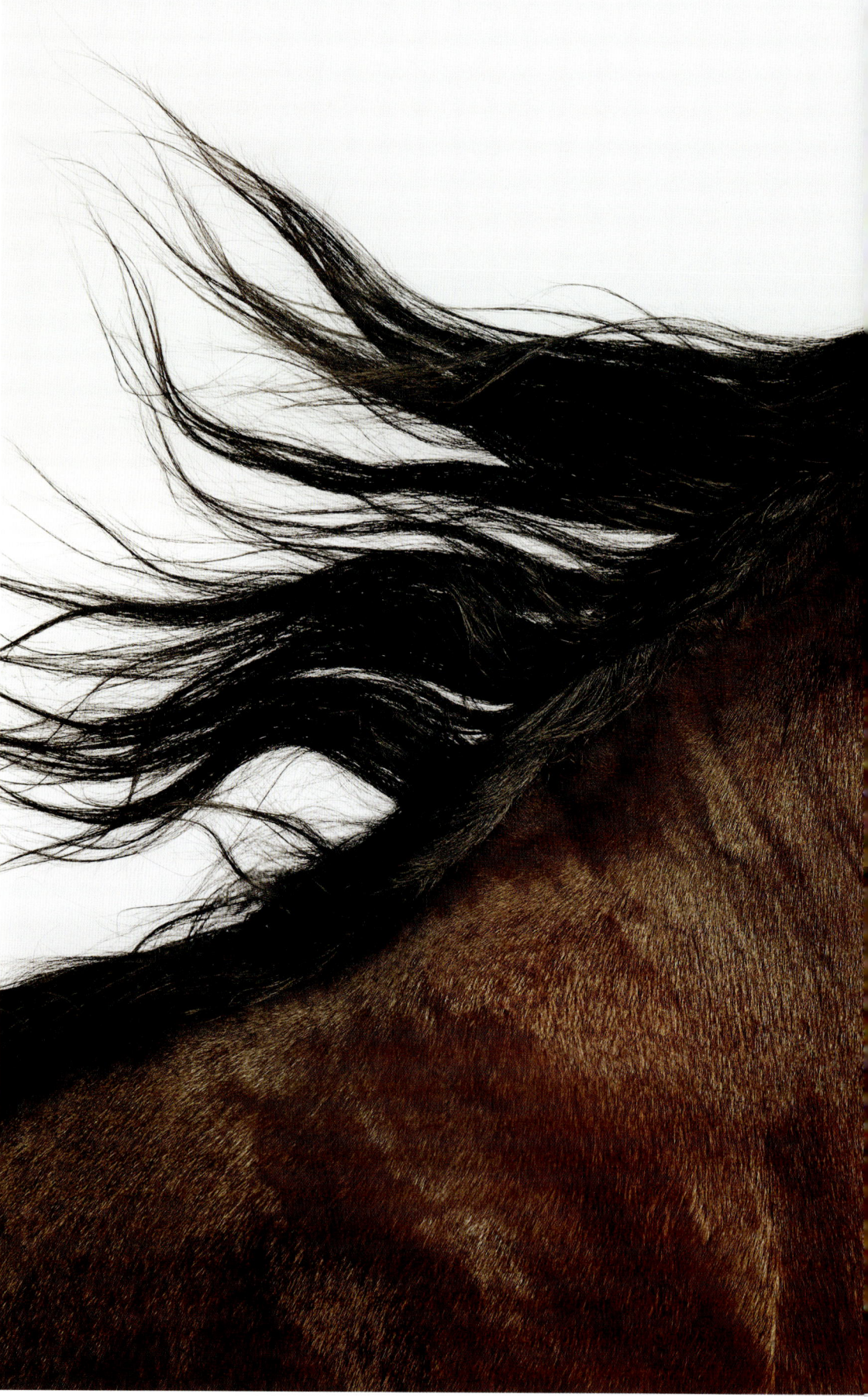

Mystery

AMERICAN SADDLEBRED HORSE

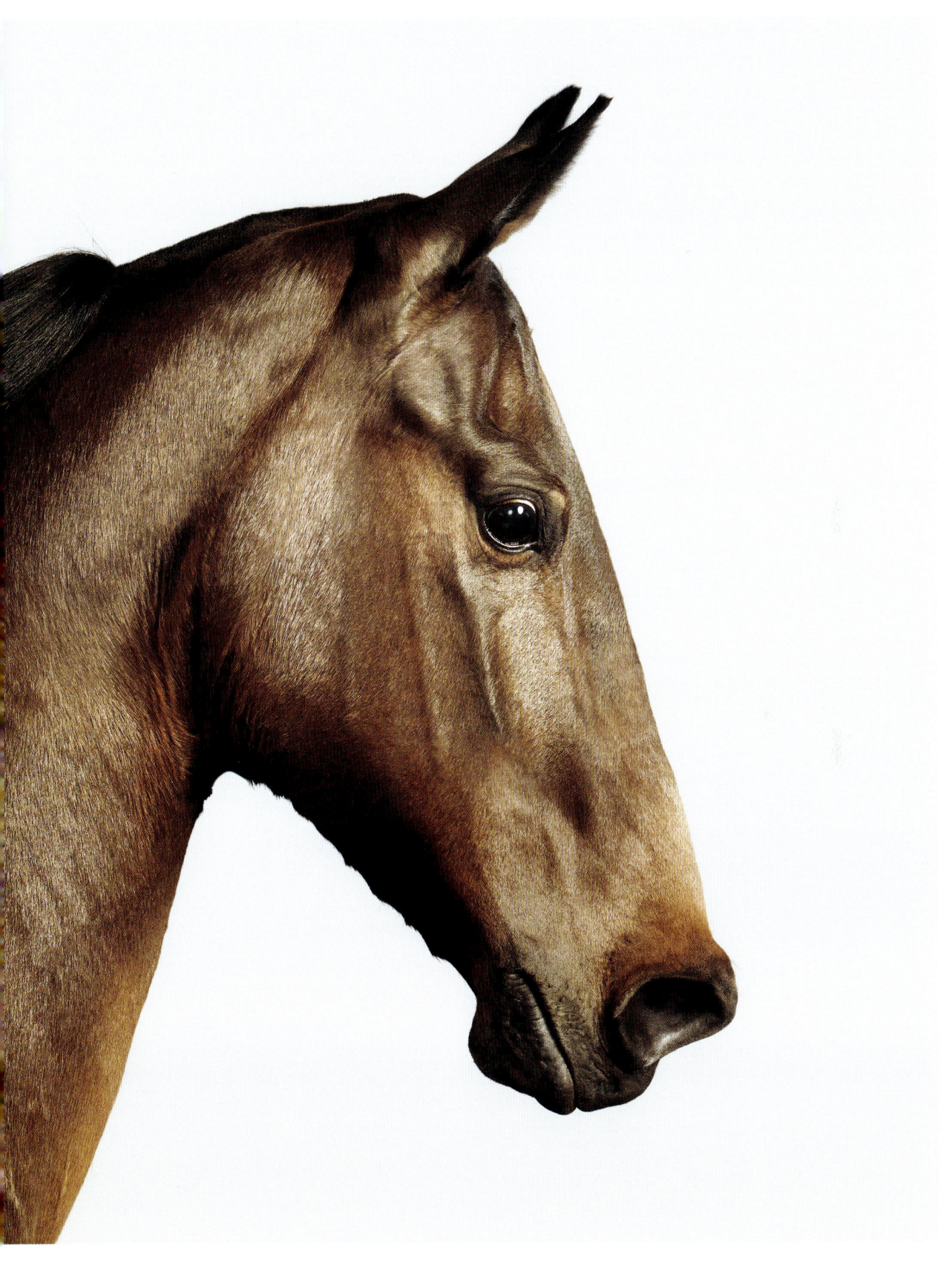

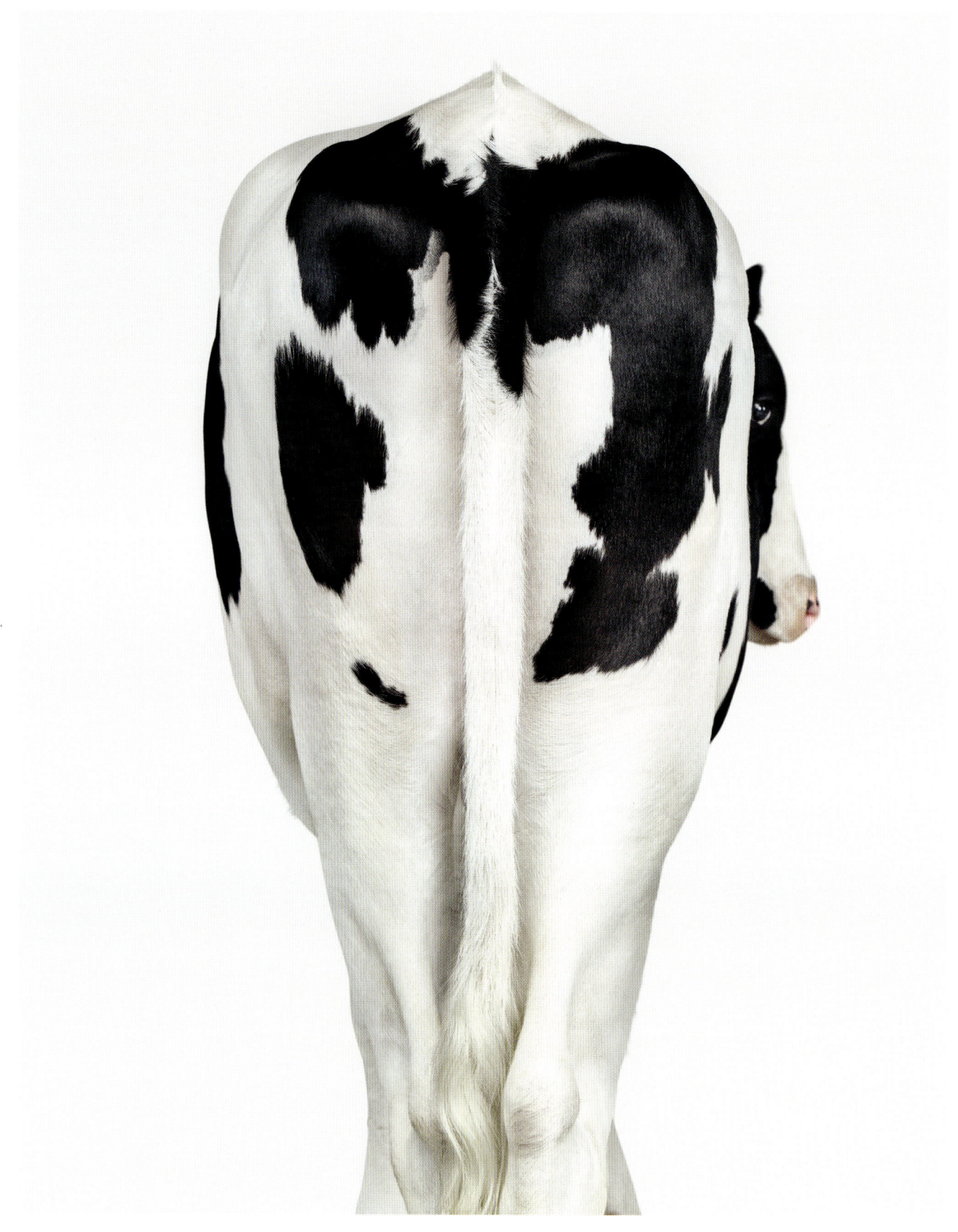

Freckles

HOLSTEIN COW

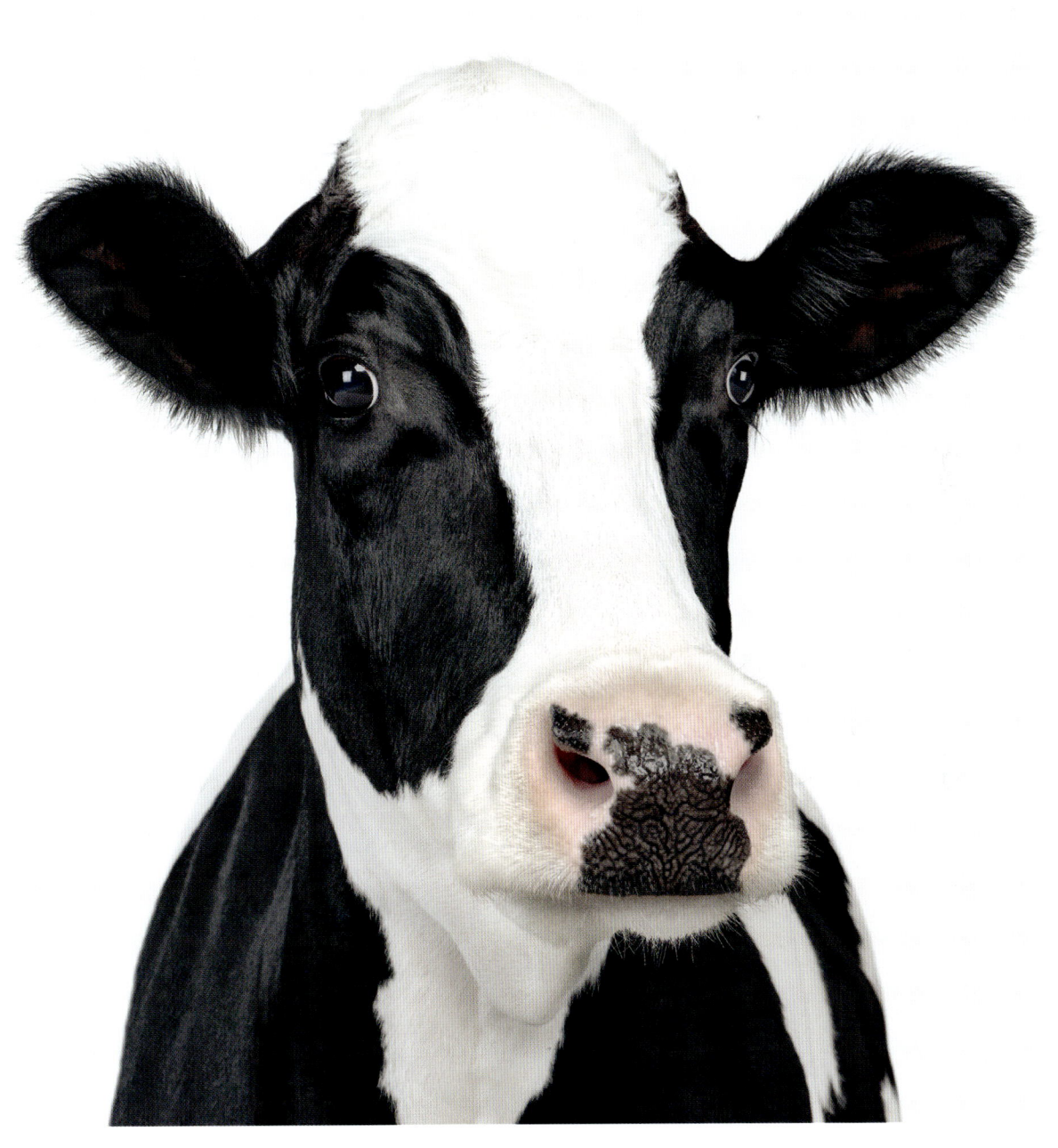

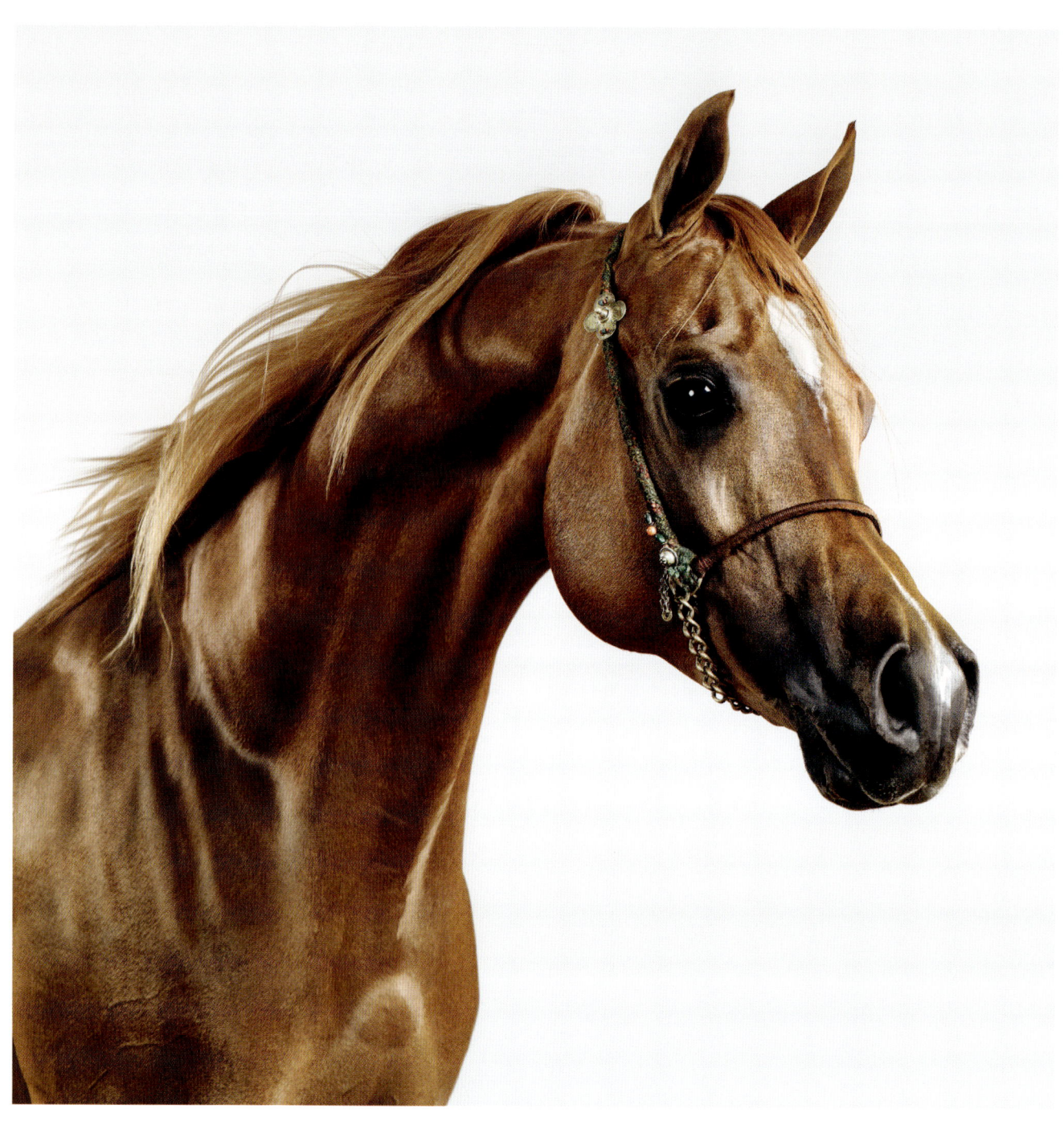

Lahab Albidayer

RED ARABIAN STALLION

ARABIAN HORSES

Arabian horses stand as a shining testament to heritage and beauty. DNA research has illuminated the pivotal role Arabians have played throughout equine evolution and revealed that nearly all modern horse breeds trace back to two ancient lineages: the Arabian horses of the Arabian Peninsula and the vanished Turkoman horses of Eurasia.

Through my lens, these ethereal beings emerge as true supermodels. Their distinctive, dished faces—coupled with mesmerizing musculature and luminescent coats—set them apart in the world of equine photography. I've had the great honor of photographing some of the world's most prized Arabians, each frame highlighting their unparalleled elegance. The difficulty often lies in capturing both their vibrant spirit and centuries-old lineage in one single frame—a challenge that is as invigorating as it is rewarding and one that I will never take for granted.

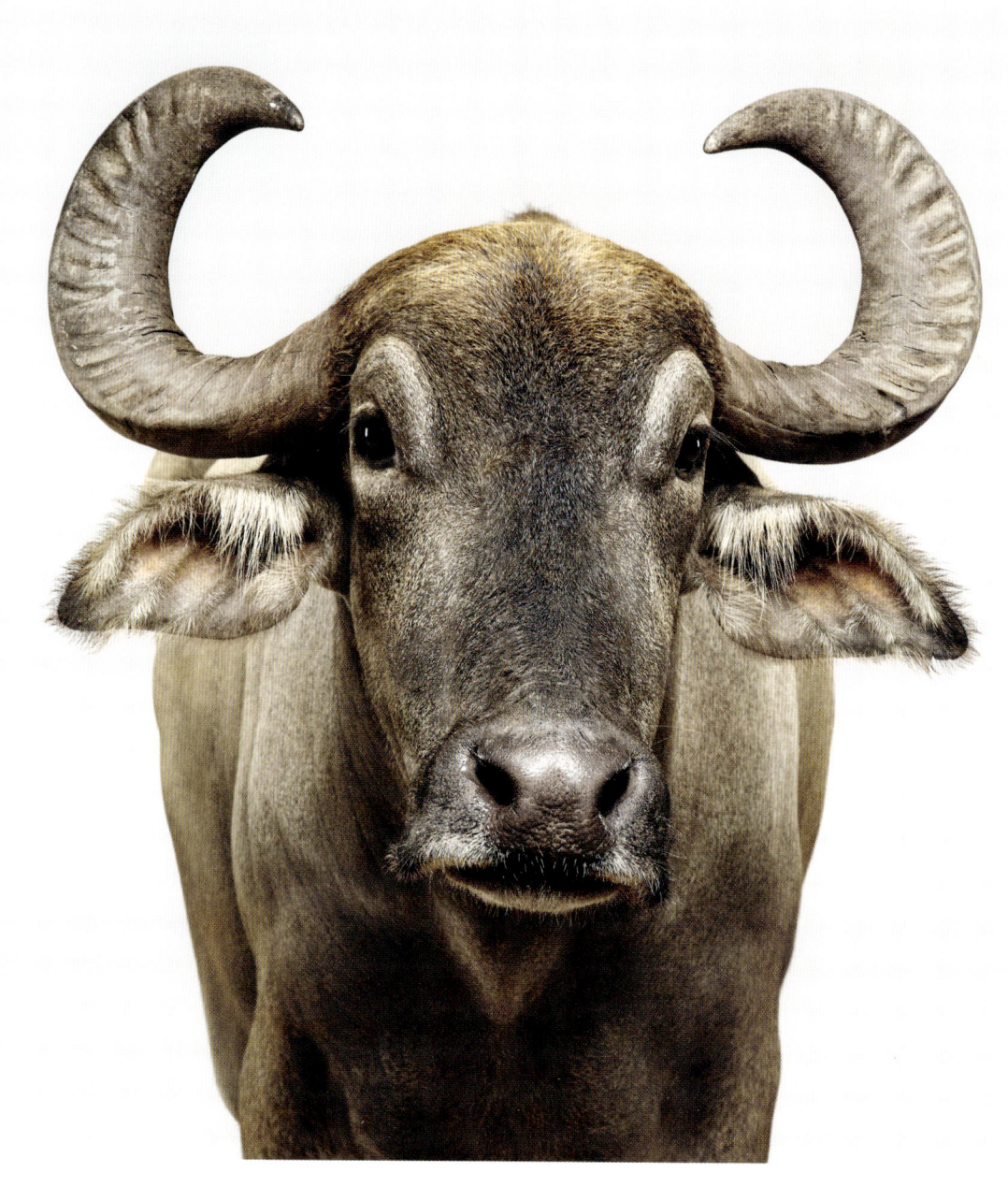

Lao Tzu

ASIAN WATER BUFFALO

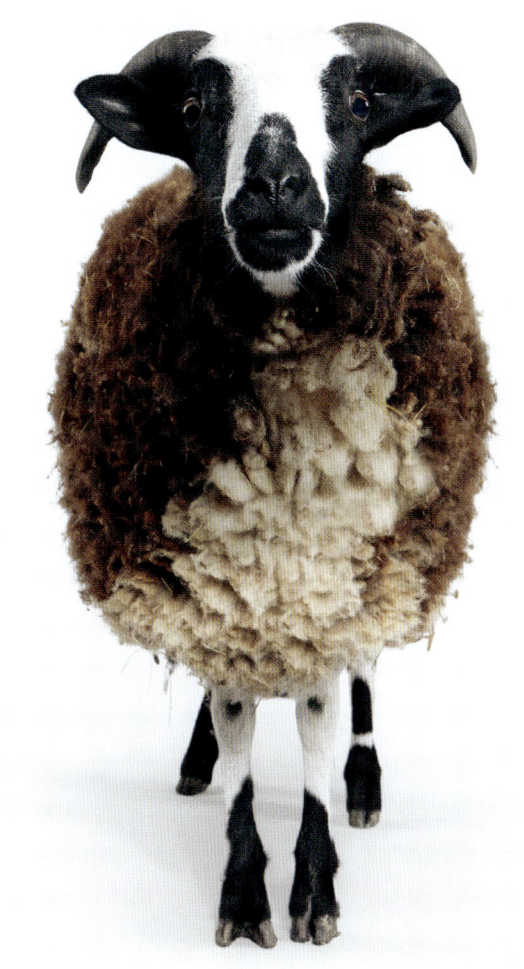

Moses

JACOB SHEEP

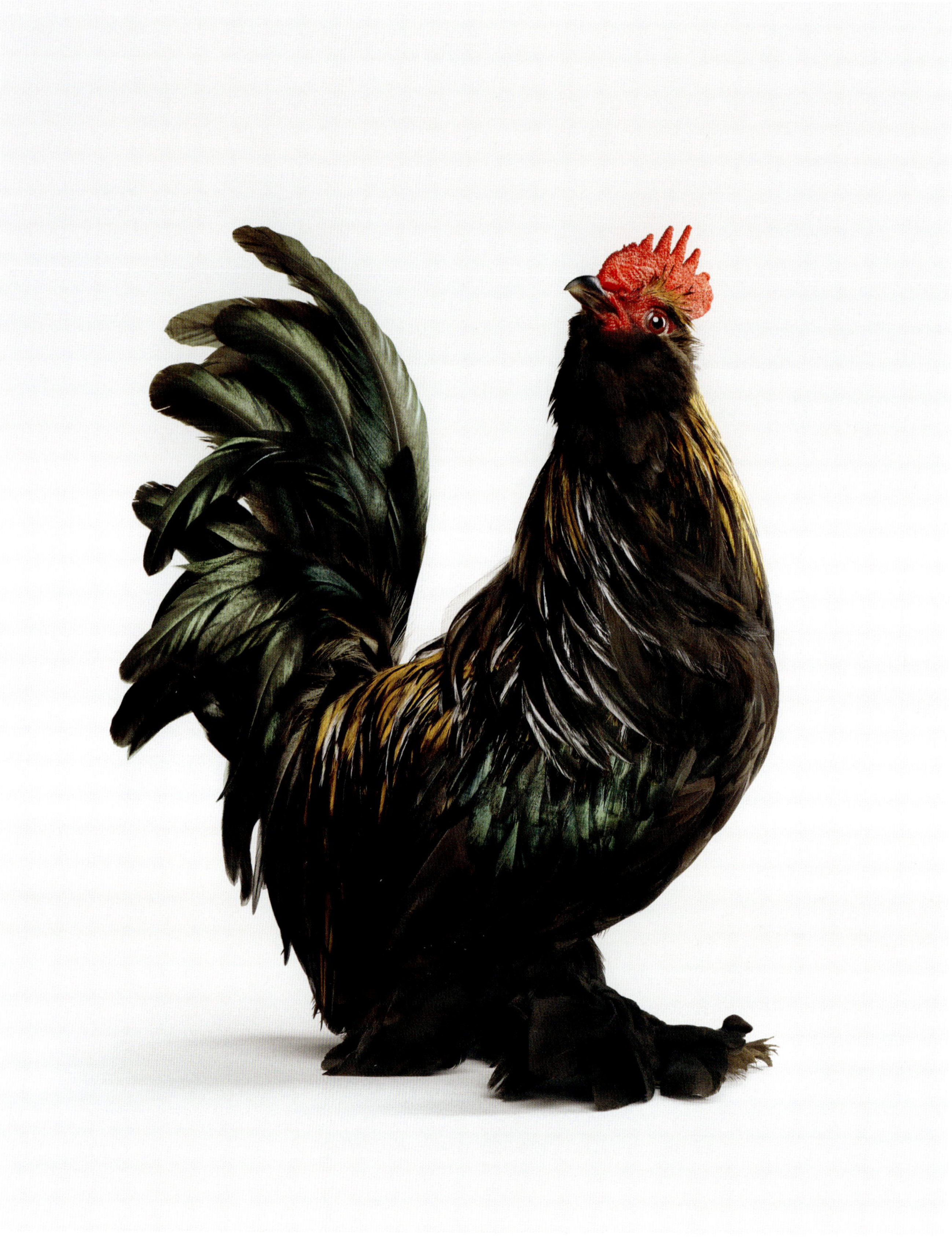

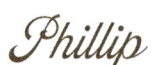

Phillip

BARBU D'UCCLE ROOSTER

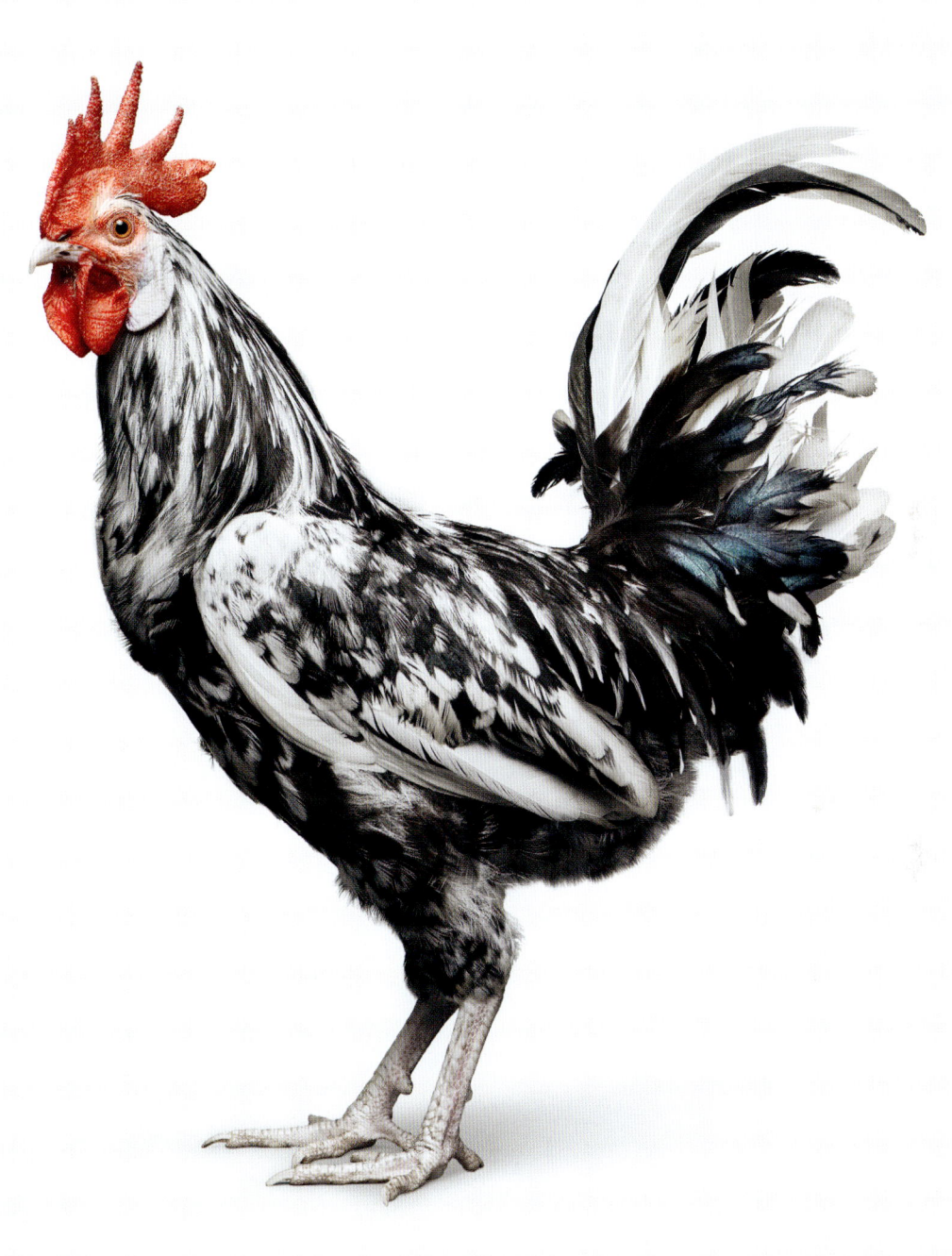

Hugo

ORUST ROOSTER

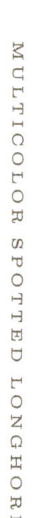

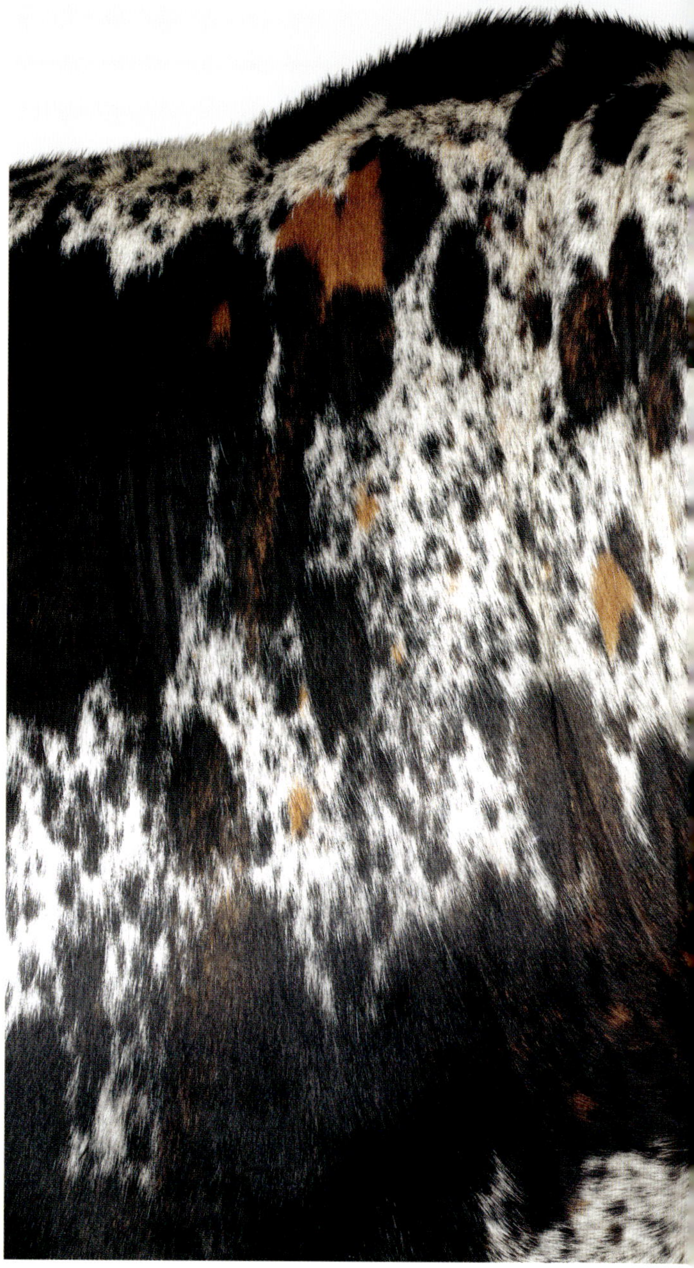

Bando

MULTICOLOR SPOTTED LONGHORN

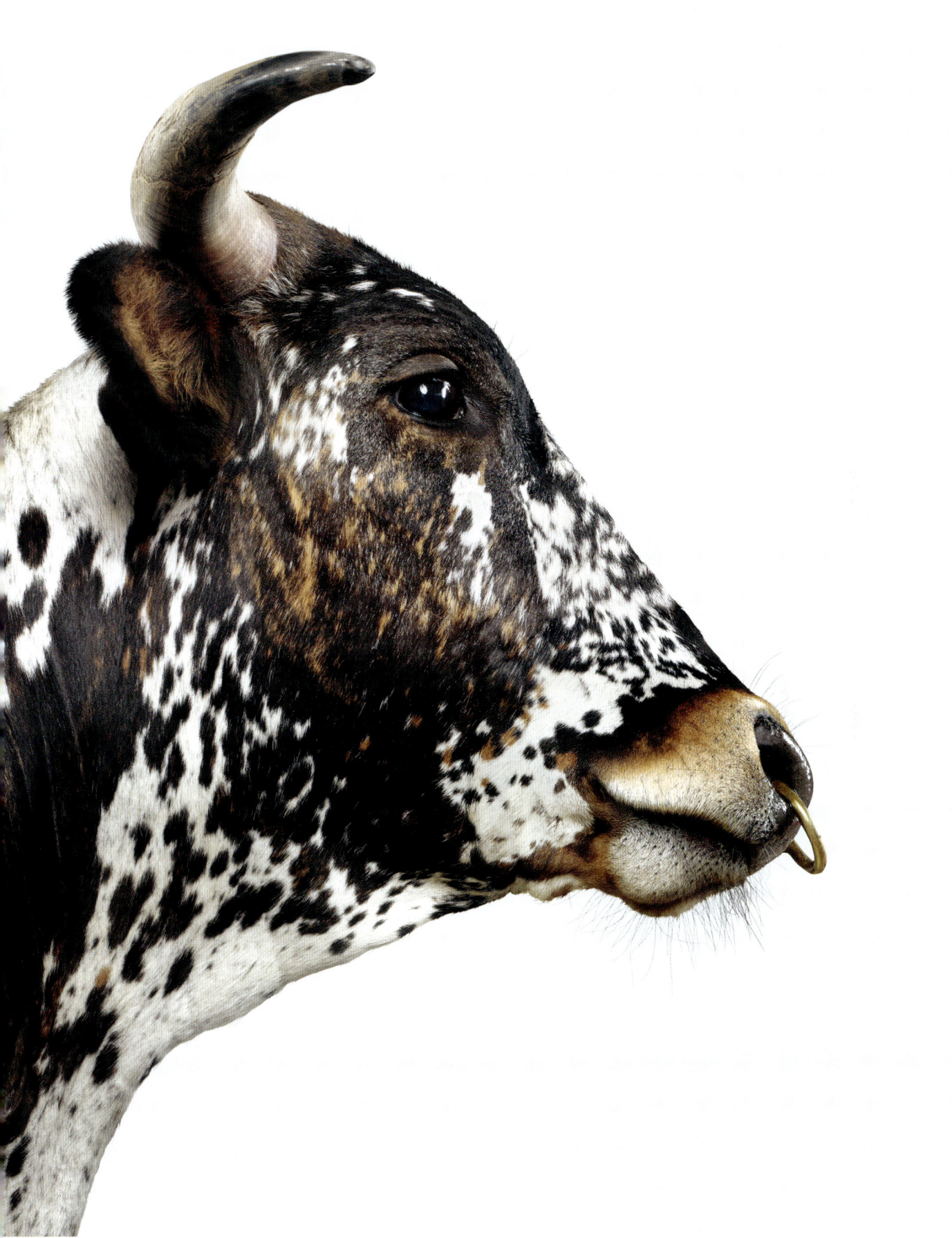

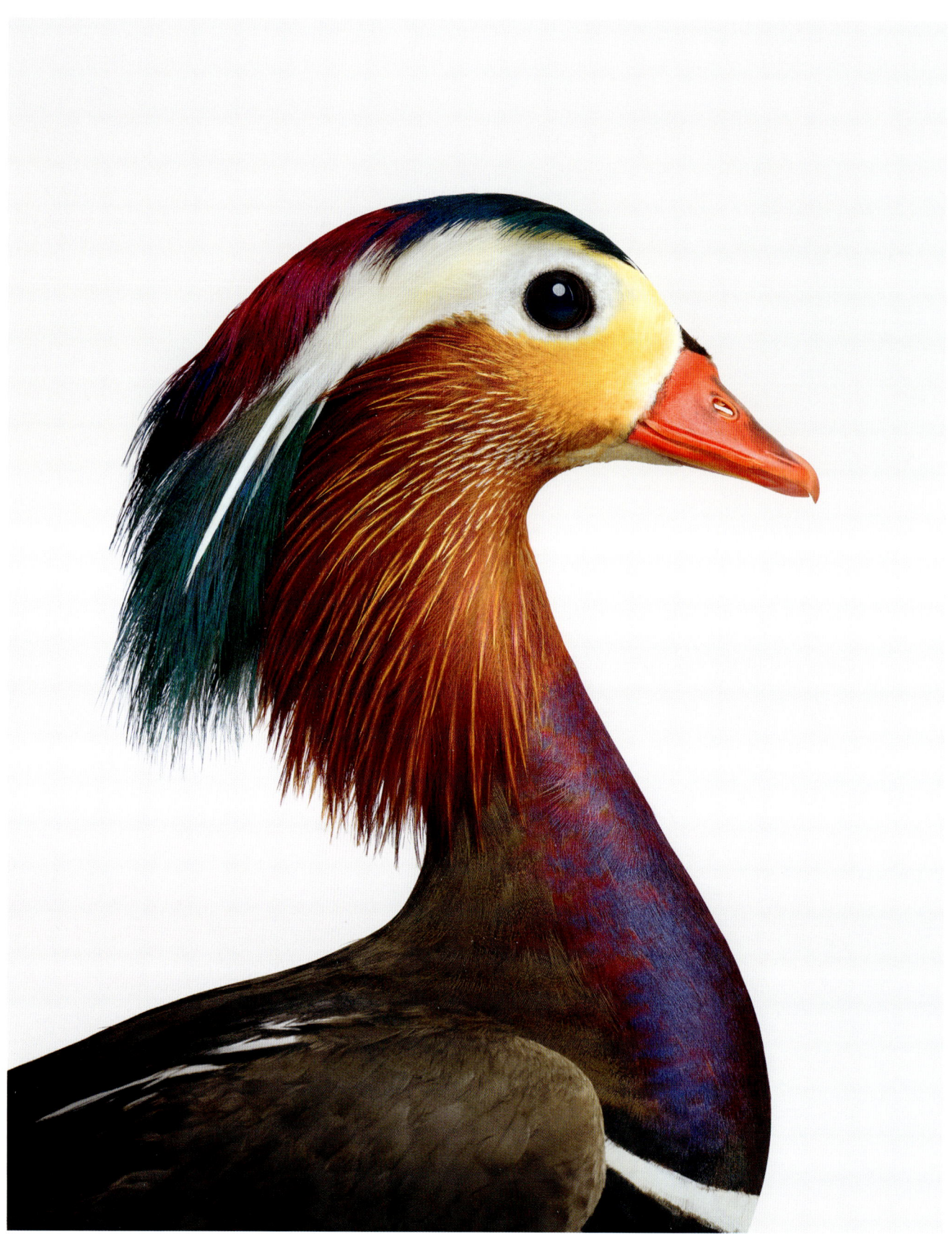

Iridian

MANDARIN DUCK

Iridian is a living masterpiece. His

extraordinary colors—unique among all

ducks—symbolize a centuries-old tale of

love and fidelity. Originating in East Asia,

mandarin ducks are revered for their

strong pair bonds and represent a lifetime

of devotion. Photographing him was an

exercise in simplicity and precision.

I used a single light source to the right

of the camera to highlight his shape

and magnificent color display.

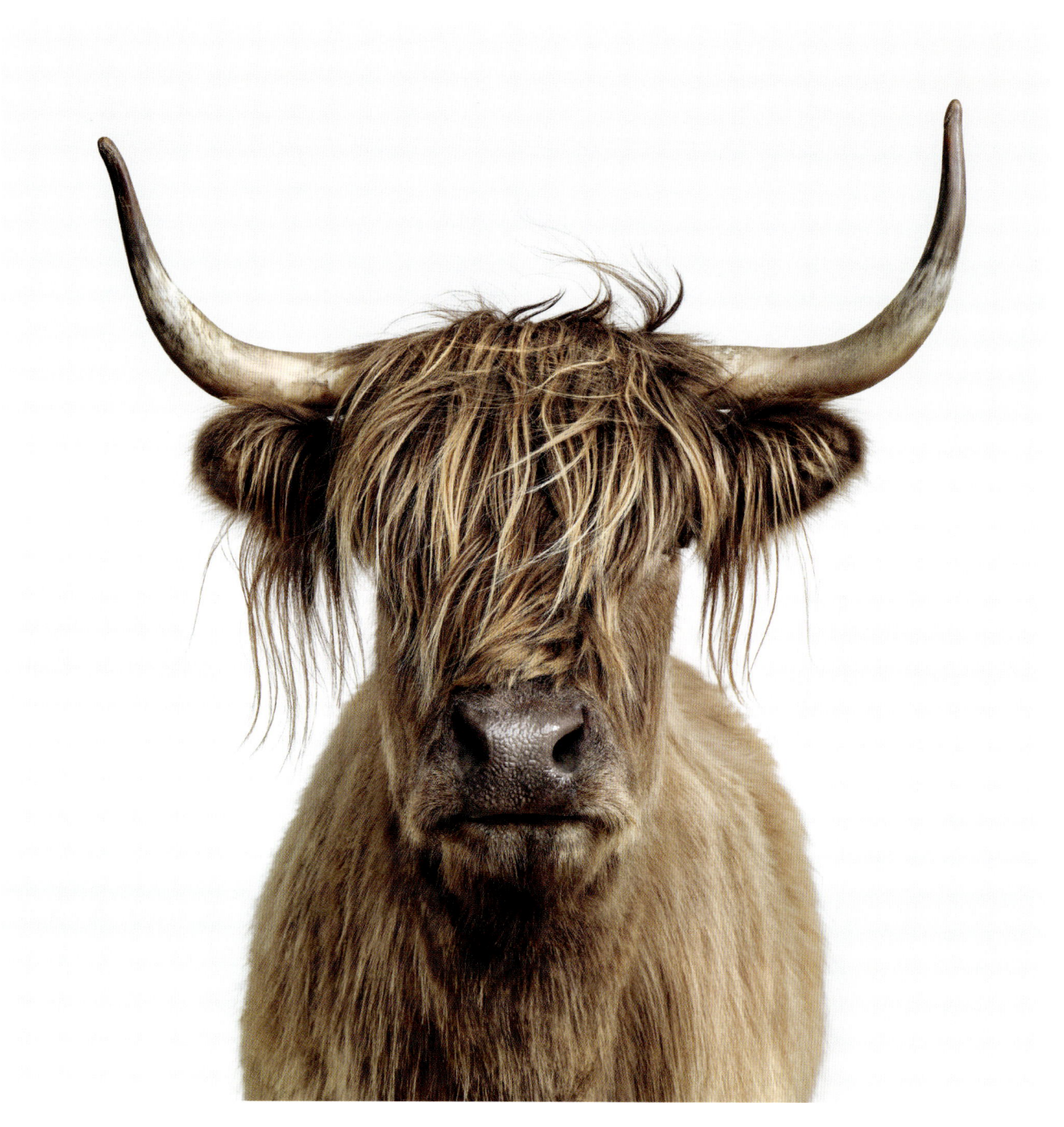

Hazel

HIGHLAND COW

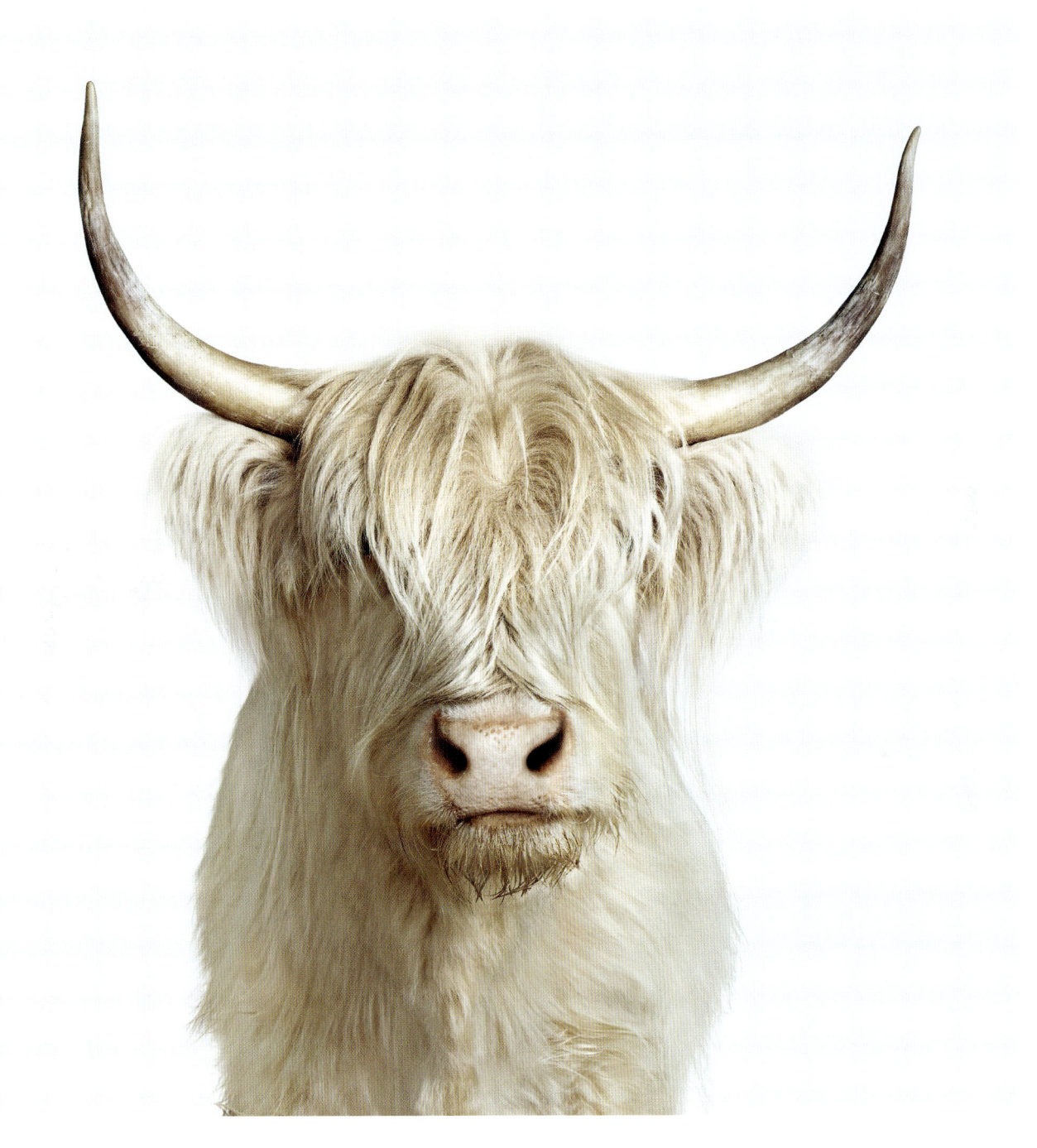

Gertrude

HIGHLAND COW

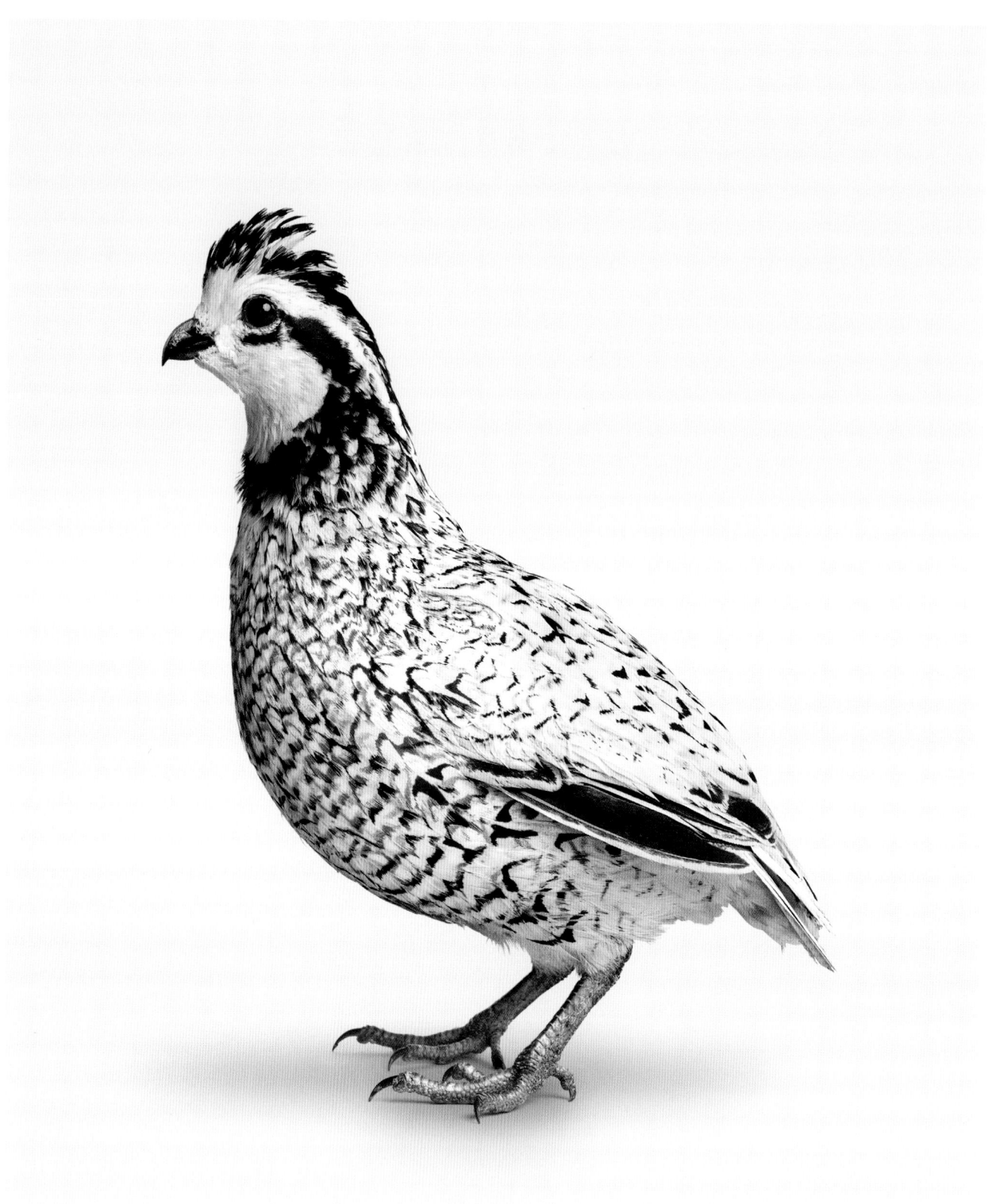

Tux

SNOWFLAKE BOBWHITE QUAIL

GAME BIRDS

Game birds—like pheasants, quail, turkeys, guinea fowl, doves, and pigeons—straddle the delicate boundary between the wild and domestic realms of the farm. They serve as vivid reminders of the wild heritage from which all farm animals once emerged. Each of these unique birds carries an untamed streak, keeping them ever connected to the wilderness within them.

This duality can be a tough challenge for a photographer, as the wilder the subject, the more unpredictable the shot. These birds—with their diverse colors, patterns, and behaviors—not only enrich the farm's biodiversity but also symbolically bridge the gap between the untamed landscapes of the past and the cultivated fields of the present.

Nothing sends a cold panic through

your blood quite like staring a bull in the

face. Titan was by far one of the most

intimidating animals I've ever stood in

front of. He was caked in black mud, with

his cavernous, onyx eyes fixed on mine,

and I could feel a shake in my fingers as

they hovered over the camera's trigger.

There are many reasons why bulls can be

aggressive; anything from fear to stress to

spikes in testosterone can trigger an uptick

in their unpredictable behavior. We always

work within the safest of standards (I shot

this portrait through a fence), but the truth

is no amount of safety measures could ever

fully relieve the instinctual fear a human

feels when at the mercy of a Titan.

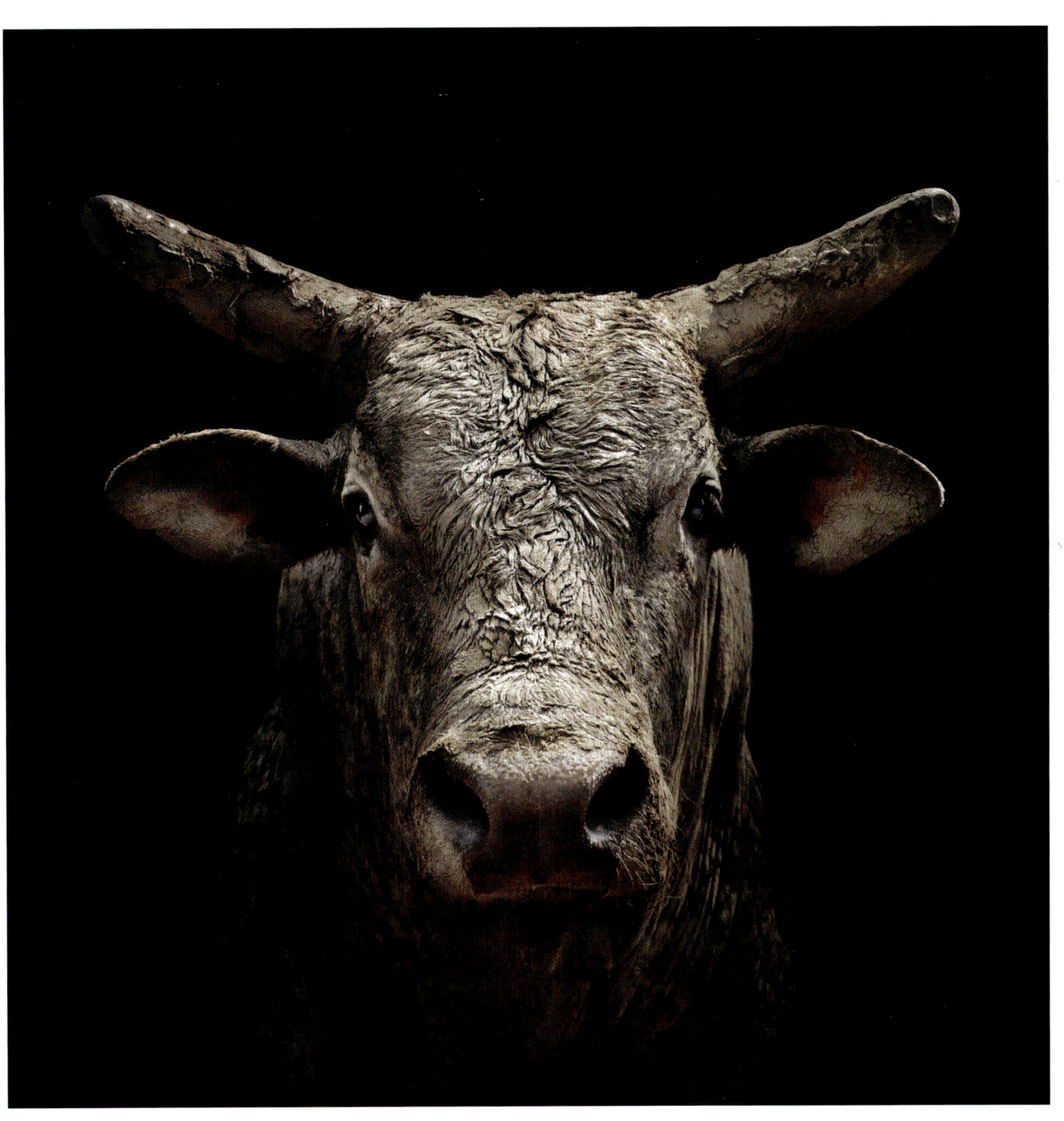

Titan

BUCKING RODEO BULL

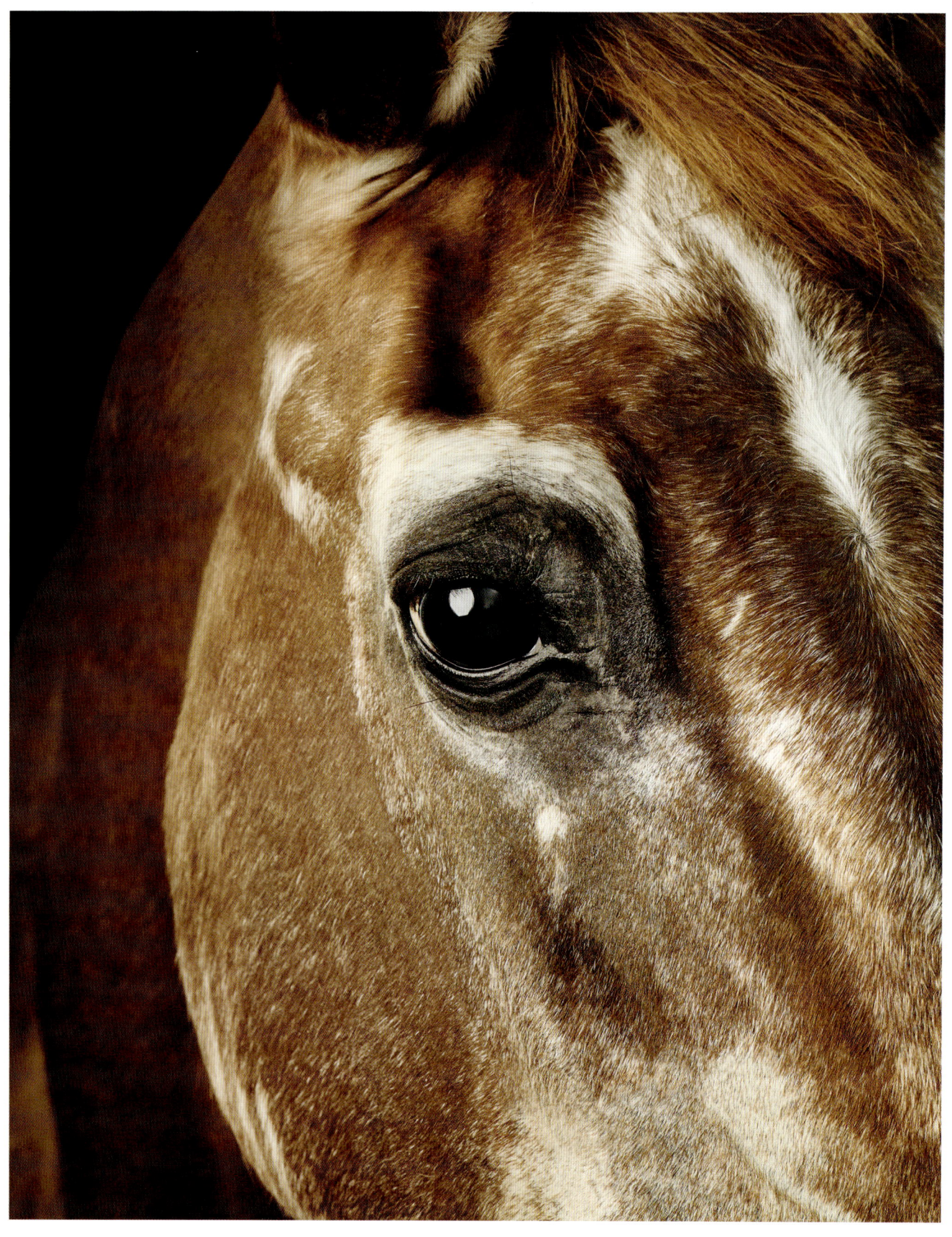

Aloha

SADDLEBRED ARABIAN MARE

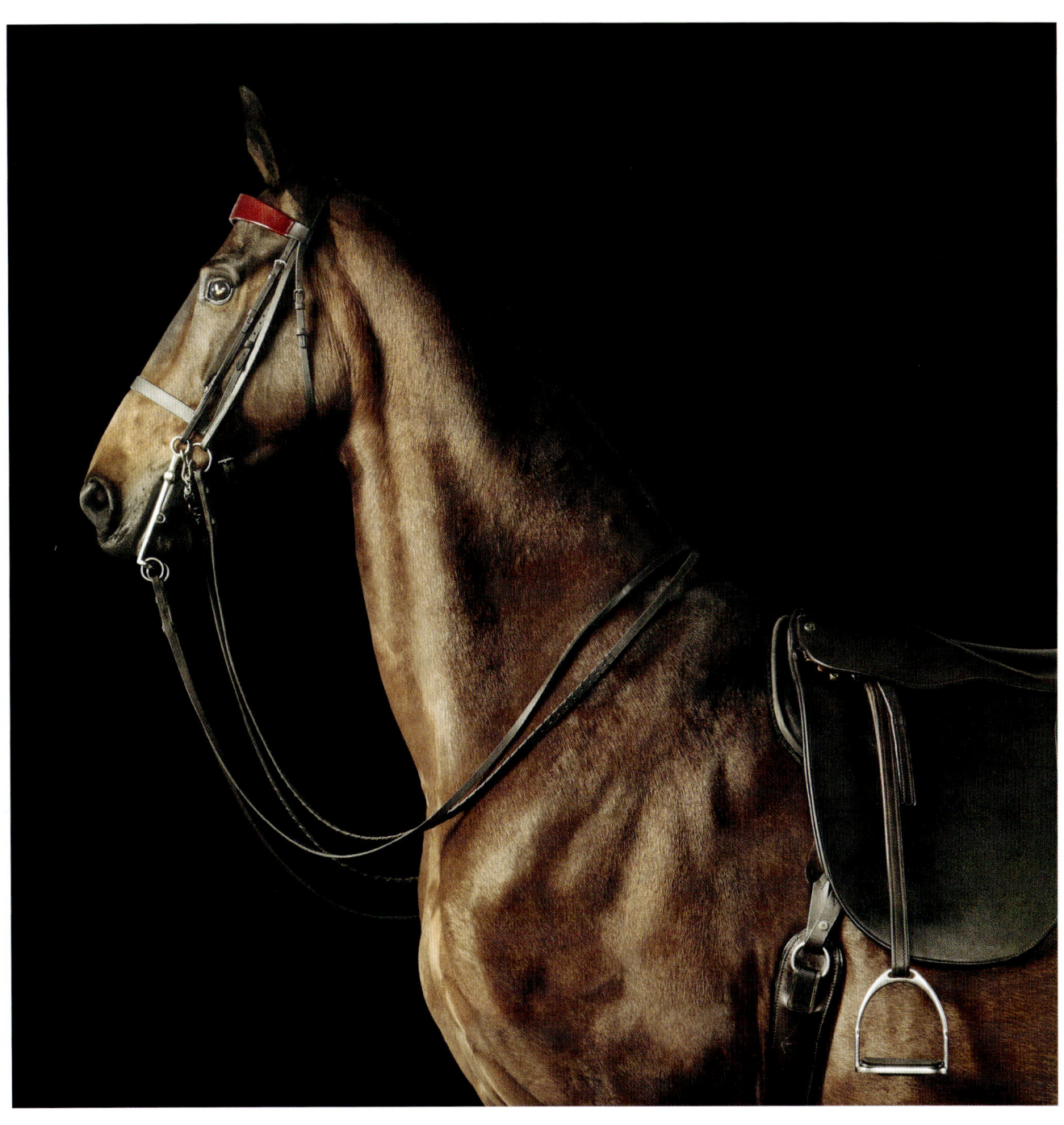

Mystery

AMERICAN SADDLEBRED HORSE

CATTLE DOGS

Cattle dogs are the unsung maestros of the pasture. These astoundingly intelligent canines guide herds with an almost telepathic comprehension of their movements. Their stealth and speed, combined with an innate sense of strategy, allow them to navigate and control large groups of powerful cattle, transforming chaos into orchestrated motion. It's like nothing I've ever seen before.

More than its skill, a cattle dog's abiding loyalty to its loving owners makes it indispensable. The harmony of a farm often hinges on the relationship between the shepherd and their dog—a bond forged in unwavering trust and mutual respect.

A pasture without a cattle dog is like an orchestra without a conductor. Their presence and precision create harmonious music across the land, faithfully reinforcing the age-old rhythms of pastoral life.

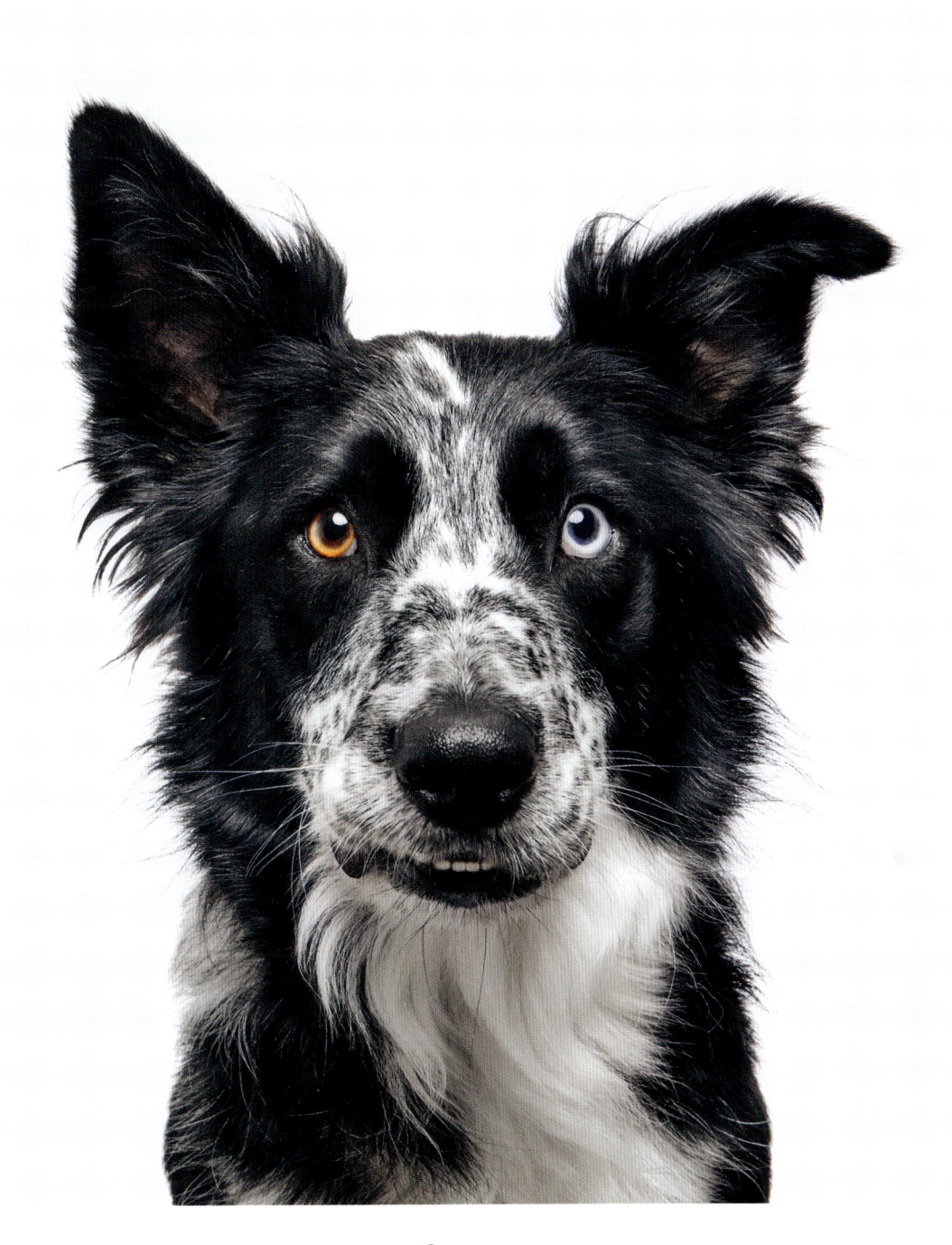

Gunner

BORDER COLLIE

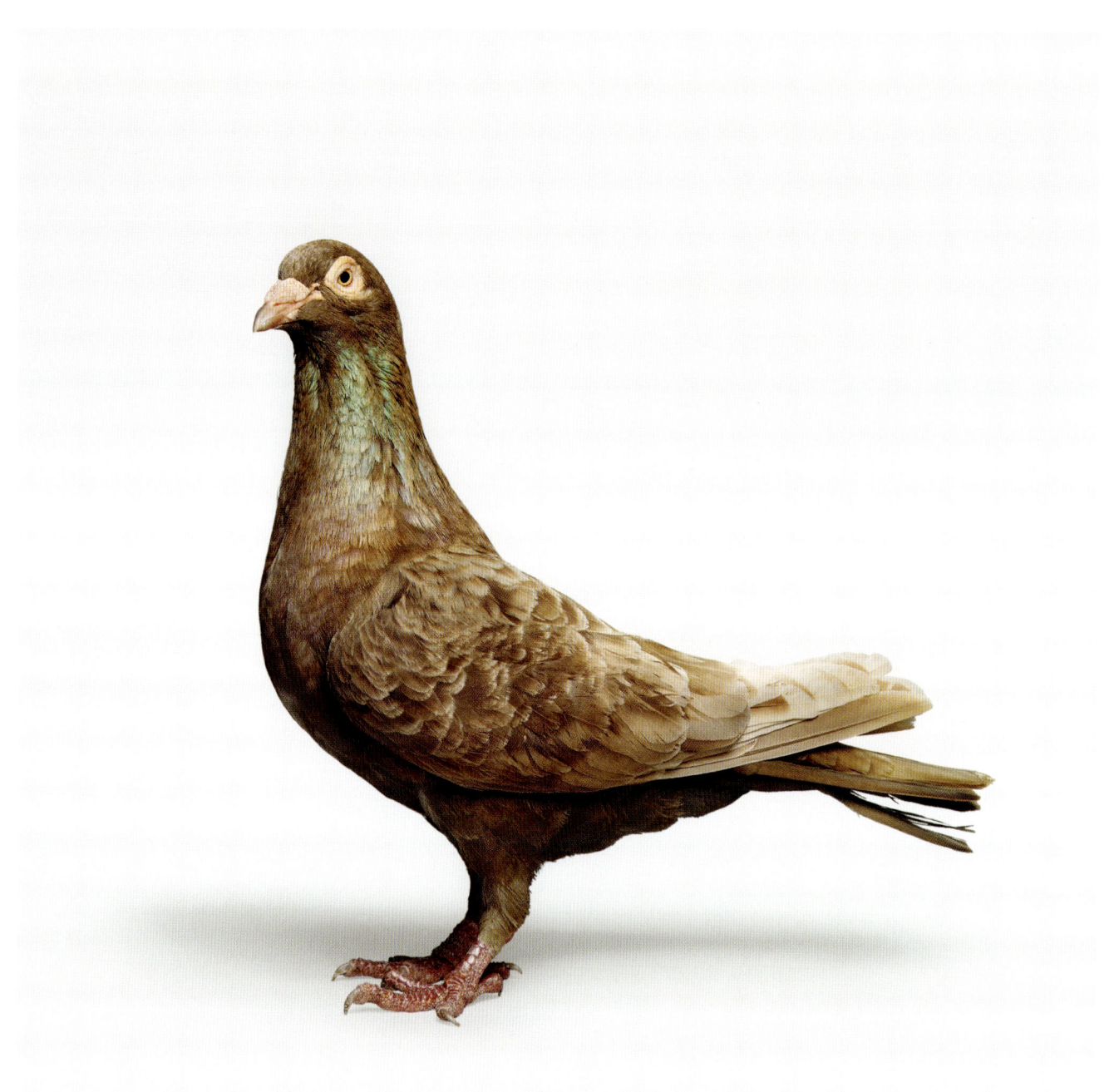

Milo

BROWN PIGEON

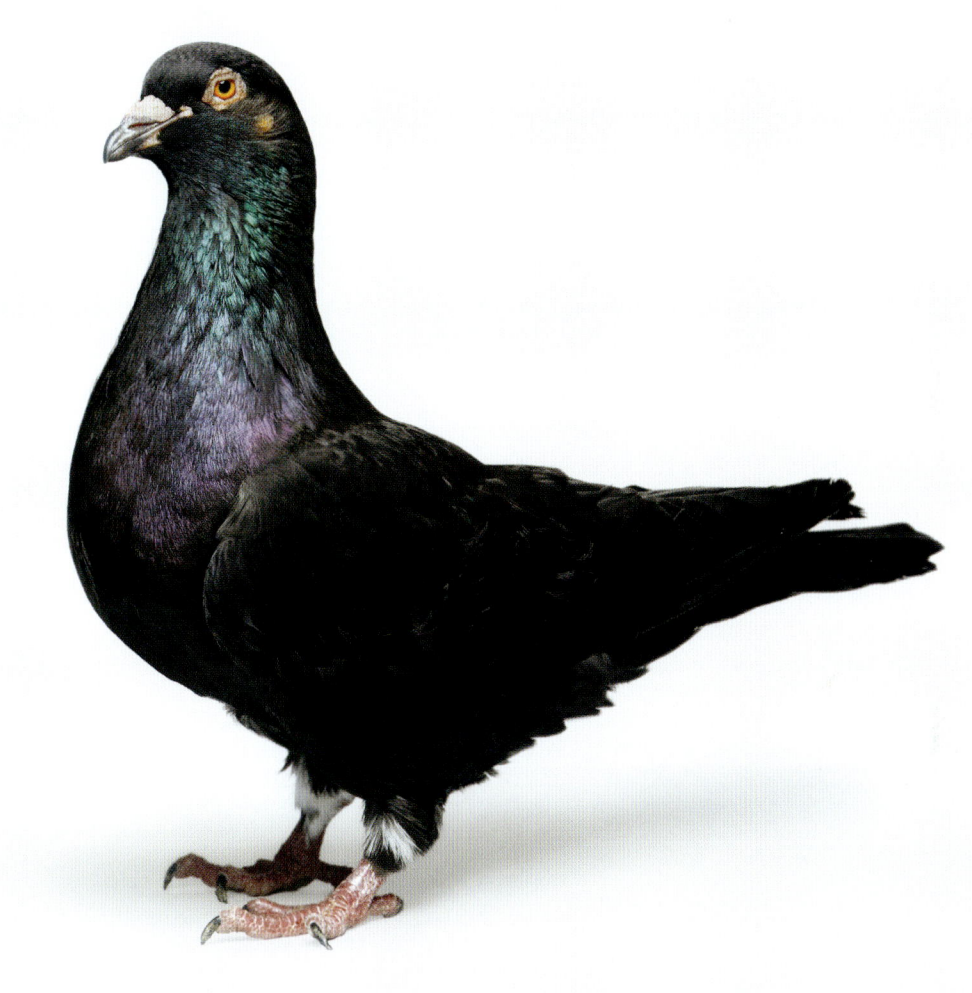

Shiloh

BLACK PIGEON

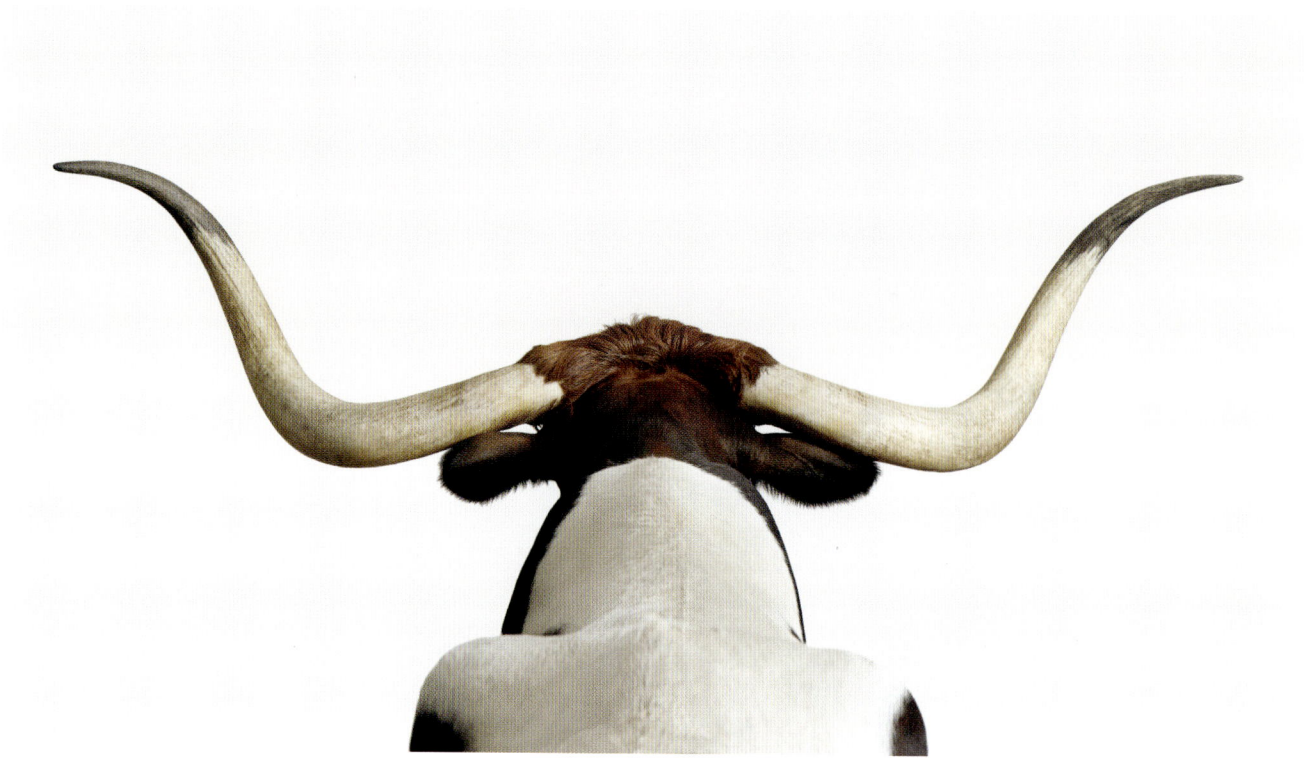

Maverick

TEXAS LONGHORN

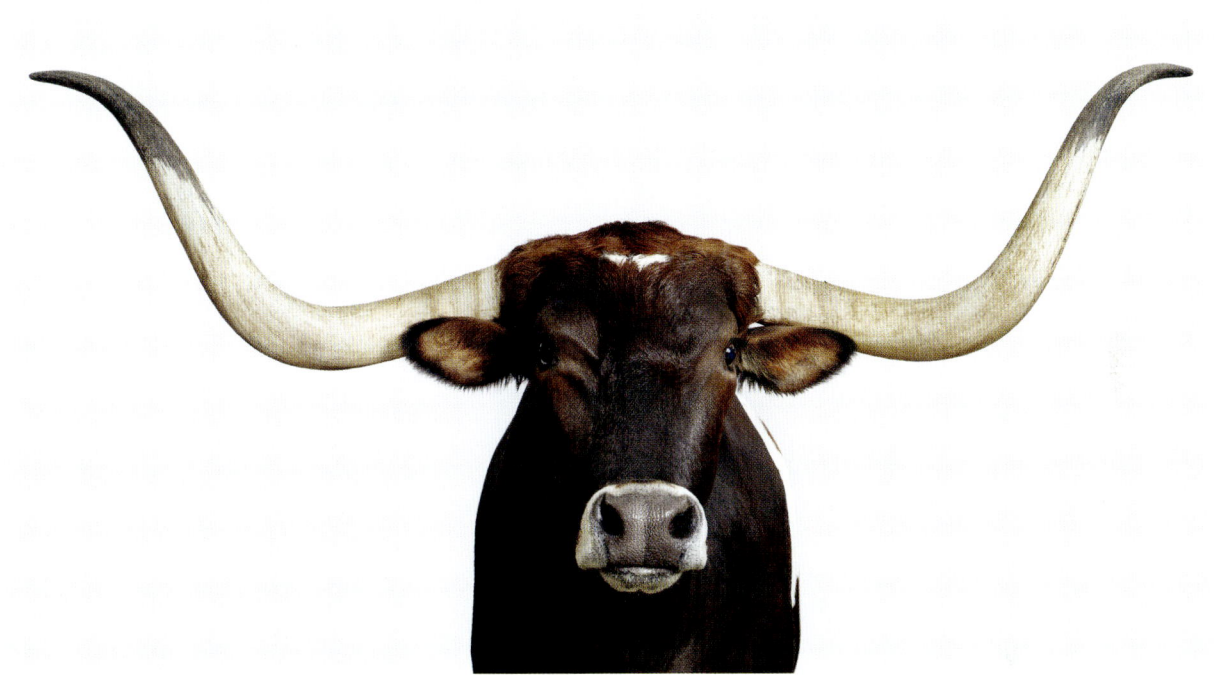

Peanut

SADDLEBRED ARABIAN MARE

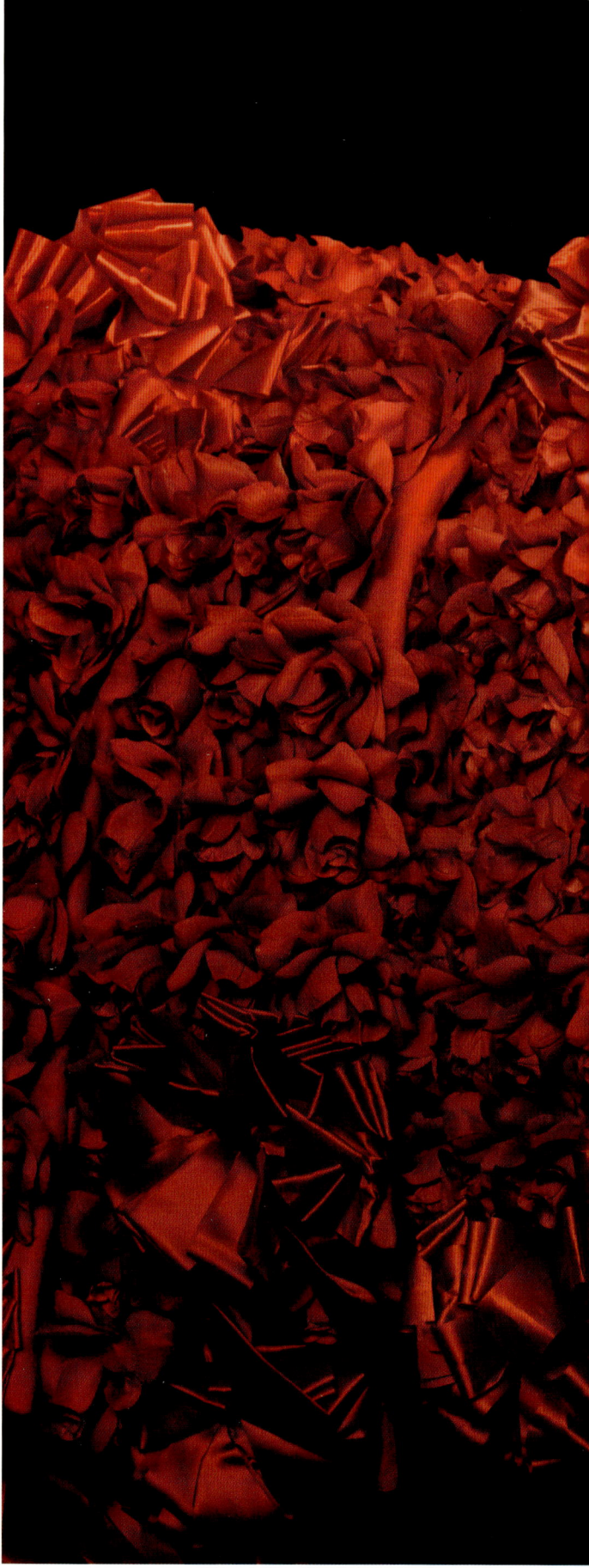

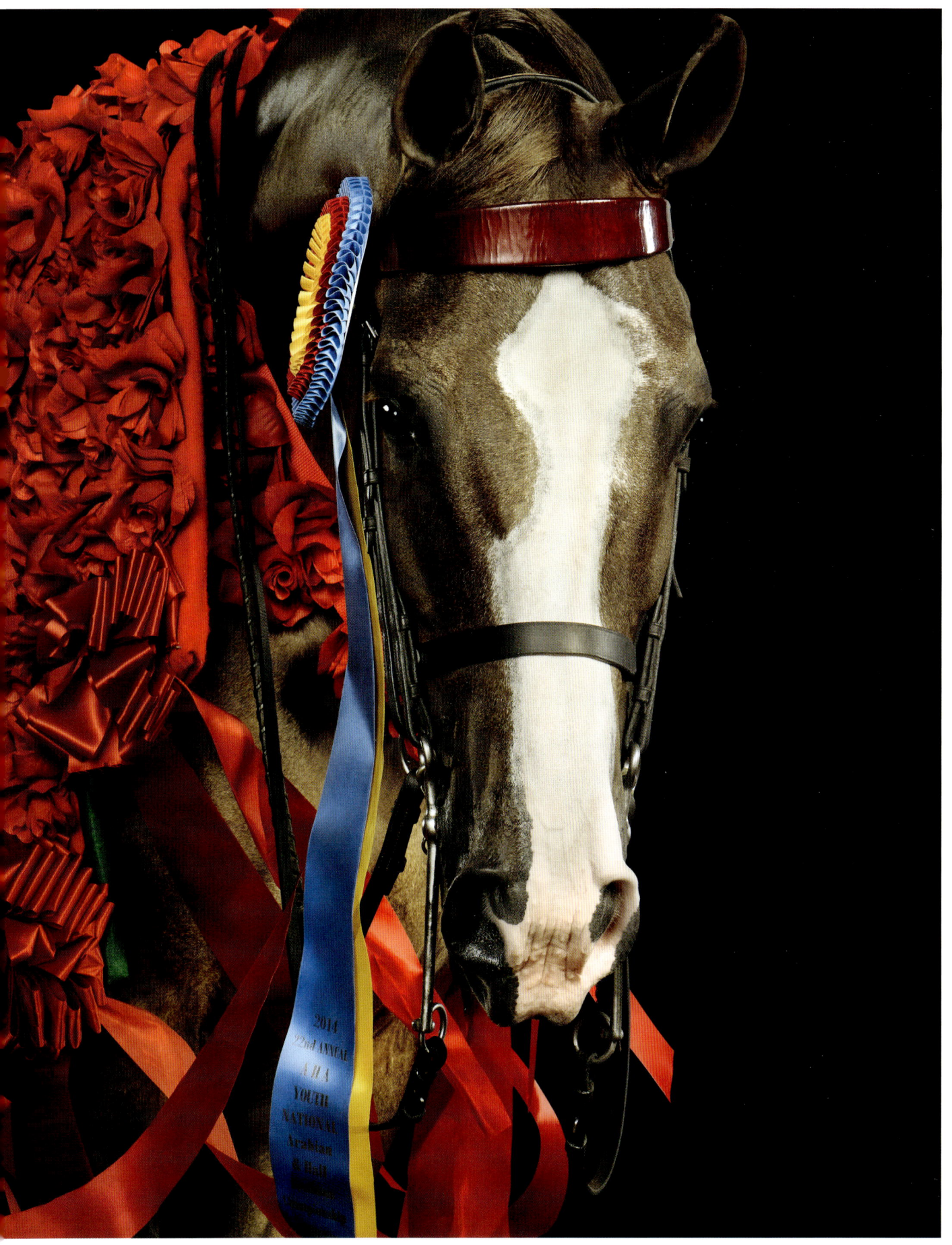

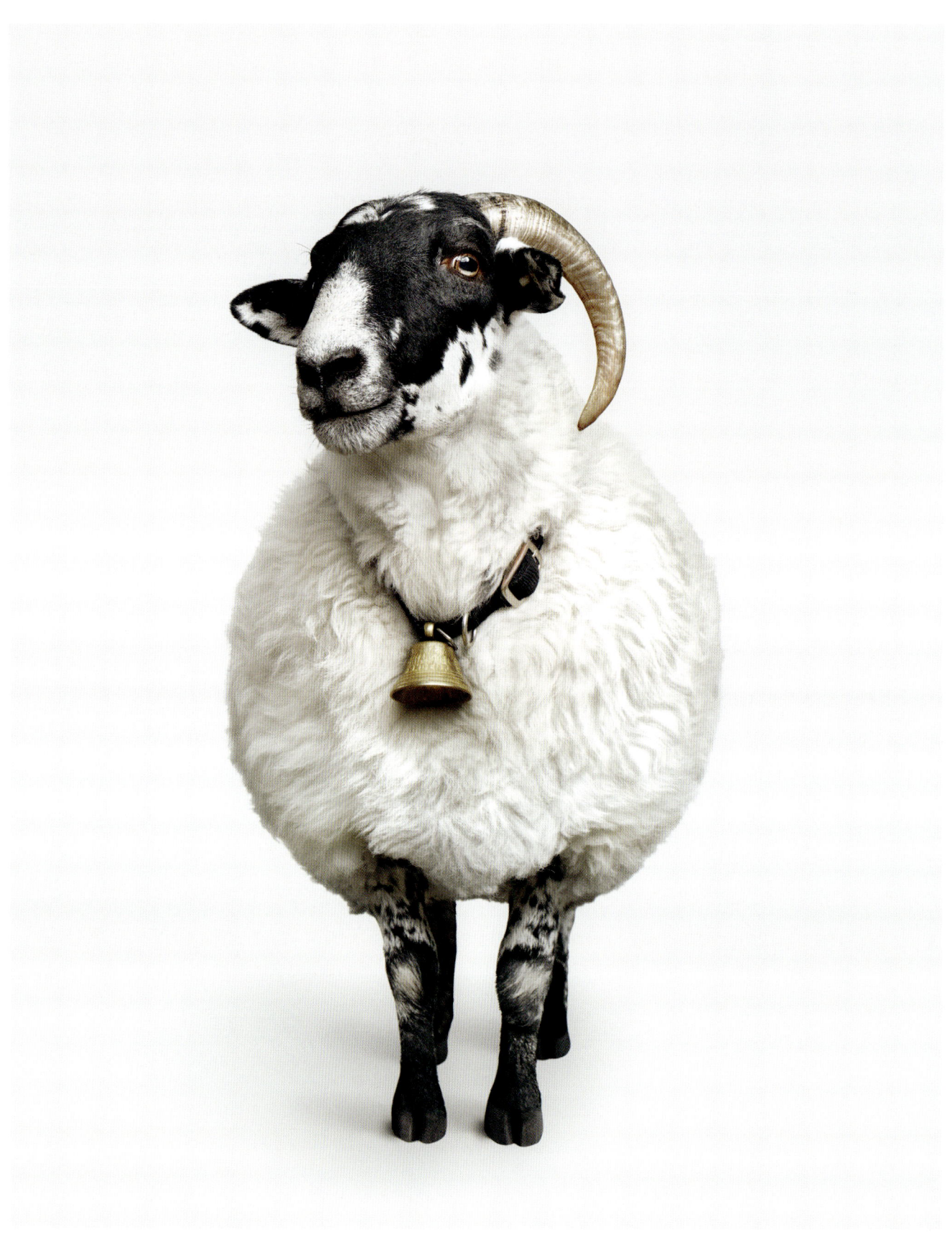

Dorothy

SCOTTISH BLACKFACE SHEEP

SHEEP

Emblematic of pastoral serenity and innocence, sheep have graciously provided humanity with warmth for millennia—from the bitter chills of the Swiss Alps to the brisk winds of America's Northern Plains. However, their significance transcends far beyond these tangible offerings.

The quiet bond between a sheep and its shepherd is symbolic, a reflection of guidance, trust, and profound mutual reliance. This ancient relationship, celebrated across various cultures, subtly mirrors biblical allegories where the shepherd guides and protects his trusting flock.

The expressive nature of sheep continually captivates me. Their soulful eyes, often seemingly illuminated with a spiritual aura, exude tales of both worldly pastures and ethereal connections. Through my lens, it's this intricate blend of the earthly and the divine that I try to encapsulate.

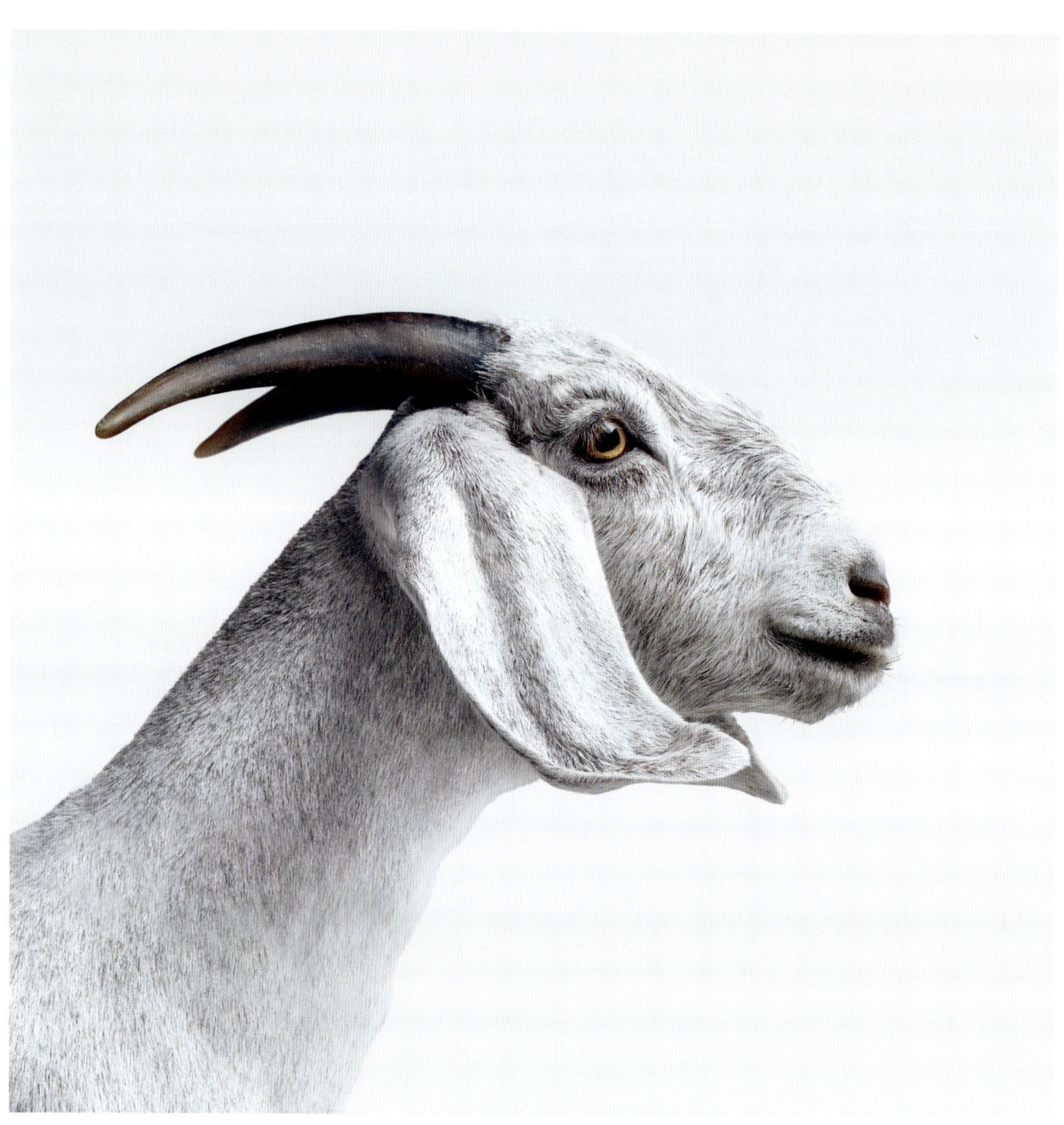

Bianca

WHITE GOAT

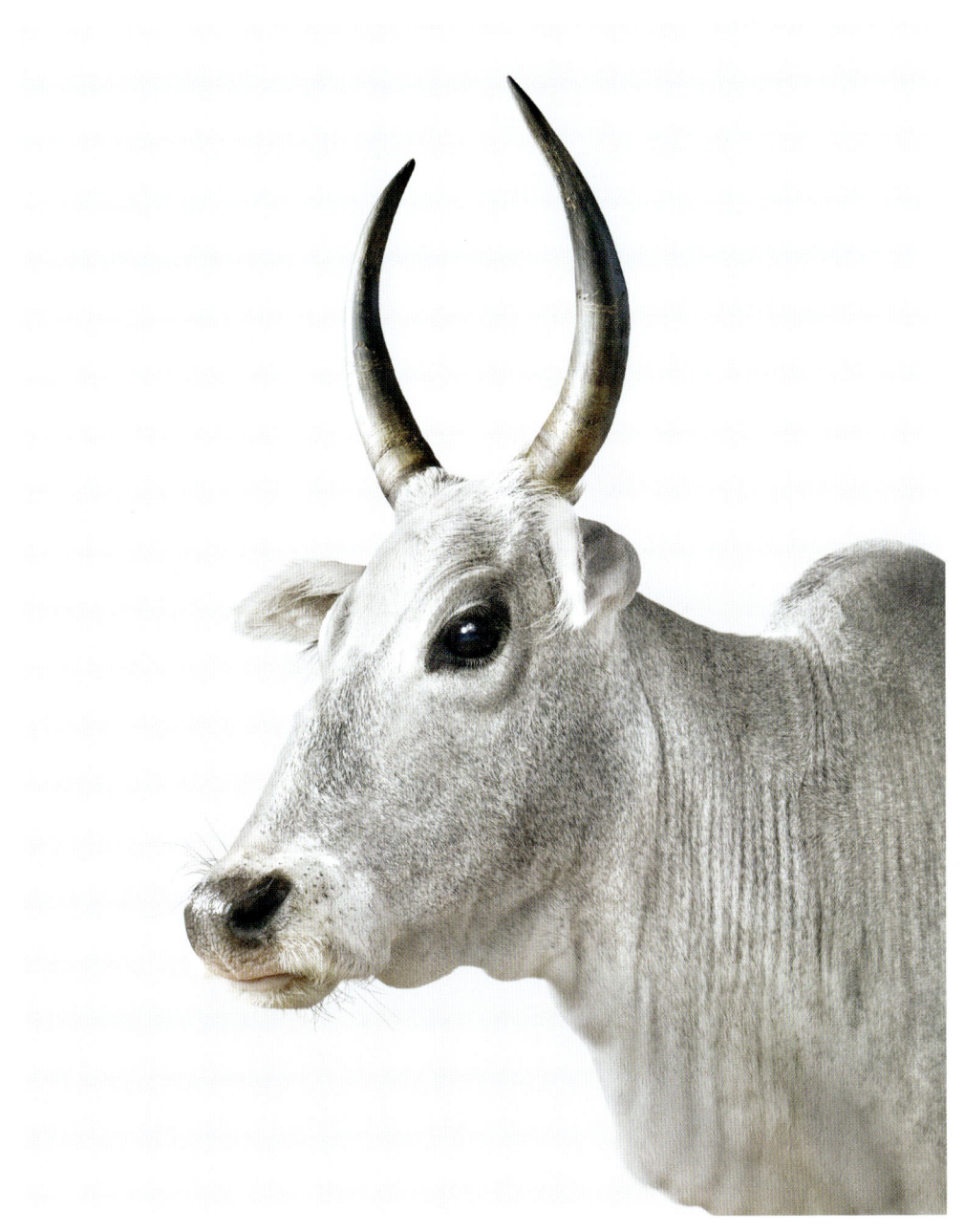

Notta Chance

ZEBU COW

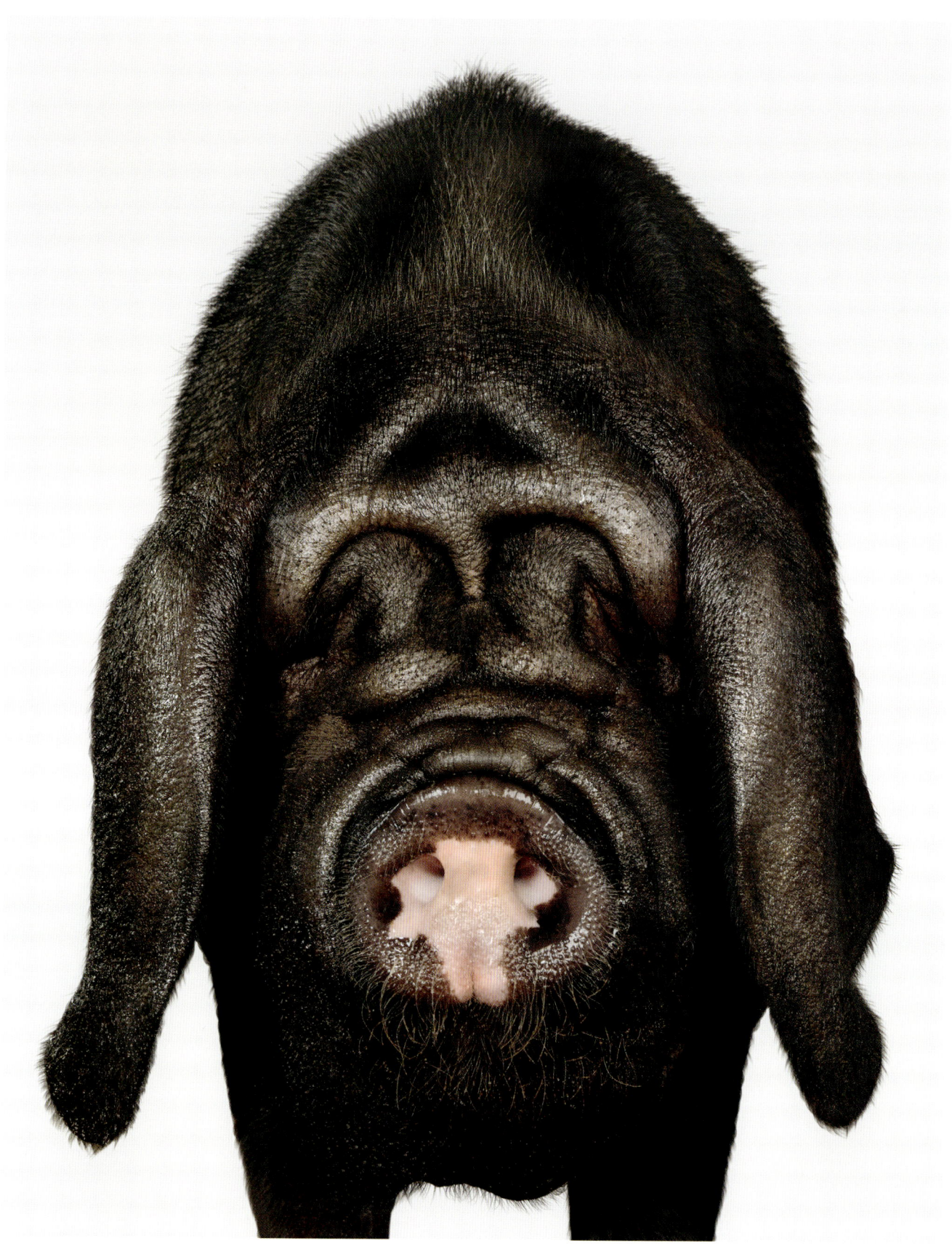

Shawn

MEISHAN PIG

Shawn the Meishan was a sight for sore

eyes—though I'm not sure he could say the

same for us. In fact, I'm not sure if he could

see us at all. Meishan pigs are known for their

squishy, shar-pei-like faces and obstructed

vision, but what they may not sense with

their eyes they make up for with their keen

sense of smell. This rare and lovable breed

is celebrated around the world for its docile

temperament and laid-back personality.

Shawn remained as cool as a cucumber on

set and glistened like one, too, thanks to the

refreshing spritzes from his favorite water

bottle. Shawn loved to be misted and would

raise his head toward the nozzle (and my lens)

each time he was ready for another spray.

Soak it up, bud, you deserve it.

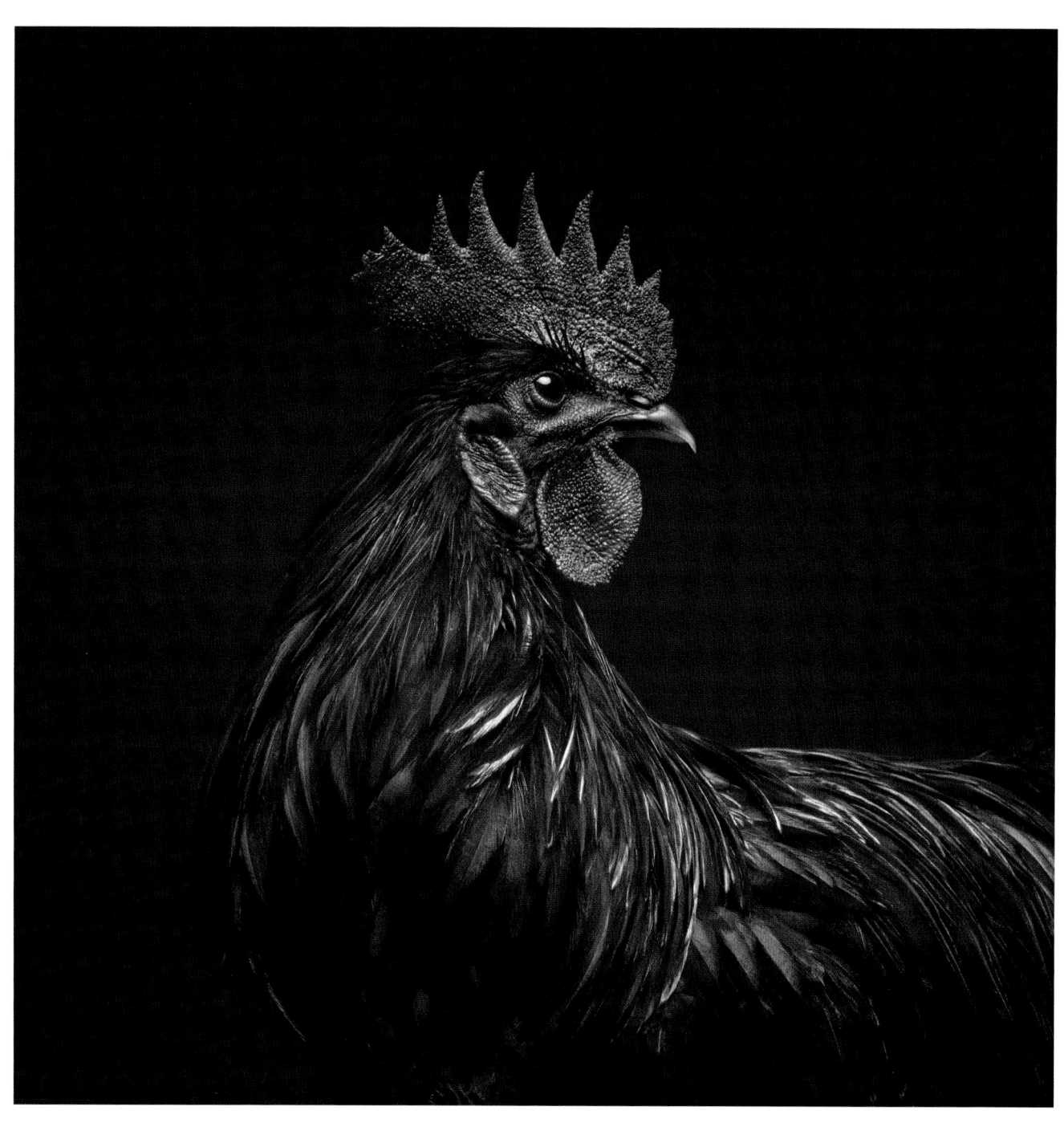

Krishna

AYAM CEMANI ROOSTER

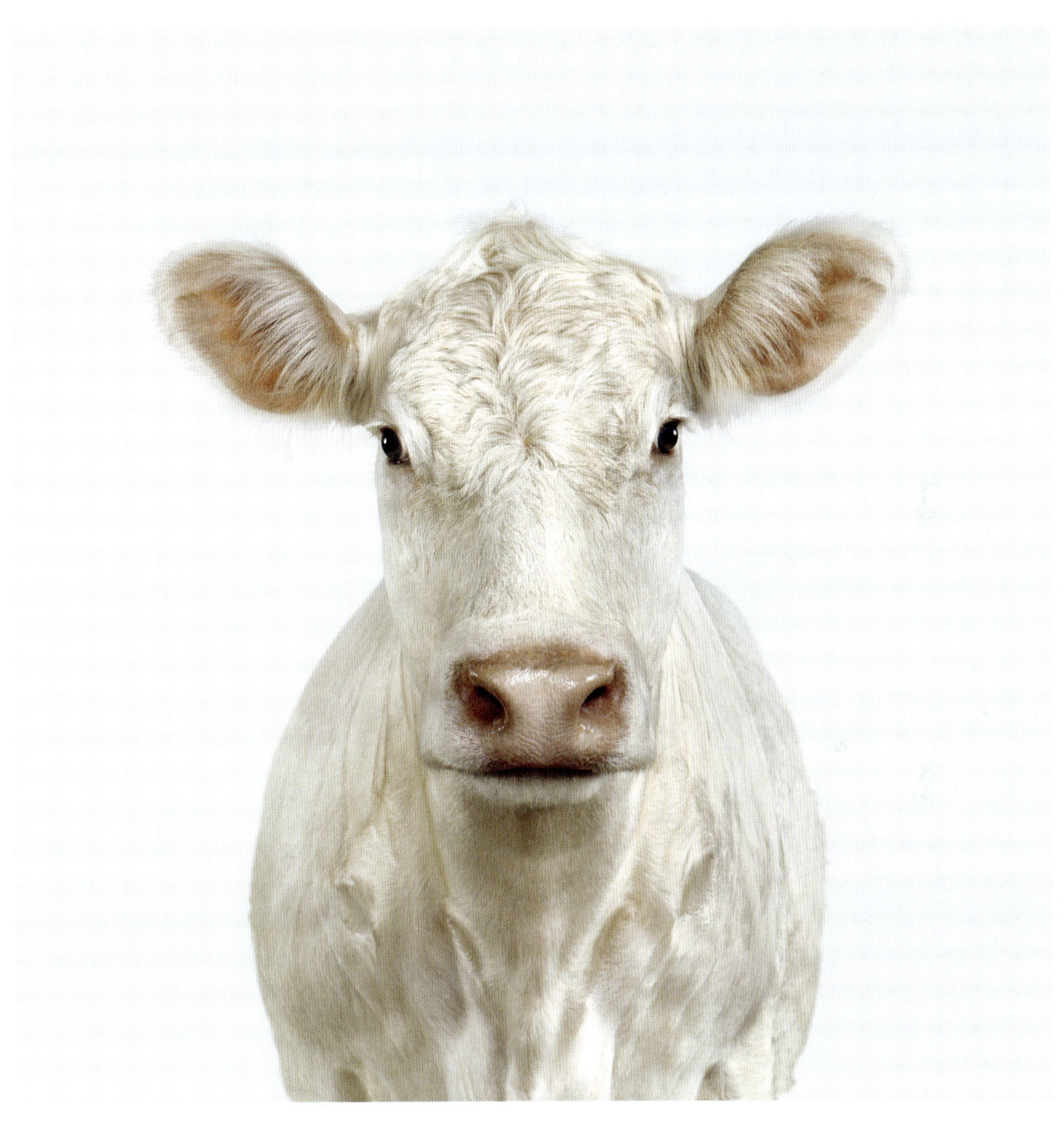

Snowflake

CHAROLAIS HEIFER

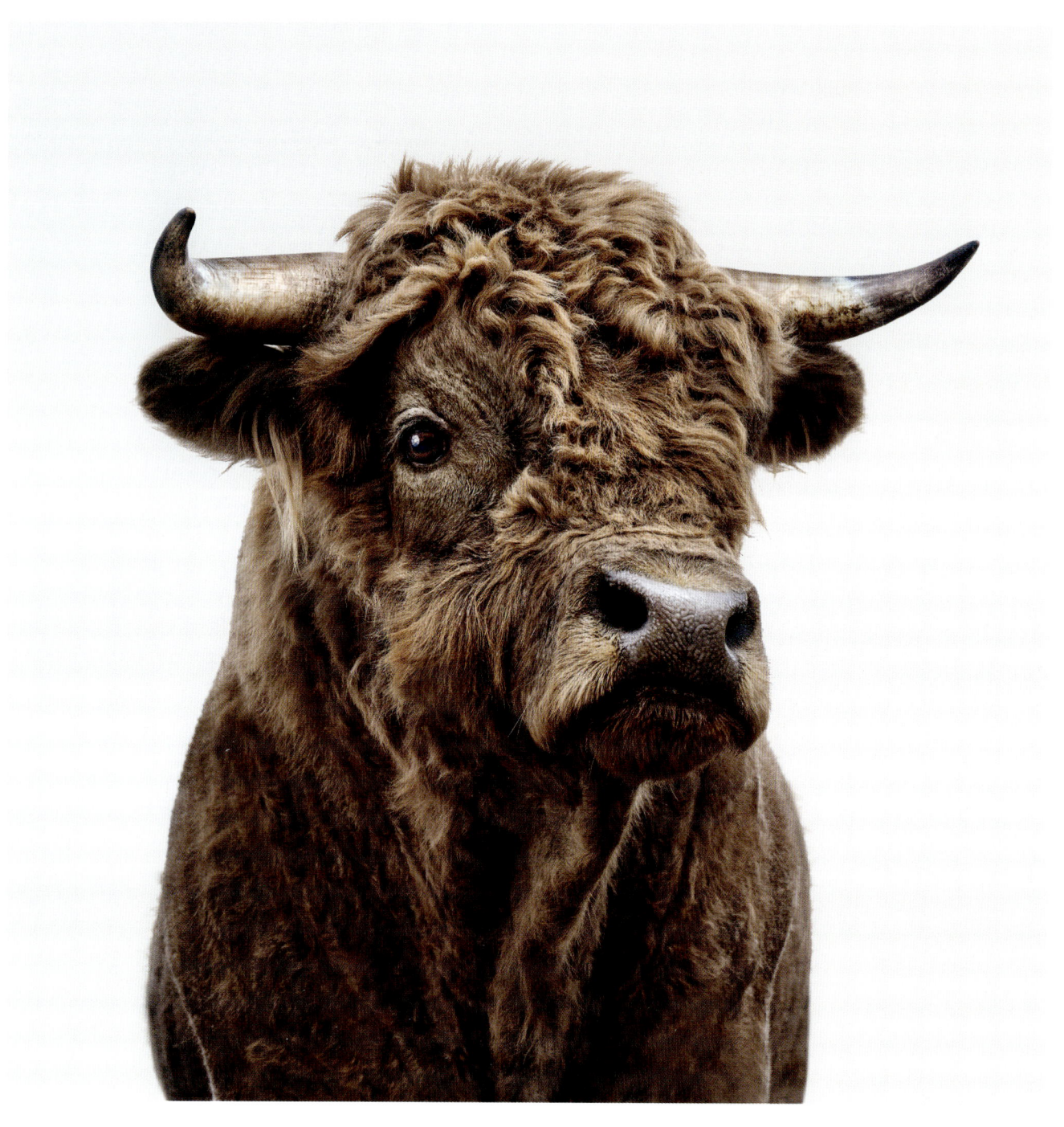

King Henry

HIGH DEX BULL

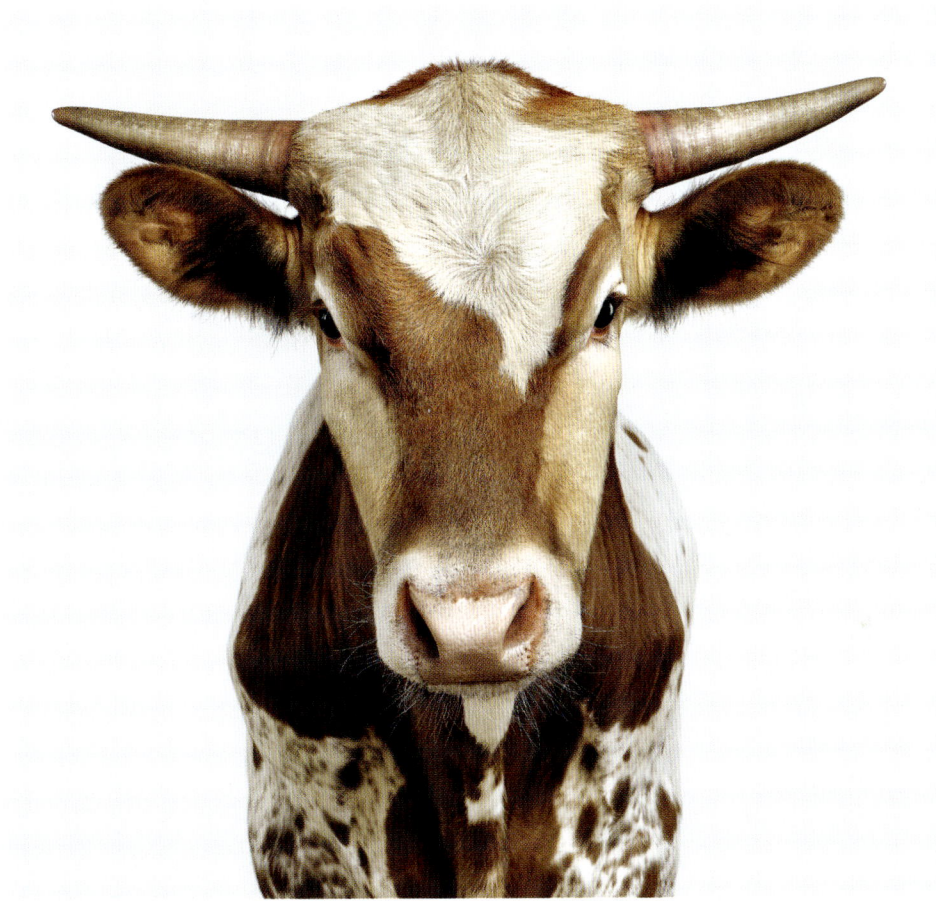

Wingman

TEXAS LONGHORN CALF

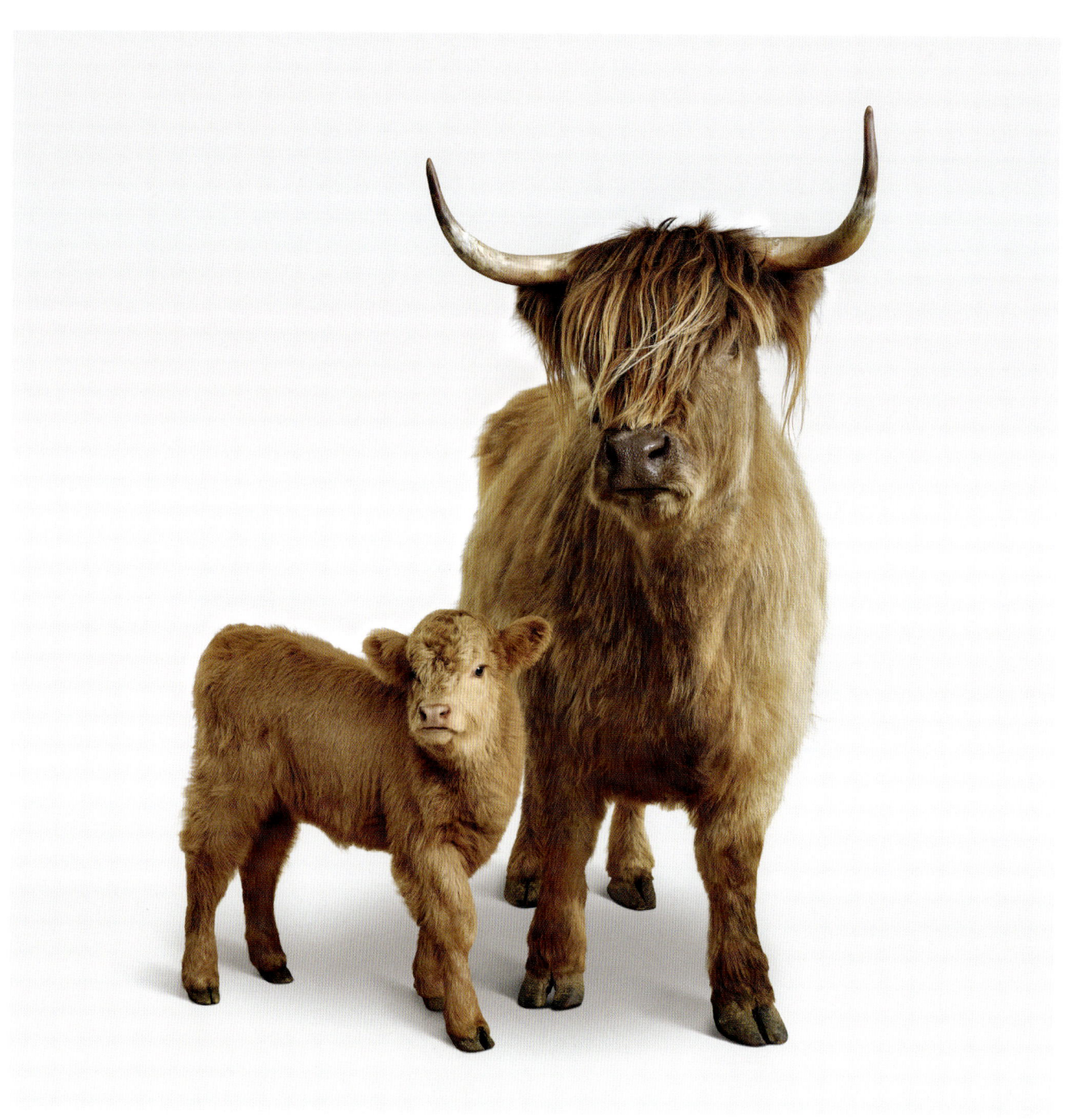

Hazel and Marigold

HIGHLAND COW AND CALF

FARM BABIES

Farm babies are the tender heartbeat of every homestead. From wobbly-legged calves followed by watchful mamas to fluffy ducklings paddling behind a proud parent, every baby animal brings a touch of magic and innocence to the world.

Capturing these moments on camera has taught me so much about the bond between mother and offspring. When coaxing a calf into the frame, we already know that its devoted mother will need to be right by its side. This same maternal dance plays out with fluffy cria nuzzling under their alpaca mothers or pink piglets curled up close to their sow moms.

Each shutter release of my camera is met with curious eyes—be they from soft brown foals, yellow baby chicks, or any other newborn fumbling around the farm. The vulnerability of baby animals, paired with the fierce love and protection of their mothers, is a powerful reminder of nature's profound connections. These moments, delicate and fleeting, underscore the eternal thread of motherhood on the farm.

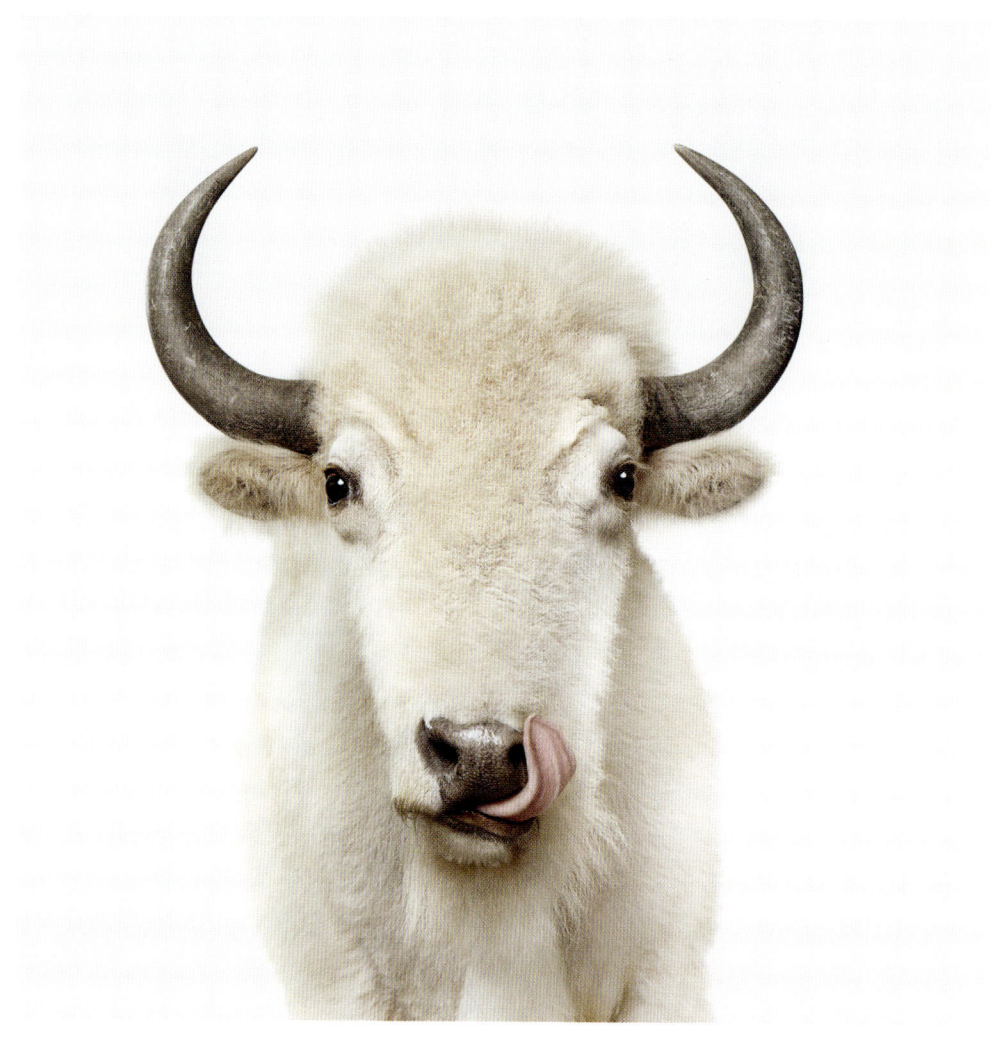

Huckleberry

AMERICAN WHITE BUFFALO

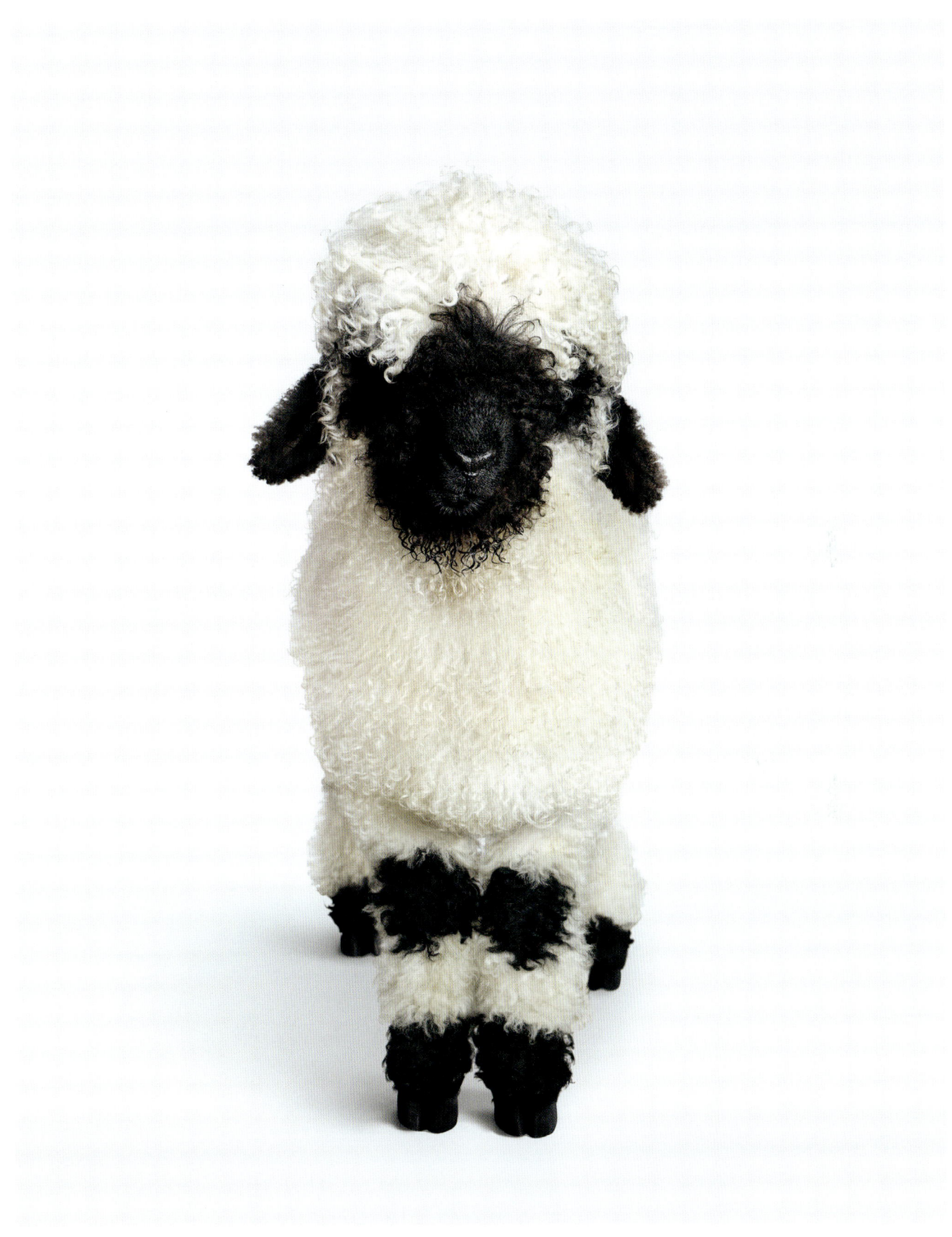

Klover

SWISS VALAIS BLACKNOSE SHEEP

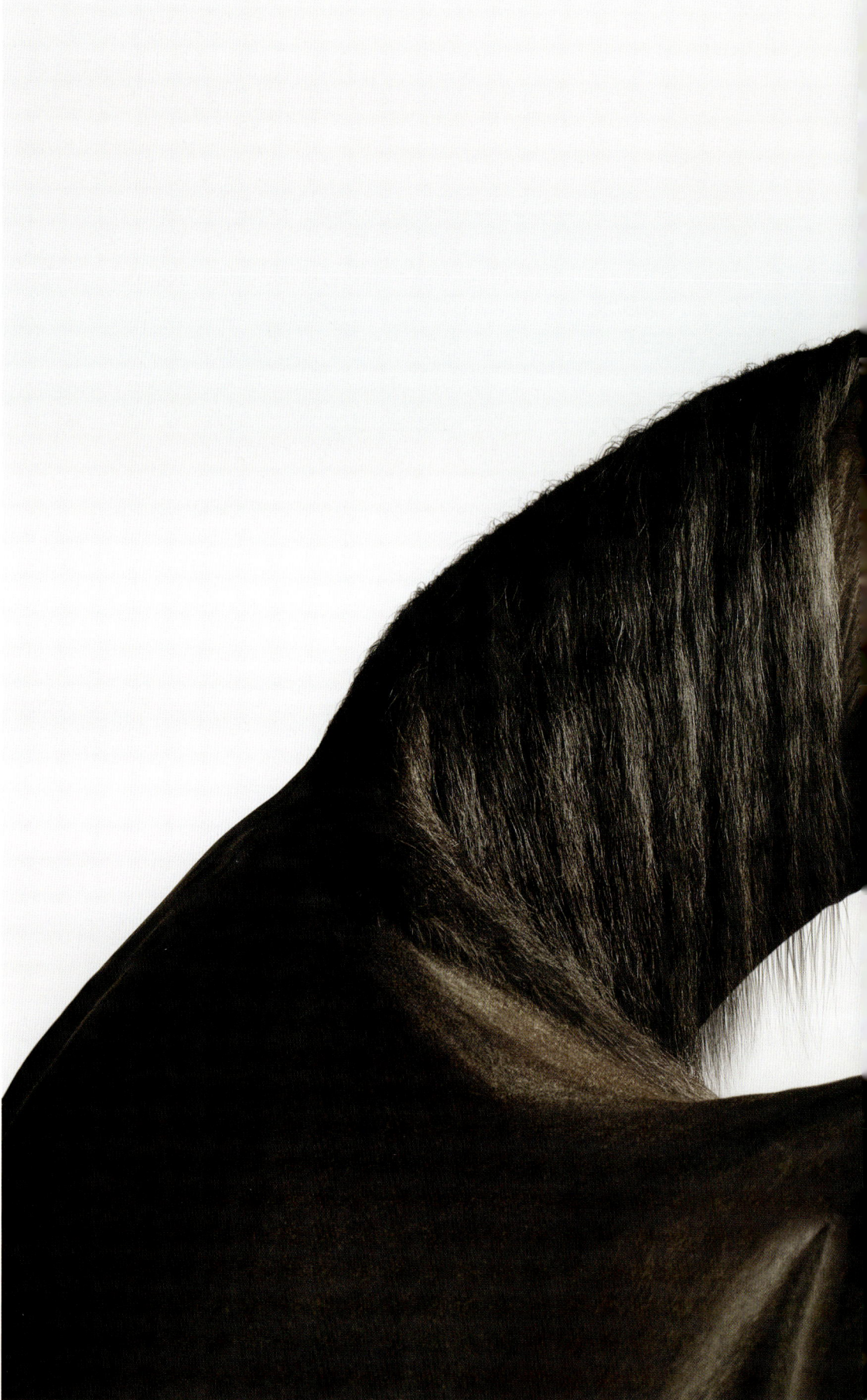

Suzie

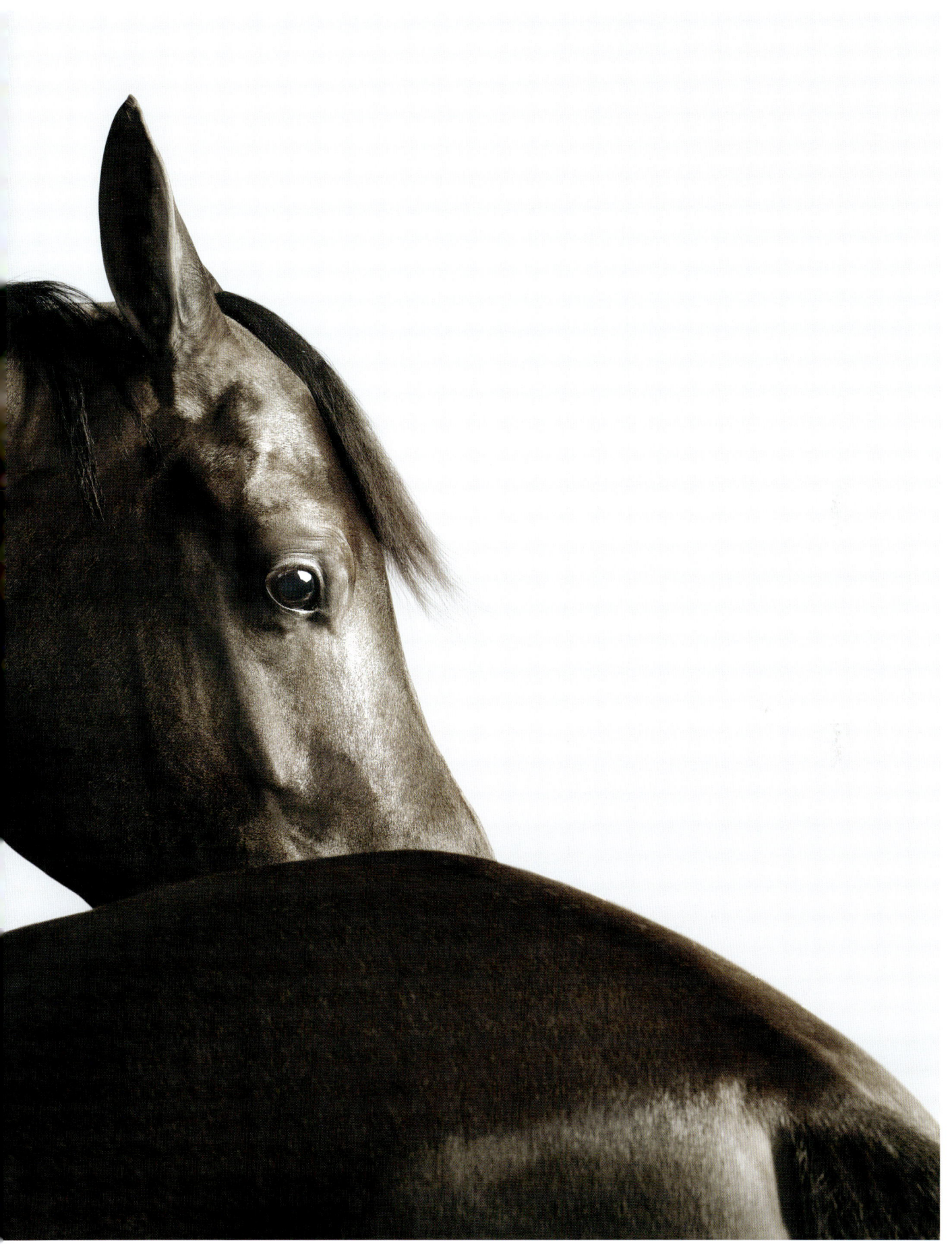

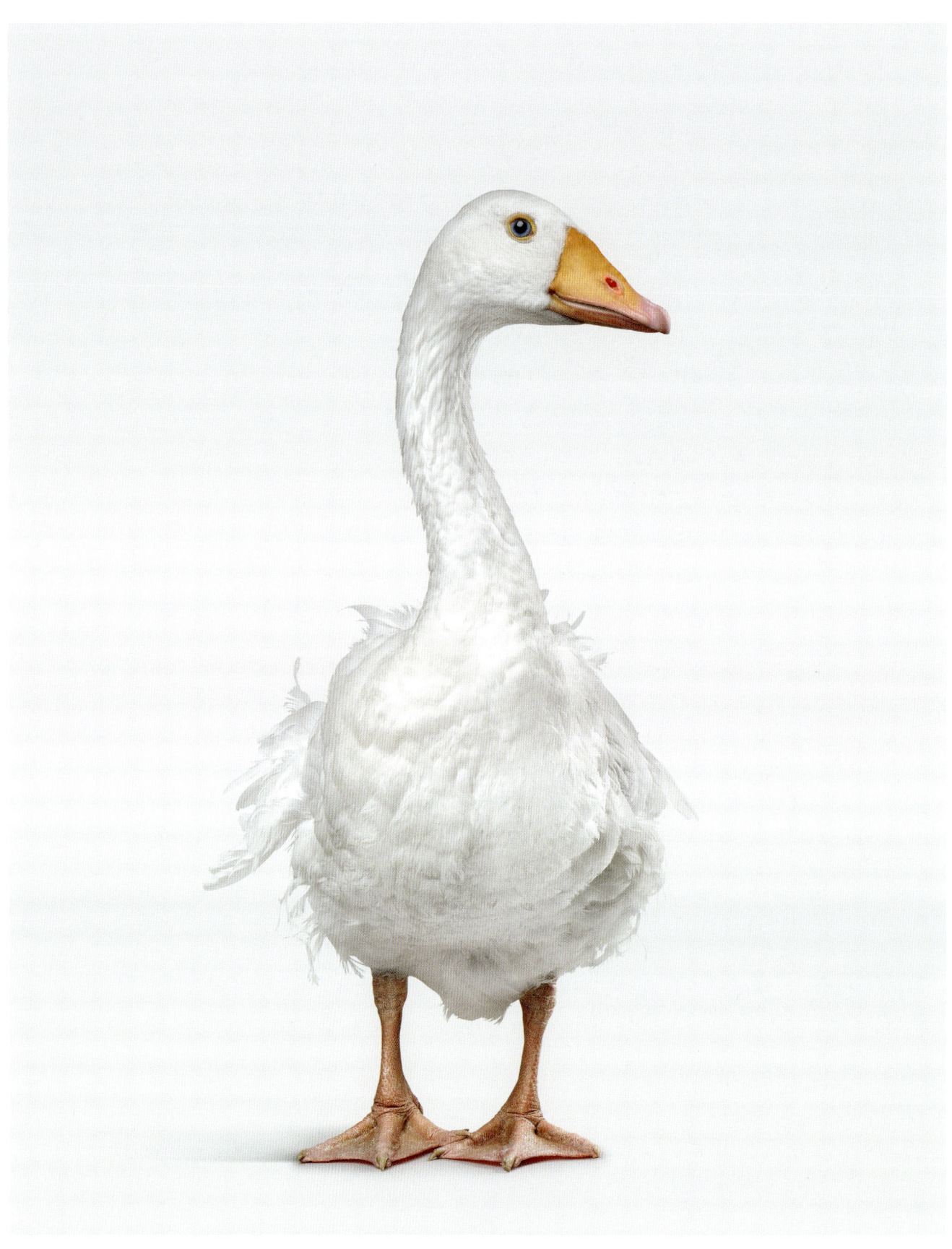

Silly

SEBASTOPOL GOOSE

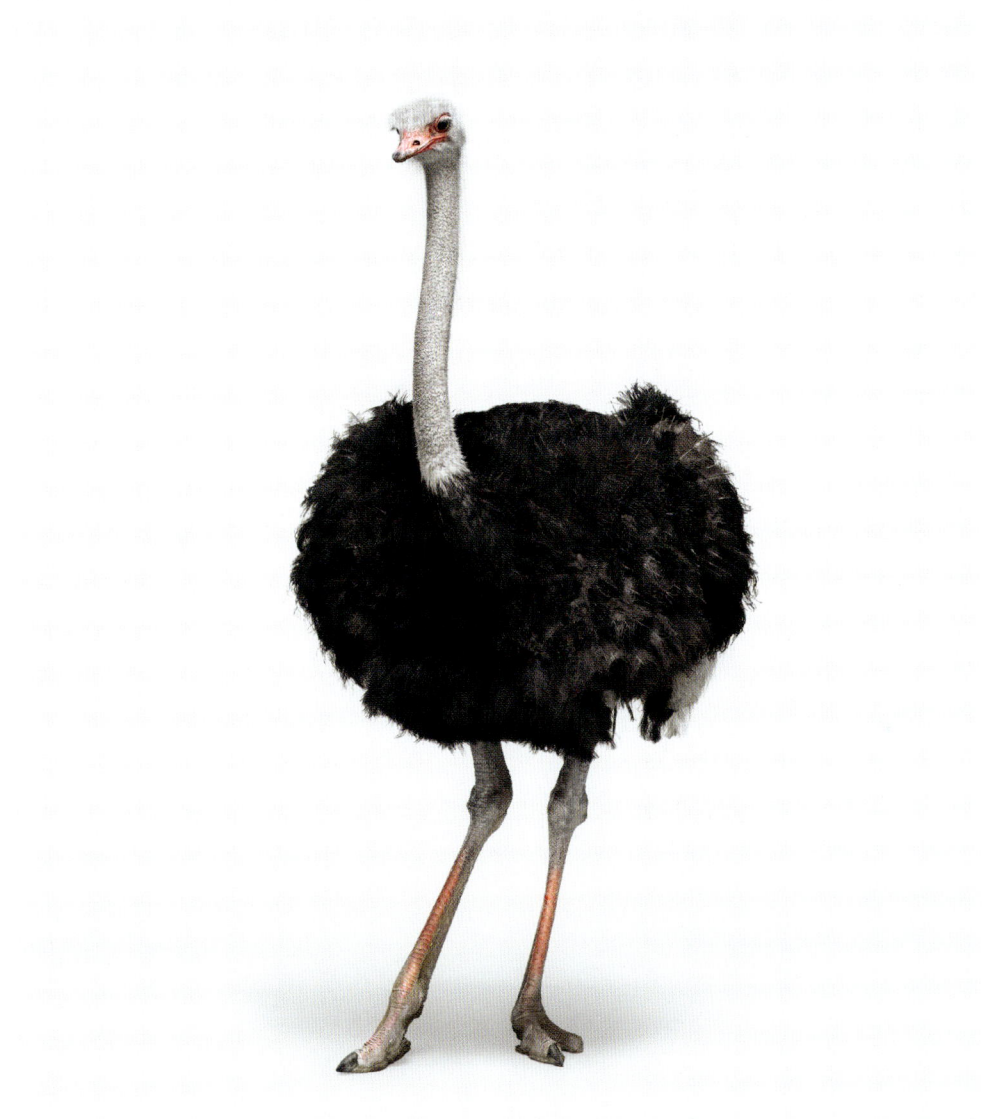

Catalina

AFRICAN OSTRICH

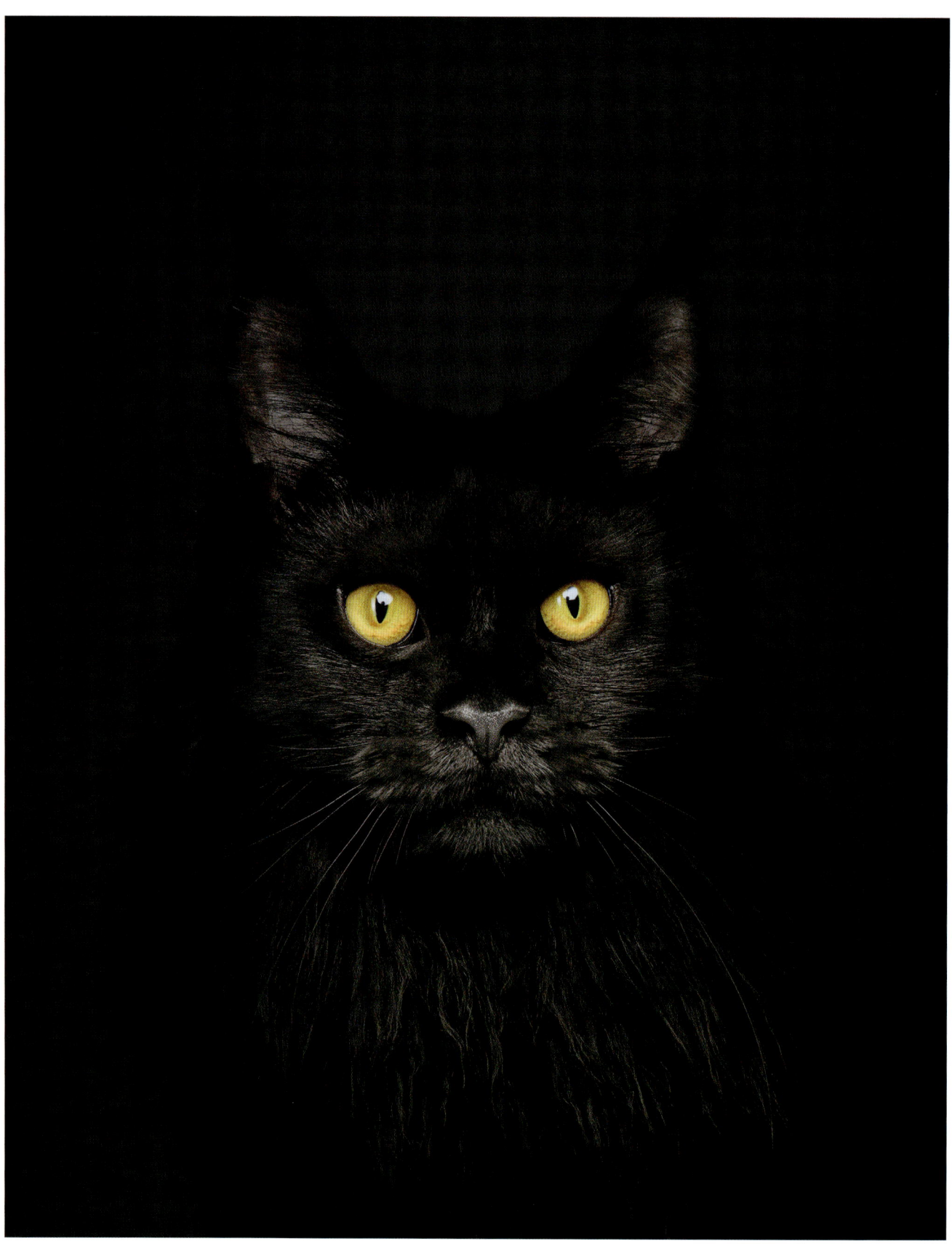

Visenya

BLACK MAINE COON

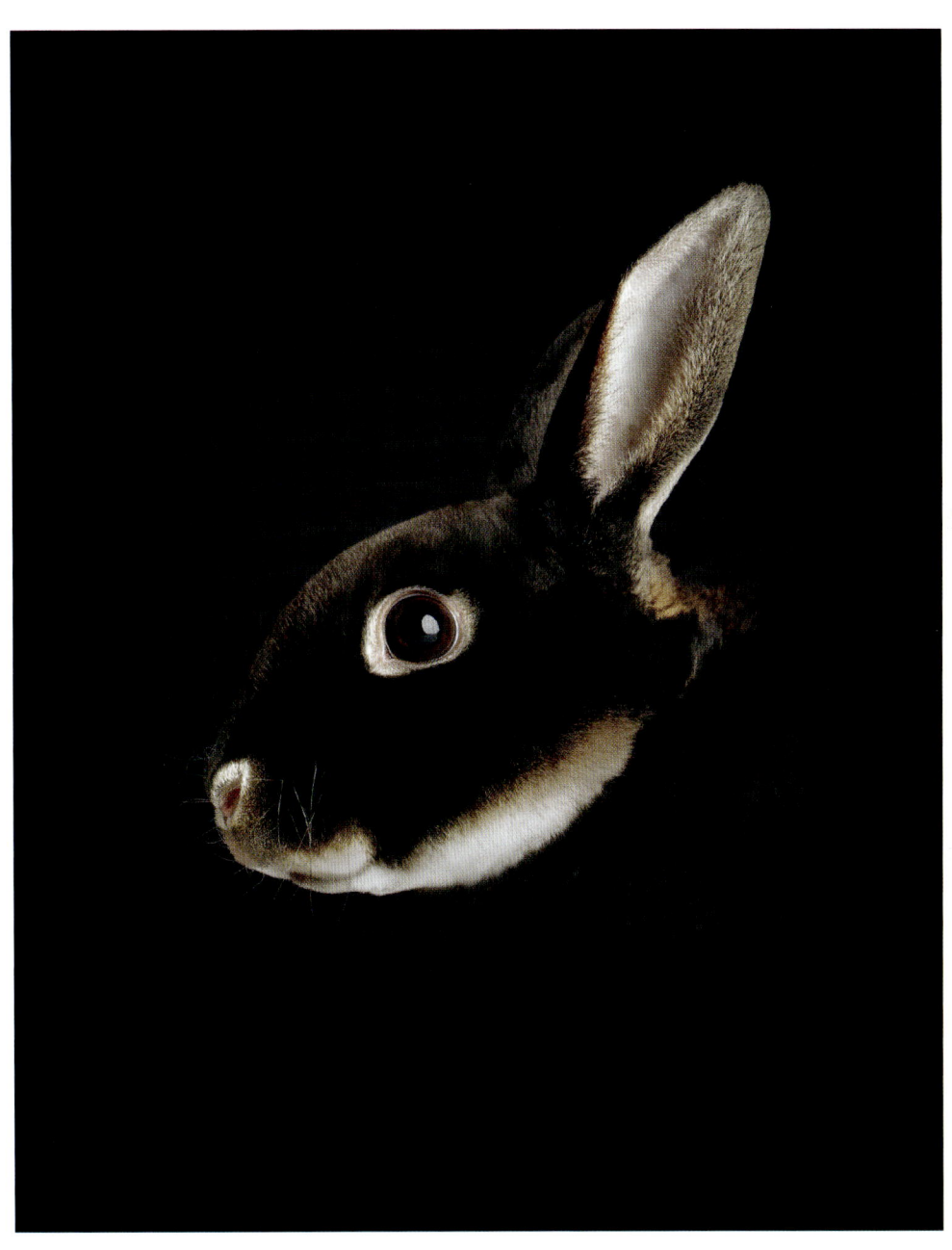

Lauren

MINI REX RABBIT

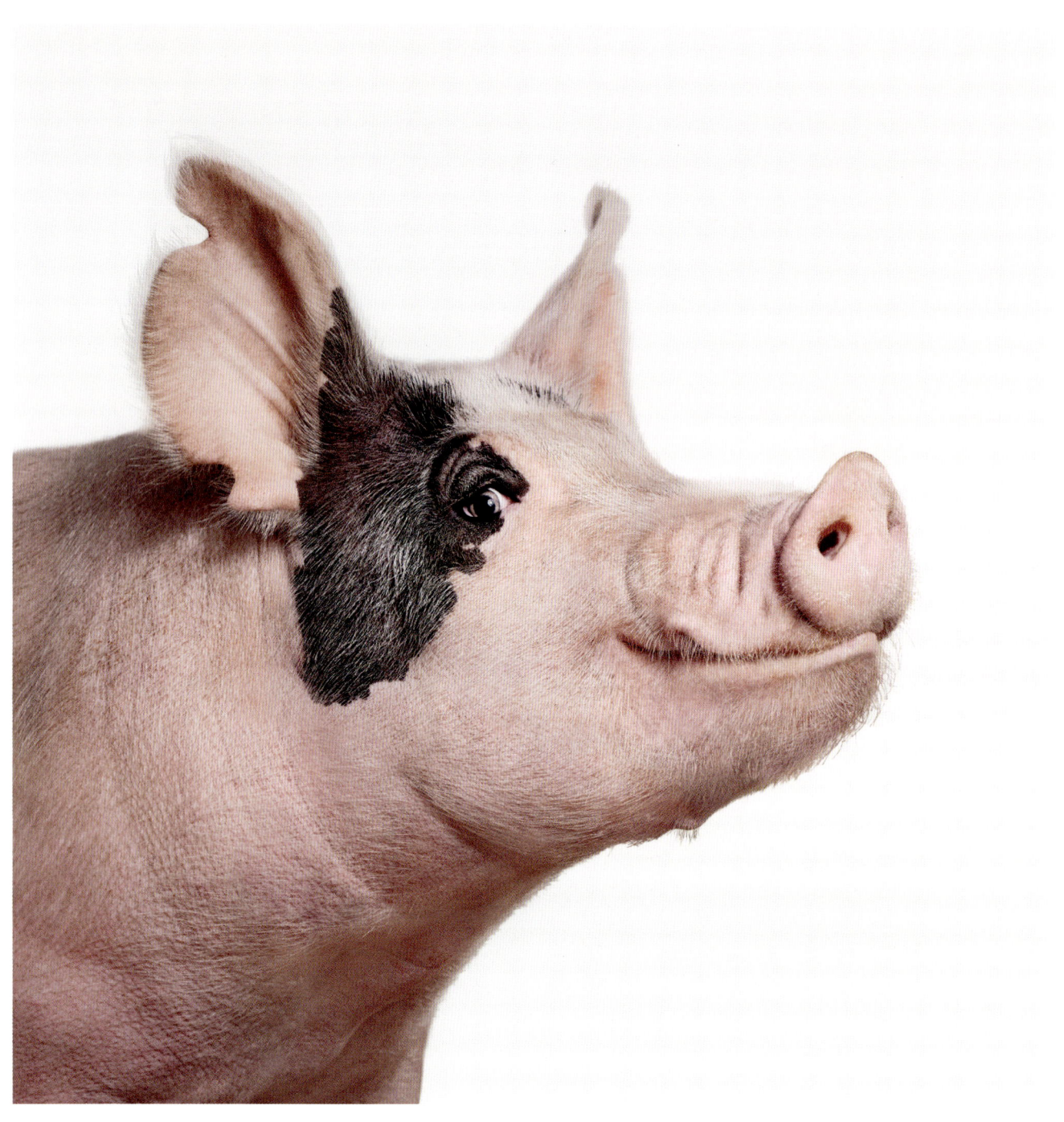

Rupert

AMERICAN WHITE CROSS PIG

PIGS

Pigs have long been sources of amusement and affection in our stories and folklore. Their affinity for carefree wallowing—especially in the muddiest of puddles—is one that often reminds us to take life a little less seriously. After all, it's good to get a little dirty sometimes.

Despite the many moments of humor pigs bring, they are paradoxically known to be among some of the most intelligent mammals on the planet. It is this contrast—goofy antics paired with extraordinary intellect—that allows us to honor the inexplicable complexities of these animals.

Capturing their essence through my lens has its challenges, no doubt. Their natural impulses—like an ever-grounded snout in constant pursuit of food—does not always lend itself to the perfect portrait pose. But every so often the stars align, and we coerce a pig to raise its head for a soft and fluffy marshmallow treat. And just like that, with a small twinkle in the eye, the quintessential piggish portrait emerges.

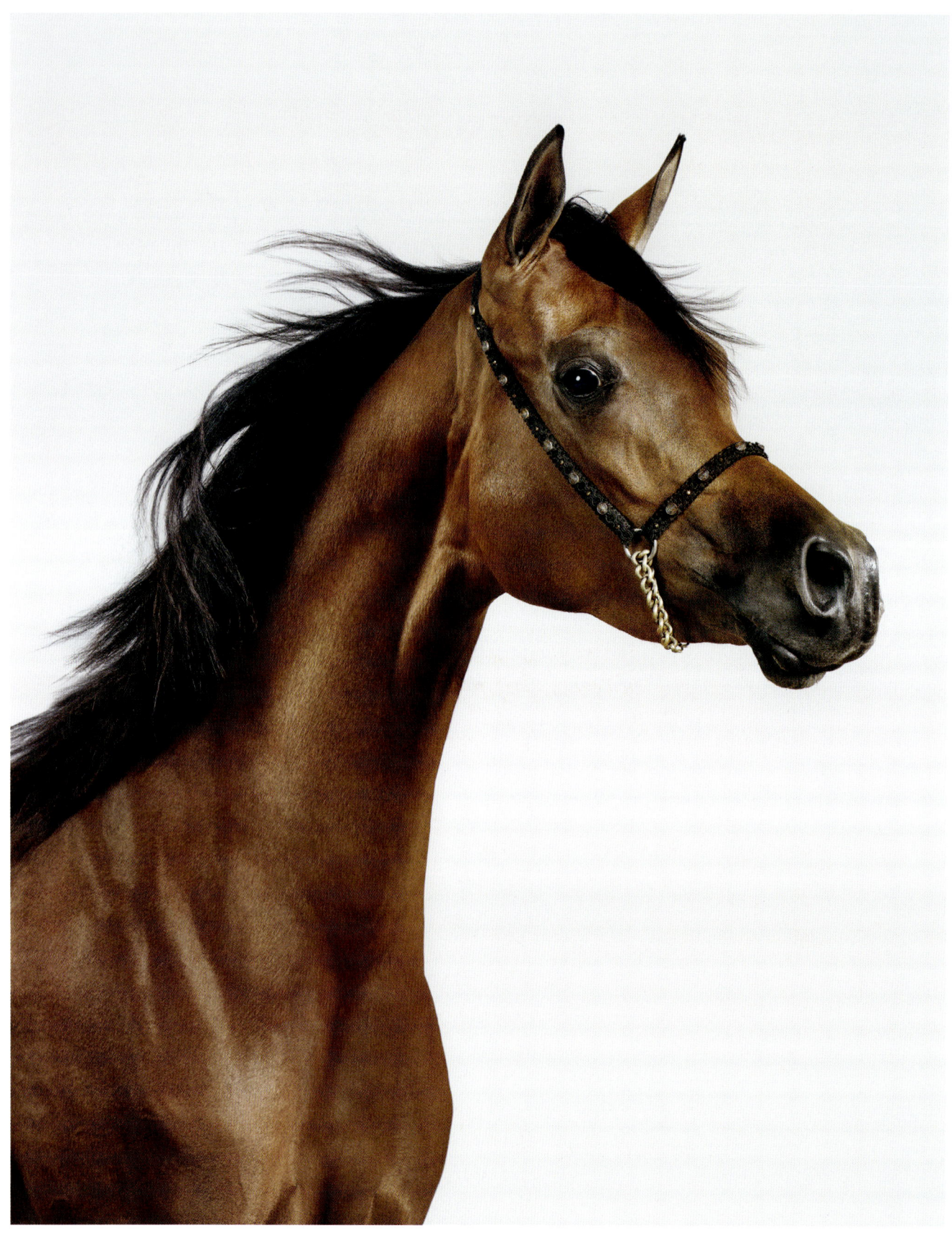

Alianna

BROWN ARABIAN MARE

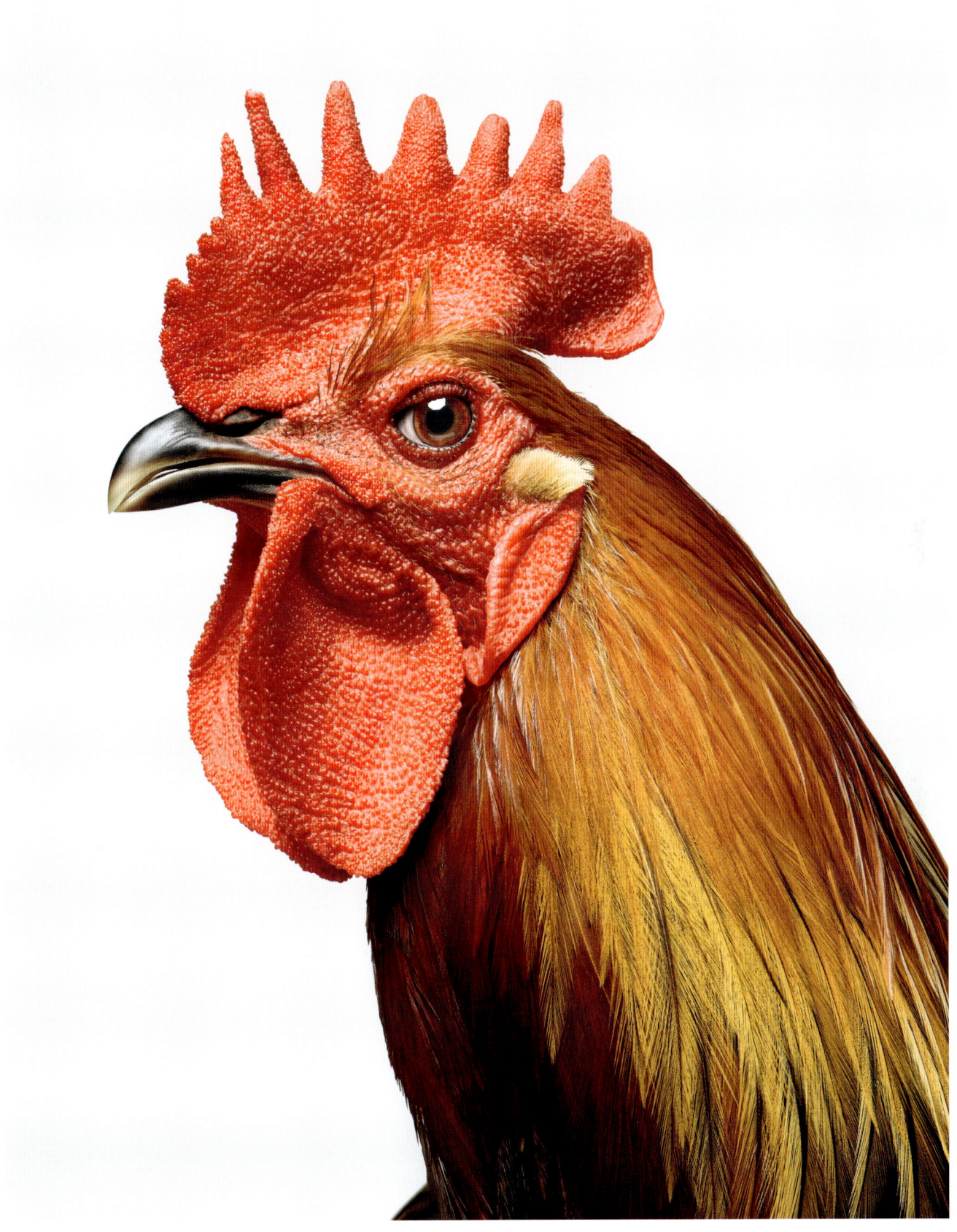

Orion

DENIZLI LONGCROWER ROOSTER

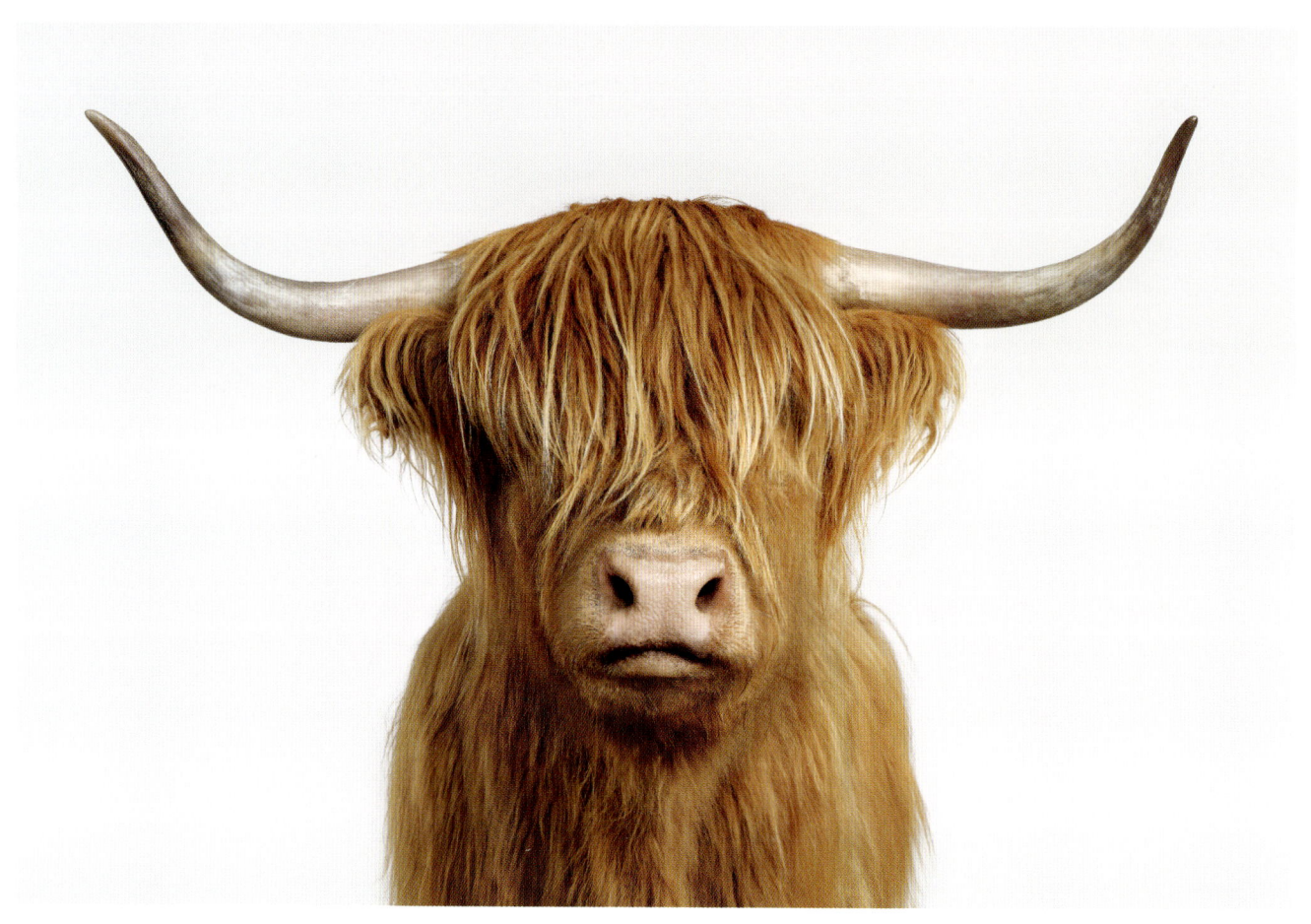

Penny

HIGHLAND COW

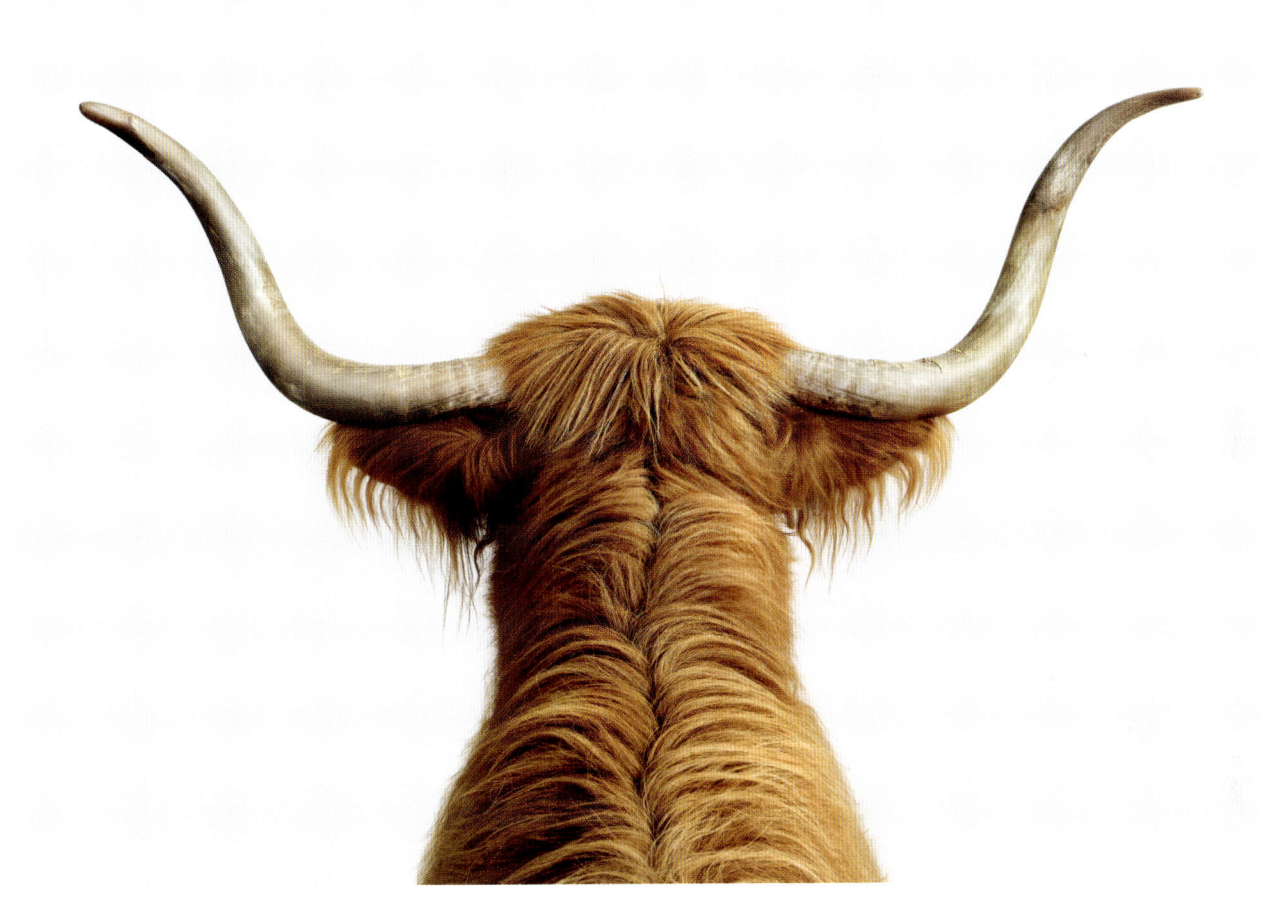

Willow

HIGHLAND COW

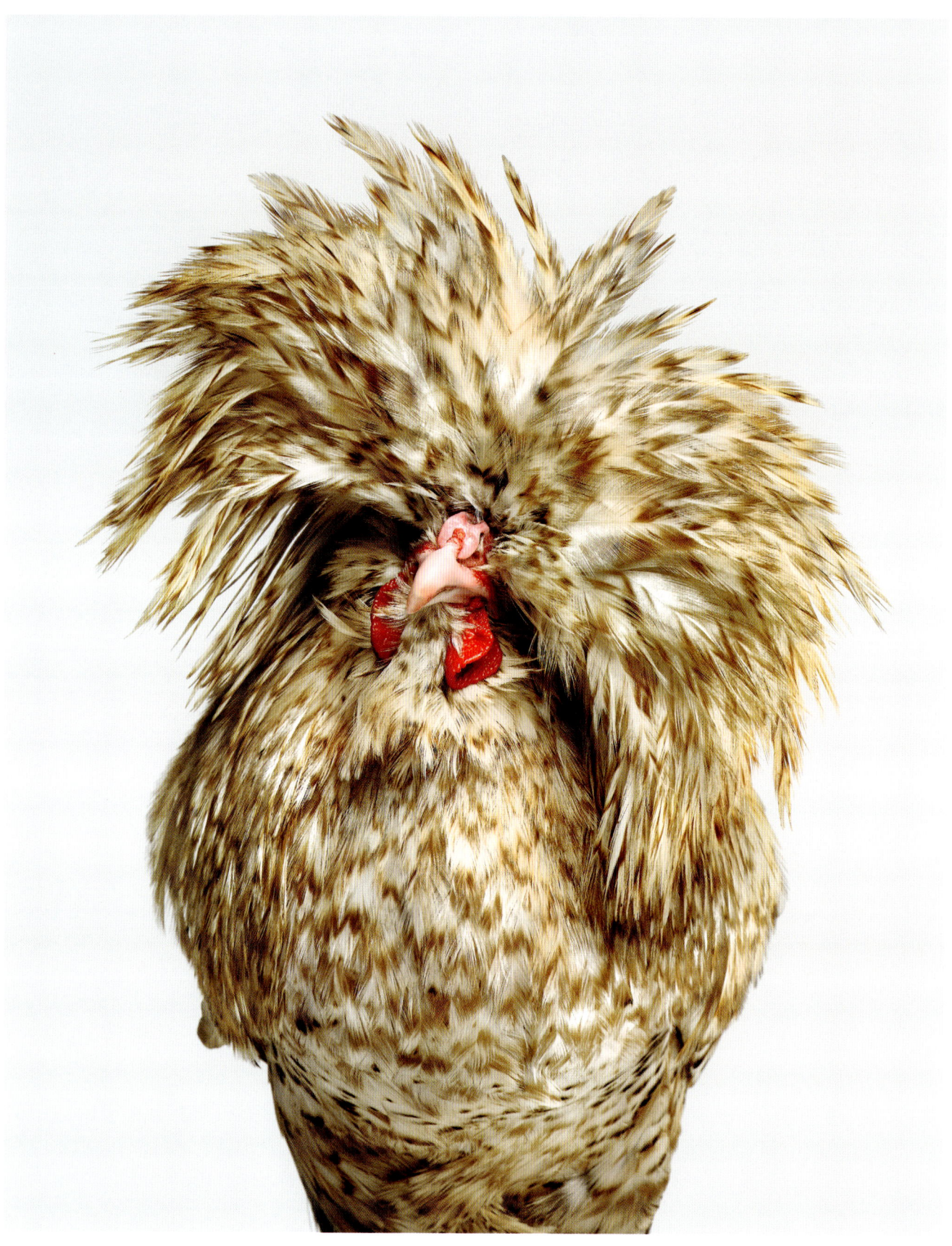

Barry

CANDY CORN POLISH ROOSTER

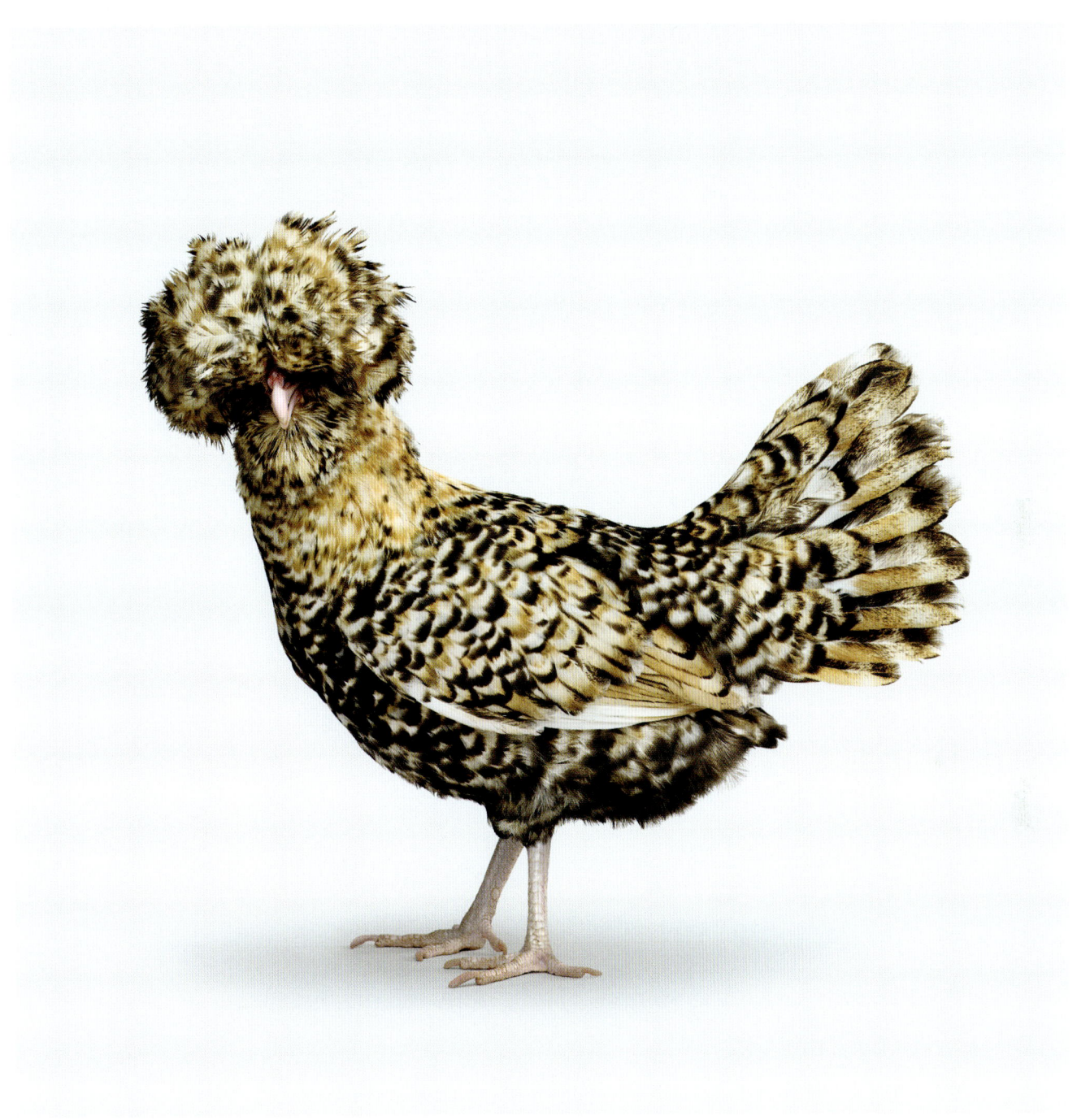

Doloris

CANDY CORN POLISH HEN

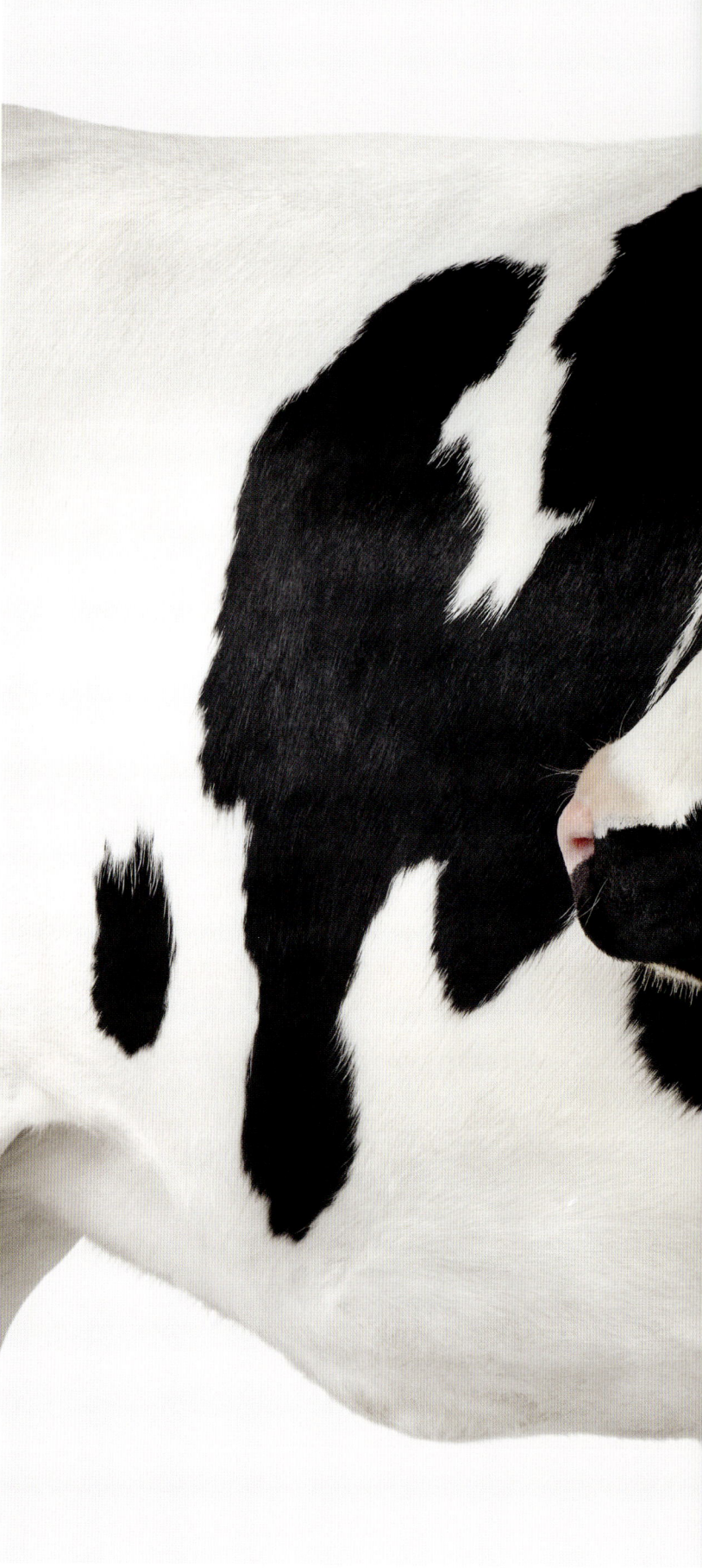

Daisy

HOLSTEIN COW

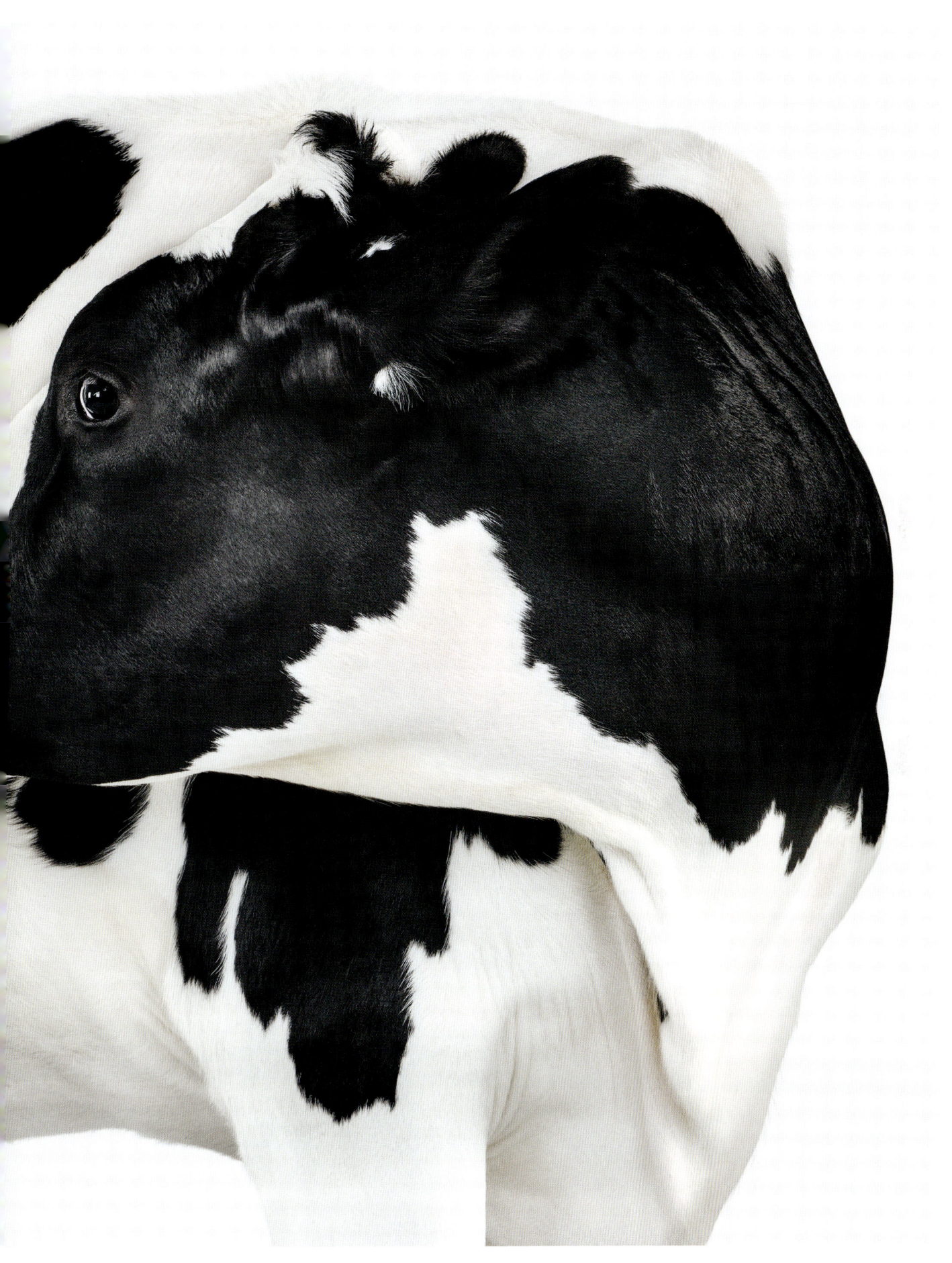

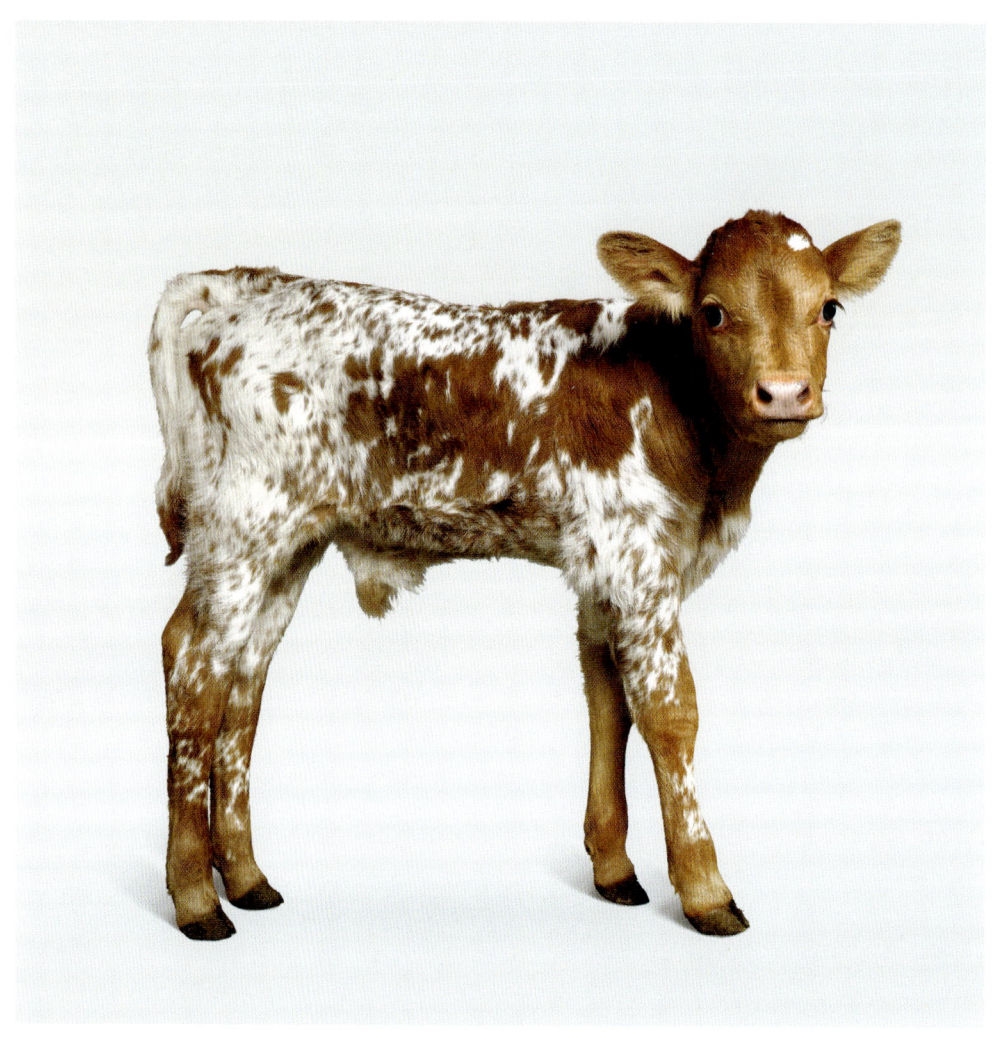

Bug

LONGHORN NEWBORN CALF

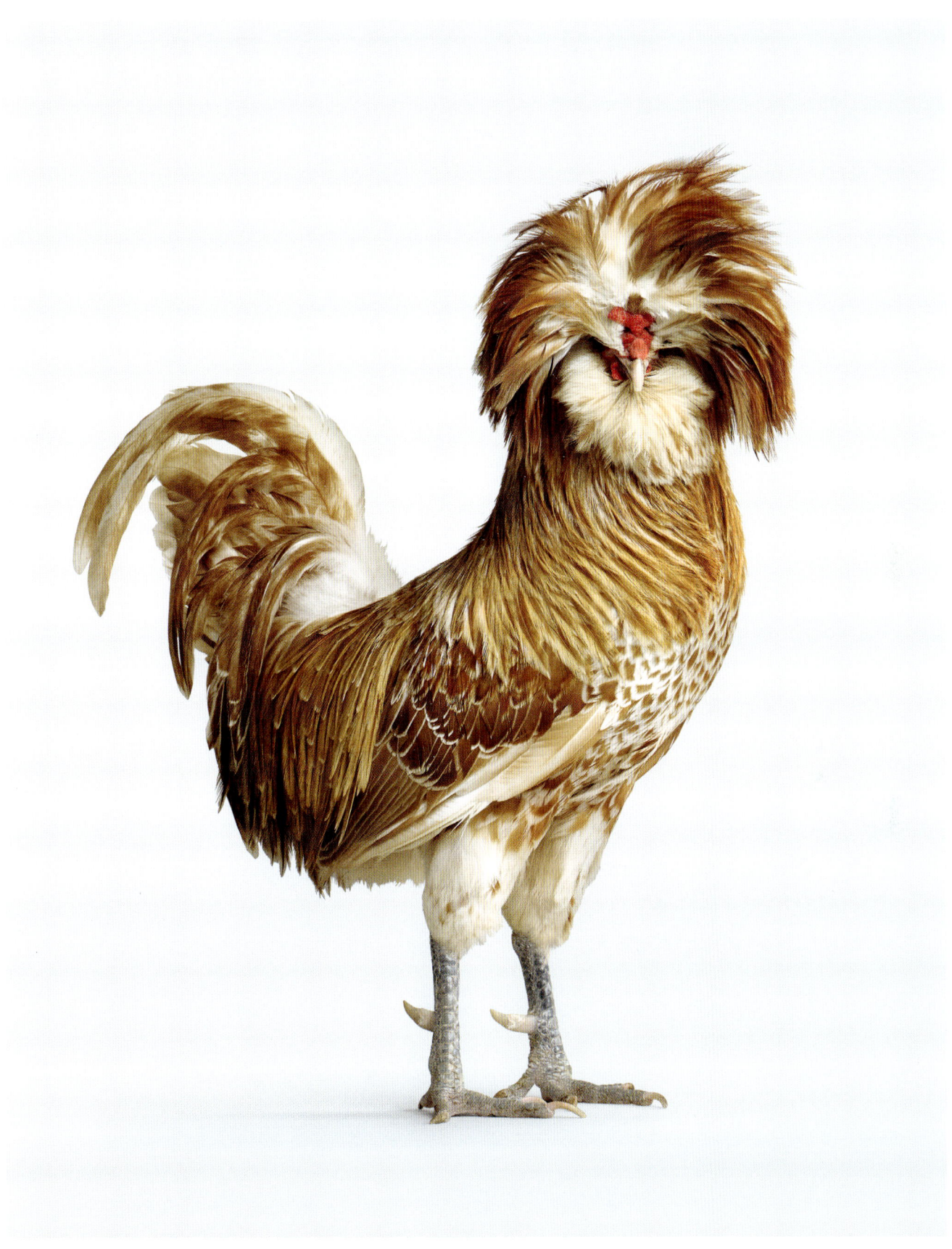

Blaze

BUFF LACED POLISH ROOSTER

AMERICAN
SADDLEBRED HORSES

The American saddlebred, often referred to as "the horse made in America," stands as a testament to equine magnificence. Born from the melding of local and imported breeds, this horse was tailored to America's diverse landscapes and demands. Majestic and powerful, the saddlebred is the embodiment of grace and symbolizes what many envision when they imagine a horse.

Photographing American saddlebreds is an exploration of elegance and dynamism. I've tried to not only chronicle their physical allure but also delve into their indomitable spirit. Every photograph is a tribute, capturing a moment of raw energy when the American saddlebred meets the soulful depths of its history, serving as a vivid reminder of our nation's rich equine legacy.

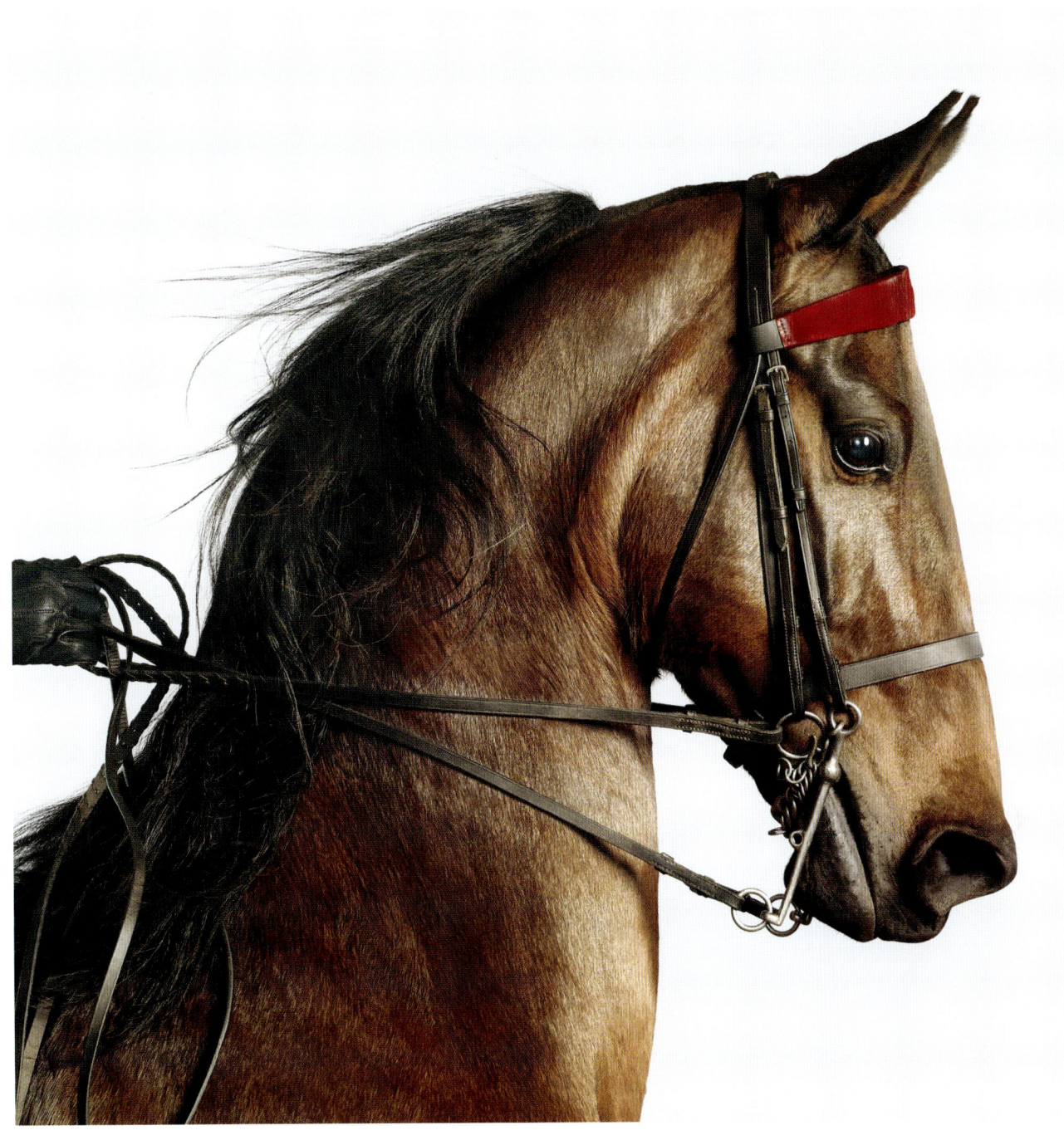

Mystery

AMERICAN SADDLEBRED HORSE

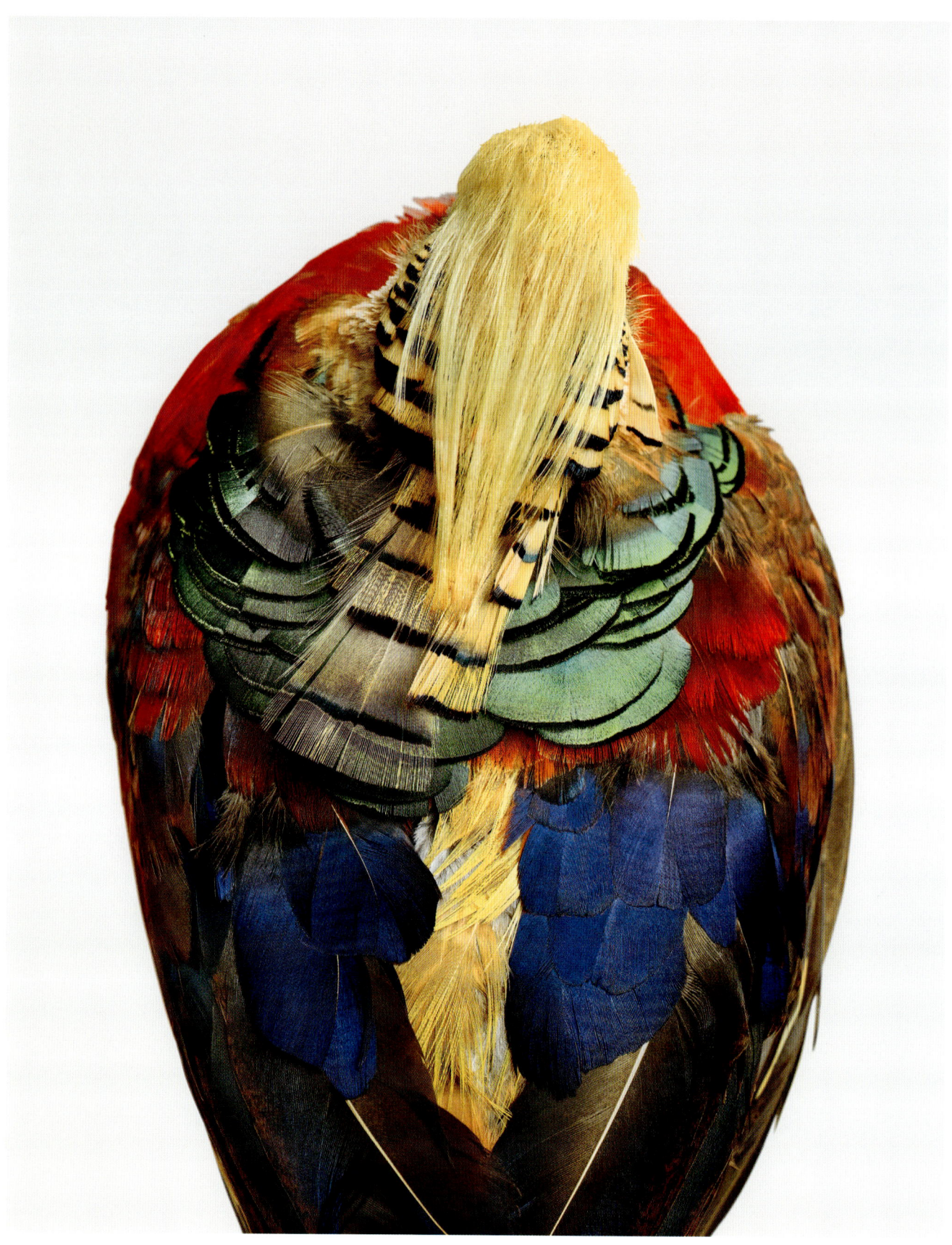

Prism

GOLDEN PHEASANT

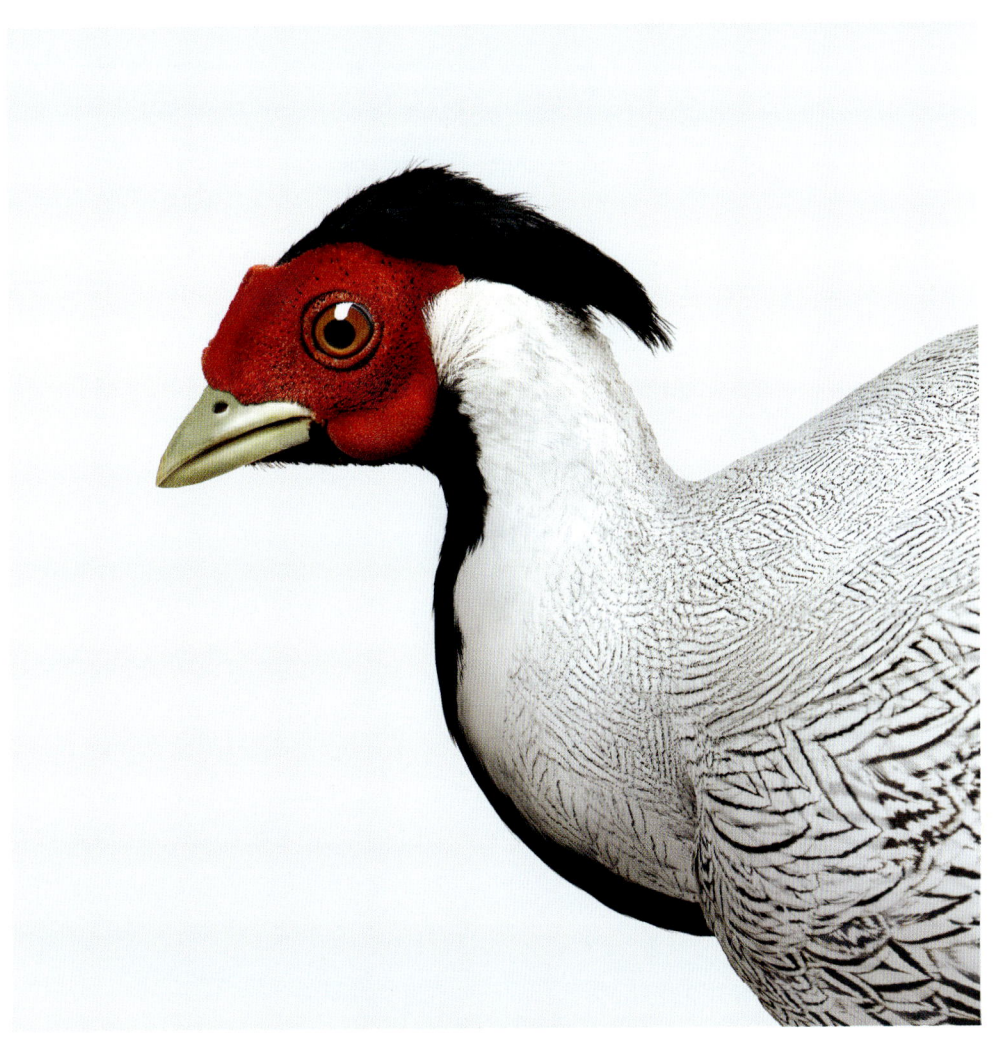

Clifford

RED GOLDEN PHEASANT

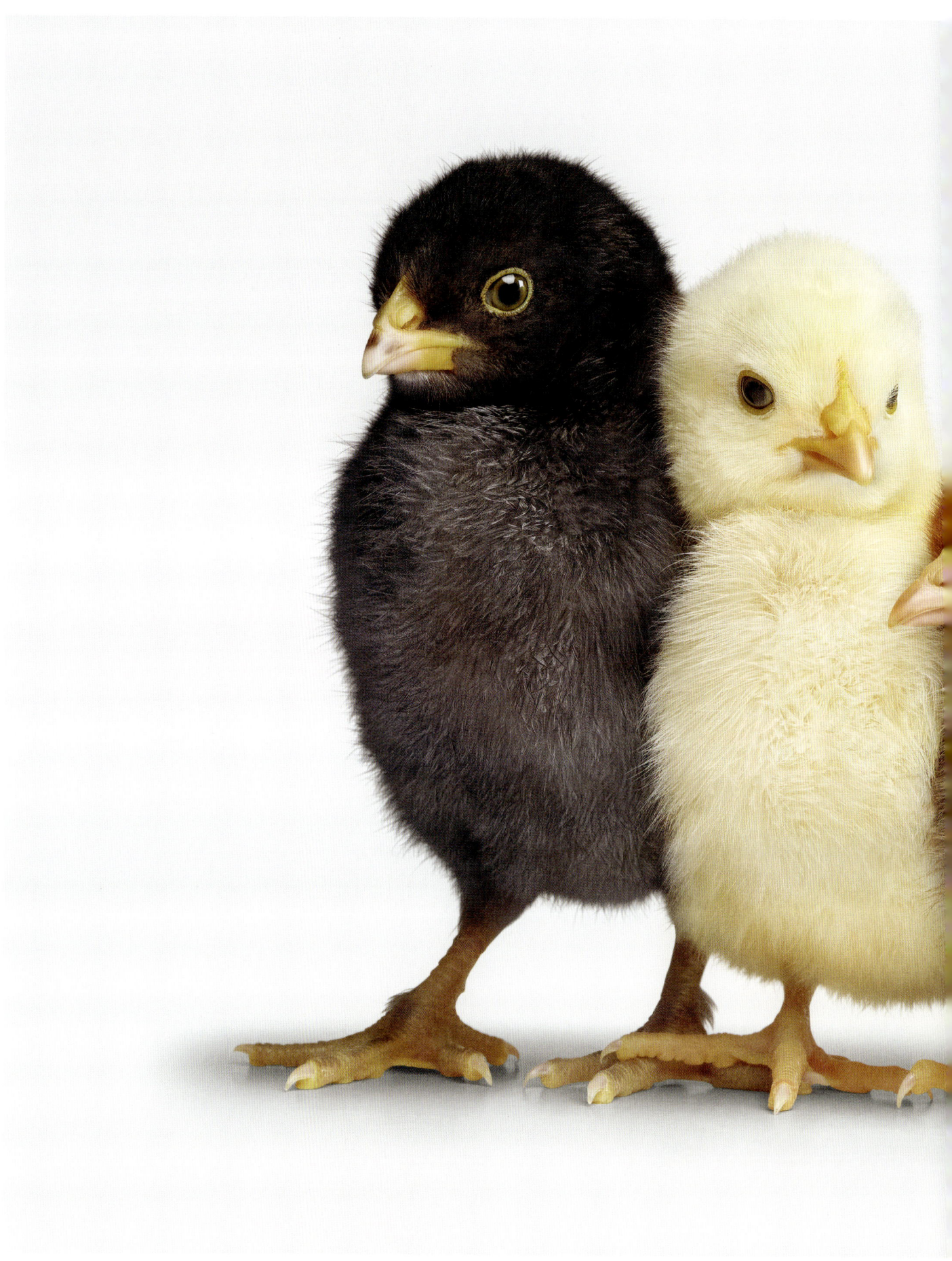

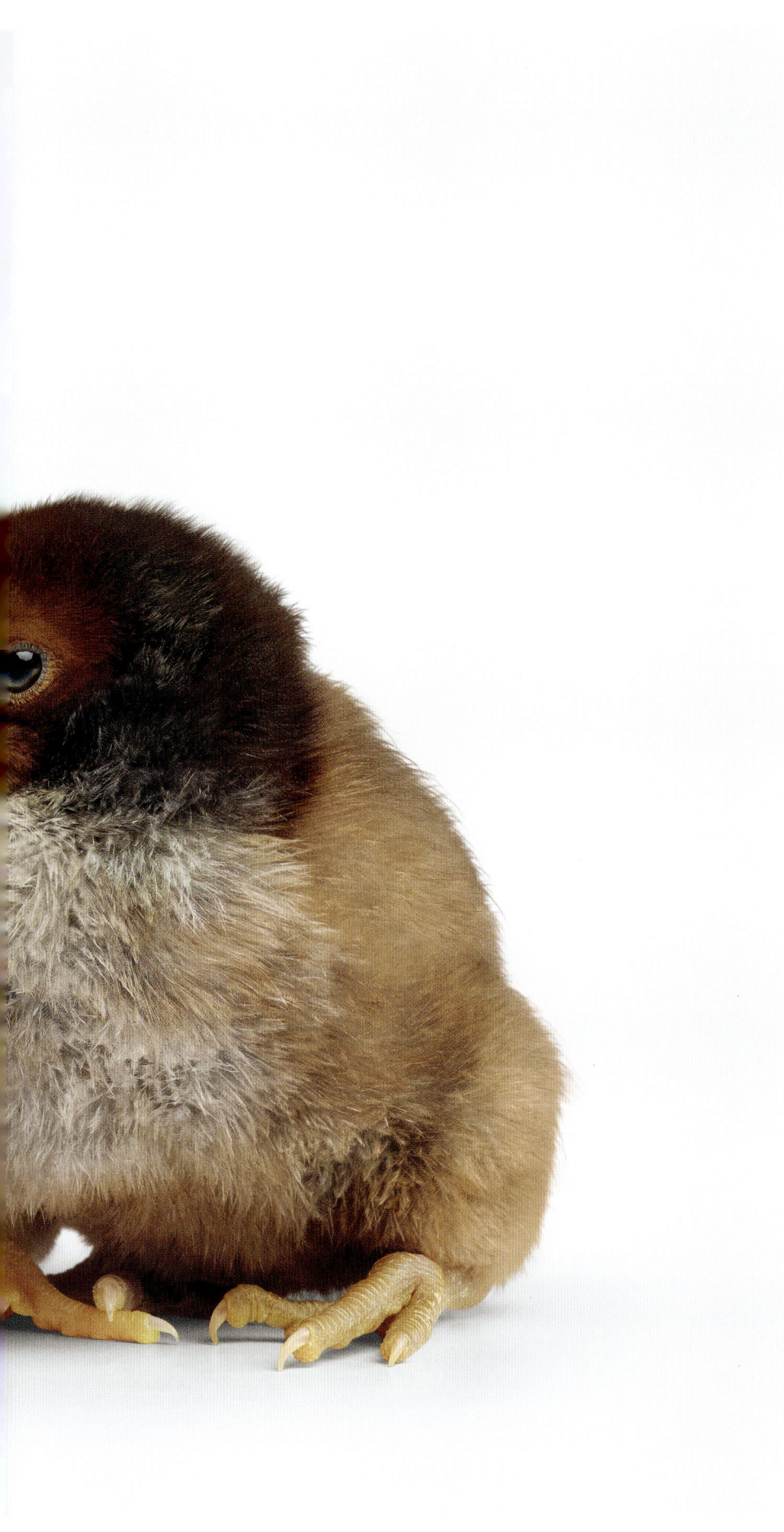

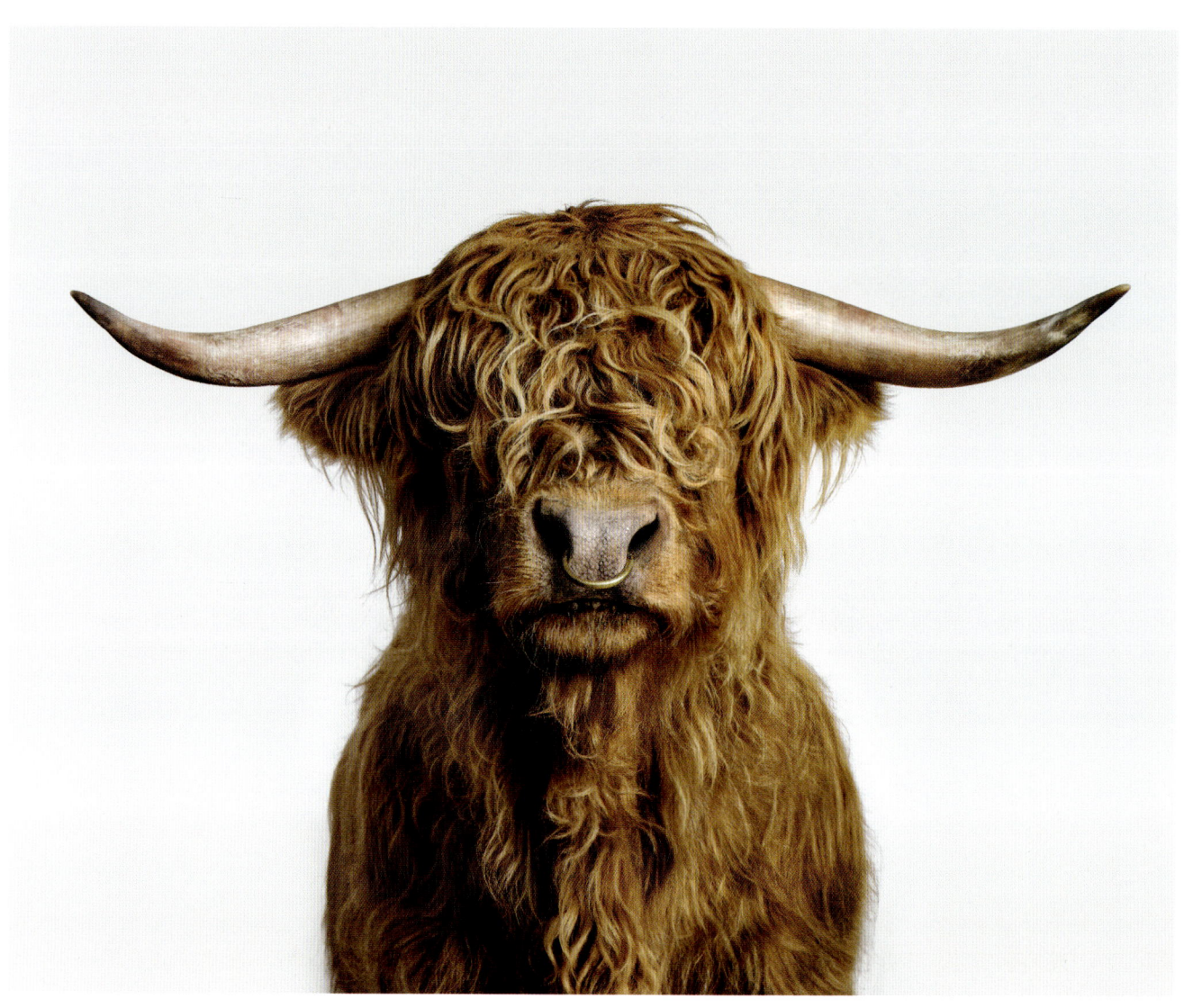

Hot Shot

HIGHLAND BULL

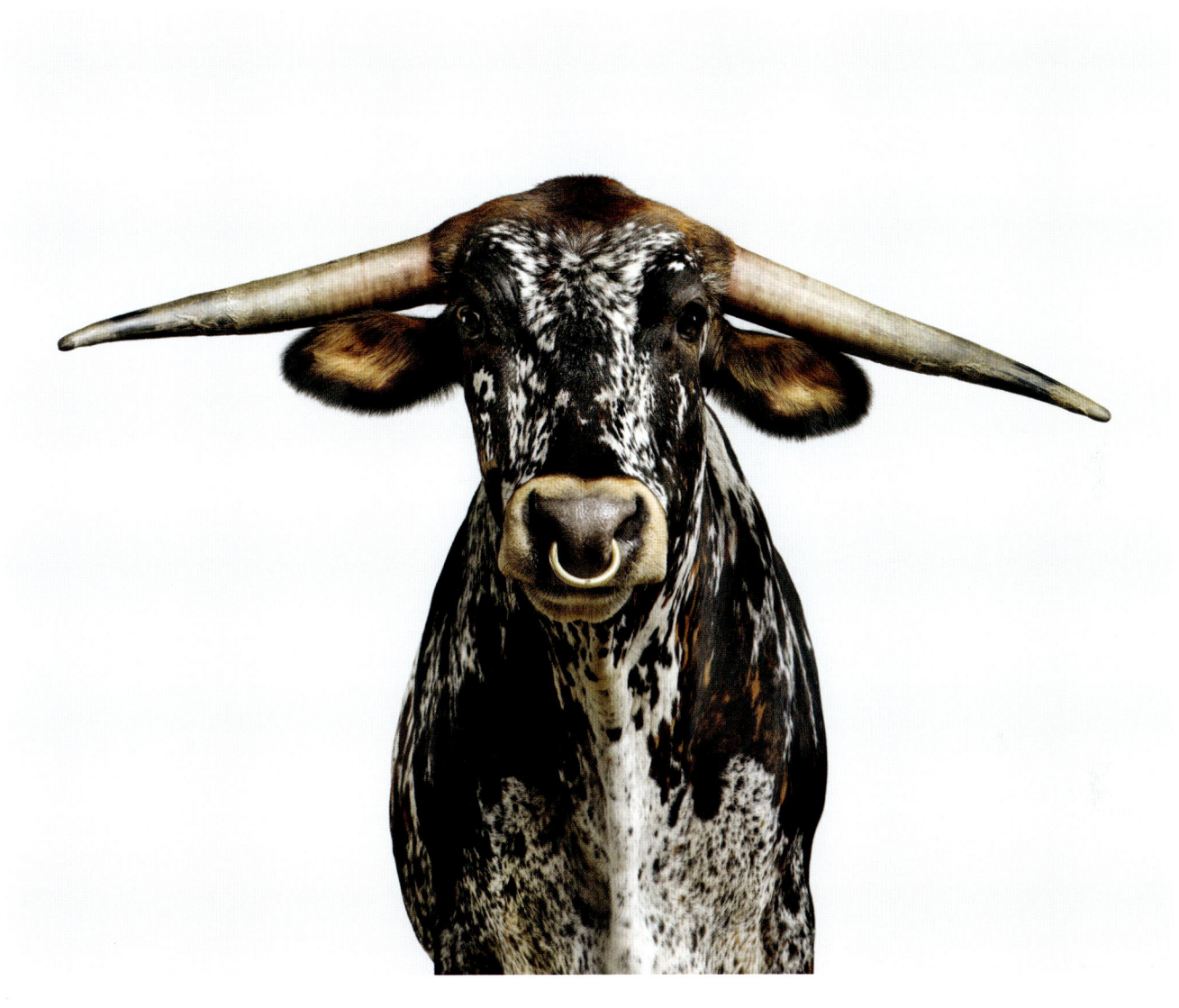

Bando

MULTICOLOR SPOTTED LONGHORN

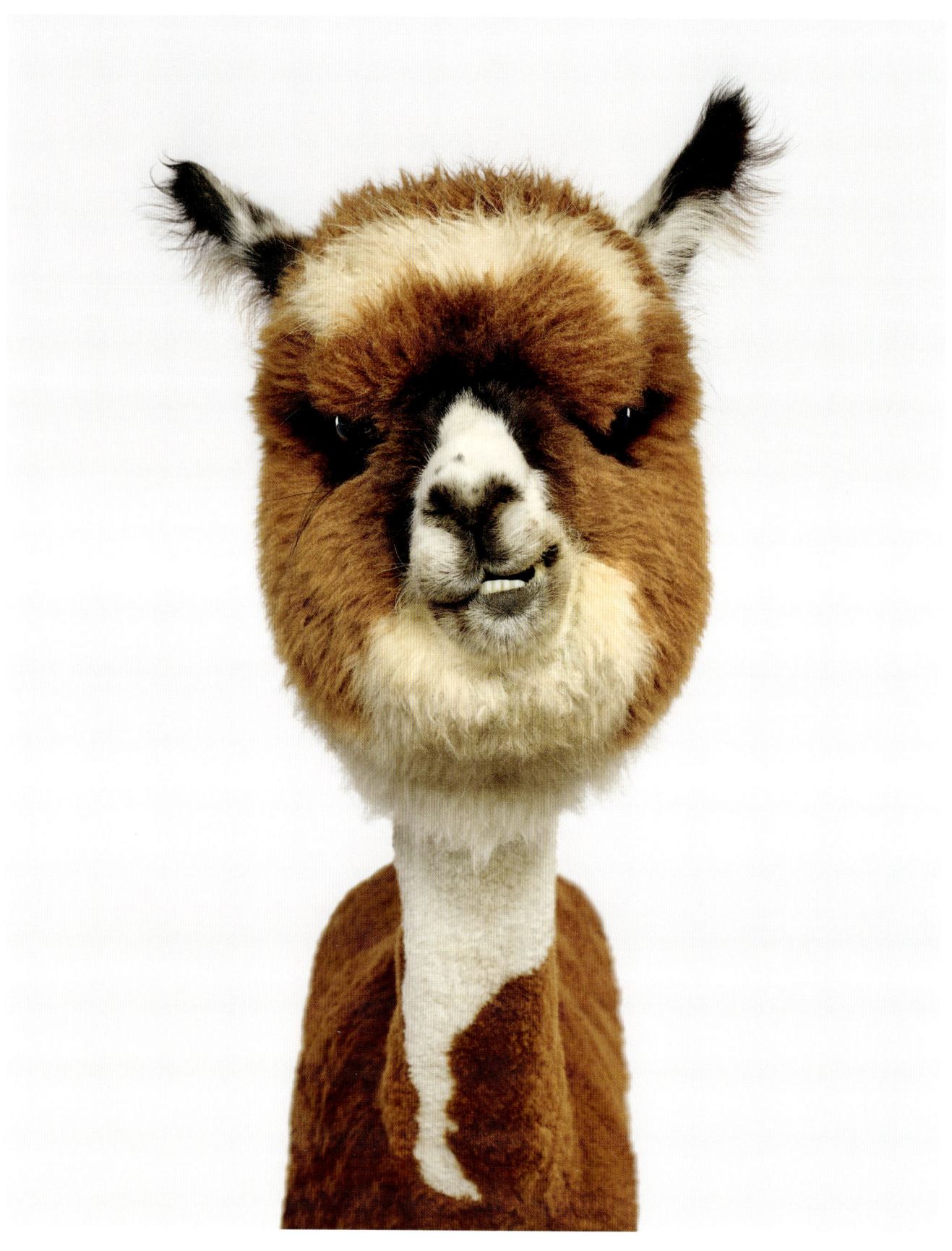

Frances

HUACAYA ALPACA CRIA

Frances is a fighter. Born five weeks early and severely underweight, this little one came close to not making it. After 48 hours of close calls and her caring owner nursing her the whole way through, baby Frances began to show more and more signs of life. Now thriving at her one-year mark, this sweet-faced cria still clings to her human hero. I love the beautiful contrast of the brown and cream colors throughout her coat and how they work together to symbolize the dark she was born into and the light she has found.

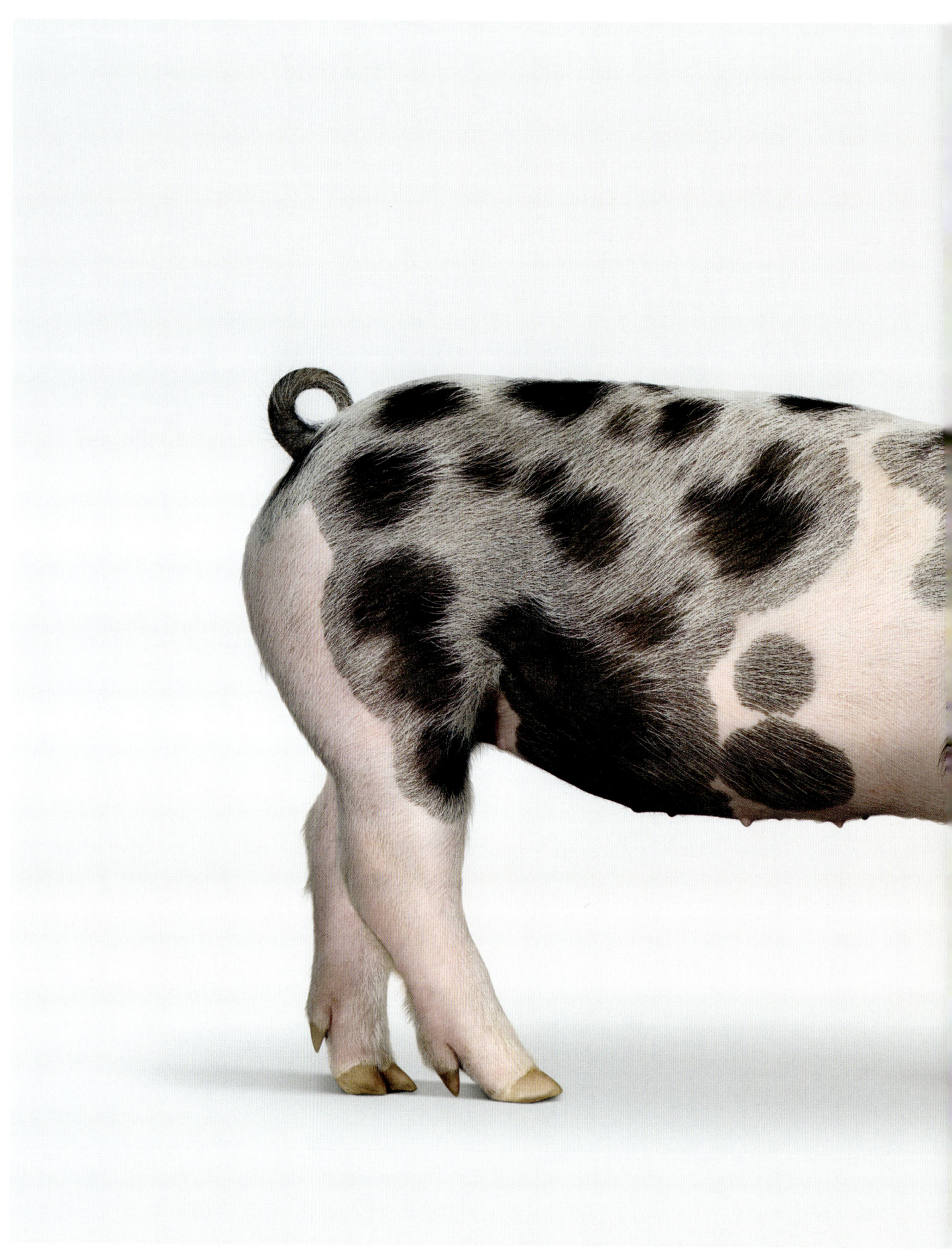

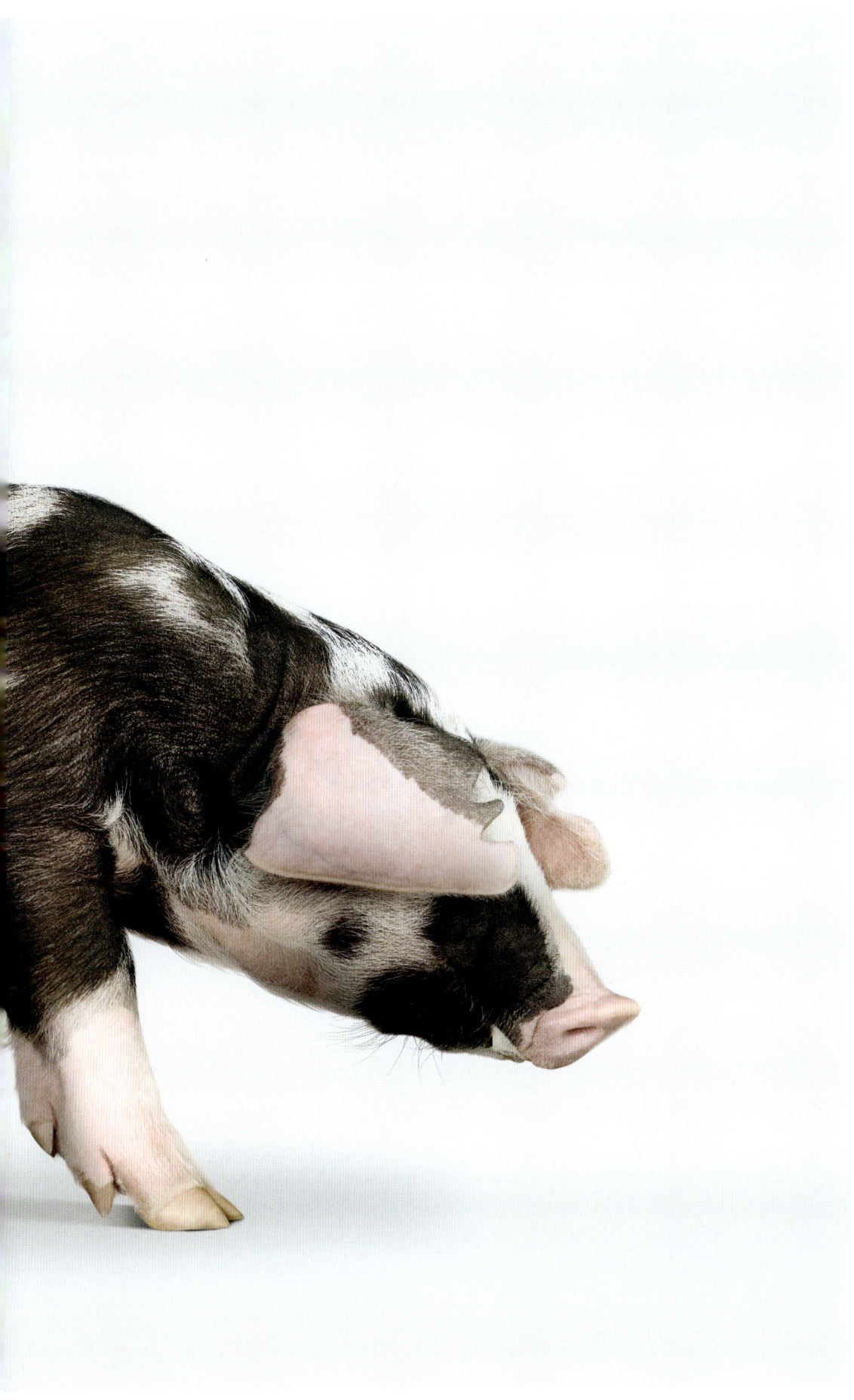

Milky Way

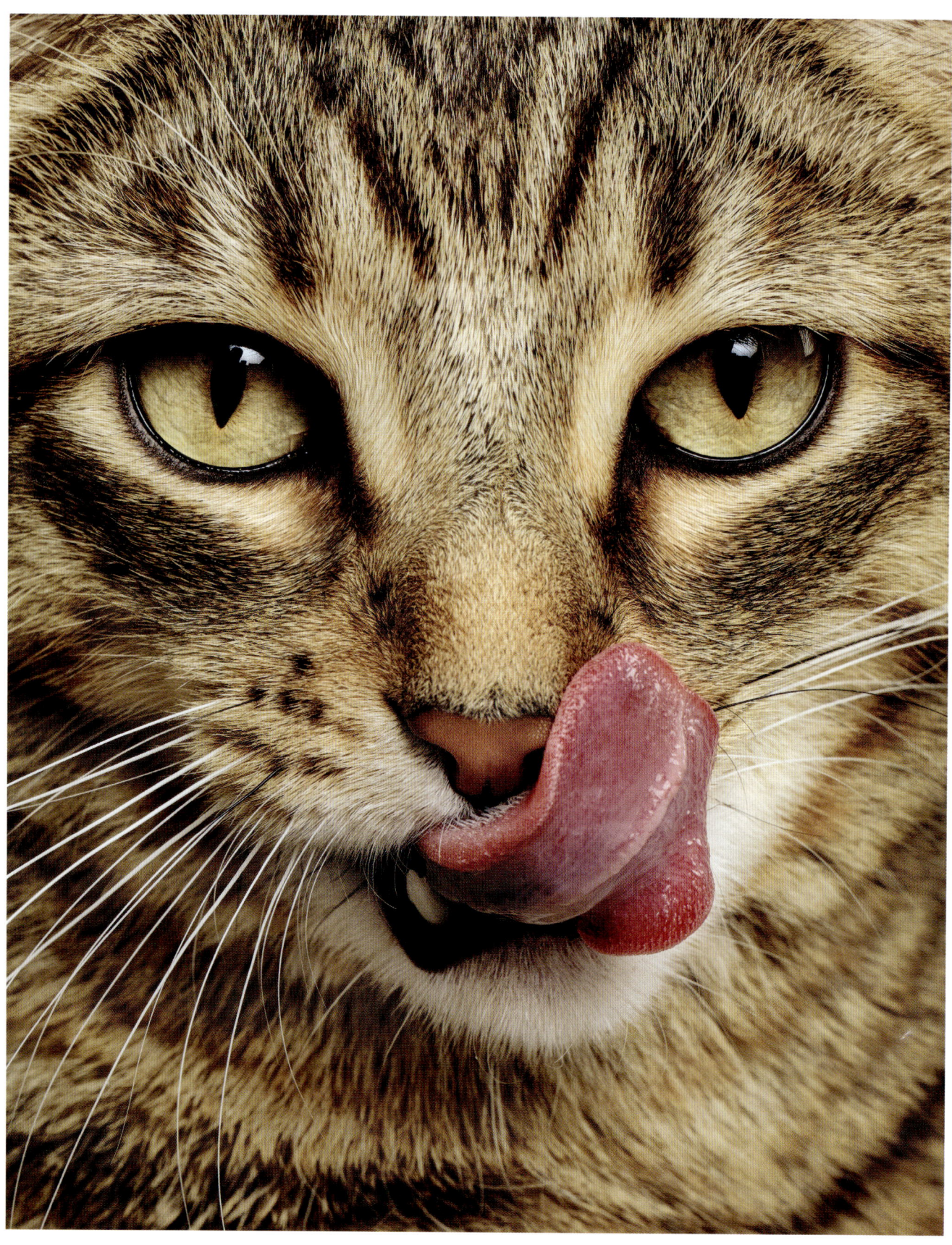

Lil Bit

BARN CATS

As night descends on the farm, sleek feline hunters patrol the barnyard almost invisibly and without a sound. While barn cats often bask in the sun or lounge in haylofts during the day, it's in the cloak of darkness that their true prowess comes to life. Their primary mission? Ridding the farm of pesky pests and rodents. With keen eyesight, razor-sharp claws, and a predatory instinct, barn cats are nature's answer to pest control. As silent guardians of the night, their stealthy work helps protect expensive grain stores from dangerous disease and mysterious disappearances.

Beyond their functional role, these cats create a sense of family on the farm and offer moments of joy, playfulness, and unexpected companionship—on their terms, of course. They often greet farmers at dawn, purring and weaving between busy feet, only to disappear at dusk to quietly prepare for the night's mission.

Photographing these enigmatic creatures presents a unique challenge—one that quickly has me feeling like the mouse on set. These crafty cats dart in and out of the shadows, each movement a sovereign decision, challenging me to a game of wit and patience. It's a game from which I rarely emerge victorious.

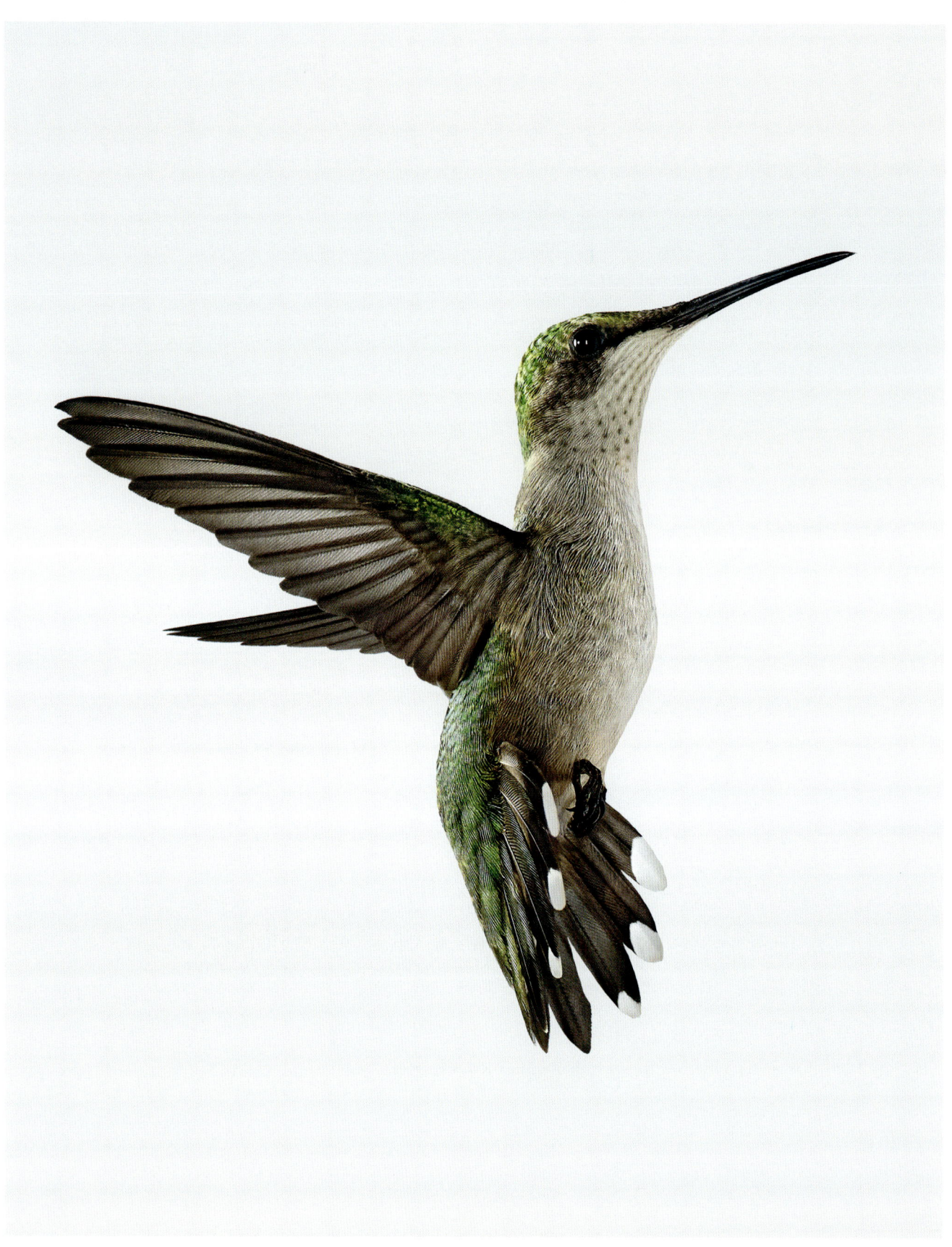

Dotty

HUMMINGBIRD

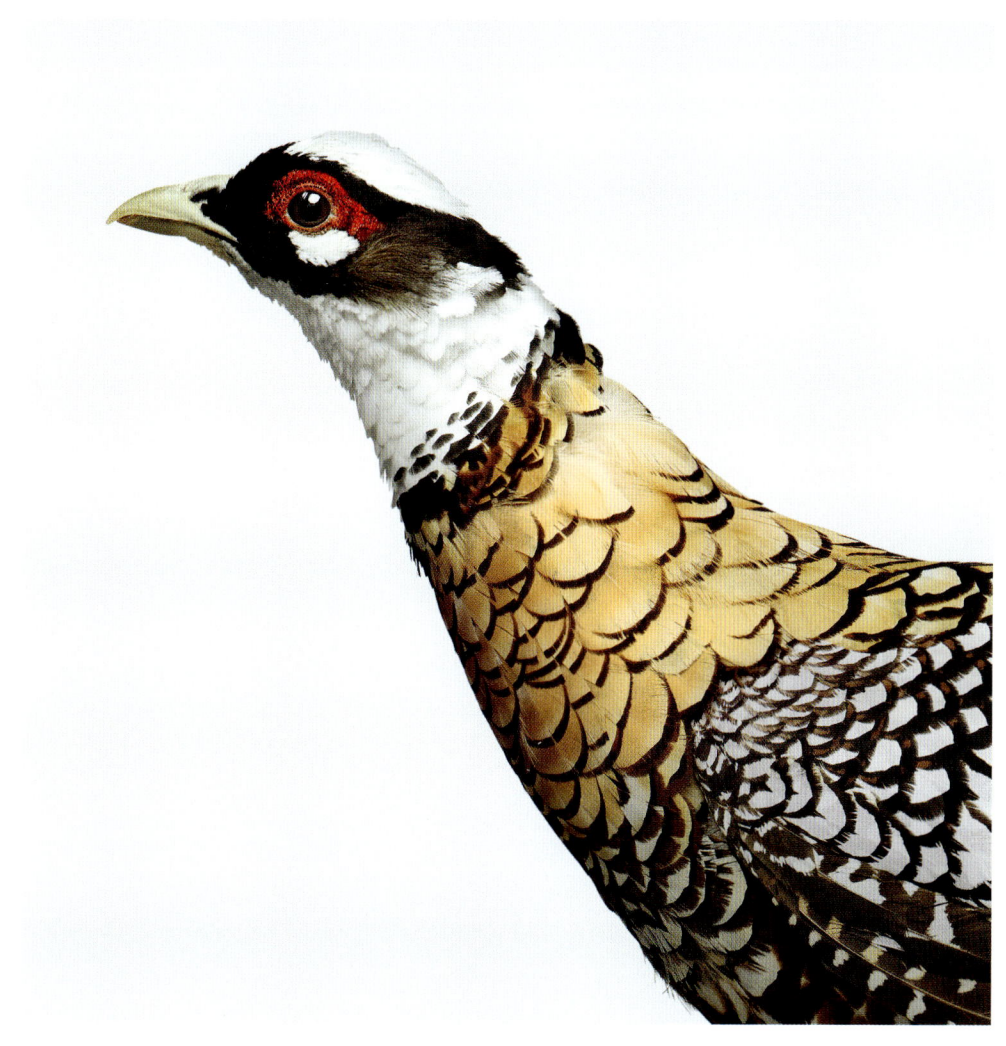

Lindor

REEVE'S PHEASANT

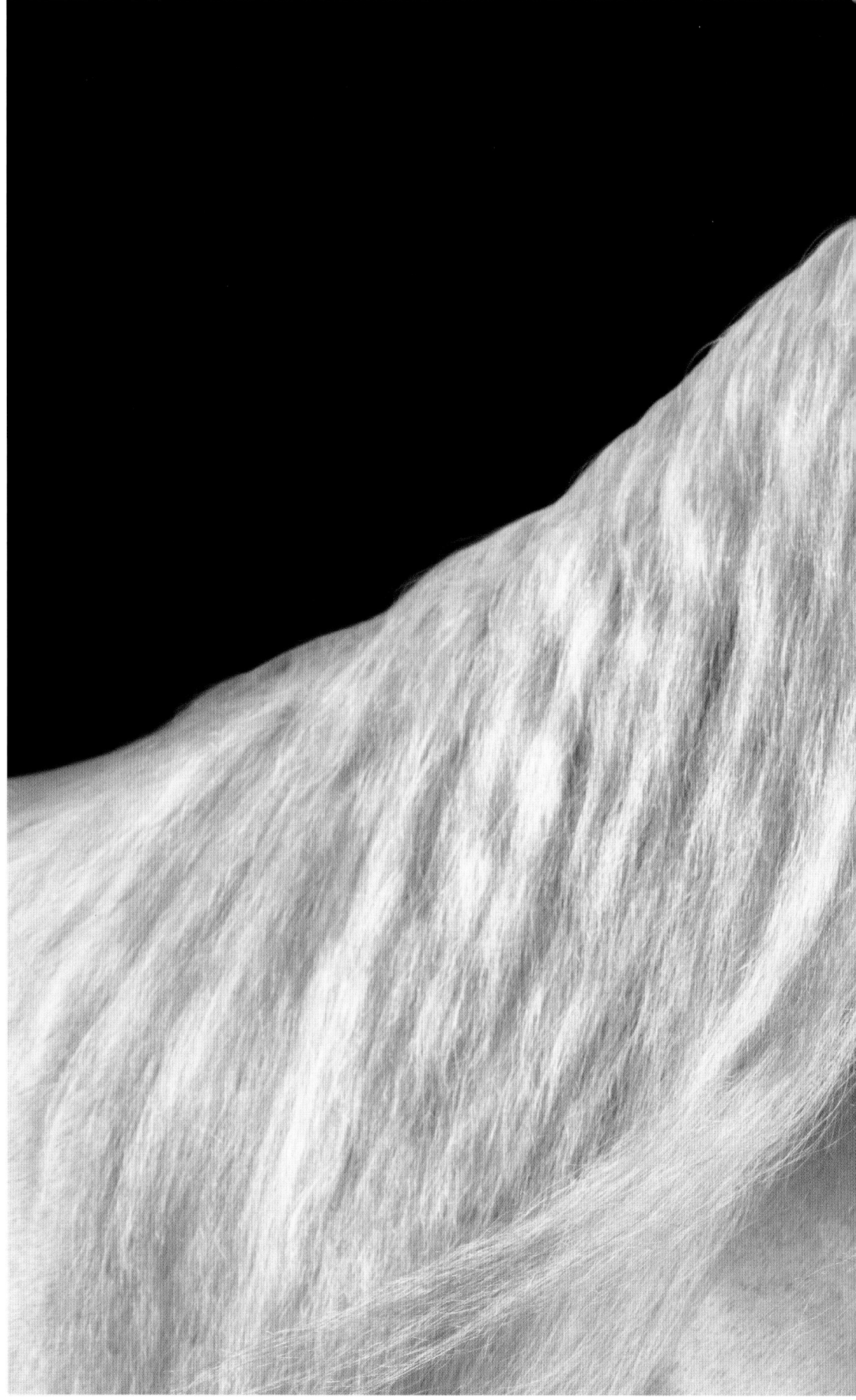

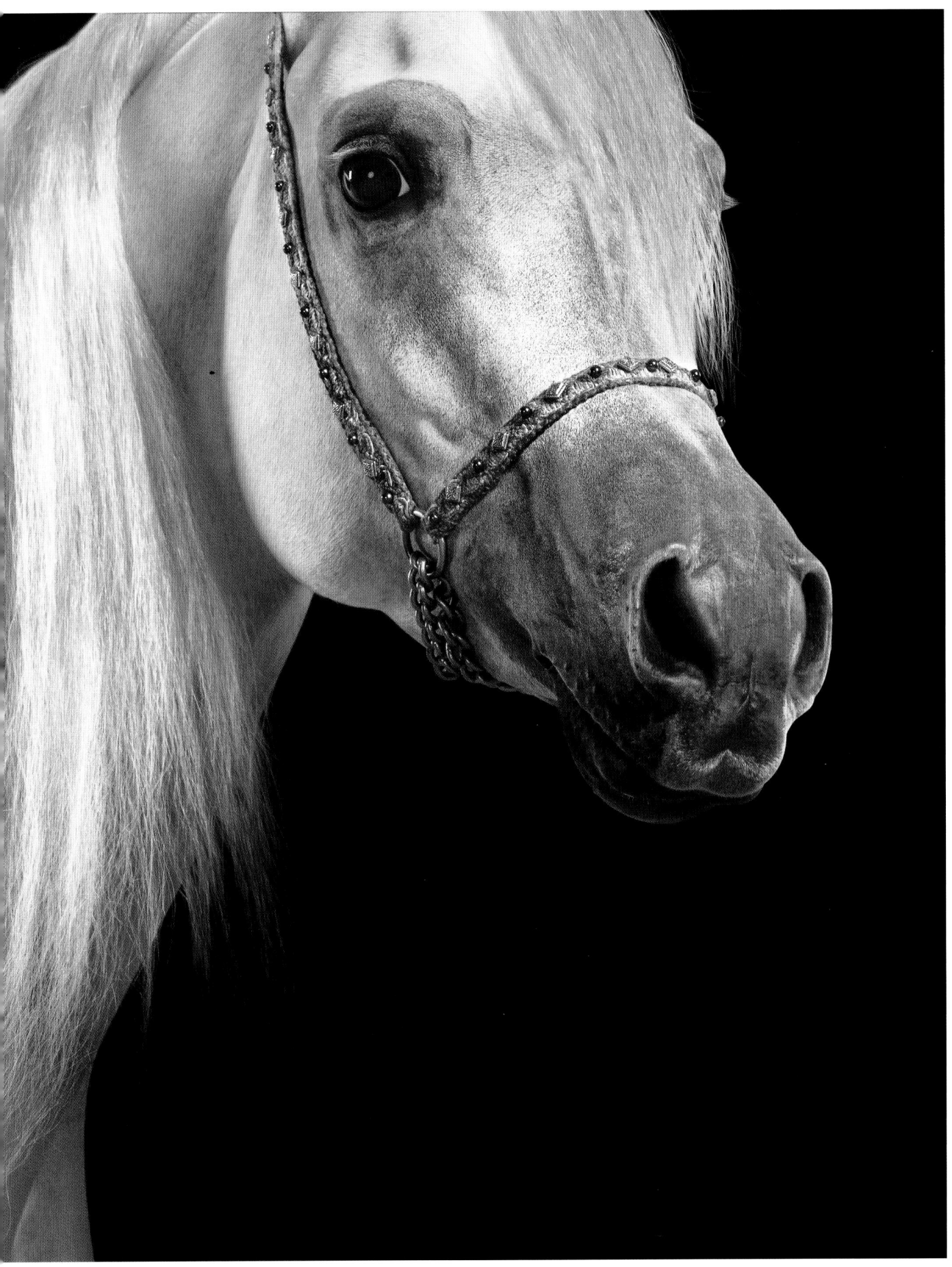

Don't worry; this sweet-faced calf is not

coming to collect. Born on April 15, The

Tax Man is anything but taxing. Cows are

some of the kindest animals there are, and

I always love working with them. From

their soft coats to their gentle nuzzles to

their endearing moos—if all tax collectors

were this friendly, the whole world would

be filing on time. Photographing calves

can be tricky, and, despite his tough name,

The Tax Man needed his mama close by. In

this portrait, I hoped to capture his soft and

symmetrical facial features, as well as the

newness of his young coat.

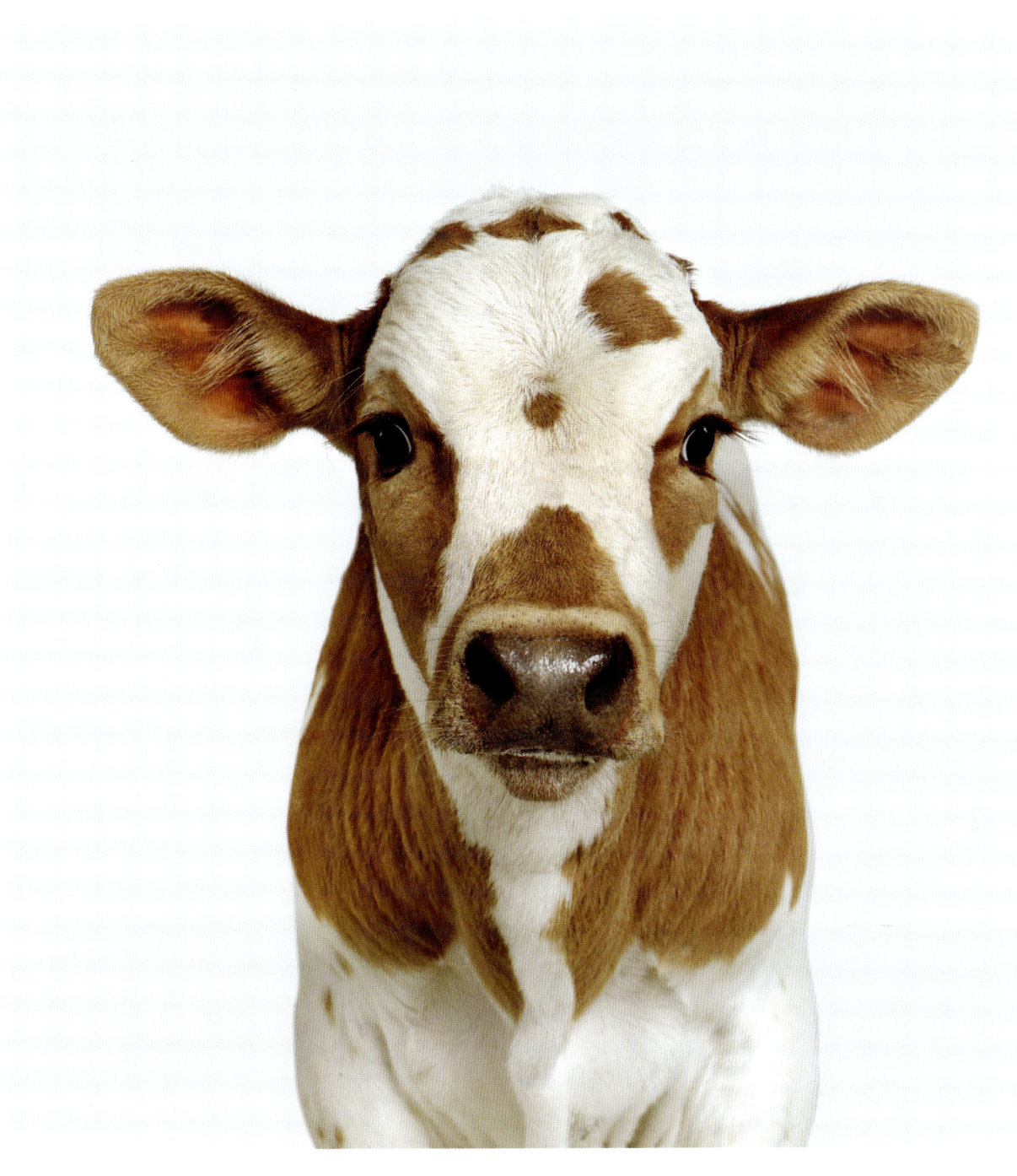

The Tax Man

TEXAS LONGHORN CALF

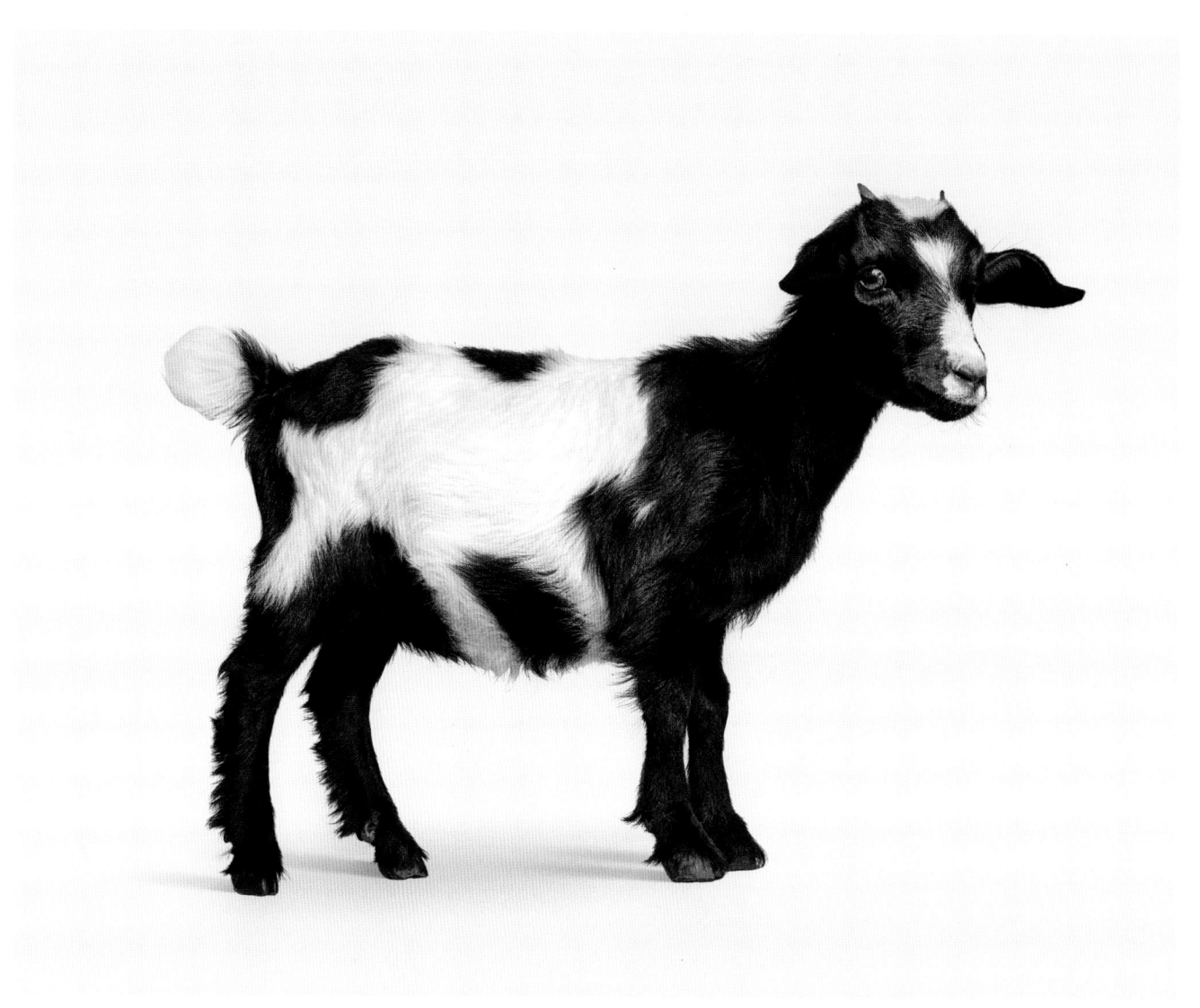

Bubbles

BABY GOAT

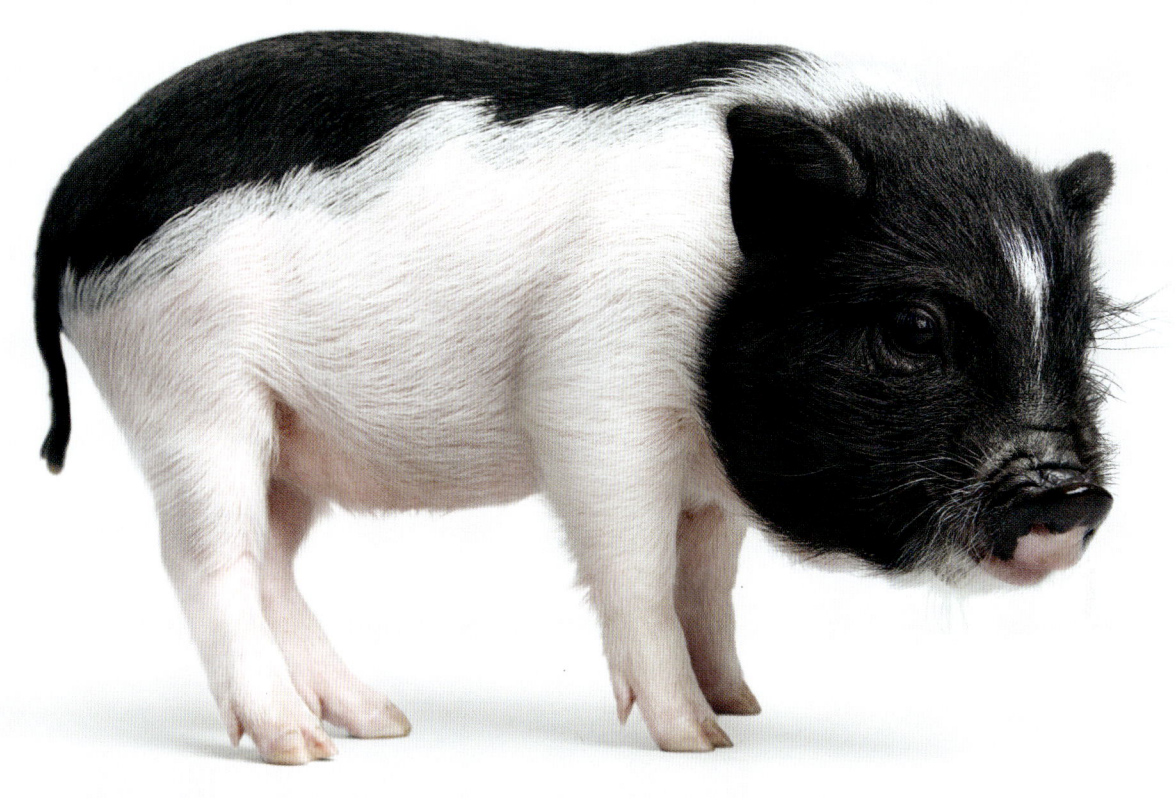

Carnita

POTBELLIED PIGLET

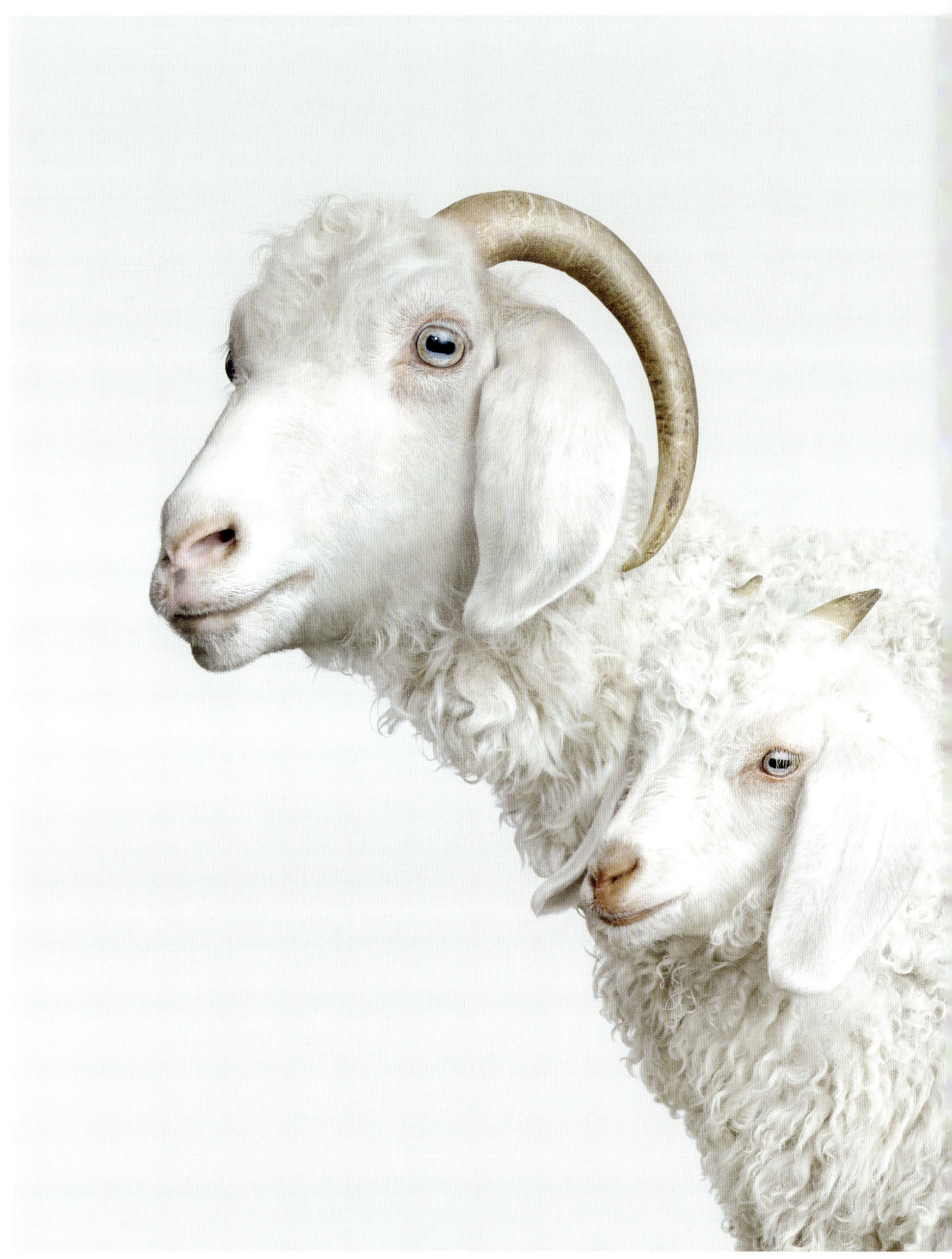

Annie and Clover

ANGORA DOE AND DOELING GOATS

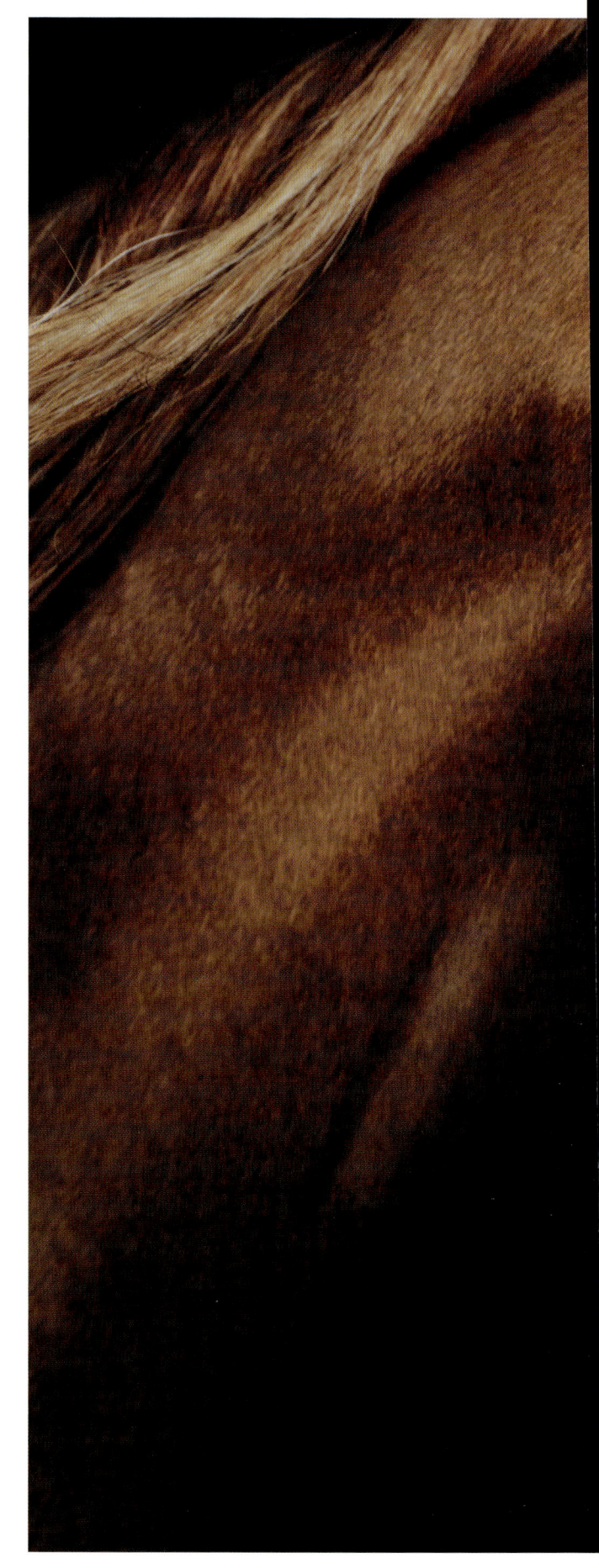

Lahab Albidayer

RED ARABIAN STALLION

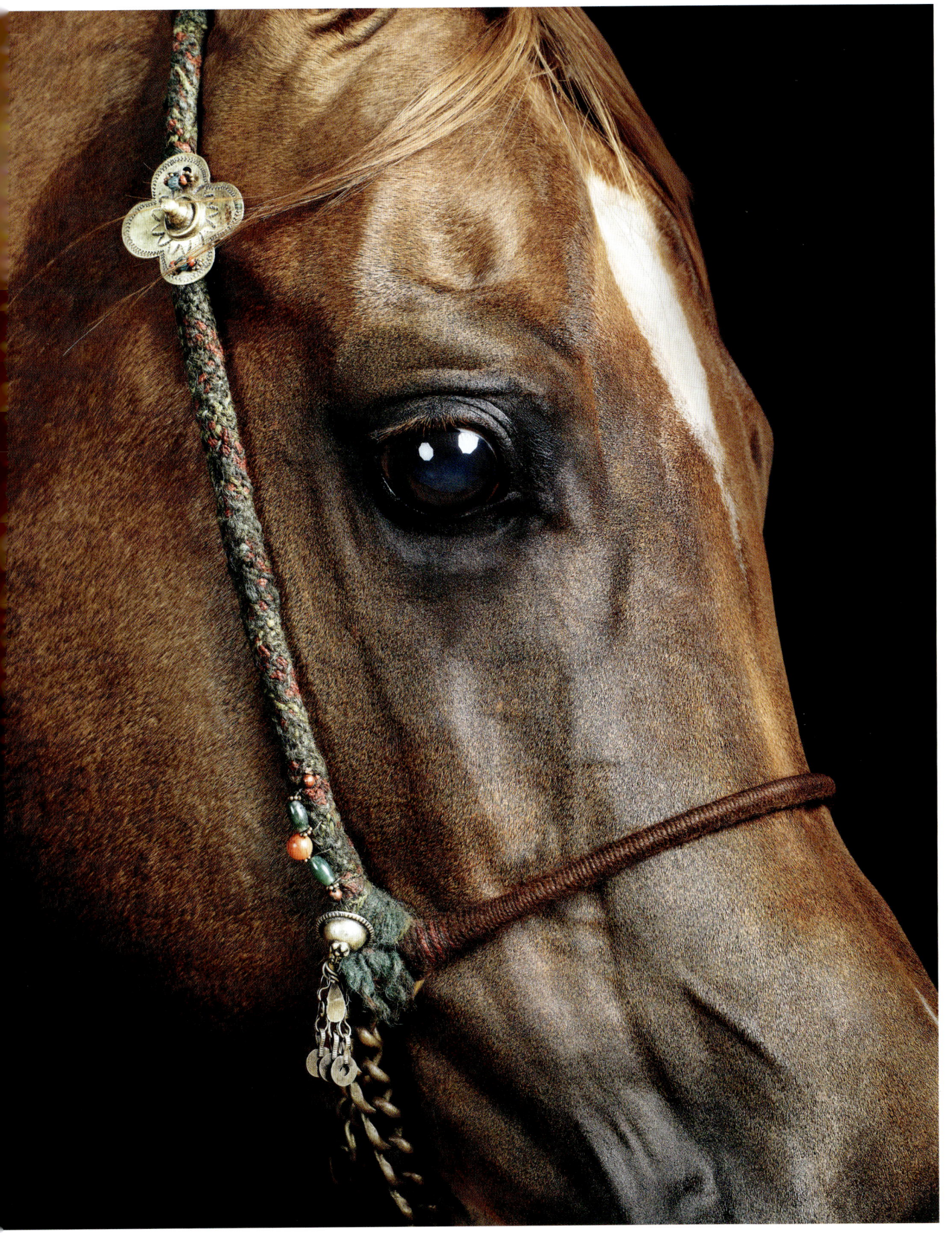

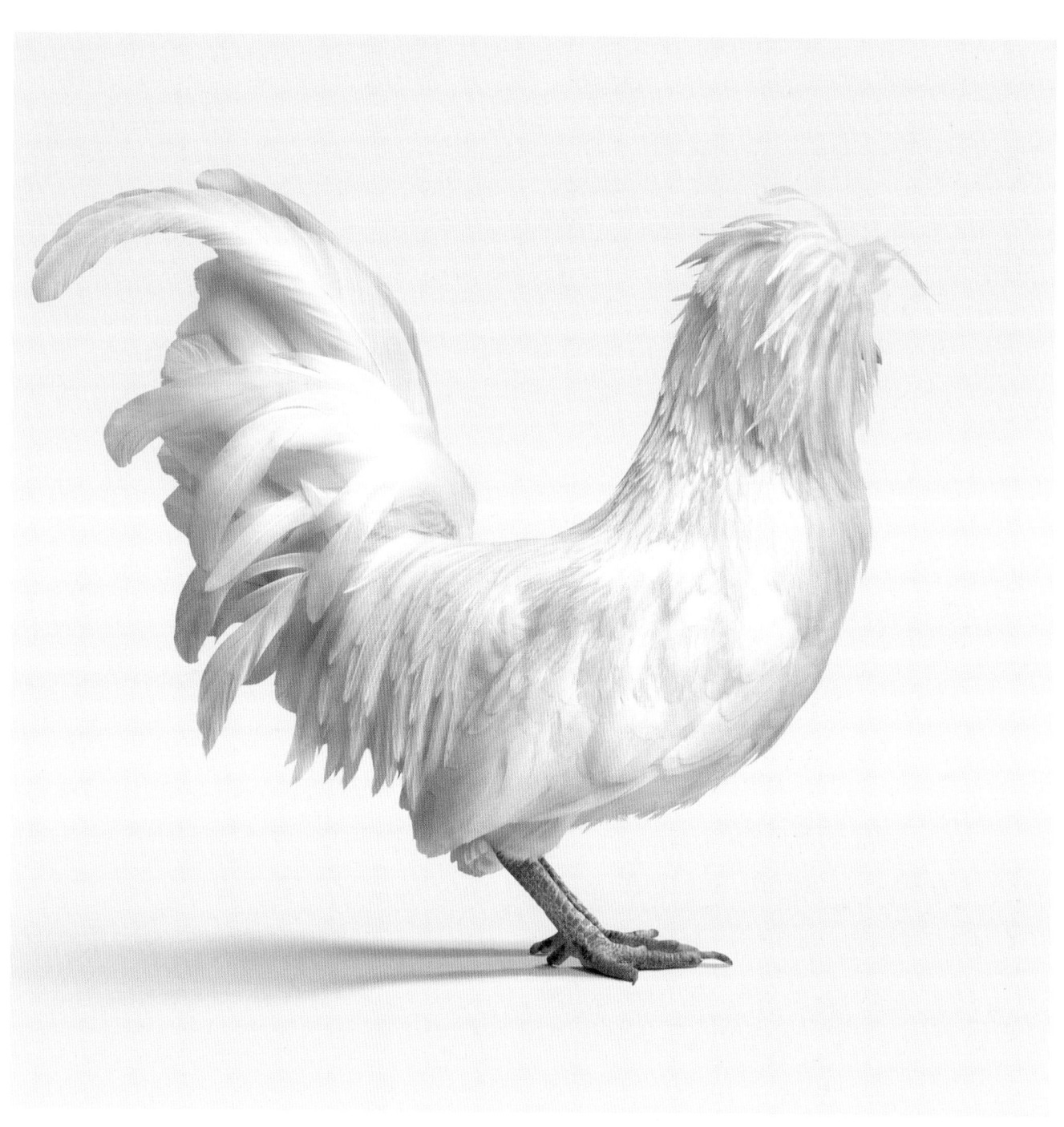

Denali

BANTAM WHITE POLISH HEN

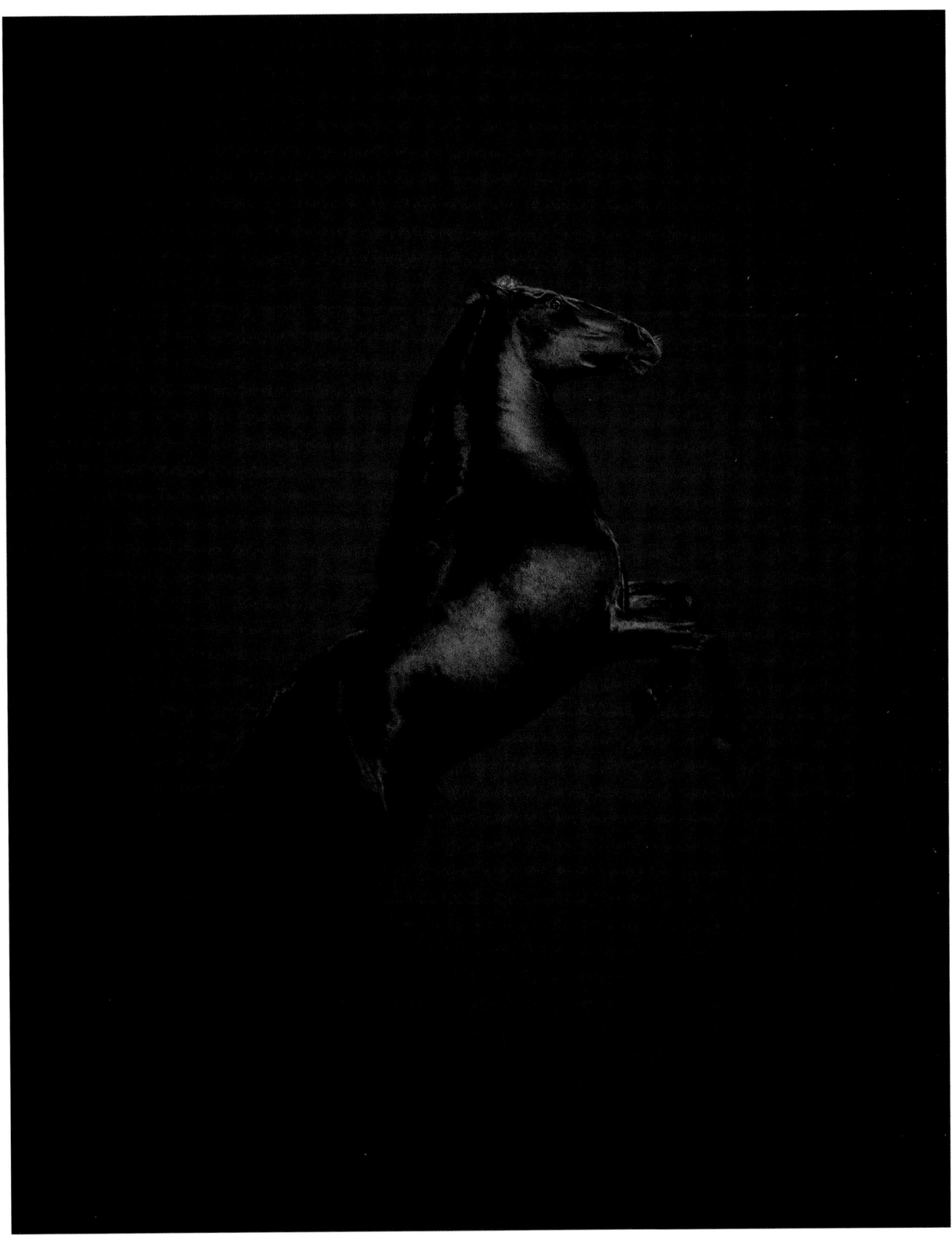

Bastina

BLACK LUSITANO MARE

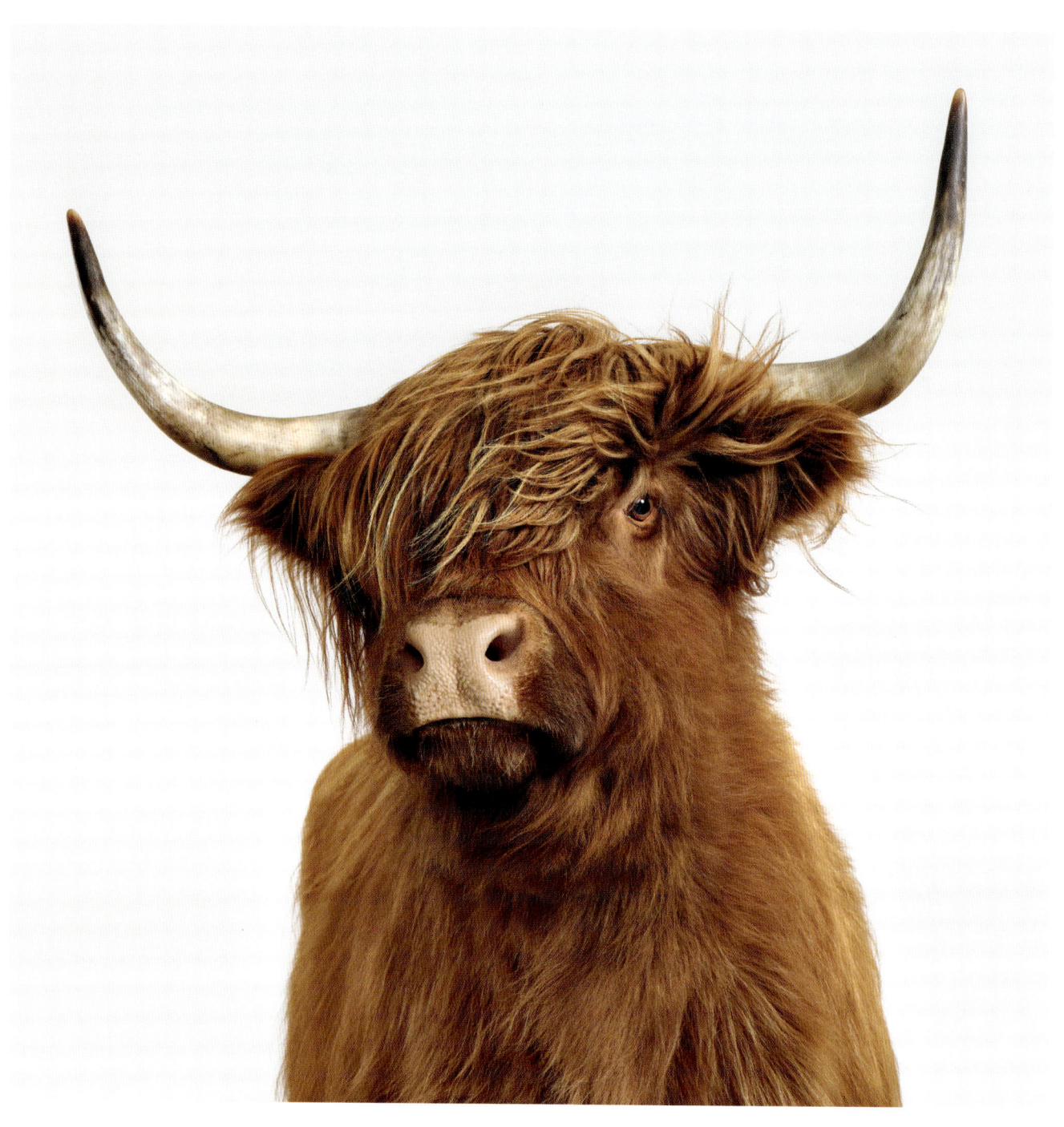

Symphony

RED HIGHLAND COW

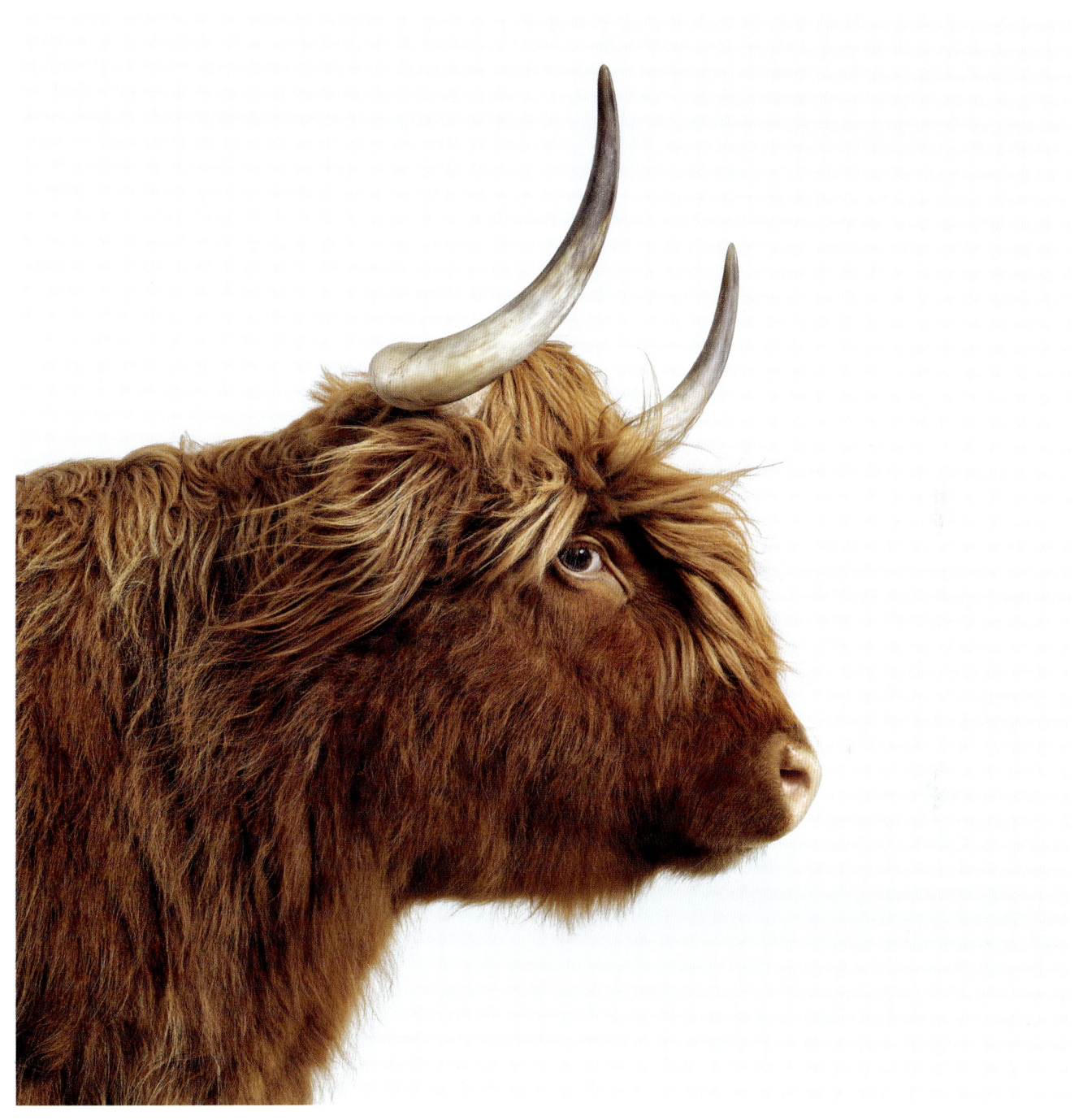

OWLS

Barn owls, with their ethereal beauty and enigmatic presence, have long been revered in folklore as harbingers of good luck. Possessing an almost ghostly appearance with their heart-shaped faces and soft, muted colors, they patrol the night skies with silent precision. One single barn owl, with a voracious appetite of three to four prey per night, can do a magnificent job of keeping unwanted farm pests away.

In my encounters photographing these sacred raptors, there is an unmistakable aura they exude, one of deep-seated wisdom and profound mystery. Their eyes, having witnessed countless nocturnal tales, seem to hold ancient secrets. Their majestic demeanors and invaluable roles in maintaining ecological balance make barn owls a stunning presence to capture.

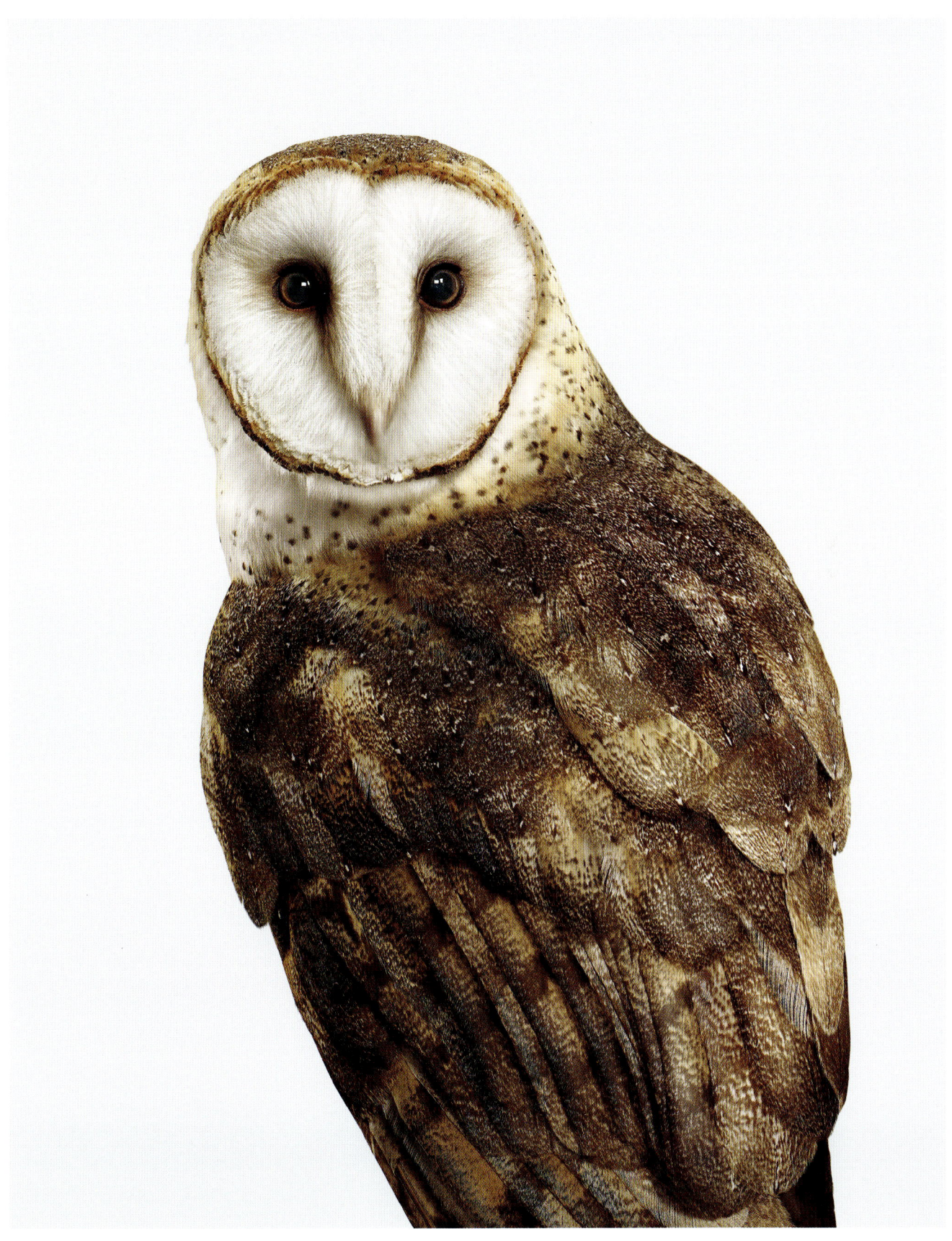

Winston

AMERICAN BARN OWL

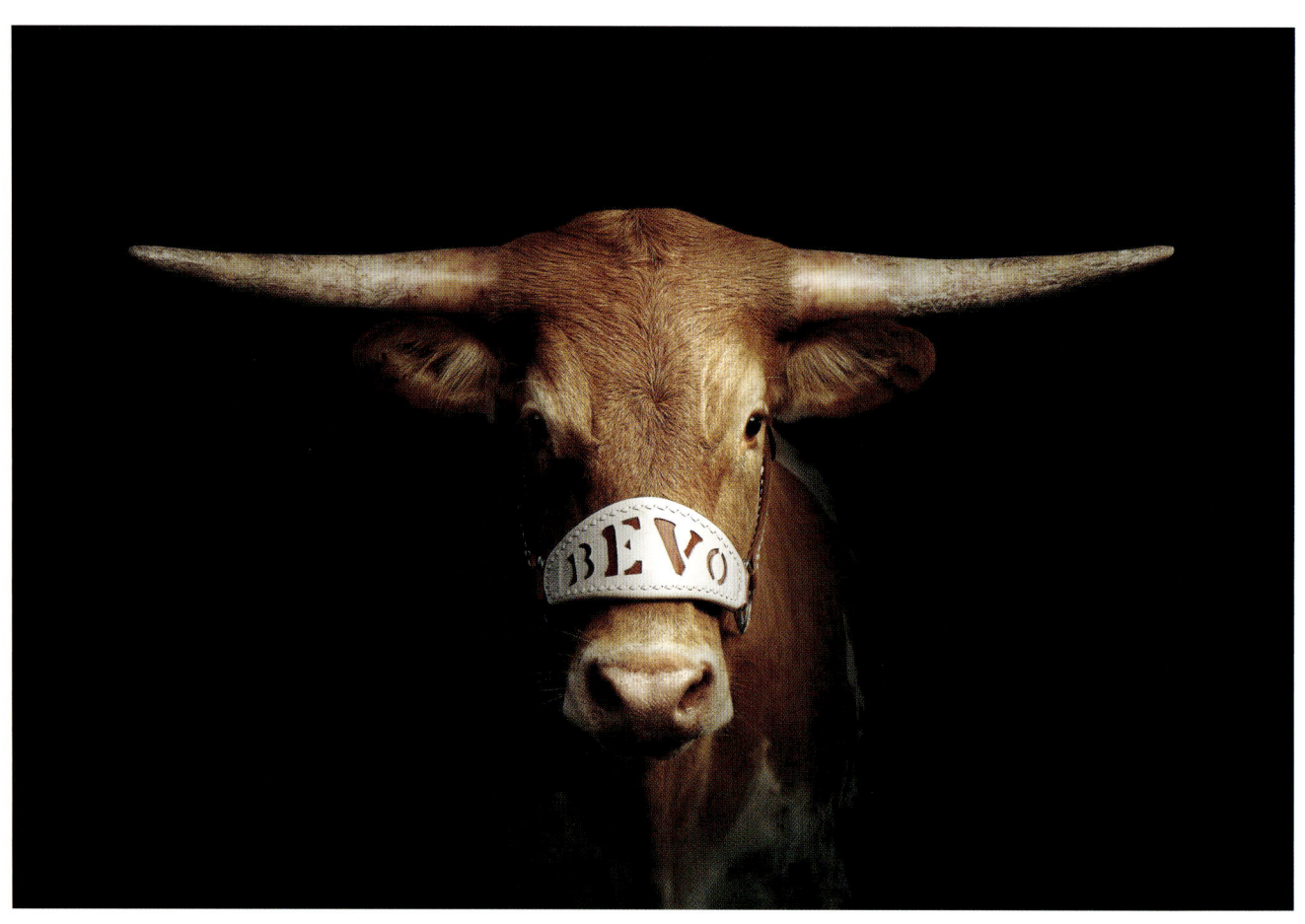

Bevo XV

TEXAS LONGHORN

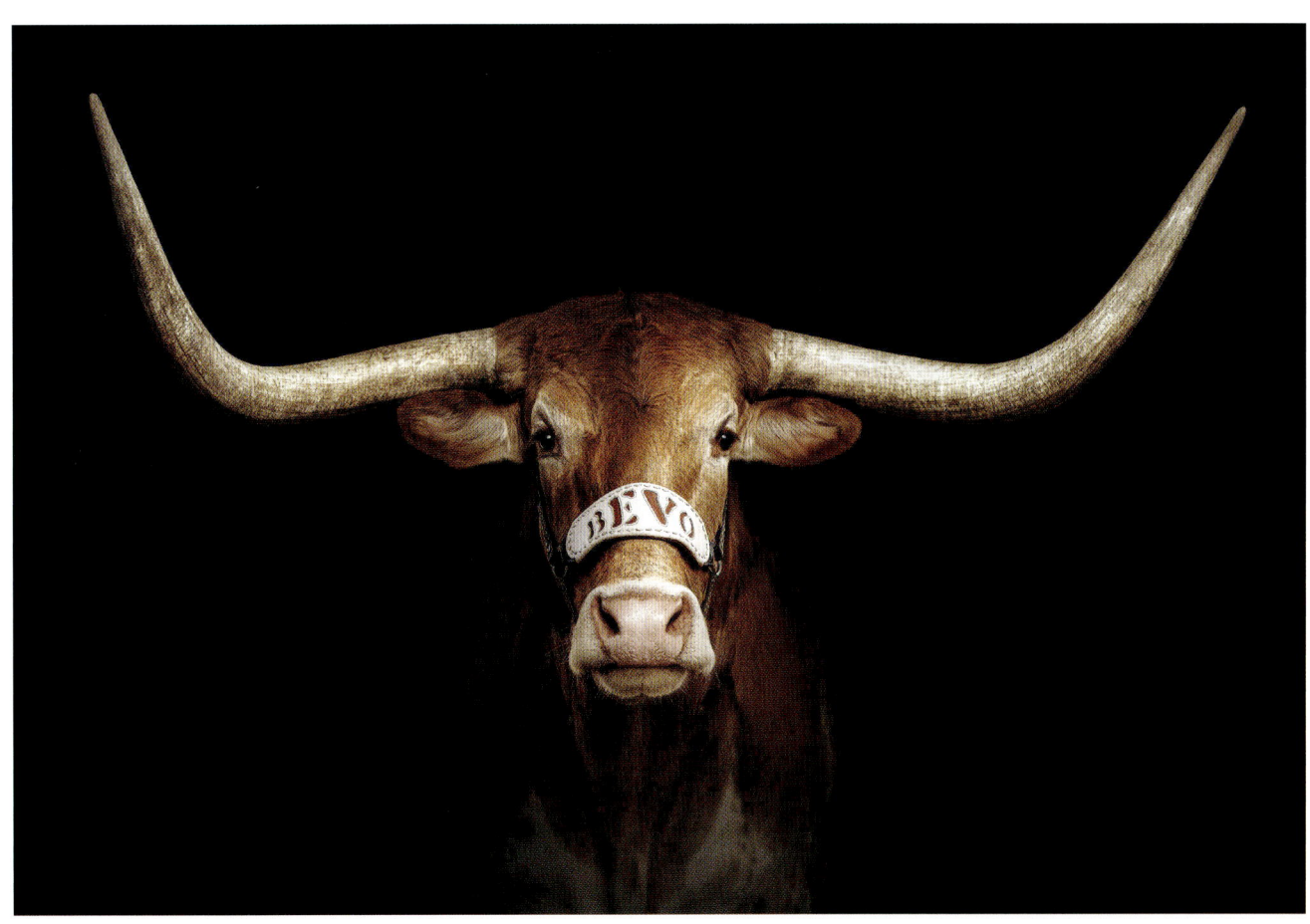

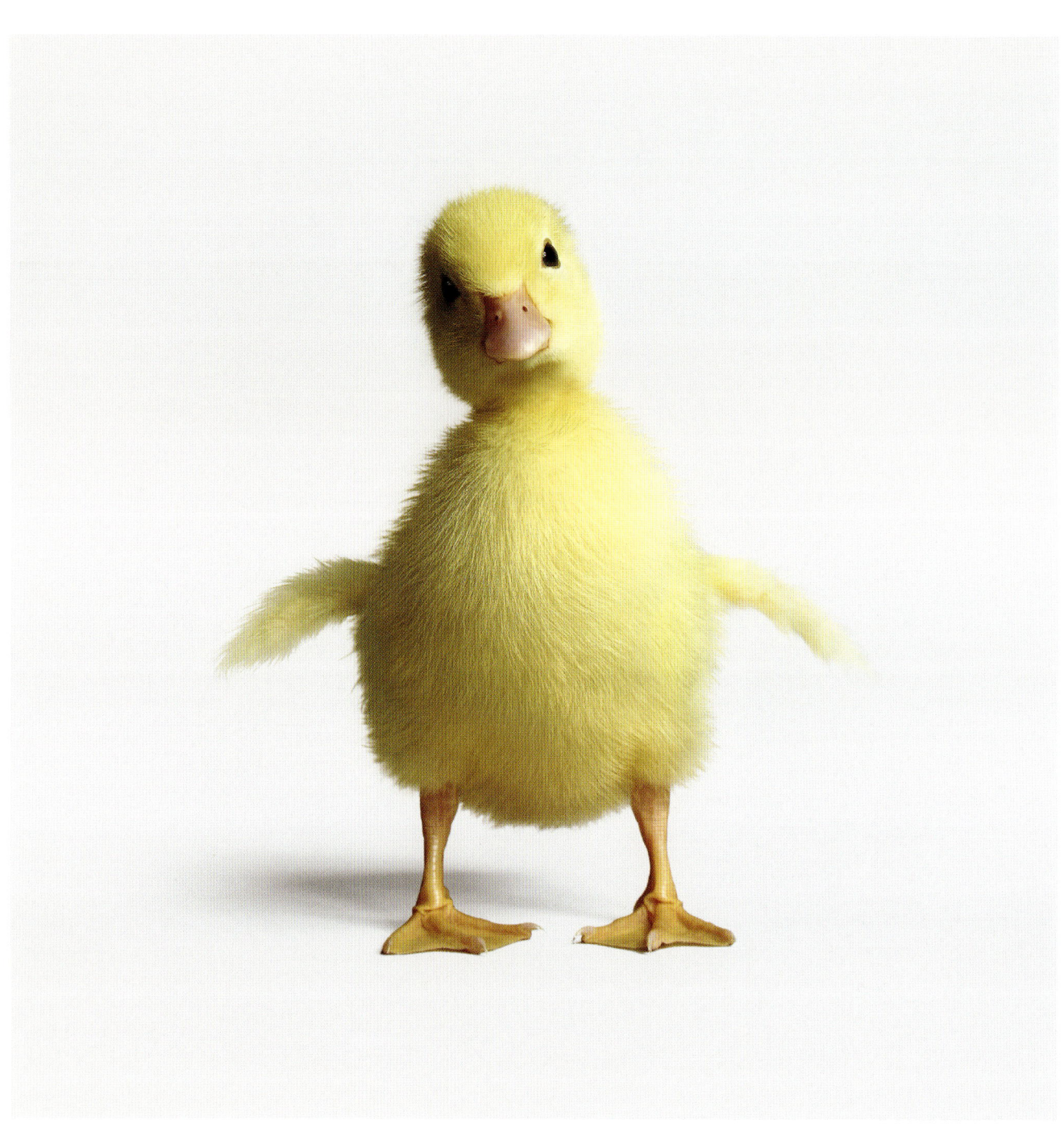

Luna

MALLARD DUCKLING

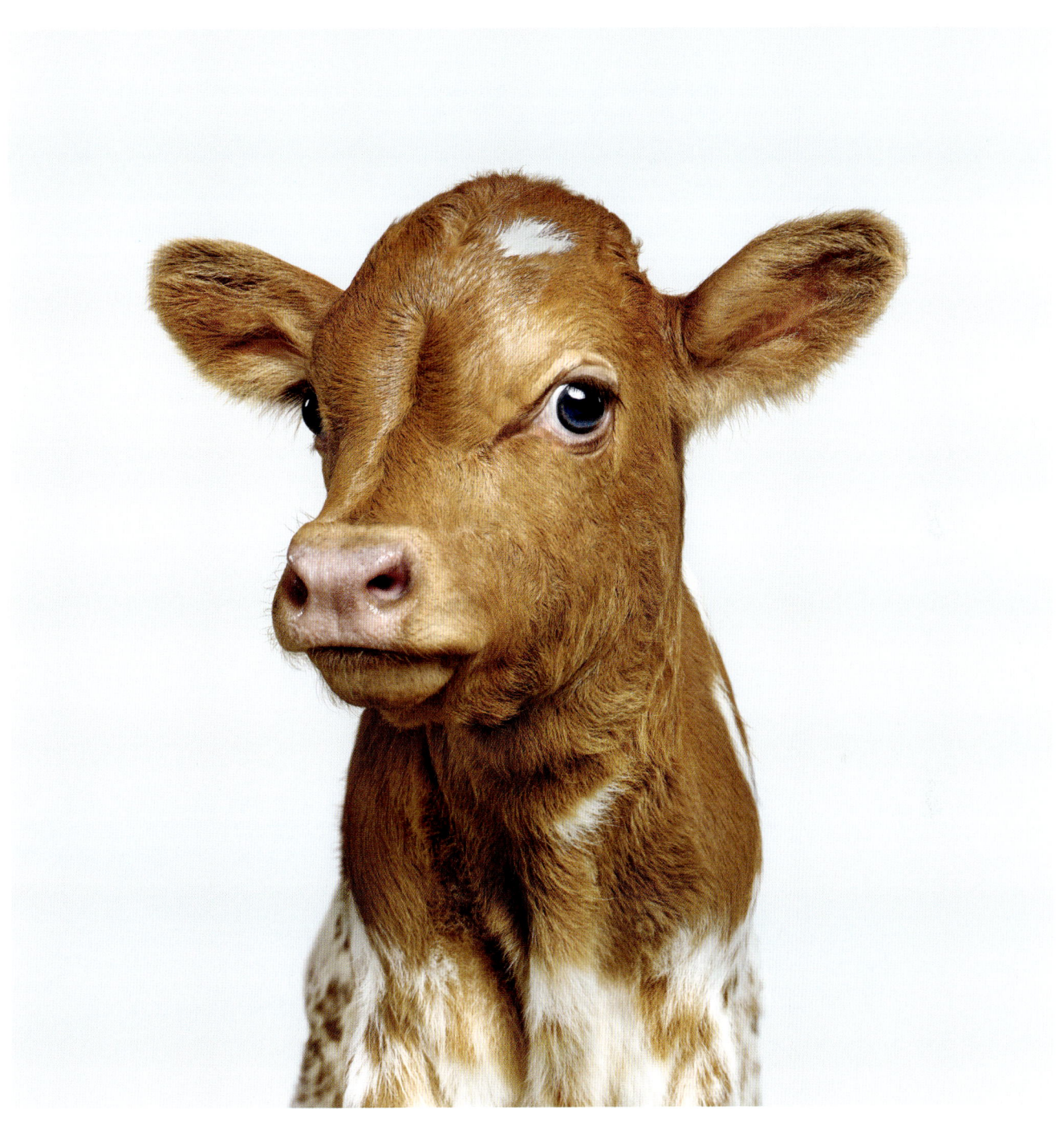

Bug

LONGHORN NEWBORN CALF

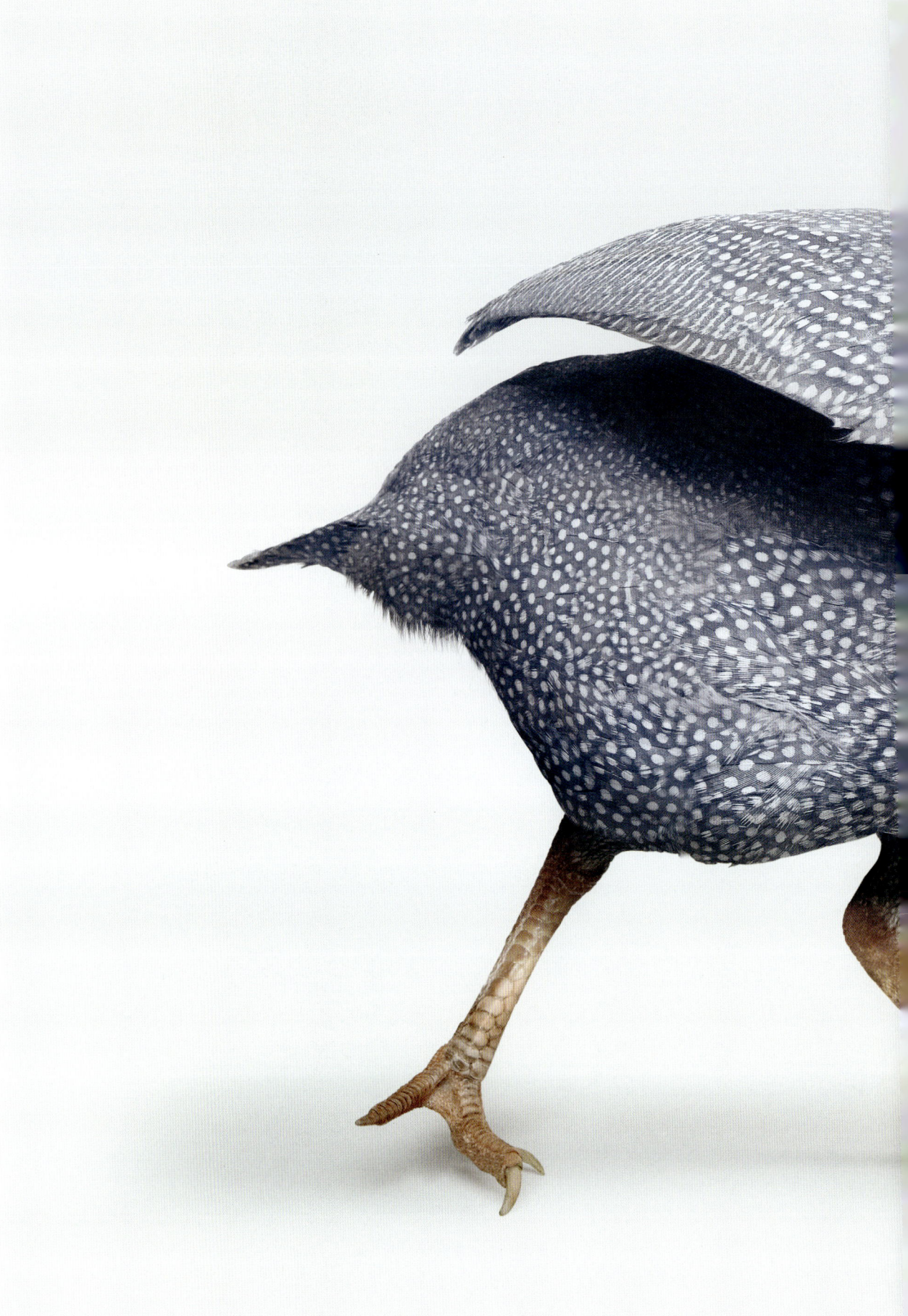

Jester

LAVENDER GUINEA HEN

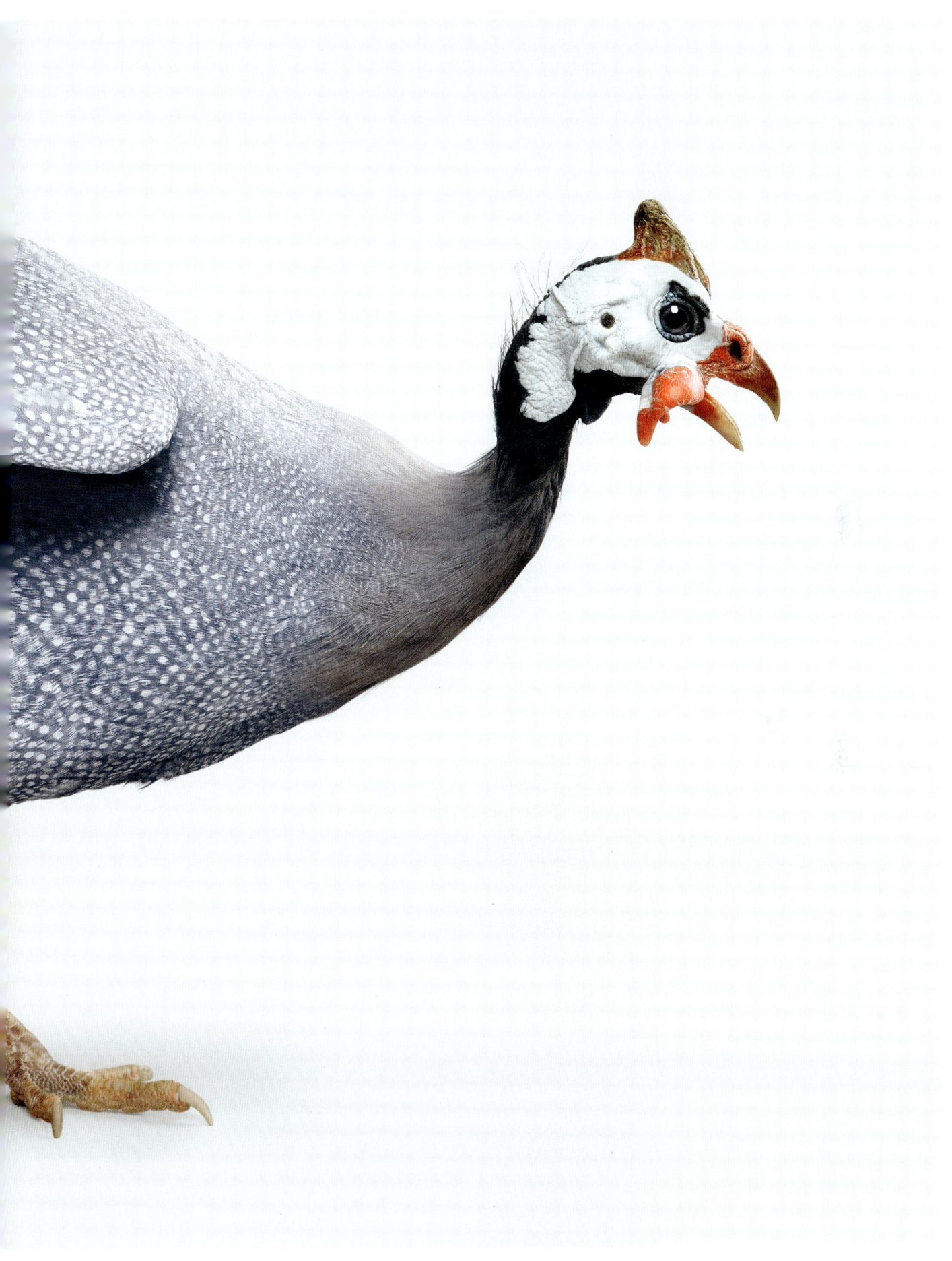

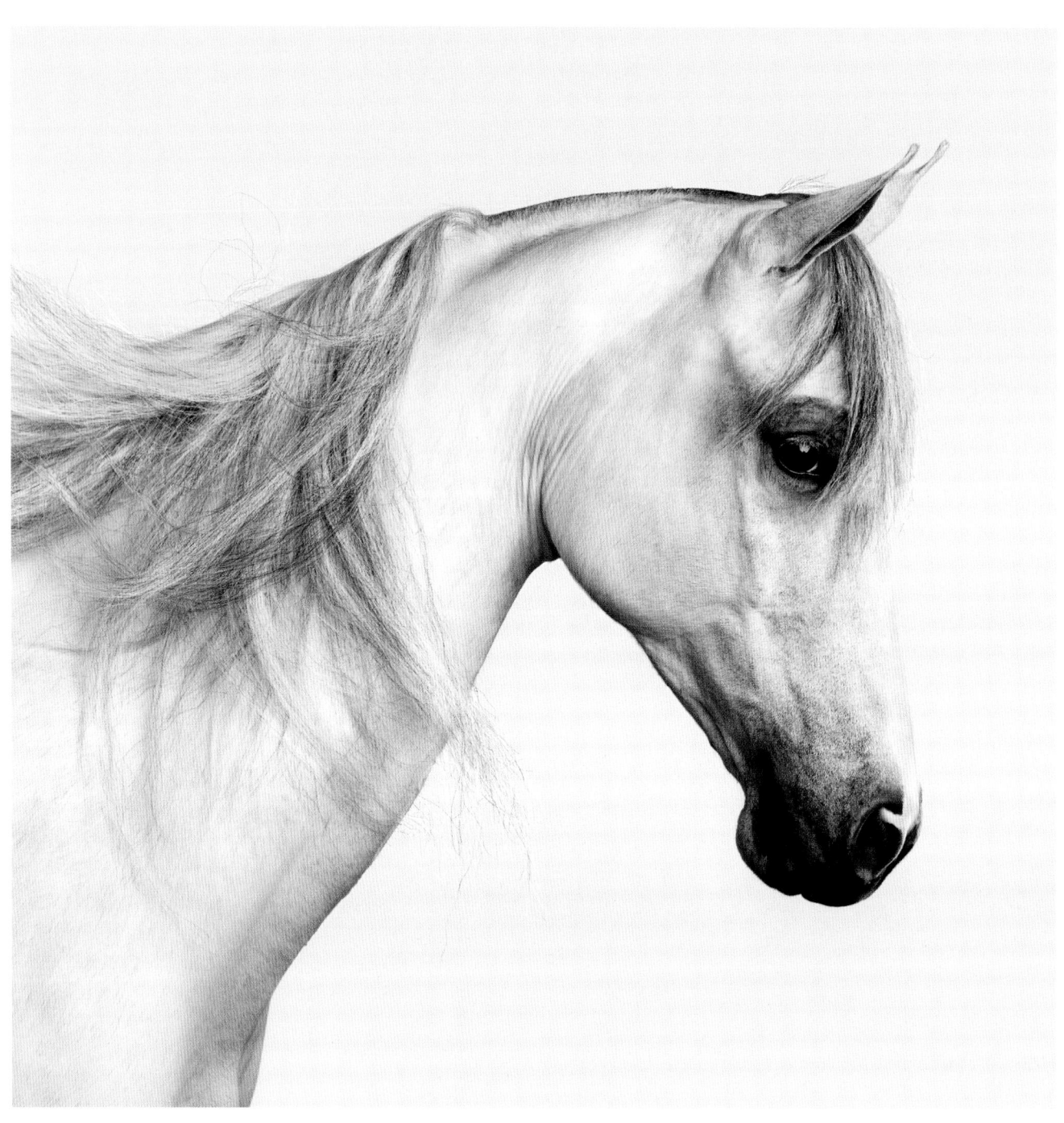

Sergeant Pepper

WHITE ARABIAN STALLION

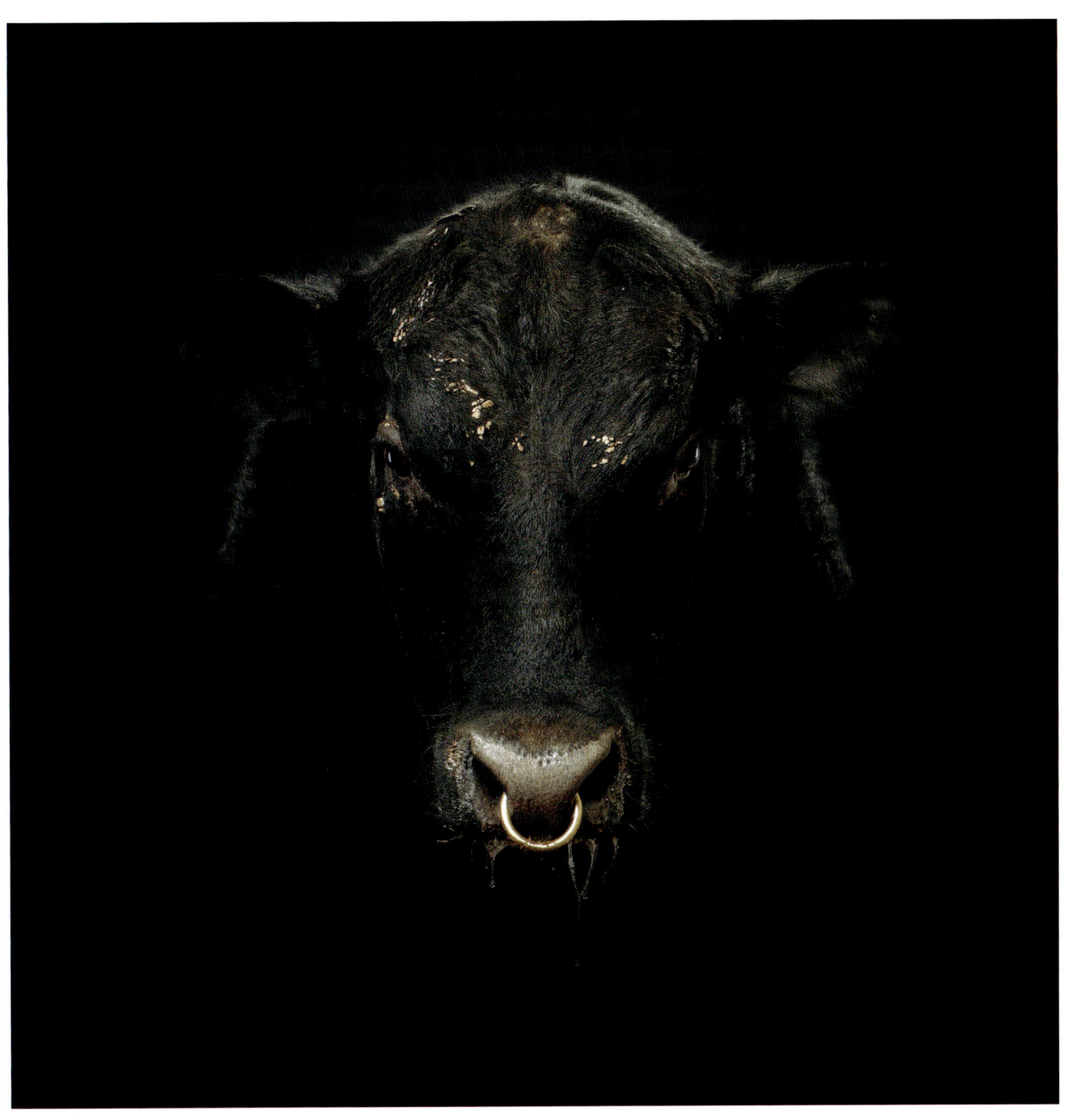

Wayne Crosby

BLACK ANGUS BULL

This girl was nothing short of a fresh

mug of coffee, with her beautiful caramel

plumage and milk-swirled poufs as proof.

You would never know it by looking at her,

but Latte was originally rescued with a

large band embedded in her leg. After the

careful nursing of her new owner and an

eventual full recovery, this feathered

beauty went on to greet each new day with

the enthusiasm of a fresh morning brew.

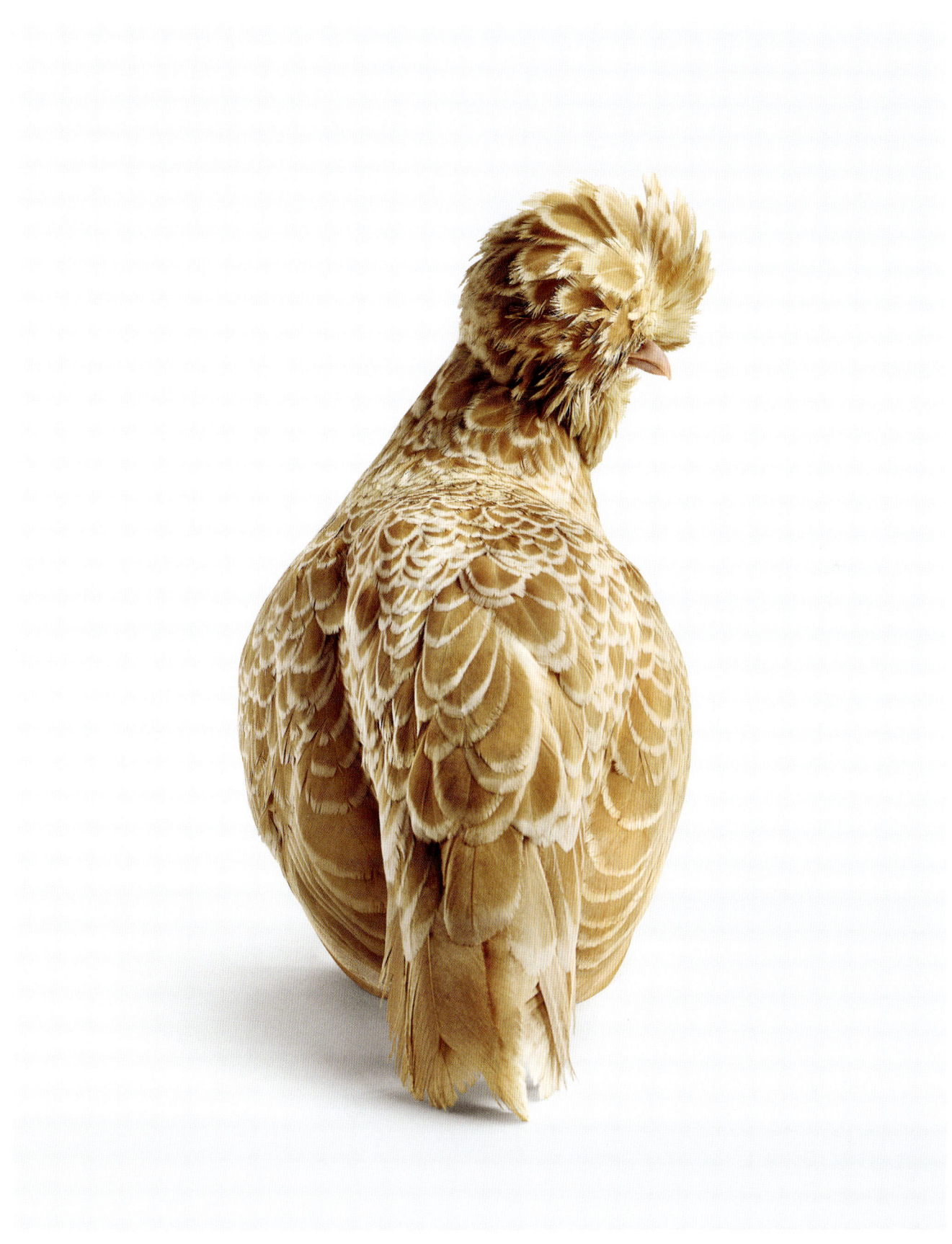

Latte

BANTAM BUFF LACED POLISH HEN

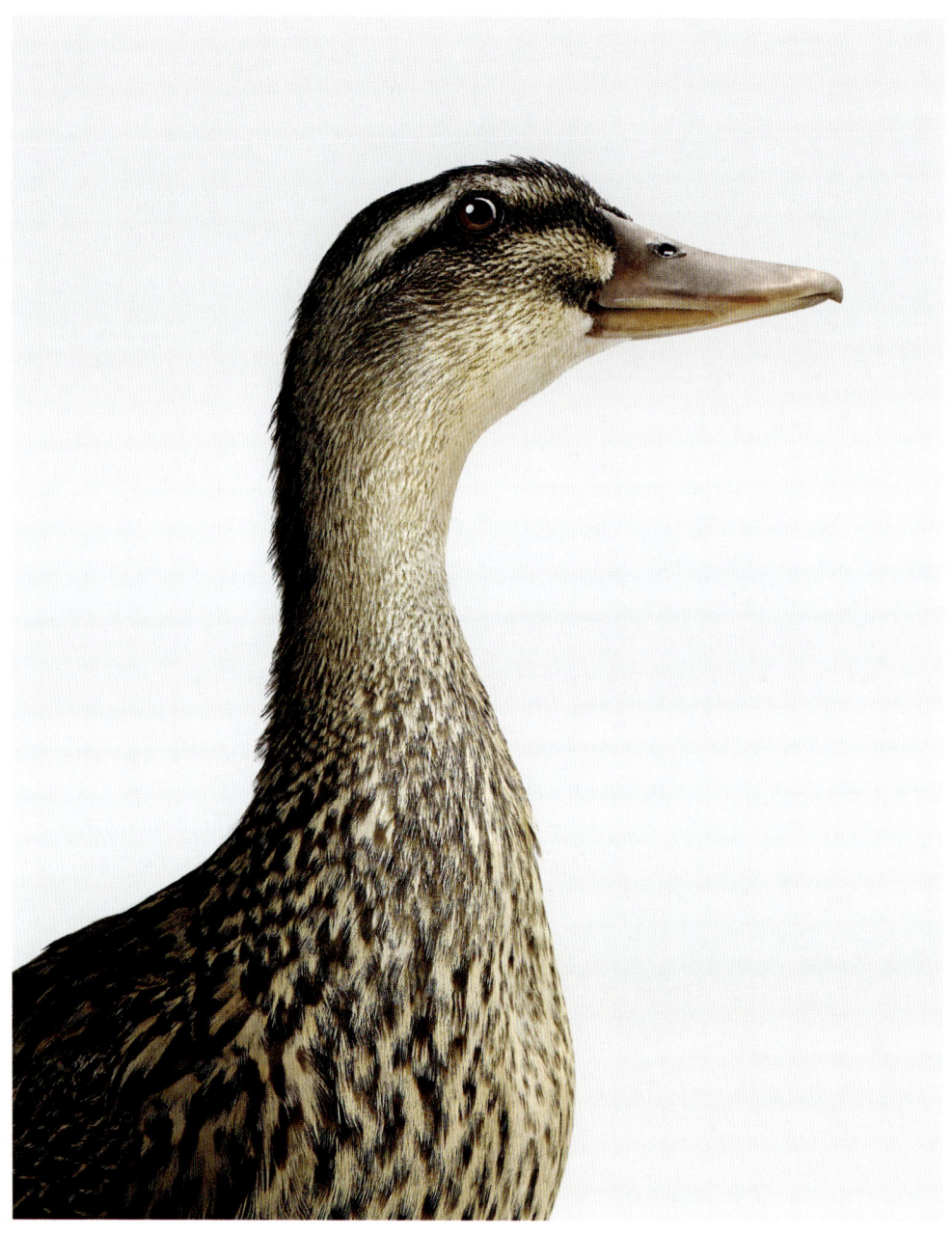

Bessie

GRAY MALLARD FEMALE DUCK

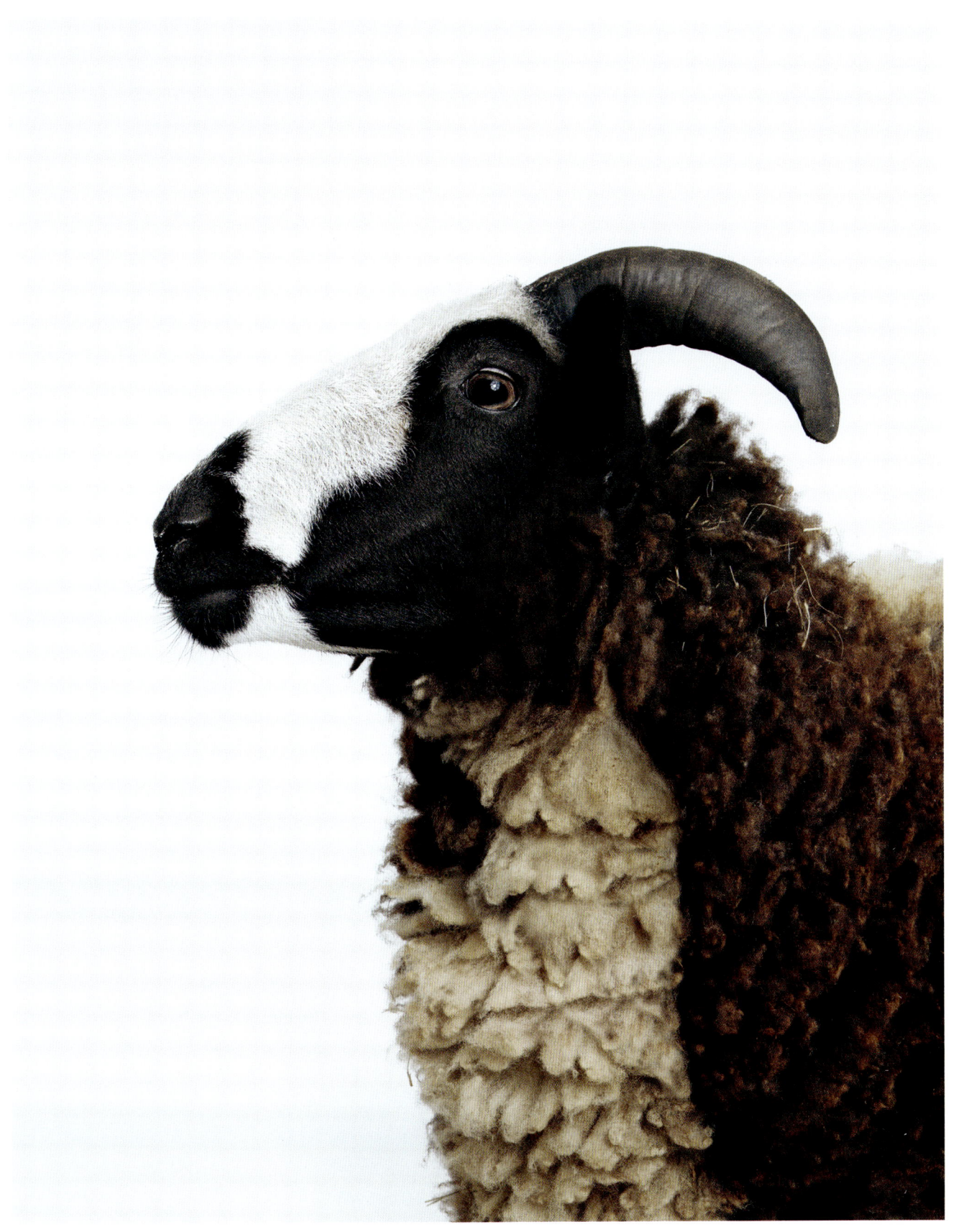

Moses

JACOB SHEEP

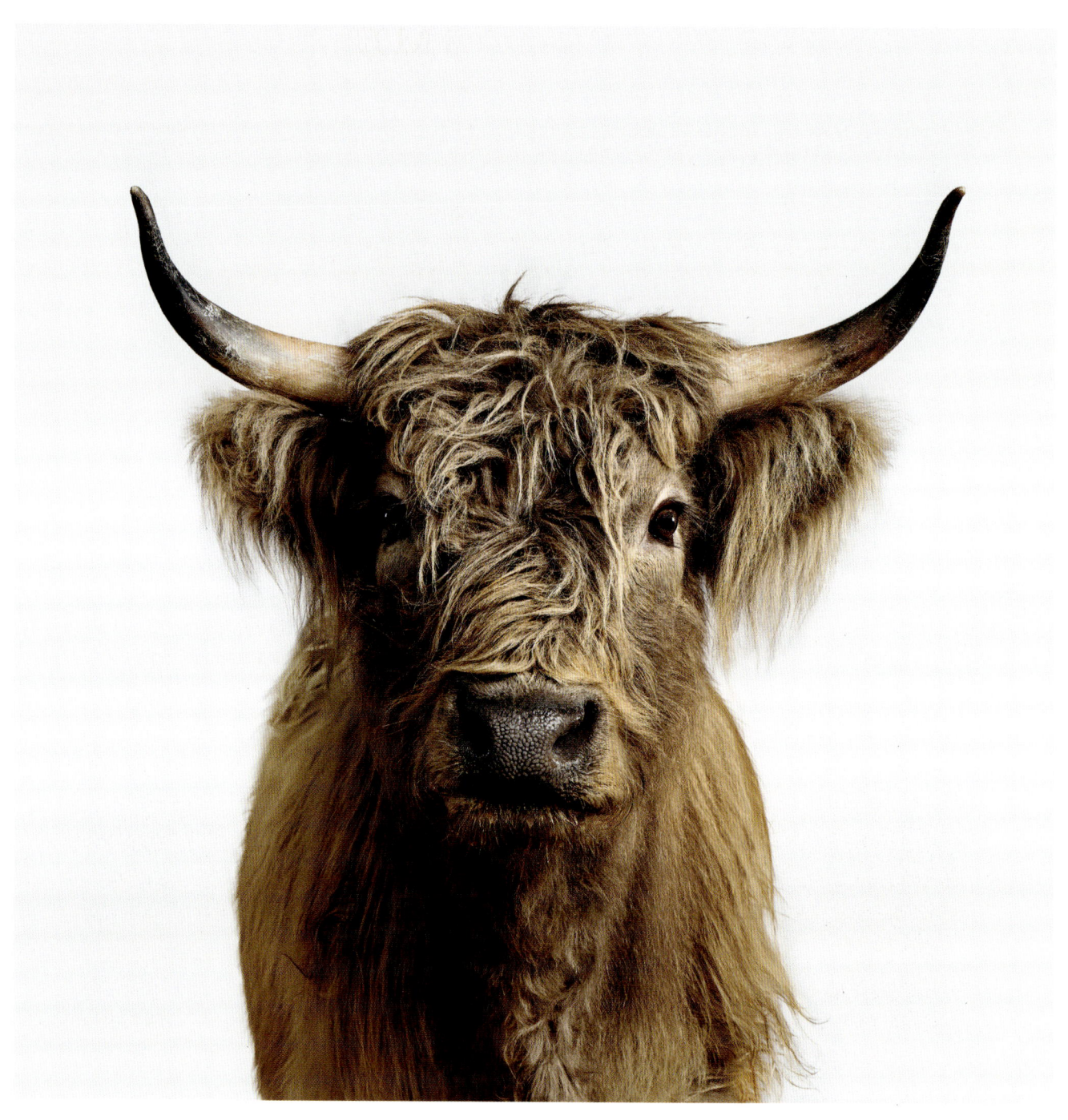

Eleanor

HIGHLAND COW

ACKNOWLEDGMENTS

Capturing the essence of farm life in this book has been a remarkable journey—one made possible by the collective effort and skill of many dedicated individuals.

I am especially thankful to the farmers and ranchers who have shared their cherished animals with us. Their commitment to preserving rare and heritage breeds is more than stewardship; it's a passion that ensures the diversity and richness of farm life continue to thrive. Their stories and dedication to these animals have added immeasurable depth to this project.

Thank you to Alicia Connor, my producer, for her role in orchestrating the photo shoots and finding the unique animals that grace these pages. Her efforts in liaising with the owners and caretakers of these animals have been key to the project's success.

Thank you to my hardworking and fun-loving photo assistants, who have helped me craft studio lighting in barns, homes, and, of course, formal studios.

A big thank-you to Stefano Cherubini, my photo retoucher, for his exceptional work in postproduction. Also, thank you to Amber Politi, who helped me retouch many of the images we used in my first book, *The Animal Kingdom*. Postproduction is the crucial final touch that brings these portraits to life, and, while I am involved in the process as well, I could not do it without Stefano and Amber.

Thank you to my cowriter, Chelsea Weber, who helped me refine and craft my message, as well as the captions and essays throughout this book. Her beautiful writing helped me communicate my stories about these animals in a heartfelt manner that connects with each and every viewer.

To my publisher, Rizzoli, which has continually believed in me and supported my craft over the course of three books and has also given me a broad scope of creative direction and control.

Thank you to DJ Stout and Stu Taylor of Pentagram Design. Thank you, Stu, for the great design and for allowing me to be so specific about how I envisioned the book. And thank you to DJ, who commissioned me to photograph my first cow portrait more than 10 years ago. Who would have thought it would lead us to a trilogy of books with a prestigious publisher and a portrait of a cow on the cover, to boot?

Thank you to my animal-loving family, especially my wife, who has provided honest and pragmatic feedback throughout this project. And to my parents and extended family, who have continually been supportive and encouraging of my work.

Thank you to my fans and collectors of my art. Without you, I would not have had this great opportunity to showcase the beauty, intrigue, and essence of so many wonderful creatures.

Finally, I want to end with a deep appreciation for the Creator. The divinity of Mother Nature never ceases to amaze and inspire me. I am continually in awe of the profound magnificence we find in the animal kingdom. *Farm Life* and my previous two books are tributes to the harmonious and sacred bond we share with animals across our world.

INDEX OF STORIES

Farm animals touch our lives in extraordinary ways, but very rarely do we get the chance to see and celebrate them up close. The following pages provide a small window into each animal's colorful story and give us the opportunity to witness their beauty in new and unexpected ways.

My hope is that each caption invites you to sit with these amazing creatures, reflect on their contributions to the world around us, and learn from them along the way.

INDEX

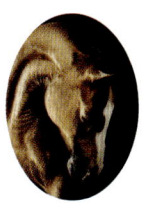 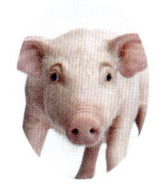 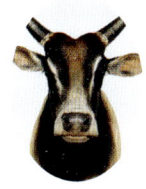 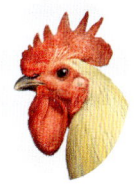 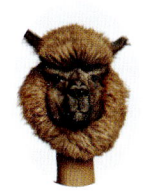 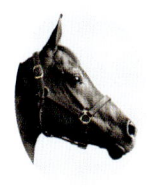 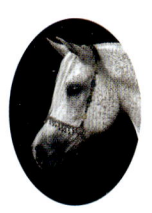

INDEX

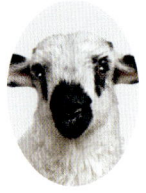 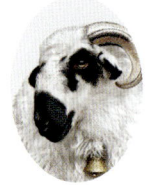 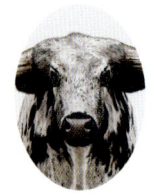 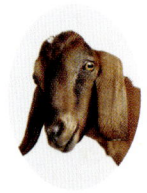 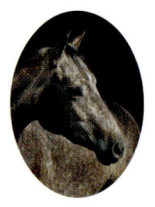 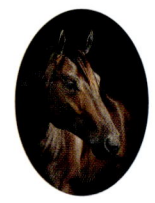 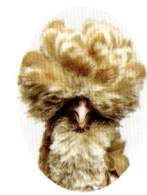

INDEX

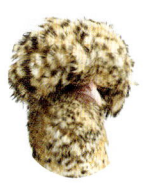

25, 155

Doloris

CANDY CORN
POLISH HEN

Doloris meant
business. As
soon as she
stepped on set,
this lady knew
what she was
working with.
Polish hens come
in a variety
of colors and
patterns, but
the scalloped
chocolate hues
on Doloris's chest
were especially
beautiful and
reminded me of
a regal red-
shouldered hawk.

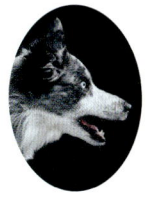

26, 86

Watson

BORDER
COLLIE

Watson got his
name from the
Sherlock Holmes
TV series, which
could not be
more perfect for
this sticky-
fingered dog
bandit. Watson
was a thief—a
very playful,
sneaky, silly
thief. While on
set, he decided to
play hide-and-
seek with every-
one's personal
belongings, and,
at one point, had
the whole crew
looking for a
shoe that he had
hidden a little
too well.

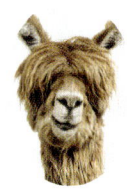

28

Goldfinch

SURI ALPACA

Goldfinch
reminded me
of a sun-soaked
surfer teen with
long, beachy
hair and a bit
of an attitude.
Throughout the
shoot, his jaw
gyrated in cir-
cles as if he were
chewing a chunk
of bubblegum
out of boredom.
I love how much
personality
alpacas have and
giggle every
time I look at
this photo. I can't
help but imagine
a pair of arms
defiantly crossed
just below the
frame.

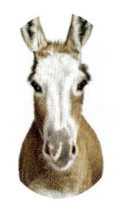

29

Daisy

DONKEY

Daisy did her
best to live up
to the stubborn
stereotype. While
trying to coax
this gregarious
donkey onto the
set, she dug her
heels into the
floor and refused
to set foot on the
soft padding we
laid out for her.
We were eventu-
ally able to lead
her to my lens
with some tasty
hay and gentle
ear scratches. In
the end, I love
the portrait we
captured of this
spirited girl.
It's as if she's
staring straight
down the barrel
of my lens and
declaring, "You
may have won
the battle, but
I'll have the
last word." And
she definitely
did. Daisy's
quiet comeback
arrived in the
form of a special
pile of you-
know-what on
the floor where
she had been
standing. Thanks
for leaving
something for us
to remember you
by, Daisy.

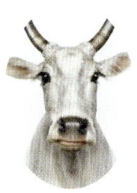

30, 131

Notta Chance

ZEBU COW

From her soft,
silvery coat to
her upright
ocher horns,
Notta Chance
was impressive
from head to toe.
She brought so
many textures to
my lens, which
is always a fun
challenge. It
takes incredibly
precise and
well-positioned
lighting to cap-
ture each unique
element in its
own complemen-
tary way. From
her dappled skin
to her wet nose
to the tiny gleam
in her eyes, I
aimed to make
this exotic zebu
shine.

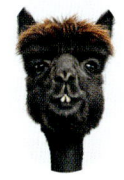

31

Venus

HUACAYA
ALPACA

Venus definitely
had us in his
orbit. From the
planetary stripe
of red across
his space-black
body to his buck
teeth and loving
personality, he
was the perfect
beholder of this
double-meaning
name. I have no
doubt that the
planet and the
goddess feel
equally proud to
have this Venus
represent them.

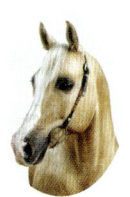

32, 48

Rhapsody in Motion

PALOMINO
ARABIAN
HORSE

Rhapsody: an
instrumental
composition ir-
regular in form
and suggestive
of improvisa-
tion. I couldn't
imagine a more
perfect name for
this gorgeous
blend of breeds.
The palomino
gold marries
beautifully with
the heavenly
sheen of his
Arabian coat
and glacial
mane. A true
piece of music,
Rhapsody sere-
nades everyone
he meets.

INDEX

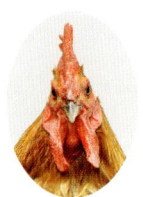 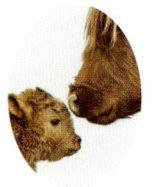 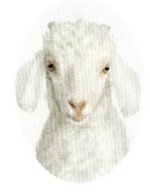 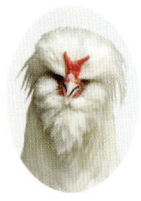 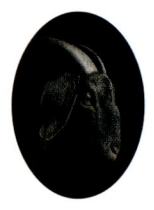 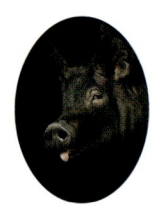 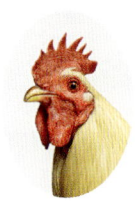

INDEX

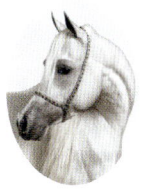

45, 83, 176

Parisii

WHITE
ARABIAN
STALLION

Horses have
always reminded
me of balleri-
nas, the way
their long necks
gracefully
bend and curve
into the most
beautiful forms. I
couldn't help but
imagine Parisii
dancing beneath
the bright lights
of the Royal
Opera House,
concluding his
performance
with a standing
ovation and a sea
of red roses. We
didn't have any
flowers for him
on set, but we
certainly gave
Parisii a stand-
ing ovation.

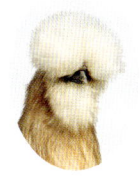

46, 55

Carmela

BUFF SILKIE
HEN

Carmela was a
character. With
their wild fluff
and laughable
likeness to a flut-
tering Muppet
from the 1970s,
silkies naturally
exude charisma
and charm. When
in motion, their
feathers become
a graceful boa, as
if floating glam-
orously past a
line of paparazzi.
Carmela was no
exception. Her
silk coat and waft-
ing crest were
definitely red-
carpet worthy.

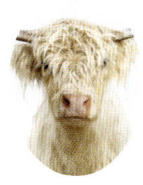

47

Rose

HIGHLAND
COW
YEARLING

Capturing
the eyes of an
animal is always
powerful but
especially so
with Highland
cows. It is almost
as if you've un-
covered a secret
or discovered a
hidden gem. And
a gem she was.
Rose was by far
the friendliest
Highland and
always seemed
eager to meet
my eye with her
gentle gaze—or
at least try to
from behind
those bangs.
Despite Highland
eyes being
hard to find,
those long locks
provide not only
warmth in harsh
winters but
also protection
against other el-
ements like wind
and rain.

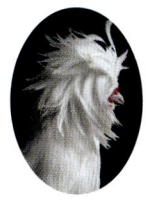

50, 51, 186

Denali

BANTAM
WHITE
POLISH HEN

With a snow-
capped crest
like that, it's no
mystery where
Denali got her
name. Origi-
nally a Native
American term
meaning "the
high one," the
word eventu-
ally became
the name of
the tallest peak
in all of North
America. But
what this Denali
couldn't make
up for in height,
she certainly
made up for in
personality. We
used a small,
battery-powered
fan to ruffle her
feathers for a
glamorous effect
fit for a crowing
queen.

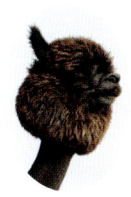

52

Pacheco

HUACAYA
ALPACA

Pacheco was
an unexpected
treat—mostly
because the cara-
mel floof around
his face had him
looking like he
was perpetually
popping out
from behind a
bush. You got us,
Pacheco! But we
wouldn't have
you any other
bobble-headed
way.

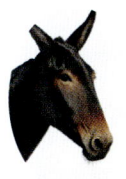

53

Milo

JOHN MULE

Just because
Milo is a mule
doesn't mean
he's not an ass
too. It's OK,
friend, we all
are sometimes.
Mules are the
offspring of a
male donkey and
a female horse—
typically taking
the wide eyes
and long ears
from the donkey
and the long face
and larger build
from the horse.
Most mules are
also completely
sterile—around
99 percent, in
fact. I loved the
way Milo's ears
formed an X
with the rest of
his body in this
image—almost
as if to say,
"Sorry, ladies,
you won't find
what you're look-
ing for here."

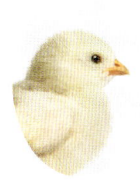

54

Curly

BUFF
ORPINGTON
CHICK

Curly was the
smallest of the
three brothers,
but he made up
for his size in
personality. A cu-
rious little chick,
he waddled his
way into all sorts
of nooks and
crannies and
was constantly
on the run, with
his two brothers
following after
him. A little may-
hem on set never
did any harm,
and we certainly
enjoyed the free
show—nyuk,
nyuk, nyuk. I
mean, cluck,
cluck, cluck.

INDEX

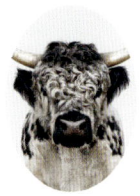 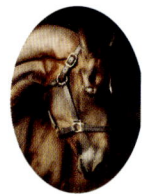 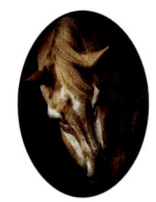 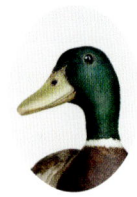 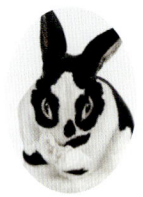 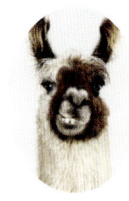 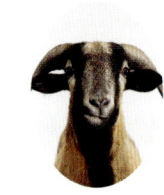

INDEX

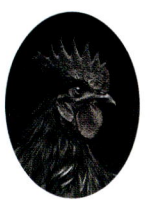

Krishna

AYAM CEMANI
ROOSTER

Krishna is real—
no Photoshop.
Ayam Cemani
roosters are
amazing. They
are entirely
black—from their
beaks to their
feathers to even
their meat. They
are quite rare in
the United States,
so it took some
time to find an
available Ayam
Cemani to photo-
graph. I eventu-
ally discovered
a small farm of
exotic chickens
and journeyed
there to capture
this captivating
portrait of
Krishna in all of
his black beauty.

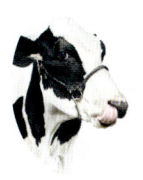

Shirley

HOLSTEIN
COW

This playful por-
trait of Shirley
is where my
work in animal
portraiture first
began. When
renowned de-
signer DJ Stout
commissioned
me to photo-
graph a fun
series of dairy
cows, I traveled
to a small dairy
farm to build a
makeshift studio
with bright
lights and color-
ful backgrounds.
The end product
beamed with
personality,
playfulness, and
charisma, and
it was this work
that made me
realize I could
photograph
animals in a way
that was just as
interesting, sin-
cere, and creative
as my portraits
of people. Since
then, this series
of cows has been
collected across
the world and
remains an inspi-
ration to me as I
continue to ex-
plore the art and
aesthetics of ani-
mal portraiture.

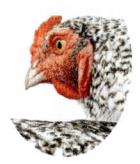

Opal

MECHELEN
TURKEY
HEAD HEN

Mother Nature is
always putting
on a show. The
endless patterns
and designs
across Opal's
plumage were
captivating.
Every feather
was completely
unique, yet they
all worked to-
gether to create
a sense of con-
trolled chaos—a
kind of random
symmetry. I
loved the beauti-
ful shape of her
rounded form
and the way her
head arched
backward, as if
giving her outfit
a quick check in
the mirror. You
look stunning,
Opal, you can be
sure of that.

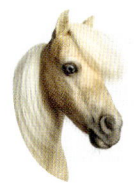

Lilly

MINIATURE
HORSE

Lilly was a true
disco cowgirl
with a bleach-
blond 1980s-style
pouf to match.
She strutted
her stuff center
stage, wide-eyed
and ready for
the bright lights.
She was the star
of her own show
and brought the
groovy dance
moves to prove
it. Although she
didn't do the
Hustle or Funky
Chicken, Lilly
loved to spin
in circles like
a roller girl on
wheels. Dance
on, darlin'.

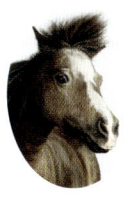

Polly

MINIATURE
HORSE

Polly was a
prancer. She
sassed her way
onto set with an
enthusiasm so
infectious it had
us all in smiles.
Her curious
gaze and playful
demeanor truly
stole the show.
Despite her
small size, Polly
pranced with
confidence and
beautifully held
her own before
my lens, as if to
say, "The best
gifts come in
small packages."

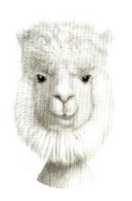

Lily

HUACAYA
ALPACA

Alpacas are
often misunder-
stood and can
be mistaken as
dopey or doltish.
Lily is a shining
example of just
how intelligent
these adorable
animals are.
Known for her
sharp intuition,
Lily has an
uncanny ability
to read and ob-
serve the people
around her. Like
a best friend,
she seems to
perceive exactly
what someone
needs, whether
it's a good laugh
or a good nuzzle.
Alpacas are
wonderful ani-
mals; while they
are incredibly
intelligent and
intuitive, they
also make room
for a lot of fun
and play. During
Lily's yearly
spring shearing,
her owners de-
cided to fashion
an Abraham
Lincoln beard
for her. You wear
it well, Lily.

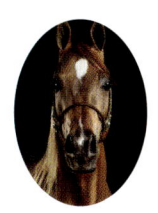

Lahab Albidayer

RED ARABIAN
STALLION

It's not often we
get to experi-
ence awe in
our day-to-day
lives. With the
many advances
we've made
in technology,
fewer and fewer
things seem
to feel new or
precious. One of
the reasons I am
passionate about
photograph-
ing animals is
because it gives
us the chance to
marvel again.
To witness these
magnificent
creatures up
close creates
a rare and
precious oppor-
tunity to be in
awe—to connect
and reflect in
a lasting way.
I am incredi-
bly grateful to
Lahab Albidayer
for allowing me
to do just that.

INDEX

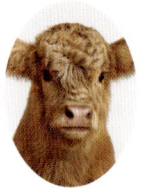

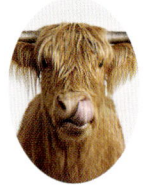

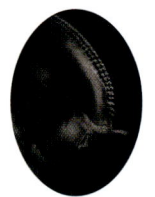

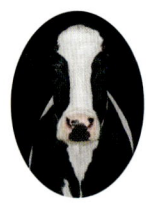

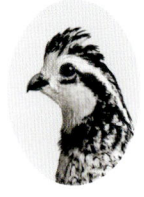

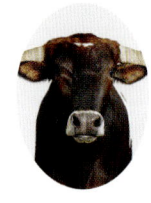

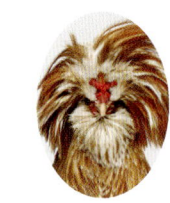

INDEX

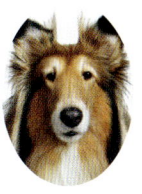

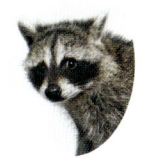

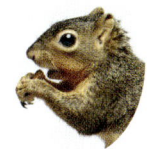

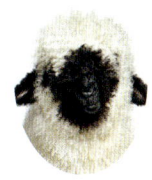

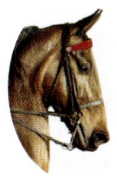

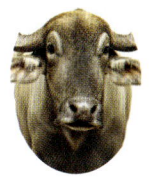

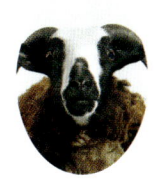

INDEX

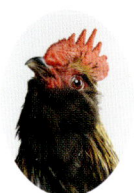 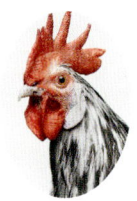 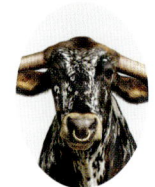 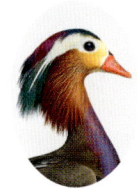 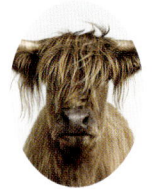 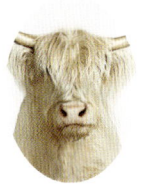 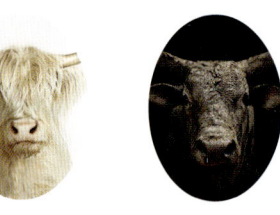

INDEX

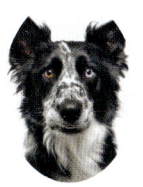 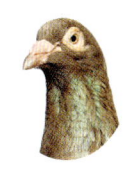 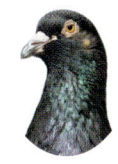 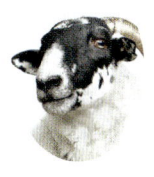 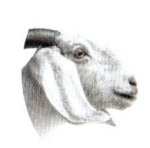 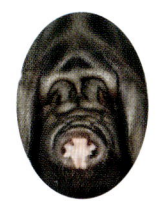 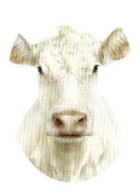

INDEX

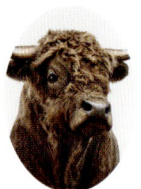 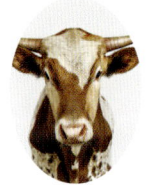 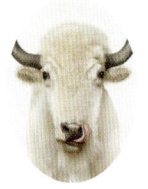 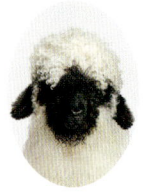 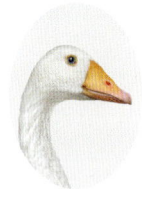 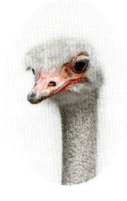 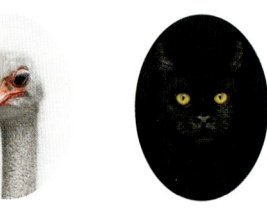

136

King Henry

HIGH DEX BULL

All hail King Henry. This beast of a bull reigns supreme over the hills of western Colorado. Whether in the summer sun or the winter snow, his presence is known. As with many bulls, when I stood face-to-face with him, I sensed his strength and power. Nothing could stop his indomitable will, but I wasn't there to try. I merely hoped to capture Henry's brute strength and intensity, with a noble aesthetic that pays homage to royal portraits from the past.

137

Wingman

TEXAS LONGHORN CALF

Wingman comes from a very special cow. His mother is a TLBAA Grand Champion female title holder, which means that this calf will be the star of his own show in no time. Until then, he's perfecting his wingman status by sticking close to his mama's award-winning side. Longhorns are quite iconic in Texas, so noticing that Wingman's white blaze was undeniably shaped like the Lone Star State was a great detail to discover.

140

Huckleberry

AMERICAN WHITE BUFFALO

A gentle giant, Huckleberry was a sweet one for sure. In person, the size and presence of a buffalo is amazing. Quite humbling, in fact. Huckleberry is a white buffalo—an extremely rare breed equaling to one out of every 10 million. Because of their rarity, white buffaloes have been considered spiritually significant in several Native American traditions and to this day are considered a sign of peace and harmony.

141

Klover

SWISS VALAIS BLACKNOSE SHEEP

Klover may not have four green leaves, but she's equally as lucky and rare. A twin to her brother, Kipply, Klover is known for her serene demeanor, a characteristic that's uncommon for her breed. Unlike the other sheep around her that feed in a frenzy, this little lady makes her way gracefully through the herd, as carefree as a clover waving in the wind.

144

Silly

SEBASTOPOL GOOSE

No surprise here, but this girl was one silly goose. She honked her way through our entire session and had everyone in tears laughing. Geese are often known for their playful (and at times menacing) ways. Her on-set shenanigans had her chasing our ankles like a bully on the playground. She meant well, though, and would abruptly lay down the second she reached our feet. Silly goose, indeed.

145

Catalina

AFRICAN OSTRICH

Sometimes you only get one frame, and it just so happens to be the perfect pose. I consider myself lucky to have captured Catalina as well as I did. We had very limited time with her because she's not only a big bird but also a fast one. Ostriches can also be very dangerous—their defense mechanism is to raise their massive talons and kick the hell out of a predator. In order to keep her and everyone on set safe, Catalina's trainers brought in a 20-by-20-foot metal fence to put around her. Each time I was ready to take a photo, the trainers would open the fence just long enough for me to get one single shot.

146

Visenya

BLACK MAINE COON

Black cats get a bad rap. Visenya was as sweet as can be and only brought good luck to set. Maine Coon cats are one of the largest domesticated cat breeds and make great pasture mascots. Social and outgoing by nature, Visenya makes her rounds each day, saying hello to all of her farm friends—dogs, birds, and every human in between. Ever since I began my series of black animals on black backgrounds, I've always wanted to photograph a black cat. After years of waiting, I got lucky with Visenya when we unexpectedly met her on a chicken farm. The stars aligned, and I just love how her stunning yellow eyes pop in the midst of her deep black hues.

INDEX

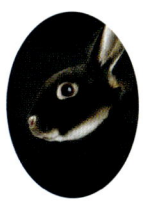 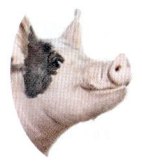 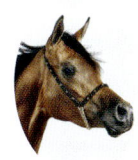 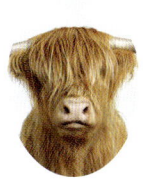 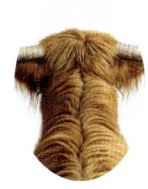 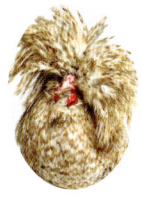 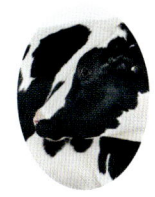

INDEX

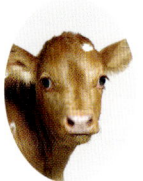

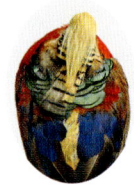

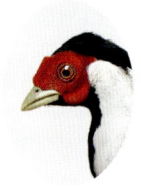

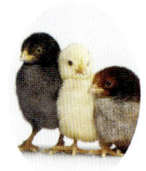

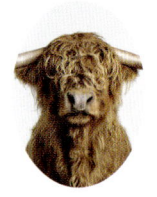

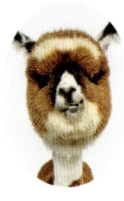

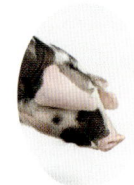

Bug

LONGHORN
NEWBORN
CALF

Bug was brand-new to the world and only a week old when his portrait was taken. With his mama close to his side, this bug-eyed baby dazzled my lens with innocence. It's rare to photograph a calf so young, but what an honor it was. Baby animals are special to us for so many reasons, but one thing I love as a photographer is how beautiful and crisp their features are. Every strand of Bug's new coat shined like a new car. His tiny nose—perfectly pink and glowing—paired with those baby blues that were disproportionately large and full of charm. Bug was a special presence who brought a lot of softness to the set.

Prism

GOLDEN
PHEASANT

Nature certainly has a way of stopping us in our tracks. Not only are Prism's colors impossible to comprehend, but the incredible shapes and patterns painted across his plumage are similar to an abstract artwork hanging in a museum. I like to play with visual angles to create new and interesting perspectives for viewers. Shooting Prism from the top created an interesting juxtaposition of parts, with the yellow-gold feathers on his head looking almost like a slicked-back coif of hair.

Clifford

RED GOLDEN
PHEASANT

Clifford's winding feather patterns reminded me of a geometric maze. I imagined myself walking through it for days, twisting and turning down various paths, until finally reaching the end with that ruby-red eye in the sky. I love a good pop of color, and Clifford's was one for the history books.

Three Stooges

BAND OF
CHICKS

These three brothers were knuckleheads on set and a welcome source of entertainment. Watching them waddle around, bump into one another, fall off surfaces, and get lost was hilarious. This adorable trio brought so much personality to the stage and had all of us quoting the old TV classic.

Hot Shot

HIGHLAND
BULL

The moment Hot Shot arrived on set, I was reminded of the way time stops when a bull enters the room. He was a fierce beauty to behold and a rare glimpse at the chilling juxtaposition of massive strength and massive restraint. I think all of our temperatures went up a bit while Hot Shot commanded the room.

Frances

HUACAYA
ALPACA CRIA

Frances is a fighter. Born five weeks early and severely underweight, this little one came close to not making it. After 48 hours of close calls and her caring owner nursing her the whole way through, baby Frances began to show more and more signs of life. Now thriving at her one-year mark, this sweet-faced cria still clings to her human hero. I love the beautiful contrast of the brown and cream colors throughout her coat and how they work together to symbolize the dark she was born into and the light she has found.

Milky Way

GLOUCES-
TERSHIRE
OLD SPOTS
PIG

Even though this pig can't fly, she sure looks like something from the sky. Milky Way was just that—a gorgeous, galactic spread of dark and light spheres across her skin. As she continues to grow, her spots will likely stretch and bleed into one another, creating an entirely new scene to witness. It never ceases to amaze me how truly huge pigs can grow to be. Milky Way will likely reach close to 500 pounds.

INDEX

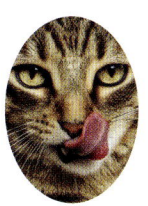

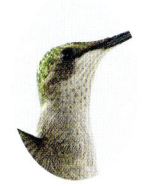

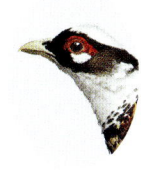

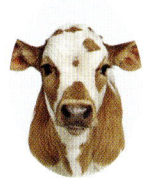

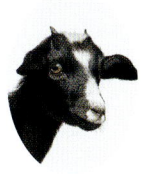

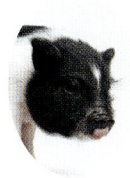

INDEX

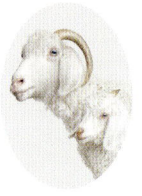

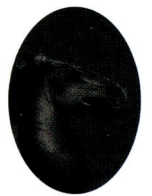

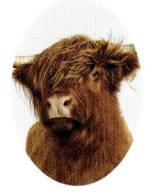

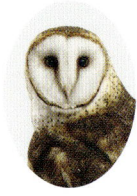

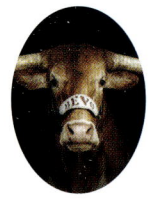

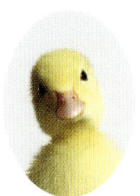

INDEX

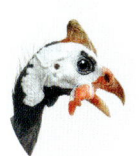

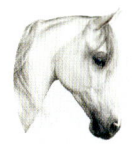

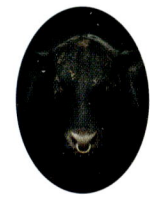

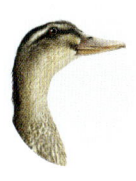

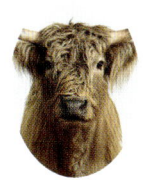

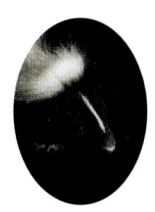

196

198

199

202

204

224

Jester

LAVENDER
GUINEA HEN

Jester was an incredible example of how features that are seemingly grotesque on their own can actually add up to a compelling piece of art. From his white leathery facial skin, furrowed Joker-like brows, and fleshy waddle to the gracefulness of his lavender wings and soft spots, Jester truly embodied both sides of the coin.

Sergeant Pepper

WHITE
ARABIAN
STALLION

The learning curve to photographing horses is significant. There are many subtleties that should be acknowledged when creating the perfect horse portrait. Those subtleties can sometimes be different depending on the breed. One of the most famous and identifiable horses is the Arabian. This art horse portrait of Sergeant Pepper embodies many of the breed's famous traits—a chiseled head, dished face, long neck, and attentive eyes. Sergeant Pepper exudes energy, intelligence, and nobility. The flowing mane says it all.

Wayne Crosby

BLACK
ANGUS BULL

Wayne Crosby squeezed us into his schedule—barely. Prior to the shoot, he spent some time in the pasture kicking up dirt, chomping on hay, and chasing after some pretty heifers. Sometimes I prefer to photograph animals that are clean and pristine, but, in Wayne Crosby's case, I wanted to photograph him in all of his dusty glory. We created a mobile set in the big red barn and were able to capture a handful of frames before he ran out on us. Thanks for your time, bud.

Bessie

GRAY
MALLARD
FEMALE
DUCK

Bessie was a sweetheart from the very start. Her kind and docile nature was calming in a way that surprised me. By the end of our session, I found myself reaching toward her in hopes of making a connection. Sure enough, sweet Bessie waddled her way over to me as if we'd known each other for years. I truly never get tired of the incredible ways humans and animals can connect with each other.

Eleanor

HIGHLAND
COW

Eleanor was a shining example of how imperfections can be oh so perfect. Unlike many other Highlands on the farm, Eleanor had messy hair, a dark sandy coat, and short asymmetrical horns. Despite her less traditional appearance, Eleanor's perfection lies in the fact that she proudly owns who she is. This girl is comfortable in her own hide and carries an air of confidence wherever she goes.

Bandit

SKUNK

When I started my animal portrait series, I always thought it would be amazing to create a portrait of a skunk. Of course, the challenge with many of my pieces is finding animals that are tame enough to sit through one of my portrait sessions. After months of emailing and weaving through a web of friends and animal owners, I found someone who had rescued a skunk when he was a baby and nursed him back to health. I've been asked many times, "Did Bandit spray you?" I'd like to leave that question open-ended.

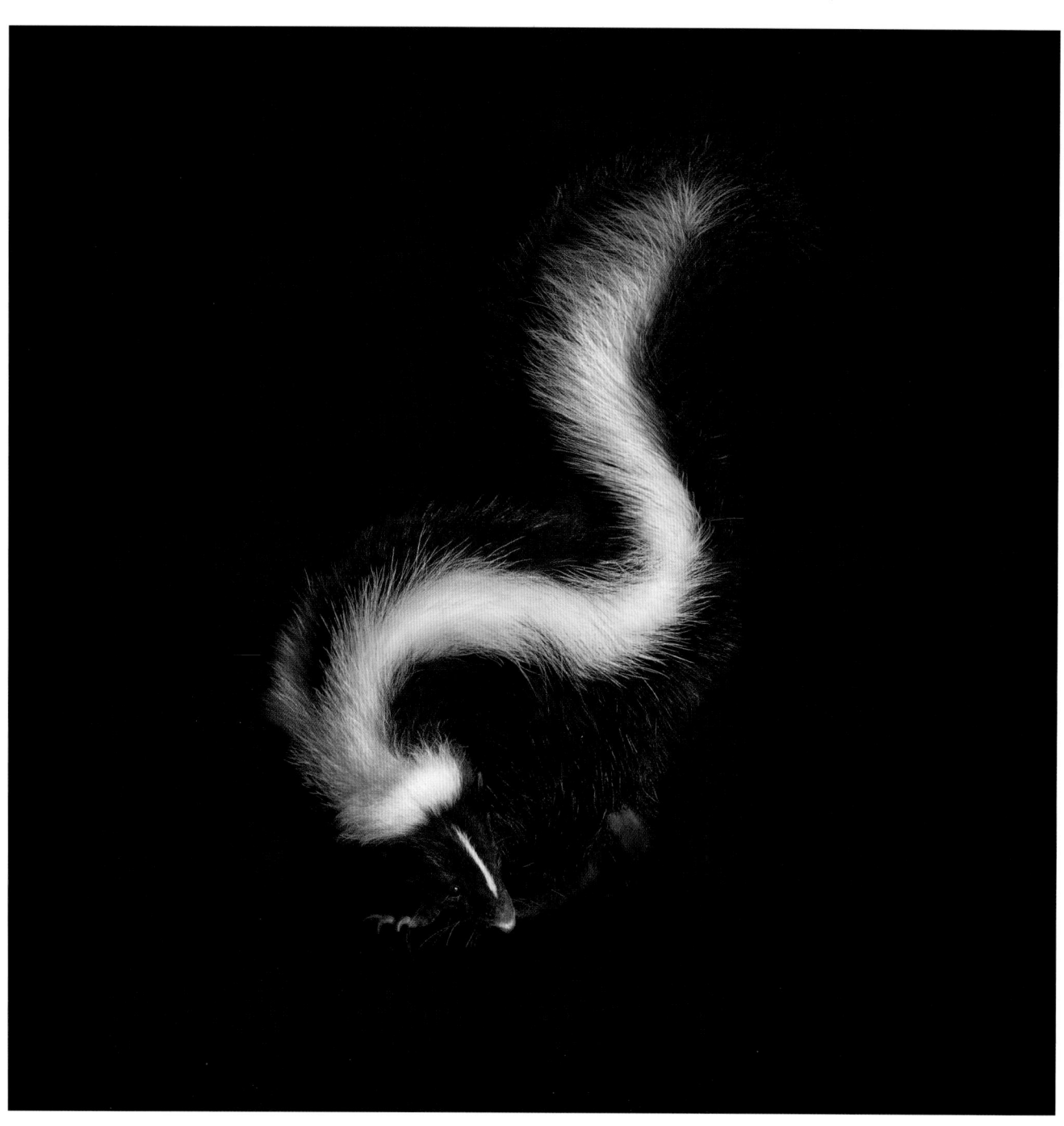

Bandit

SKUNK